REAL ESTATE OFFICE
MANAGEMENT

People, Functions, Systems

2nd Edition

REAL ESTATE OFFICE MANAGEMENT

People, Functions, Systems

2nd Edition

A publication of the
Real Estate Brokerage Council™ of the
REALTORS NATIONAL MARKETING INSTITUTE®,
an affiliate of the
NATIONAL ASSOCIATION OF REALTORS®.

Real Estate Brokerage Council™
430 N. Michigan Ave.
Chicago, IL 60611-4092

Copyright

International Standard Book Number: 0-913652-64-4
Real Estate Brokerage Council™ Catalog Number: BK 113

Library of Congress Cataloging-in-Publication Data

Reat estate office management.

    Bibliography: p.
    Includes index.
    1. Real estate business - Management.   2. Office management.   I. Real Estate Brokerage Council (Chicago: IL.)
HD1375.R3928   1988   333.33'068   88-31636
ISBN 0-913652-64-4

Printed in the United States of America
1st Edition
First printing, 1975, 10,085
Second printing, 1976, 10,427
Third printing, 1977, 10,253
Fourth printing, 1978, 10,251
Fifth printing, 1980, 9,984
Sixth printing, 1981, 10,000
Seventh printing, 1985, 5,000
Eighth printing, 1986, 5,000
Ninth printing, 1987, 5,000
2nd Edition
Tenth printing, 1988, 5,000
Eleventh printing, 1989, 5,000

"Evolution and Revolution as Organizations Grow,"
by Larry E. Greiner, Harvard Business Review.
July-August 1972 © Copyright 1972 by the President and Fellows of Harvard College; all rights reserved.

Data "Hierarchy of Needs" from MOTIVATION AND PERSONALITY,
2nd Edition by Abraham H. Maslow
© Copyright 1970 by Abraham H. Maslow
By Permission of Harper & Row, Publishers, Inc.

Foreword

As I assisted in the revision of *Real Estate Office Management: People, Functions, Systems*, I was amazed at how current most of the 15-year-old text was. Though the original book was slanted toward sales management and the Real Estate Brokerage Council™ now teaches marketing management with relatively minor changes, it remains an accurate testimonial to what real estate office management is today.

I guess it only goes to prove that "management is management is management"; that the true essence of managing people and "things" doesn't change dramatically. While it's true that there always seems to be a new management fad that everyone swears by, rather than being the "right way" to manage, such fads only offer additional alternatives.

Many management skills and disciplines are scientific, but managing by and large is still an art. The ability of a manager to *carry out* scientific truisms is far more important than the truisms themselves. In other words, the manager's style and method of imparting his message to subordinates will always be the key factor in managing successfully.

This book was originally gleaned from the knowledge and experience of many of the leading real estate managers and professional educators in the country. It was not meant to be a treatment of the general principles of management, nor was it intended to replace the RB Council's real estate brokerage courses, but rather to compliment them. Though in a somewhat different manner than the courses, this book focuses on the four basic resources of management: plans, capital or finances, marketing, and people.

The challenges faced by today's managers are many and truly require the proper utilization and balancing of these four resources. Not only must the manager be concerned about people relationships, he must also understand the functions and systems that make the firm as well as the people relationships work.

This book discusses the manager's role in recruiting, hiring and retaining sales associates, and in training associates to employ the systems and techniques that produce a profitable operation.

The many new challenges confronting the real estate business today require managers to be more learned than ever before. As sales become more complex, so do management challenges. The sales associate of today demands better education, training and management communications to guide him to a successful career. In short, the burden is upon management's shoulders to help sales associates meet the challenges of change for now and the future.

In-depth reading and practical application of the major tenets of this book will give today's management practitioner a sound basis for achieving the goal of being an outstanding manager.

REALTOR® Albert J. Mayer, III, CRB, CRS, GRI, RM
Technical Advisor
Theodore Mayer & Bro., REALTOR®
Cincinnati, Ohio
September 1988

Acknowledgement

Back in the early 1970s, the office administration courses of the REALTORS NATIONAL MARKETING INSTITUTE® achieved prominence in the field of management education for REALTORS®. As the number of brokers attending the courses increased it became apparent that a book was needed to assist students in their studies and to aid brokers in managing their real estate businesses successfully.

Real Estate Office Management: People, Functions, Systems was originally planned by the Editorial Book Development Subcommittee of RNMI® under the chairmanship of REALTOR® Albert J. Mayer III, CRB, CRS, GRI, RM, who served as technical advisor. The book rolled off the press for the first time in 1975.

The structure of RNMI® has changed since those days. The Institute is no longer a single entity, but is comprised of three distinct Councils: the Real Estate Brokerage Council™, the Residential Sales Council™, and the Commercial-Investment Real Estate Council. The primary function of these Councils is to provide real estate education for industry members. As such, each Council offers its own educational designation to its members who meet the respective Council's professional and course-related requirements. The RB Council awards the Certified Real Estate Brokerage Manager (CRB®) designation, the RS Council awards the Certified Residential Specialist (CRS®) designation, and the CI Council awards the Certified Commercial-Investment Manager (CCIM®) designation.

Real Estate Office Management is now published by the RB Council as part of its commitment to educating real estate brokerage managers. The Council offers a variety of other books and products as well, including educational programs on audiocassette and videocassette.

Many RNMI® members and office administration course instructors shared their knowledge and expertise to produce the original version of *Real Estate Office Management*. Their names are listed here with grateful acknowledgement for their time and effort.

Contributors

Edward J. Boleman
F. C. Tucker Company
Indianapolis, Indiana

Joseph B. Carnahan
Paul-White-Carnahan
Realty Co., Inc.
Mission Hills, California

Richard M. Caruso
Rich Port, REALTOR®
LaGrange, Illinois

Fred E. Case
University of California
Los Angeles, California

Arthur R. Close
Portland, Oregon

H. Harland Crowell
Crowell & Co., Inc.
McLean, Virginia

Carl Deremo
Real Estate One, Inc.
Farmington, Michigan

David B. Doeleman
Gibson Bowles, Inc., REALTORS®
Portland, Oregon

William M. Ellis
Shannon & Luchs Company
McLean, Virginia

Richard C. Farrer
Hayward Realty Investment Co.
Hayward, California

Gary Fugere
Real Estate 10, Inc., REALTORS®
Minneapolis, Minnesota

Art Godi
Art Godi Associates
Stockton, California

Larry E. Greiner
University of Southern California
Los Angeles, California

Joseph F. Hanauer
Thorsen, REALTORS®
Oak Brook, Illinois

Henry S. Harrison
Harrison-Durocher Incorporated
New Haven, Connecticut

Darrel Johnson
Real Estate 10 Inc., REALTORS®
Minneapolis, Minnesota

Earl J. Keim, Jr.
Earl Keim Realty
Dearborn, Michigan

Joseph P. Klock
The Klock Co.
Miami, Florida

Henry A. Leist
Henry A. Leist, Inc.
Cincinnati, Ohio

Bernard J. MacElhenny, Jr.
MacElhenny, Levy & Co., Inc.
Santa Barbara, California

Albert J. Mayer, III
Theodore Mayer & Bro.,
REALTOR®
Cincinnati, Ohio

Bruce T. Mulhearn
Bruce Mulhearn, Inc.
Bellflower, California

Ross C. Munro
React Realty
Cherry Hills, New Jersey

Robert H. Murray, Jr.
Schindler-Cummins
Houston, Texas

George A. Nash
Bermel-Smaby, REALTORS®
Burnsville, Minnesota

William D. North
Kirkland & Ellis
Chicago, Illinois

Roger Pettiford
Columbia Realty Co.
Colorado Springs, Colorado

Rich Port
Rich Port, REALTOR®
La Grange, Illinois

Barry G. Posner
University of Massachusetts
Amherst, Massachusetts

Ralph W. Pritchard, Jr.
Thorsen, REALTORS®
Oak Brook, Illinois

Kenneth J. Reyhons
Ken Reyhons, REALTORS®
Colorado Springs, Colorado

Clifford A. Robedeaux
Robedeaux, Inc.
Milwaukee, Wisconsin

Don C. Roberts
Don C. Roberts, Inc.
Whittier, California

Richard Ryan
Shannon & Luchs Company
McLean, Virginia

Ronald A. Schmaedick
Rams Realty Inc.
Eugene, Oregon

John W. Steffey
Chas. H. Steffey, Inc.
Baltimore, Maryland

Warren H. Schmidt
University of California
Los Angeles, California

Wayne R. Weld
Indian Hills Realty
Columbus, Ohio

Norman B. Sigband
University of Southern California
Los Angeles, California

Leonard L. Westdale
Westdale Company
Holland, Michigan

Edward L. Sowards
Sowards Inc.
Rockford, Illinois

Florence Willess
Ebby Halliday
Dallas, Texas

Original Reviewers

Joseph B. Carnahan
Paul-White-Carnahan
Realty Co., Inc.
Mission Hills, California

Albert J. Mayer, III
Theodore Mayer & Bro.,
REALTOR®
Cincinnati, Ohio

William M. Ellis
Shannon & Luchs
McLean, Virginia

Ralph A. Pritchard
Thorsen, REALTORS®
Oak Brook, Illinois

Lydia Franz
Century 21-Country Squire,
REALTORS®
Barrington, Illinois

Clifford A. Robedeaux
Robedeaux, Inc.
Milwaukee, Wisconsin

Joseph F. Hanauer
Thorsen, REALTORS®
Oak Brook, Illinois

RNMI® members who reviewed single chapters of the book include
Robert A. Doyle, Amery Dunn, Helen Hirt, Dorothy J. Peterson and
George R. Winters.

Reviewers for 2nd Edition

Drexanne Evers, CRB
Drexsells Real Estate
Clarksville, Ohio

Neil D. Lyon, CRB, GRI
Hunneman & Company
Boston, Massachusetts

John W. Lane, CRB, CRS, GRI
Spectrum Marketing Group of
America, Inc.
St. Charles, Illinois

Albert J. Mayer, III
CRB, CRS, GRI, RM
Theodore Mayer & Bro.,
REALTOR®
Cincinnati, Ohio

Henry A. Leist,
CRB, CRS, GRI
Henry A. Leist, Inc.
Cincinnati, Ohio

Ronald P. Noyes, CRB, GRI
Ron Noyes and Assoc.
Swarthmore, Pennsylvania

Contents

Dimensions of Management   1

Knowledge and understanding of the principles and background of any field are basic to effective functioning within that field. Management is an area in general; real estate marketing management is a field in particular. Managers of all types of organizations, ranging from government to business to military, perform essentially the same functions. Successful managers have two different sets of knowledge and understanding. They know management and they know the business which they are managing.

Just as selling real estate requires a knowledge of the principles of selling, so does managing a real estate business require understanding management practices and how they evolved. This chapter provides a brief introduction to the history of management, its concepts, theories and disciplines. It can be used as a reference to aid in applying the specific techniques of managing a real estate business discussed throughout the book.

Dimensions of Management

You are probably a manager today because you were unusually good at doing something else earlier in your career. At least that's the way it is with most persons in executive positions. Few have been trained specifically to be managers; most have risen to their positions of responsibility by being exceptionally good specialists in sales, engineering, teaching, law or finance. Now they must manage the activities of others.

The job of a manager involves very different kinds of sensitivities, judgments and skills than are required of sales associates. Fig. 1 compares the competencies required by the good manager and the good sales associate.

Fig. 1. Key tasks of the manager and the sales associate

The Manager:	The Sales Associate:
• must employ the strategic planning process	• must employ a personal business plan
• must identify problems and opportunites (or make sure they are identified)	• must identify problems and opportunities
• must analyze (or make sure they are analyzed)	• must analyze
• must communicate decisions to others	• must consider alternatives and make decisions
• must gain the acceptance of others for the decisions	**And then**
So that	must participate in the achievement of the company and personal business plan objectives
others participate in the achievement of the plan's objectives	
Courtesy: Warren H. Schmidt	

Obviously the most important parts of the lists in Fig. 1 are planning and implementing. Identifying and analyzing problems or opportunities and even decision-making can be done superbly. But if the persons who are to implement the decision do not understand, do not care or do not want to take action, then all the energy invested in problem solving goes down the drain. This is the most frustrating part of many managers' jobs. The manager gets all excited about a new program, a new approach or a new method of operation only to discover that others in the organization want to keep things as they are.

Consider what happens when someone gets instructions from the boss. The subordinate's active mind immediately entertains questions like, "Does this make sense?" "Is this something I really should do?" "Is this something I can do?" "Is this something I want to do?" If the answer comes out "No" to any of these questions, the clever subordinate has many courses of action available even without arguing with the boss. He can "misunderstand" the instructions and continue to do what he thinks ought to be done. He can delay. He can give lip service to the new approach but carry on as usual. He can even mislay the paper on which the new program was outlined. This kind of passive resistance can eventually drive a manager up the wall. Franklin Roosevelt once said that trying to change the Navy was like punching a featherbed. When you're all tired out it's still in about the same shape as when you started.

This awareness of his dependence on others has caused many a manager to look more carefully into the literature of management and psychology for strategies and techniques to increase his influence and control over the organization he leads. Experience with hundreds of managers in real estate and other fields suggests examination of concepts that seem most useful to the practicing manager. They are:

Key psychological concepts: three formulations that help you to understand why people behave the way they do

Major theories of management: an overview of the four principal schools of management and how they define the manager's responsibilities

Major theories of motivation: three widely recognized and used formulations of what determines where people choose to invest their initiative, energy and creativity.

The manager who has a grasp of these key concepts will be more effective in giving leadership to his organization. Since this can only be an overview rather than an in depth discussion of any one approach, the interested reader can look for further understanding of these areas in management literature suggested in the bibliography.

Key Psychological Concepts
We all know something about people and we all have theories why people behave the way they do. The most successful managers are not limited by their personal experience and their own common sense knowledge of human behavior. They take the trouble to become aware of theories developed from systematic studies of people in various settings—particularly research undertaken in business and industrial settings. Three such formulations involve:

Behavior

Motivation

Perception.

Two Determinants of Behavior
The formula can be stated very simply: $B = f(p + e)$. Behavior is a function (or result) of a person and that person's environment.

The implication is that when you want to change behavior, you have two variables to work with: the person and the environment. Changing people is usually a long and costly process; changing environments is generally an easier place to begin. Just as you behave differently in different settings (sometimes you're casual, relaxed; sometimes uptight and cautious), other individuals also change with different environments.

When you want to change someone's behavior, therefore, a good place to begin is to ask: "How can I change the situation so that Charlie is more likely to produce the behavior that I want?" This is usually a better question than, "What's wrong with Charlie?"

Process of Motivation

A second key psychological concept involves the basic process of motivation. Understanding the sequence of events that occur when we say a person is motivated can give the manager useful clues on how to influence those around him. The basic process is described in Fig. 2.

When a need arises in a person, e.g. too little fluid in the body, that need sets off a signal in the form of a tension—tightness in the throat—and the individual says, "I'm thirsty!" Through learning, we have discovered that when that particular tension occurs we should get something to drink so we head for a drinking fountain or bar. We are now motivated (aware of a need and heading for a goal that will satisfy it). When the goal, drink, is attained, we feel satisfied for a time.

Since people are always feeling and satisfying needs, everyone is motivated. You do not really motivate the people who work for the firm (they are motivated); the question is whether they are motivated to do what you think is important. This depends on the extent to which they feel their needs are being met in your organization.

Think of it this way: the extent to which a person is motivated to act in the interests of the organization depends on the extent to which he feels there is an overlap of his needs and the needs of the organization (see Fig. 3). The greater the overlap, the greater the effort that person will expend in achieving the organization's goals. Think of all the organizations you belong to, including your business. In some you are a fringe member, or unmotivated, some would say; in others you are deeply involved and committed. The degree of your involvement depends on the extent to which your needs are being met in the organization.

The implications for the manager are clear: get to know what the priority needs of your people are; figure out how to meet those needs more fully on the job; and make sure they understand how large that overlap area is. Later in this chapter we discuss the major theories of how this can be done.

Concept of Perception

A third key psychological concept of importance to the manager involves perception. Simply put, each of us behaves in terms of our perception of reality and that perception is determined partly by what's outside of us and partly by what's inside us.

The formula is $P = f(s + pe)$. Perception is a function or result of the stimulus (what we see, hear, etc.) and our past experience.

Fig. 2 Elements of motivation

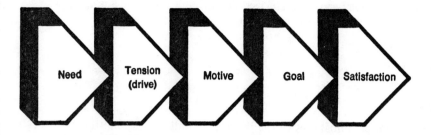

Need → Tension (drive) → Motive → Goal → Satisfaction

Dimensions of Management

Courtesy: Warren H. Schmidt

Your perception of your organization and any person in it is a bit different from any other person's perception because you carry with you a different set of past experiences.

The implications for the manager are fairly clear. Don't expect other people to view things exactly the way you do, no matter how clear things seem to you and how certain you are of your point of view. Expect differences since each person filters the same information through a different screen. The wise manager takes time to find out how his colleagues perceive things, knowing that their perceptions are the reality to which they respond.

These are basic psychological processes to keep in mind. The point to emphasize here is that there is now a significant and growing body of psychological research that is shedding important light on the people problems managers must deal with.

There is another set of concepts that shed light on the position of being a manager.

Fig. 3 Relation of individual and organizational needs

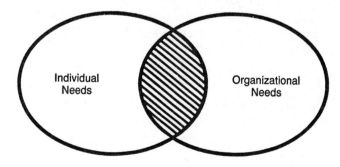

Individual Needs

Organizational Needs

Courtesy: Warren H. Schmidt

Major Theories of Management

While management theory cannot supply answers, it does provide a framework for understanding and a systematic guide for action. Management has been characterized by different people in a number of ways. These schools of thought have been referred to as:

Bureaucratic-process

Behavioral

Quantitative

Systems.

Each school contributes to the integrative and operational theory of management. The best test of any of them is to see to what extent they help you understand better what is happening in your organization.

Bureaucratic-Process

This school has often been called the traditional or classical school of management. It is concerned primarily with the structure and functioning of the formal organization. It is represented at one level by a concern with determining the one best way and at a second level with the specific administrative responsibilities and roles.

Frederick W. Taylor, founder of scientific management, and his followers were essentially concerned with production. They analyzed and focused on the basic physical activities involved in the production of the individual workers. Their aim was to reduce the contributions of each worker to the smallest and most specialized unit of work possible and to eliminate any uncertainty about the expected output. Taylor emphasized that there was one best way to do a job and it was management's responsibility to find it and train workers to conform to this best way.

Max Weber provided a model for administrative responsibility in an ideal type of organization which he referred to as a bureaucracy. It was and is characterized by a rational division of labor, coordination by a hierarchical pyramid, consistent and prescribed sets of rules for organizational behavior, authority based upon expert knowledge, the idea that employment is based upon technical qualifications, promotion based on loyalty and achievement and finally the impersonal, formalistic conduct of responsibility.

The principles emanating from the Bureaucratic-process school are generally well recognized. Warren Haynes and Joseph Massie have codified these principles as follows:[1]

The Unity of Command principle: no member of an organization should report to more than one superior

The Span of Control principle: no superior should have responsibility for the activities of more than five to eight subordinates

The Exception principle: a superior should delegate responsibility for routine matters to subordinates

The Scalar principle: every organization should have a well defined hierarchial structure.

16

Behavioral

The Behavioral school is concerned with the role of individual and group behavior on the functioning of the formal and informal organization. Key behavioral concepts from the disciplines of psychology, sociology and anthropology which provide a focus for this school include: motivation, perception, learning, personality, group dynamics, leadership, satisfaction, morale and organizational change. In large part this approach developed out of a feeling that the essentially human character of the business organization was being ignored.

The beginnings of this school of thought and the so-called Human Relations Movement are generally marked by the Hawthorne (Western Electric Co.) studies of the 1930s conducted by Elton Mayo and his associates. They originally set out to study the relationship between productivity and physical working conditions. The researchers discovered that productivity was largely a function of the human element in the work environment.

One of the early writers to dramatize the impact of the human factor directly was Douglas McGregor. In *The Human Side of Enterprise* he suggested that individuals in an organization will behave in a particular manner based upon the manager's assumption, Theory X and Theory Y, about human nature.[2]

Theory X assumptions about people are that they are basically lazy, unreliable, dislike work, avoid responsibility and prefer to be directed. A manager who holds these beliefs leans toward a management style marked by close supervision, centralized authority, autocratic leadership and minimal participation of subordinates in decision making.

Theory Y is based on vastly different assumptions: people are reliable, like to work, not only learn to accept but seek responsibility and will exercise self-direction and self-control when committed to organizational goals. Consequently this management has looser, more general supervision, greater decentralization of authority, less reliance on external controls and coercion, democratic leadership and more participation in decision making.

Quantitative

This school, identified by such terms as operations research, operations analysis or management science, sees management largely as a system of mathematical models and processes. Its primary emphasis is on the development of structured decision making and control models. William Newman and his associates suggest that this approach "is primarily a technique for selecting a course of action."[3] It has three key distinguishing features:

Problems are stated in mathematical symbols. Thus the statement is concise and can be manipulated easily by a mathematician.

A set of equations, or 'model,' is designed for each problem. This model shows the various factors that should be taken into account and points out the relationships among them.

Quantitative data must be provided for each of the variables and their weights. To achieve this quantification requires a tremendous amount of digging for facts and the expression of subjective judgments and values in numerical terms. Then a highly rational decision can be made by injecting the data into the model.

The Quantitative school's approach generally requires the manager to make a systematic analysis of problems and take a comprehensive rather than segmented view of them. Operations research and management science are not so much types of management as they are aids to the manager in his efforts to achieve the best results for the whole company.

Systems
The essential scope and thrust of the Systems approach is the "processes that transform inputs into outputs and the major emphasis is upon the interrelations, interdependencies and the dynamics or the flow of activities in the organization."[4] According to this school, the organization is a highly complex system with management acting as the force which integrates, coordinates and directs the enterprise as an entity toward the achievement of organizational objectives.

In addition, the organization is described as an open rather than closed system. This means that the organization engages in dynamic

Fig. 4 Contributions of the various schools of management

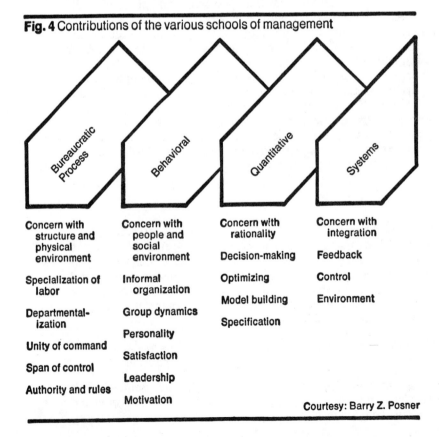

Bureaucratic Process	Behavioral	Quantitative	Systems
Concern with structure and physical environment	Concern with people and social environment	Concern with rationality	Concern with integration
Specialization of labor	Informal organization	Decision-making	Feedback
Departmental-ization	Group dynamics	Optimizing	Control
Unity of command	Personality	Model building	Environment
Span of control	Satisfaction	Specification	
Authority and rules	Leadership		
	Motivation		

Courtesy: Barry Z. Posner

interaction with its environment and that managers must establish and maintain adequate feedback mechanisms. Viewed from this perspective the Systems school is an application of cybernetic theory.

How to Use These Theories

Each of these schools of thought have relevance for the real estate manager. As Stephen Michael and Halsey Jones have suggested, "A manager must be able to anticipate, coordinate, and control the behavior of his subordinates. To do so, he should know something about human behavior. If he must make a decision about replacing equipment or purchasing materials for inventory, he is sensible if he uses available mathematical techniques. Finally, if he wants to improve the efficiency of a production or administrative task, systems analysis provides a means for dealing with the problem; if he has to integrate a new task into his existing routine, he can find useful suggestions in the Bureaucratic-process school."[5]

The debate among researchers, academics and theoreticians regarding the relative advantages and limitations of each "school" may be spirited and interesting but is of little importance to the practicing manager. A more important concern is the manager's need to be both cognizant and conversant in the applications and perspectives each major approach offers.

Management Process

A widely used method for integrating the various schools of management has been to conceive of management as a process comprising a series of actions which lead to the achievement of goals. This viewpoint has been developed as still another school of thought, the Operational school. This approach and the universal components of the management process are represented in the basic management text *Principles of Management: An Analysis of Managerial Functions.*[6]

Strategic Planning/Goal Setting

"Setting goals and objectives for the organization and determining appropriate strategies and tactics to achieve them."

Goal setting simply means that whoever is organizing and operating the firm must know what objectives that firm is supposed to achieve. These goals must be expressed so they can be communicated to whomever can use them to measure the quality of his own performance. Someone likened an organization to a piece of cooked spaghetti. The basic management principle thus applied is that a manager cannot push a piece of spaghetti; he has to pull it. This says the manager must be out in front giving direction, studying the kinds of goals that will maximize the resources of the firm.

Planning evolves out of goal setting. It expresses the separate objectives in ways that point to the kinds of programs, policies or procedures necessary to achieve the objectives. Goal setting means that many kinds of alternative opportunities are identified for the real estate marketing office. Planning examines the alternatives with care, selecting among viable alternatives the things the firm will do.

An important element for a real estate brokerage office in planning is to set up the policies and procedures, the generalized rules of

Fig. 5: Functions of management in process

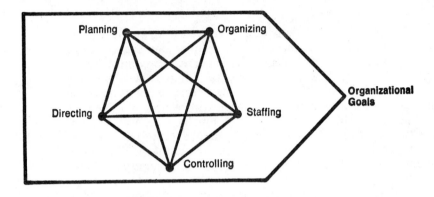

Courtesy: Barry Z. Posner

action necessary to accomplish the plan and achieve goals. The operations manual therefore helps each person determine how he will do his job. Planning should be done so well that those not connected with management understand where the firm is going, how it intends to get there and where they fit within the whole plan.

Organizing

"Establishing a formal structure of roles, tasks, and authority to achieve organizational objectives and coordinate human and material resources."

Organizing means identifying the relationships which should prevail among the people in the office. It is a matter of telling each person what his job is and explaining how it fits with other jobs that have to be done.

The most important result of good organization is that routine functions necessary to maintain the operations are done consistently and not overlooked. Organization is the means by which routines are welded into a smooth-functioning operation.

An important purpose of an organizational arrangement is to identify who can give the orders and who carries them out. The two words responsibility and authority are most important in an organizational arrangement. A basic management principle is that if a person is given the responsibility for doing something he must also be given sufficient authority or power to accomplish that task. If the sales manager is given responsibility for achieving sales quotas, he must have the authority to select methods to reach them. If he does not, he is powerless and his ability to function is hampered.

20

Staffing

"The recruitment, selection, appraisal and development of people to fill the roles and positions provided for in the organizational structure."

Staffing is a continuous function. Any real estate brokerage office that is doing well and planning to expand is always searching for good salespeople. Staffing involves the use of a combination of management tools. Psychological tools are used to select people, motivate them and measure their performances and attitudes. Financial controls are used to determine how effectively the staff is using the resources provided.

Staffing is the job of finding the right people for the right position so the combination of the two will support the achievement of the firm's goals.

Directing

"The interpersonal aspect of guiding, motivating and leading subordinates."

In a sales staff made up of independent contractors, directing cannot be construed as telling people what to do. In this case, directing consists of such functions as setting goals, helping the sales staff set goals, providing resources and assistance and developing an adequate set of working procedures. An operations manual setting out guiding rules of action can be an important tool in a real estate office. Direction in the form of training is vital to company image and to reduce traditionally high turnover.

While direction of employees is best accomplished by guidance and motivation, it is here that the manager can exercise a firmer hand by telling when necessary, due to the nature of the relationship.

Controlling

"Comparing actual operations with planned operations and making appropriate adjustments when deviations exist."

Controlling includes all those functions a manager does to ensure that all activities are proceeding in accordance with the goals of the firm and within the limits of the resources provided. Controlling can mean that a real estate firm has a bookkeeper who keeps account of all the financial transactions of the office or that the sales manager has a sales chart and reports periodically on listing and sales performance. Controlling is the act of keeping track of what people do and how resources are used, comparing what has happened to goals and then trying to identify the nature and reasons for the discrepancies which emerge and making whatever changes are indicated.

A controlling function of management which is not often discussed but which an experienced manager understands is called follow-up. When a manager assigns someone a job, it is necessary that he determine whether the individual has done it and how well. Follow-up is based on the assumption that since an organization is made up of people who will make errors and that since communication is often imperfect, the manager not only assigns individuals to jobs but develops means of measuring their performances.

Even though these management functions are stated separately, it is important to keep in mind that they are interrelated and in most cases occur simultaneously, although at any point in time one or more may be predominant.

These functions are considered central to the process of management. They are relevant and operational regardless of the level of management or type of organization with which one is concerned. As Koontz and O'Donnell have said, "Acting in their managerial capacity presidents, department heads, foremen, supervisors, college deans, bishops and heads of governmental agencies all do the same thing. As a manager, each must at one time or another carry out all the duties characteristic of managers."[7]

Having reviewed briefly the various ways to conceptualize the job *you* have as a manager, we turn again to a closer look at the people through whom you must get work done.

Major Theories of Motivation

"How do I get people to take their jobs seriously?" "How can I get some of these bright people to take initiative rather than just doing a marginal job?" "How can I get my salespeople turned on?" These are the kinds of questions managers often want answered, knowing how dependent they are on the voluntary commitment of energy, initiative and creativity of the people they manage.

In the first section of this chapter we gave the formula: human behavior is designed to meet needs. People will do the things they think will meet their needs. To better understand how to view human needs you may find it useful to consider the formulations of the three best known students of motivation: Abraham Maslow, Frederick Herzberg and David McClelland. Each of their approaches may suggest

Fig. 6. The effective manager is aware of the major theories and approaches to management

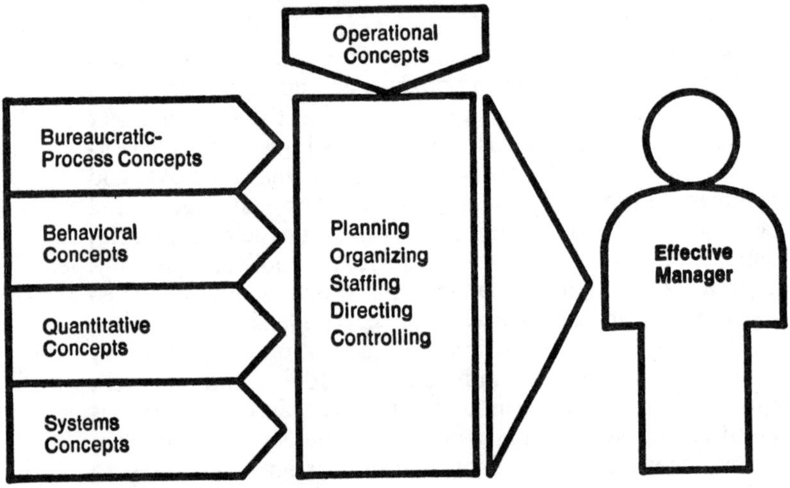

Courtesy: Barry Z. Posner

ways in which you can provide greater satisfaction on the job for the people who work in your organization.

Maslow's Hierarchy of Needs

In the most widely accepted formulation of human needs, Maslow suggests that human beings are constantly seeking to fulfill their wants. When one level of need is satisfied, another comes into focus and determines where the individual's energy is expended. Five levels of needs can be thought of as a pyramid with the base being the lowest unmet need that has the most influence on the individual.

Five Basic Needs

Physiological needs—food, shelter and air—are the most basic of all human needs. Fulfilling these needs is essential to keep the individual alive. They therefore take top priority until they are satisfied.

Security needs are next most important. These are the needs to protect oneself from outside danger, both present and future. They become the primary determinants of our behavior after physiological needs have been satisfied at least to some extent. A starving person may risk his life for food, ignoring security needs to respond to the lower, more basic physiological needs.

Social needs come into the picture after physiological and security

Fig. 7 Hierarchy of needs

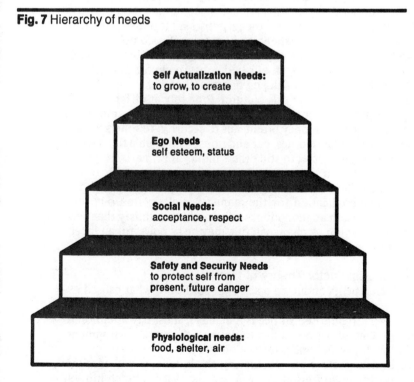

*Adapted from *Motivation and Personality,* 2nd edition, 1970, by permission of Harper & Row publishers.

needs have been met. Here we think of the need to be loved, to be accepted by others and to belong to a group. Think of all the things we do to make ourselves attractive to other human beings and how painful it is when we are ignored or rejected.

Ego needs for self esteem and status are next in the hierarchy. We want to think well of ourselves and be proud of who and what we are. We also want others to recognize our worth by according us the respect we deserve. Ego needs become a powerful force after the physiological security and social needs are at least partially met. Think of how much it can mean to a person to have an important title, a nice office and other symbols of status that remind him and others of his importance.

Self-actualizing needs are at the top of the pyramid. These are the needs to develop, to create and to contribute. "If an acorn could dream it would dream of becoming an oak tree." In the same way, most human beings have a desire to become more fully human, to use themselves more effectively and to fulfill their potential. There are occasions when a task is so enjoyable, interesting and challenging that we lose ourselves in it and no external reward is necessary to keep us at it.

Their Implication

As you look over this hierarchy of needs, reflect for a few moments on the best job you ever had, a job that really "turned you on." What was so great about that job? In a typical group of managers or workers who are asked this question, the responses almost always include words and phrases like "challenging," "personal accomplishment," "demanding," "exciting," "creative," "had responsibility," "lots of freedom" or "recognition." In our best jobs we almost always have our social, ego and self-actualizing needs well met.

Where does money fit in this picture? Probably at different levels for different people. To some people money is important to put bread on the table; to others money is a means to security; to others money is important to buy the clothes, car and house that enable them to socialize with certain people; to still others money is primarily a symbol of self-worth. And to some people money is important because it makes possible the freedom to grow and develop, to do things "on my own." The implication for the manager is clear: find out what need is uppermost in an individual's mind and try to satisfy that need more fully on the job. A change in title may be as powerful an incentive to someone as a salary increase.

Herzberg's Dual Factor Theory of Motivation

Frederick Herzberg conducted a series of studies of what caused extreme satisfaction and dissatisfaction on the job. He concluded that there are two different sets of needs a manager must pay attention to on the job. One set of needs has to do with the work environment; the other with psychological factors on the job.

If the hygiene factors are satisfactory, the individual will continue to work for the organization but will not necessarily stretch himself to do the best possible job. Factors like a decent salary, security, fringe benefits and good working conditions tend to be taken for

Fig. 8 Factors influencing worker satisfaction

Hygiene Factors (Dissatisfiers)	Motivators (Satisfiers)
Salary	Achievement
Security	Recognition
Fringe benefits	Nature of work
Work conditions	Responsibility
Status	Chance for growth, development
Adequate relations	Opportunity for advancement

Credit: Fred Herzberg

granted after awhile and do not motivate a person to extend himself. A salary increase may cause a temporary spurt in effort but soon ceases to be a motivator. The absence of hygiene factors causes dissatisfaction but their presence does not guarantee satisfaction.

On the other hand, certain factors do serve as motivators in the work situation. Factors like achievement, recognition, responsibility, the chance to grow or the chance to advance have the power to turn a person on. Again, you might check this against your own experience in the best job you ever had.

The implications for the manager are fairly clear. If you want your colleagues to extend themselves, make sure that they have plenty of opportunities to feel a sense of achievement, feel that their efforts are recognized and appreciated and feel that they have been given responsibility. Few things are more demoralizing on the job than to be taken for granted or to feel there is no chance to grow into larger responsibilities. The person who does a consistently good job needs to be recognized for that consistency. It is sometimes surprising how much a simple word of commendation can mean.

McClelland's Hidden Motives
At another level, David McClelland has identified three very pervasive motives that influence people's behavior on the job:

The need for achievement

The need for affiliation

The need for power.

These needs exist in different people with varying degrees of intensity. In some the need for achievement is predominant; in other the need for affiliation or the need for power is strongest.

Achievement
Persons with a high need for achievement have a strong desire for success and a strong desire to avoid failure. They are always looking

for ways to move ahead. They want responsibility and challenge. They tend to set fairly realistic goals and are willing to take reasonable risks.

When you are dealing with this kind of person, make sure his goals are clear and that he gets prompt feedback on his progress toward meeting them. This is where he gets his satisfaction and what propels him forward toward the next goal.

Affiliation

Persons with a high need for affiliation want most to be loved by others. They enjoy and seek out intimate, understanding relationships. They want to help others and they feel very uncomfortable when there is dissension. They thrive on personal attention and evidence of appreciation.

When you are working with this kind of person, make sure you take an interest in them as persons, not just as employees or salespeople. You might use them sometimes to help resolve conflicts between others in the organization. Seek their advice whenever appropriate, remembering that they enjoy being helpful. Many salespeople have high affiliation needs.

Power

Persons with a high need for power want to influence and control other people. They seek positions of leadership and are usually aggressive in stating their positions. They enjoy situations where they can persuade others. How the individual uses power depends more on his other needs and values than on the strength of the power motive alone.

When you are supervising a person with strong power needs, take care not to demean or push him around. His aggressiveness and desire to persuade others can be a great asset if the aggressiveness is directed toward achieving the organization's goals.

Using These Theories

Each of these concepts can help us think about human motivation in a more systematic way. They are not mutually exclusive. Their general thrust is quite consistent. Each supplements the other. You may find that in trying to understand the behavior of a given individual one approach is more helpful than another.

The most basic point to keep in mind is that the people around you are doing the things they think will help them meet the needs they feel. If you want to influence someone's behavior, the best question to ask yourself is, "What need is he trying to meet?" From this diagnosis you will get better leads on the satisfactions you might provide that will make sense to him.

What then can a real estate broker learn from this survey of management? He can learn that there are many ways of being a manager and that if he understands what the functions of management are he is more likely to be successful than if he concerns himself with the details of how to be a manager. What he hopes to achieve should determine how he operates. And once he knows what he hopes to achieve and understands the environment within which he is operating, he can then select from any of these schools of management to help him become a more effective manager.

Understanding which need is predominant in an individual helps you understand better why that person behaves as he does and what kind of influence he is most likely to respond to.

To quote from a study of successful real estate brokerage offices: "The real estate brokerage firms that are successful achieve this status because they are managed in one of two ways. The most numerous of the successful offices are managed by owners who recognized their lack of business ability in any field except that of selling and therefore organize and operate their businesses so that they are little more than sales organizations. The second group represents the evolving real estate office and anchor their activities in selling; but having done this either develop or acquire the necessary managerial talent which must accompany growth."[8]

Dimensions of Management

[1] Haynes and Massie, *Management,* pp. 39–43; as quoted by Gibson in *Academy of Management Journal,...* September 1966.

[2] McGregor, *The Human Side of Enterprise,* pp. 33–34, 47–48.

[3] Newman, Summer and Warren, *The Process of Management,* 3rd ed., p. 9.

[4] Michael and Jones, *Organization Management,* p. 473.

[5] Michael and Jones, *Organization Management,* p. 12.

[6] Koontz and O'Donnell, *Principles of Management,* 5th ed., pp. 46–49.

[7] Koontz and O'Donnell, *Principles of Management,* 4th ed., p. 53.

[8] Frederick E. Case, *Real Estate Brokerage,* p. 3.

Characteristics Essential to Success   2

There exists neither a formula to follow nor a set of questions to ask that will assure a person's being qualified to manage a real estate business. But experience and a study of many people who have succeeded reveal some of the skills and practices essential to success in this field and some of the questions to be asked as a self examination of one's general qualification for management.

The information in this chapter can serve as a guide to measuring people and their skills and aptitudes for management positions. It's information that can be helpful to people already in management positions, who are interested in analyzing their skills and methods and improving them; and it will interest salespeople and other staff members who want to know more about management techniques and challenges. It can help the latter group decide whether or not to work toward a management position.

There is a list of questions at the end of the chapter which management people or candidates for such positions can ask themselves. Answered honestly, these questions can help people to decide the direction they want their careers in real estate to go.

Characteristics Essential to Success

What are the characteristics of a successful real estate broker? What traits are essential to generating the best efforts of others?

The general brokerage operation, no matter what its size, has three managerial components: corporate, office and sales or line management. The person operating a small brokerage firm will be involved in all three; the larger the firm the more likely management people's responsibilities will be limited to just one of the components. But large or small, certain characteristics are essential to successful management, to generating the best efforts of all subordinates. What are they?

The list of desirable characteristics will invariably include:

Stability

Knowledge

Dedication

Integrity

Flexibility

Ability to make decisions

Desire

Ability to manage oneself.

People at the management level in real estate have a specific purpose: to provide the direction by which an organization functions continuously and successfully. They know how to work with and through other people to attain reasonable goals. They are able to recognize problems and know how to attack and solve them. As experienced business people they know the positive value of making mistakes, admitting them and correcting them. These abilities enable them to achieve the purpose to which the real estate business is dedicated: service and profit for all.

Without effective management even the best trained, most enthusiastic salespeople will fall short of their goals. Strong, continuous management is the glue that holds a business together. Good managers know that well made plans are worthless without an enthused, well-trained team to carry them out.

Stability
Stability of mind and purpose is essential to successful management practices. The manager who is strong will focus on the goal to be achieved and not allow himself to be diverted from it by anything less than a better idea for ways to achieve the goal. In this sense, stability

does not imply rigidity. There always exists the possibility of a better way of doing things. The talent to recognize and act on plausible suggestions is a mark of stability.

There are three facets to stability in management: *physical, emotional* and *financial*.

Physical Stability

Good health is essential. Real estate business managers must be equal to the same demanding work schedule salespeople follow plus be ready to extend themselves and go that extra mile. Physical stability is an essential quality to successful leadership.

Characteristics Essential to Success

There's a saying that "when you've got your health, you've got just about everything." Whether or not this is fact, it is a fair reminder that good health is essential to doing one's job well. History has examples of people who overcame health handicaps to go on to great achievements. But most of us require a sturdy constitution to meet the onslaughts of the day whether we're in management or some other position.

This book is not a primer on how to stay healthy. But the mention of health as one of the essential elements of successful management is germane. Without good health, any manager will soon weaken under the stresses and strains of his responsibilities.

Several years ago High Downs, speaking at an American Medical Association forum on health in the middle years, focused attention on the changing concepts of our working habits in the latter part of the twentieth century. Downs questioned the viability of the old Puritan ethic of work, work, work; the lifetime routine that wore a man out by the time he reached retirement age. All he had left at 65 was a new gold watch and a worn out body with only enough energy to sit in a rocking chair for his remaining years.

Today's smart management people, in fact most working Americans, are not ready to accept such a restricting work style and its outcome. They believe in and practice a balance of work and play. They seek recreation that is completely free of work relationships.

Find Outside Pleasure

Peter F. Drucker of the Claremont Graduate School of the Claremont Colleges stated in an "Op-Ed" article in the *New York Times* of May 5, 1974, that at the beginning of this century organizations and managers were quite insignificant. "In this century, the United States has become a society of organizations," he wrote, "each requiring a great many managers and a high degree of management.

"This means," Drucker continued, "that more and more of the people, especially most of the highly educated ones, can expect to work sometime during their lives as managers or as professionals in an organization and to participate actively in managerial work." He concluded that this group had increasingly become the central leadership group in our society and collectively its decision makers.

Drucker's thesis was that because so much of a manager's time and effort is devoted to his "public" (organization) life, he needs a private life with wholly different concerns, different values and above all different personal ties and different friendships. He needs not just a hobby but a serious outside interest in which he can excel and be recognized as an accomplished performer.

Why are such pleasures necessary for management people? Precisely because they form the armor against the gossiping, the inevitable defeats and the setbacks sure to be encountered in managerial life. They provide the needed, refreshing breakaway from the pressures and responsibilities of leadership.

Emotional Stability

The manager's emotional stability needs to be at its best when those he supervises are in the throes of emotional turmoil. When other tempers flare, when arguments assume the tensions of a pitched battle and when "team effort" threatens to go up in a cloud of smoke, it's the manager's emotional stability that is needed to calm things down.

It's a mark of emotional stability to understand there is more than one way to attack a problem and to know how to employ the better way. It's the talent to fight the fight in the manner of a healthy debate and not let it turn into a name-calling, finger-pointing free-for-all. In another time emotional stability might have been labeled a serene spirit: today it is called being "unflappable."

There are times management is called upon to listen calmly to both sides of a heated argument. A classic example common to real estate offices is the competing claim for a sales commission between two sales associates when the situation is not covered by the operations manual.

Whatever the controversy, try to avoid making judgments. There is seldom a single, right answer to any problem. Your role as manager will be more effective if it consists of asking the right questions, leading those engaged in the controversy to find a reasonable solution.

Whether major or minor differences, wise handling of emotional situations will result in fewer such incidents in the future. Effective management learns how to handle differences fairly and amicably and teaches staff people to do the same. When a problem is solved on the basis of what is right rather than who is right, you've not only solved a problem, you've strengthened the organization and its people.

A busy or unheeding manager compounds problems in his office.

Salesperson: "Hey, Fred, I've got a problem. I'm putting together a listing for the Miles property and..."

Manager: "Sorry, Jim, I'm just leaving on an appraisal job."

A week later...

Salesperson: "Fred, can you help me shape up this financing problem?"

Manager: "Jim, I'm on my way to a board meeting right now."

A month later...

Salesperson: "There's this argument between Joe and me over who's entitled to the commission on the Brown sale. Got a minute?"

Manager:	"Sorry, I've just got to leave right now for an executive meeting."
	Much later...
Manager:	"Hey, Jim, how come you never bring your problems to me any more?"
Comment:	He doesn't come to the manager anymore because the manager turned away every time he needed help. If the manager had said, "Jim, I can't do it right now. But let's set up a date now when we can both go over this..." Or, if it were a real emergency, he could have said: "I've only got five minutes right now. Tell me your problem; I'll think about it as I drive to the board meeting and get back to you as soon as I return. Is later this afternoon okay?"

A good manager is one who makes it look like he's doing nothing at all. He finds time to sit down and talk to people about their problems. He does it not by dropping the matter but by making an appointment if he can't handle it at the moment.

Emotional stability is needed to bolster sagging spirits. When, for example, a salesperson fails to get the listing he's working on diligently or when sustained effort to make a sale fails, it's the manager's role to sit down and *listen*. Listen as that salesperson tells you what happened. Ask a few relevant questions if he hasn't given you all the information you need. Then help him analyze how he might have done it differently. Finally, give him the guts and heart to go out and give the next opportunity all he's got.

Emotional stability relating to the job is also needed at home. When one's mate and family are relentlessly reminded of the burdens of the job, it inevitably leads to stresses and strains that have a bad effect on both business and home life. If, for example, you dwell endlessly on your office problems and ignore your mate's frustrations, you're heading for trouble.

Marriage counselors tell us it's *healthy* to communicate frustrations. You, in effect, are sharing your burdens with your mate. But it's *unhealthy* to so concentrate on those burdens that they close out all other interests and diversions. Soon your mate will resent your job, the firm and the bad effect it's having on family life.

The other side of this coin of emotional stability is the problem of coping with home difficulties so they do not have a negative effect on business life. Some people have a unique ability to seal off personal problems from business hours. In fact, there have been people who have achieved success by burying themselves in work to escape an unpleasant home situation.

It's a wise manager who sustains open communications with his staff so he is aware of the existence of personal problems. Helping them keep things in perspective, being understanding and supportive when they're going through difficult phases, not only cements personal relationships between the manager and his staff but also strengthens loyalties to the firm.

Financial Stability

Financial stability is a necessity to good management of a real estate office. It is difficult to succeed when hounded by creditors, whether for personal or company indebtedness. A poor personal credit reputation in the community can have a direct, negative bearing on the credit rating of the firm as well.

Tardiness in paying other brokers their share of commissions will quickly cripple the operation of a real estate business in the eyes of competitors. This careless practice is likely to result in losing top salespeople to a more reliable firm. It is easier to be financially stable if you apply your sense of fairness to designing a procedure that insures prompt payment.

Companies set up on a proper financial basis plan to plow back into the business a reasonable percentage of profit dollars. Financial stability demands that the manager not overspend profit dollars merely to keep his salespeople happy. Many real estate office managers have given away their businesses through overspending on things like contests and unreasonably high commissions to attract or hold salespeople. This practice is self-defeating because there is nothing left to manage.

Market fluctuations in the real estate business are as inevitable as in any other field. Whatever the reason for a down market, firms that are prepared to cope with severe market slumps maintain adequate cash reserves. They can weather the vicissitudes of market downswings while other less provident firms surrender to the first wave of reverses. The unprepared ones are first to merge, sell out or simply close down.

Salespeople respect managers who budget the finances of a company carefully. They want to know why a certain number of dollars are being spent in certain ways and how they are likely to profit from it. People are happier when working for a financially stable organization. It helps assure their personal financial security.

As an example of how sharing budget information with a staff pays off, consider the following experience of a successful, medium-sized real estate firm.

The manager shares his budget plan with his staff each year. This is done before the budget is finalized. He shares it with his salespeople so they know it's a realistic plan, based on what he expects the firm to produce. He goes over the general classifications, telling the salespeople what is planned and why. Then he asks for their opinions as to whether or not it's practical. Let's say they "buy" it (though he has remained open to their suggestions for possible revisions).

Three months later one of the salespeople comes to the manager and says, "We're not spending enough on advertising." The manager then responds, "But Joe, this is exactly what we budgeted to spend. Remember the day we went over the whole budget together? You thought then—three months ago—it would be enough."

Knowledge

No newcomer to real estate office management can possibly bring to the job all the knowledge he'll need. But what he doesn't bring with him he can surely get.

Three specific kinds of knowledge will be needed:

Knowledge of the real estate business

Knowledge of people

Knowledge of sound management practices.

Plan your program to continually add to your knowledge in all three areas.

Knowledge of the Business

This includes everything from how to get listings, write ads that attract prospects and find customers to buy the properties listed, to sales psychology and financing. Information about the community in which you do business should include schools, industries, churches, parks, libraries, shopping, banking, zoning restrictions, tax rates, history, civic and cultural opportunities and socio-economic data.

New information should be shared with staff. It is the kind of knowledge needed by the salespeople as they pursue their daily work. It's important that you be a fount of information for them. But you should carry it a step beyond that. When a manager stops teaching he stops leading and can soon lose credibility. As the leader, it is your duty to show them where to get information and how to develop their own contacts. If you do this, you'll not only help them grow but you'll also strengthen the firm's image in the community.

Knowledge of People

Second, you'll need to have and to keep on acquiring knowledge of people, how to motivate them and how to establish empathy with them. The people in this case are those associated with you in business as well as the customers, clients and all other people you deal with including bankers, mortgage company personnel, city officials, builders, lawyers and business, civic and cultural leaders in your community.

Psychologists have brought the word *empathy* into common usage but it is not always understood. Empathy is defined as the ability to accurately sense the reactions of another person. Empathy is the capacity to recognize the clues and cues provided by others in order to relate effectively to them. *Empathy is not sympathy.* Sympathy involves over-identifying with another person, thereby losing sight of one's own objectives. This blocks the ability to deal effectively with others. The individual with empathy is able to accurately and objectively perceive the other person's feelings without necessarily agreeing with those feelings. This invaluable, indispensable ability to get powerful feedback enables him to appropriately adjust his own behavior in order to deal effectively with others.

Translated to the practical management of a real estate brokerage, a manager with empathy listens to a salesperson's problem and helps him analyze it. But he remains objective and helps the salesperson find a workable solution. Salespeople are often involved with the emotions of a transaction. When a manager shares these emotions he is unable to give salespeople the help they really need. When he empathizes, he understands but stops short of becoming involved emotionally. When a manager feels himself getting emotionally involved in a salesperson's problem it is a good practice to defer his answer to their call for help. Don't rush into suggesting a solution. Wait several hours (or even several days if necessary and if possible) before you make a judgment or suggest a course of action. Taking this necessary time will make it more likely you will come up with a truly objective decision.

Knowledge of Sound Business Practices

A manager will also need all the knowledge he can get on sound management practices. This includes knowing how to recruit a good sales staff and office staff, understanding financial systems and records, developing budgets, setting up marketing and statistical controls, developing a policy and procedures manual, planning, organizing and supervising the overall survival, growth and profit goals of the firm. Beyond such basics as knowing how to rent office space, develop a floor plan for it, equip and furnish it, a well-informed manager will know how to keep up to date on what's going on in the real estate profession locally and nationally.

Training and information on good real estate marketing management practices are available from a variety of sources.

Management development courses are scheduled regularly by the Real Estate Brokerage Council™. Instructors are professional REALTORS® with a wealth of management knowledge and experience to share. Role-playing sessions offer training in actual real estate office problems. After-hours informal sessions enable students to talk with their peers.

Other kinds of personal development sessions are available in many communities. While they may not be programmed to fill your particular needs, you are likely to find them a profitable investment of your time. Wherever you find it, whatever form it takes, additional learning will help expand your horizons and enable you to become a better manager. Individual study will be important, too.

The greatest collection of real estate books outside the Library of Congress is located in the NATIONAL ASSOCIATION OF REALTORS® library in Chicago. Any REALTORS NATIONAL MARKETING INSTITUTE® member may borrow from this collection at any time. A letter or phone call will elicit prompt service.

Your local public library can be a valuable source of business reference materials. Even the smallest public library has access to a wealth of material from its state library. And in heavy populated areas most public libraries are now part of a unit system offering reciprocal use of all nearby collections. If you cannot conveniently go there, your librarian can have their books sent.

Remember to build your own business library, too. Encourage those on your staff to use it and to suggest titles and publications they'd like to have available. Learning of this kind soon becomes contagious and leads to profitable discussions and exchanges of ideas.

Dedication

Real estate is a service business where, with dedication, a manager can enjoy the satisfactions known only to people who help others solve their problems and realize their ambitions.

The manager who is dedicated to his job can find satisfaction from three sources: his own accomplishments, his staff's accomplishments and the satisfaction of the customers and/or clients they all serve.

Total dedication to the real estate business starts with being there.

In his tersely written book on management, *Up the Organization,* Robert Townsend draws the analogy between managers and playing coaches. He believes managers should be first on the field in the morning, last to leave at night. They should be ready to help their salespeople at any time. If they're not, they're not good managers in Townsend's opinion.

People who have other people reporting to them should be on hand to reassure the hesitant, give a green light at the proper moment, be calm in a time of crises and do whatever else is necessary to help the "players" advance toward their objectives.

A good manager makes being there a two-way street. Just as he is available to them at all hours for important action, they understand he may call on them on the same terms. Neither, it is understood, abuses this right.

Anything short of this, according to Townsend, and a manager's people will lose satisfaction, then interest and zeal.[1]

Dedication to the success of the business does not have to be at the sacrifice of one's dedication to his family. People's work habits vary as much as their thumbprints. What takes one man only eight hours to accomplish may require an additional two or four hours of effort for another. The job may be everything to a single person and his life-style can accommodate his work habits. To another, family-oriented person, dedication to family comes first. He may plan his working time to allow large blocks of time with his family. A good manager will understand these differences, help each set realistic goals and respect varying work habits so long as they do not interfere with job performance.

What of managers' and salespeople's dedication to the public they serve? Certainly any marked degree of indifference to the public will soon be reflected in a downward sales curve. Missed appointments, tardy arrivals, inaccurate handling of records and details all indicate indifference. They soon result in a poor reputation for performance and loss of referrals and repeat business.

Integrity

One of the most important traits salespeople observe about the manager is whether he has integrity.

What is integrity? "Integrity" is perhaps too solemn a word for the characteristic we're talking about. The old-fashioned phrase "all of a piece" is more like it. H. L. Mencken, who in his time was regarded as an outrageous man, was a person of unquestioned integrity. Like many other writers of great talent he was offered huge sums to do some other man's bidding. But he turned down the big money and never wrote a piece he didn't want to write. He was impervious to the seductions of wealth because he liked his life; he enjoyed what he was doing. He lived by his code of values.

People may forgive a manager's lack of some other important traits of good leadership but they will not overlook a lack of integrity. And they will fault top management for having placed such a person in a position of authority.

Flexibility

Flexibility is the fine art of maintaining a healthy balance between being firm and bending to every suggested change. When written goals are established and communicated effectively to a sales staff, a flexible manager will be willing to adapt to changing situations and make reasonable compromises when it seems the sensible thing to do. This does not imply surrendering to every pressure that comes along, for to do so is to become known as a wishy-washy manager.

Some two years following the publication of Alvin Toffler's best seller, *Future Shock,* a speaker quoted from it in addressing a small group of businessmen. "Must get that and read it," commented a member of the group. "It's too late," retorted the speaker. "Most of it is already behind us." That's how fast the world changes. Leaders who do not respond quickly to changing business patterns are soon left behind.

But there's a fine line between knowing what changes are taking place and participating in them. This is where a combination of knowledge and flexibility can be most productive.

Do you know the best sources or can you develop new methods for mortgage financing? Are you aware of vacant land that may be coming on the market and how that land might be developed to fit into the growth pattern in your community? Have you investigated how television might be serving your market better than print media? Have you made the acquaintance of top management people for the new factory that's being built near your town? What new marketing techniques might you develop to attract these company workers to buy your listings? If your salespeople suggest a rearrangement of the office and present it to you with logical reasons, do you sit down and discuss it with them or are you likely to reject it out of hand?

Develop friendships with the better minds in the business. A number of groups exist today that are made up of successful brokers from a broad area. They are not in the position of being competitive in any particular market. They are simply people who like to get together from time to time to exchange new ideas and techniques in the real estate marketing business.

Continuing education is an essential part of being flexible. This not only implies fact-finding knowledge but also a better understanding of behavioral sciences and decision-making skills. As these are developed a good manager learns how to really listen and how to respond in a positive manner. He encourages those working under him to continue to bring in ideas even though a great many of them will prove unworkable. Differences of opinion need not be a negative part of the day's management work if a manager knows how to communicate the difference between what's right and who's right, between opinion and fact.

As new ideas and change become part of a manager's daily thinking, he naturally begins to consider change in his own business position. A manager can never promote himself until he trains his successor. Some managers shun this facet of flexibility because of a fear that the successor may do a better job! When a manager stays on in the same position year after year, stagnation of the organization is a predictable result. An important facet of flexibility is to have as many people as possible know how to perform all the duties within the office. Encourage everyone to flex their business muscles, to try new ideas and to work in creative ways to help the organization grow.

Dr. James Batten, in *Tough-Minded Management,* points out that almost every staff in any kind of business includes innovators and "abominable no-man" types and all the others that lie somewhere in between.[2] Flexible managers are able to recognize many types and learn how to fit the useful ones into their organizations.

Let's look at the major types according to Batten and as they appear to a real estate manager: "The bright-eyed zealot who feels anything connected with growth and newness must be good, regardless of cost or net profit." He is interested in buying everything new on the market, urges use of every gimmick offered and can lead a manager to bankrupting the company.

"The man who waits for the boss to tip his hand so he can agree"; a yes-man. He's gutless and can often cause an otherwise successful manager to make poor decisions if that manager believes others really agree with him when, in fact, they're simply currying his favor.

"The suave individual who makes progressive-sounding comments, uses words like 'dynamic' often and contrives largely to hold his job." This person tries to impress others with his progressive language but really never moves off dead center. He generates a lot of nebulous conversation as he tries to cover his own ignorance.

"The tough-minded [person] who demands facts, a blueprint for action and realistic controls, yet is impatient to get something done." This type person is ideal when he also has the talents of the bright-eyed zealot. But if he lacks that "let's do it now" drive, he may find that by the time all his blueprints and plans of action are thoroughly analyzed, the opportunity for change has passed him by.

"The [person] who is opposed to innovation of any kind if it involves courage and positive action. His usual reaction to new ideas is 'Come on, now, let's be realistic.' " He tries to defend the status quo by always putting down new ideas. He fears change and tries to make the new idea look like one that was tried before. He may be able to persuade others not to try new ideas. Some of his fear has to do with not wanting others to get ahead of him.

The flexible manager not only knows how to recognize the foregoing types, he also understands when and how to fit their ways into established practices and planned changes.

Ability to Make Decisions

People look to a manager for answers. Unless he can provide them, they will start looking elsewhere. Although some decisions will have to be made more quickly than the following might indicate, it is a useful guide to the mental process.

First, be sure you understand the problem and the ramifications of any solution.

Review the problem in terms of existing policy. Ask if it is similar to past problems or if it is completely new.

Ask if it is similar to problems found before, if former solutions apply.

What would be an ideal solution? List all you can think of.

Gather all the data, get the facts and interview every person involved.

Separate fact from opinion. Weigh the information to determine what is true and can be substantiated and what is opinion. Discard the latter.

Determine the objective you want to reach. Review exactly what you want to accomplish in solving this problem. Is it simply a matter of settling an argument between salespeople or will it have ramifications throughout the entire organization?

List the possible solutions and their results. In a previous suggestion you listed all the ideal solutions. Now list only those which comply with the policy of the firm.

Determine the course of action most likely to succeed. You must now decide how you are going to present the solution to the staff. A management decision is always limited by two factors: the sophistication of the people who will carry out the decision and your ability to convince others that it is the best solution.

If you come up with a decision that is beyond the understanding or capabilities of the staff, they will not respond. Though it may have looked good on paper, it will be of no practical use.

Also, if you may come up with a wonderful solution but cannot show others how it will help them, they will not respond. Therefore, you must be sure how you will convince others of the benefits involved.

Put the solution into action. Don't wait until tomorrow or next week. Implement the action today. A good manager goes through the decision-making process constantly and is never reticent to put the solution into action.

Remember that people make decisions work. Therefore they are always considered limiting factors in whatever area, human or material, your decision may affect. You must tell the people the reasons for a particular decision. Make sure everyone understands.

Don't worry about a decision after it is made. You cannot always be right. A poor decision is usually better than no decision at all. One who never makes a decision loses his ability to lead others and therefore is not effective as a manager.

Finally, follow up on the decision. Evaluate it. If necessary, revise it. Talk to the people involved to see if the decision is solving the problem. If, in fact, it is not, then it is necessary to revise the decision.

Desire

Desire plays a major role in successful management. A good manager wants to solve problems. He enjoys people and likes to see them succeed. And he certainly wants to succeed himself.

A good manager actually seeks problems that need to be solved. He relishes analyzing them and working out solutions. He also enjoys sharing his knowledge. He wants to teach salespeople where to find answers. And he's able to communicate it all in a direct, understandable way.

Desire can be the means of making poor salespeople great. It's what enables a person to commit himself to others and to their success. A manager knows that if his staff succeeds it is a direct result of his leadership; if they do not, the failure is at his doorstep and he has failed, too.

Managing Oneself

Finally, a good manager can manage himself. It has been implied throughout this chapter in a variety of ways. It has been said that too frequently the last person we study is ourself. Here is a list of questions to examine to see if you have some basic management characteristics.

Do I really want the responsibility of managing others?
Am I sensitive to people, their desires, their fears? Do I have empathy?
Can I motivate, direct and lead others?
Do I manage my time effectively?
Am I creative? Can I bring new ideas to the sales staff?
Can I make decisions?
Do I listen only to what I want to hear?
Do I create an atmosphere where others can express themselves?
Do I understand the principles of two-way communication?
Do I give full attention to people when problems are discussed?
Do I lose my temper when my decisions are questioned?
How much criticism can I take from the salespeople?
Do I recognize that people are my real strength?
Do I realize that my program will not work without complete and eager participation of the salespeople?
Do I treat everyone fairly or do I tend to have favorites?
Do I have the courage to carry out company policy, no matter who it may hurt?
Do I really want to see other people succeed?
Do I understand when I have to be the boss in control of my people?
Do I know how to make a profit and develop my business?
Am I willing to pay the price to be a manager?

If the foregoing kind of self-examination does not appeal to you, there's another way to have a good look at yourself and your management talents.

Take a piece of paper, draw a line down the center. Put a plus sign at the top of the left column, a minus sign at the top of the right column. For the next few hours or even a couple days, list in the plus column all the areas in which you believe you control situations that confront you. Under the minus sign list those areas you feel you do not control or which you know can be improved.

When you've listed everything you can think of, ask yourself, "Am I a manager or am I being managed by others?"

If the minus column outweighs the plus column you may want to review this chapter to see if you have the basic characteristics for a management position. You may conclude that you are fighting yourself to accomplish something you honestly do not want. As the philosopher Seneca put it, "Do not ask for what you will wish you had not got."

If the plus column outweighs the minus column, you have the promise of being a successful manager.

---

[1] Townsend, *Up the Organization,* p. 84.   [2] Batten, *Tough-Minded Management,* p. 36.

Transition 3

A person moving into management in the real estate business is usually one who has had experience in selling real estate. He is likely to be a person whose advice and counsel is sought by fellow salespeople. In other words, he has proven his ability to acquire knowledge, use it himself and share it with others. His plan of action and at least to a degree his thought processes agree with those in top management. He not only gives his best to "this sale" but also plans ahead to next week, next month, even next year and what he wants to achieve then.

As a new manager begins his work he understands that an effective, efficient, high quality real estate business operation is his primary function. He wants his salespeople to succeed. Their growth and recognition come first in his thinking and actions. A manager knows the success of others helps assure his own.

He is a practical person and knows that the transition from sales to management cannot happen overnight. The time required to make a successful transition will vary with the individual and the firm. Depending on his prior role in the firm and whether or not he has any management experience and/or formal training a number of personal adjustments have to be made and training acquired. He'll likely develop a job description for himself outlining how he will perform in his new role and how he expects to grow.

One of his first personal considerations will be to make certain that in learning new skills and adding them to his business repertory he is careful not to change his personal style, his way of doing things and relating to others, the qualities that brought him to a management position.

Perhaps the greatest challenge to the new person in management is making the transition from being "one of the bunch" to becoming their leader. This is a major psychological transition. When attacked a step at a time it's not the traumatic experience some people expect or fear.

Transition

Transition can be tough. Ask anyone who's been through it. It's tough to change from doing things to directing others to do them. It's tough to move from being one of the bunch to being the boss and being accepted in your new role. It's tough to learn where to turn to find out many of the things you'll need to know. Tough as it all is, it isn't impossible. People do it everyday. Many make the transition from doing to directing with only a minimum of trauma.

How you make the transition to management will depend on the needs of your firm and what you bring to the job. Write out a job description for your new position. It should cover both the needs of the business and your personal needs. Get this down on paper before you start in the new job. What will you be doing now that you did not do before? How many functions from your old job will still be required of you? Will your needs be satisfied more fully in the new job? Do your needs fit the company's plans for the future? How will your time organization differ on the new job? If it looks like you will be doing more of the same old thing or doing it faster or doing it for the salespeople, you have not described a true management position.

Your personal job description will vary according to the set up of your firm. You may be a selling broker, a sales manager/broker or a full time administrator. The principles of management apply in all these roles. How you fulfill your management role will depend on your skills, traits and needs. The way you do it should be very authentically your own. The big challenge is to get organized and get going.

Professor Theodore Levitt of the Harvard Business School, discussing the crucial factors that impact on managerial success or failure, once made the point that there is no such thing as the right way for a manager to behave or to do his work.

Each person brings to a management position his own traits and talents. He may share with his peers some skills and the desire to succeed; but in the end it is the manager himself who will do the job and he'll do it in whatever way he sees it, working within the established structure.

Levitt asserted that one can be taught about management but he cannot be taught management.

He further said that it is altogether proper to try to learn better, more practical technologies of management including planning, budgeting, control systems, communication, manpower development and the like. But it is not desirable to try to change the personality of the manager. His interpersonal skills in dealing with people and situations, the most important aspect of his basic working method, are not appropriate subjects for arbitrary manipulation. They are, however, subjects to be studied to increase understanding of people.

First Step

Once the owner of a real estate business adds a salesperson on any basis other than that of equal and co-determinor of the firm's policy and procedure, the functions of that broker change to a management role. He is no longer free to engage in total self-determination and a program of personal action. That broker becomes a manager of the behavior of at least one other person. The manager immediately takes on a role in which he has to plan things the firm must undertake, organize his own energies and those of his salesperson, direct and motivate the salesperson, and control or review the results of the action of the salesperson. The manager decides in which areas the salesperson is free to work, sets the standards by which actions may be taken and reviews the results of the salesperson's performance.

The reluctance or inability of brokers to manage their business is considered by many the greatest single force suppressing prestige and status for the real estate industry.

In precise management terms, a manager decides upon goals, quotas, deadlines, standards and budgets. He uses the management process which is planning, organizing, directing, motivating and controlling work effort to organize people, money and time. The legal relationship of the independent contractor or employee has no bearing on the need for good management or the need for individuals associated with the firm to fit into the managed program.

Real estate sales and management are quite different worlds. Your situation may require you to move back and forth from one to the other or you may move wholly into the field of management. Your management role will depend on the size of your firm and whether you continue to sell. Whatever your role, remember that real estate salespeople need management and that without real estate sales there is nothing to manage.

Three Management Positions

Three basic types of management positions are generally found in real estate offices:

Selling brokers

Sales managers/brokers

Administrative brokers.

Selling Brokers

Selling brokers are usually found in relatively small offices of three to ten people. Selling brokers continue to depend on their own sales production as their primary source of income. They sell in competition with their own salespeople. Learning how to do this in the fairest way possible is extremely important.

It is estimated that approximately 85 percent of all real estate firms in the U.S. are in the small office category just described. Thus, the selling broker is by far the most common type of real estate business manager.

When salespeople understand how a selling broker operates and know he makes every effort to be fair with them, his competitive selling role will be accepted. For example, a selling broker who is fair does not take all company leads but works primarily on listing property and representing buyers from his own personal referrals. He does not take the best company leads and service them himself nor does he allocate all the undesirable leads to his salespeople.

One of the advantages of a selling broker is that he is constantly aware of every aspect of the market being encountered by his salespeople. In the parlance of the business, he's "out there where the leather meets the road." And because he is, he doesn't have to rely on their reporting back to him the changing situations and new problems they encounter day by day. Whether it's a softening of the market, difficulties developing in mortgage funding or rumors of a proposed zoning change, the selling broker has it too. He has given it thought and is often prepared to act on it by the time his people communicate it to him.

Another advantage of a selling broker is that he's alongside his people as they work and can spot bad habits as soon as they begin to develop. Such an early warning system can save time and dollars in taking corrective action quickly. Such counseling can be on a one-to-one basis or may be incorporated in the firm's continuing training program. In the latter case, such training can also prevent the same bad habits in other salespeople.

A marked disadvantage of a selling broker is that he must bother with details rather than manage.

Sales Managers/Brokers

Sales manager/broker management situations are usually found in firms with a staff of 15 to 20 people. In this type operation the manager spends most of his time bringing good people into the business, training them and helping them achieve their goals. Although a portion of this manager's income continues to come from his own sales production, the major part is derived from the bottom line.

The dual role enables the manager to do a thorough job of in-house training as well as provide leadership in selling. It is a delicate balance, calling for a keen sense of fairness. But the total effort is aimed toward the ultimate achievement of the firm's sales goals.

In a larger firm, the manager can often delegate more non-selling responsibilities to others than might be possible in a smaller operation. Even part-time sales work restricts the amount of time such a manager can devote to planning growth, setting objectives, planning and controlling the budget and measuring results on a regular basis. This manager's skillful use of the talents of several staff people in helping with these tasks or even doing some of them for him can add measurably to his success as a manager. Such help need not come from salespeople. Secretaries, accountants, clerks or receptionists are a few of the sources for such help.

Administrative Brokers

Administrative brokers are usually found in large firms, often those having multiple offices. Their primary management responsibilities are to plan the firm's operations and supervise a sales manager or managers who in turn direct the salespeople. Administrative brokers do little or no listing or selling. On occasion they may assist in bringing in account type sales.

These managers spend a great deal of their time planning the overall destiny of the firm, both short-term and long-range. They work with sales managers rather than salespeople. Their income derives almost entirely from the bottom line of individual offices and the whole company.

The owner of a modest size real estate business sometimes plays a similar role as he administers everything that goes on in the business. The smaller the firm, the higher the production per person needed to make it all fit together into a successful operation.

Three Levels of Management

No matter which of the three foregoing types of real estate business management position you hold, you will find yourself managing people at two, and in some cases three levels:

You manage yourself

You manage others

You manage others who manage others.

With such diverse combinations of business styles it is important to keep your thinking free of restricting rules that limit how any one owner or firm operates. Each has been described briefly to enable you to identify in a general way how your firm and your job fits the most common types of brokerage firms.

Certain generalizations can show the ways a real estate business can be organized. Whatever the size of your firm, whichever type management you choose as being best suited to your needs, all share the goal of a successful, profitable operation. Each also shares the problem of keeping abreast of how things are going with salespeople and being alert to those who need help or closer direction or supervision. Everyone in management shares the challenge of being a continuing source of encouragement and enthusiasm.

Some Common Transition Problems

Management training courses conducted by the Real Estate Brokerage Council™ of the REALTORS NATIONAL MARKETING INSTITUTE® each year serve thousands of members and offer them an opportunity to share ideas and problems. In addition to discovering that their problems are shared by many, real estate managers learn how to overcome the difficulties of a period of transition as they move from selling positions to management.

Four problems seem to be shared by most new managers:

The tendency to do it yourself

The belief that you not only know how to do it but that you can get it done a lot faster

The fear of losing a listing or a sale

The tendency to motivate the way you like to be motivated.

"Do It Yourself" Syndrome

Ego contributes a lot to this problem. Wanting to "do it yourself" is really lacking confidence in your salespeople. You don't want to believe they will ever be quite as good as you are because you have both the knowledge and the experience needed.

At this point it's a good idea to remind yourself that you've been appointed, not annointed. Let go of your own ego a little and build up the salesperson's. Give him the knowledge and confidence to go out and do it himself. Be sure to encourage him to do it his own way.

As long as you continue to do it yourself there's no arguing with you when things go wrong. If you fail, you can come back and say you failed because of the "dumb seller," "tight buyer" or because somebody "didn't understand the market." Whatever your reason chosen to hide your failure, there's no arguing with you when you're the boss. No one is likely to have the temerity to sit you down and review, step by step, the course of events.

And the salesperson hasn't learned a thing except, perhaps, that you're not the leader he thought you would be. Until he fails, he really hasn't learned. If the salesperson sent out on his own fails, a skilled manager encourages thorough feedback on exactly what happened. Careful, relevant questioning can tell the manager what happened and help the salesperson understand what went wrong, why and how to try to correct it this time and prevent its recurrence.

A good manager maximizes reward situations and minimizes anxiety situations. When a salesperson succeeds, be prompt and generous with your praise. Spread the good news. This soon results in his coming to you with his successes as well as his problems. You'll be better informed on all counts. Your salespeople's successes will stroke your ego, too.

Still another facet of the "do it yourself" syndrome is a natural reluctance to give up doing what you enjoyed. Everyone who likes selling likes the competition, relishes the contacts with buyers and sellers and enjoys helping them realize their dreams and ambitions.

As a successful salesperson you enjoyed the one-to-one confrontation of selling. Learn to transmit this sense of competition to your salespeople in a selling sense, not a managerial sense. Successful salespeople have a habit of feeling they've got to win. When you send them out to do that, that's good management. But if you use that same one-to-one confrontation in a management encounter and you win, you've lost! If a salesperson is put down because of your competitive spirit, which is really ego acting, and you tell him in an abrasive way that he's doing it all wrong, the very determination that made you a success in selling will defeat you in management.

Enjoyment of direct contact with people was perhaps one of your major reasons for going into real estate in the first place. You like people, like dealing with people and like to be with people. Now your challenge is to move away from that particular set of people, buyers and sellers, and develop new contacts. These new people will be important to your success as a manager: bankers, builders, civic leaders, developers, local government and other management people. Soon this new mix of people will replace the buyers and sellers of the past who now become part of your management routine only occasionally.

"I Can Do It Faster" Syndrome

The belief that you not only know how to do it but you can do it faster is another facet of the "do it yourself" syndrome.

Lack of confidence in salespeople is rooted in failure to give them adequate training. If you succeed as a teacher you'll set them free to go out and use your teaching, knowing you'll both benefit, personally and financially. Teach them, trust them and turn them loose to do the job in their own way. Your way worked for you. Somebody let you do it your way and didn't force you to follow theirs. Steer clear of trying to force people to do things your way. It might not work for them. Give them the necessary guidelines and train them to develop their own techniques.

As you learn to do this you will be developing your management skills and you will win the respect of the people you've trained. Be there to answer their questions and make suggestions when asked but let them do the job themselves.

Fear of Losing Income

Fear of losing a listing or a sale is the third of the four most common problems. Every listing and sale may be extremely important to your immediate income needs. That's understandable. But it's equally important to let the salesperson do his job. It affects your immediate relationship with him and the long range success of both the salesperson and your firm. Put in that perspective, it becomes easier to keep hands off. It's important that you do.

If the salesperson gets the listing or makes the sale, you'll both have reason to celebrate. But if you take the transaction out of his hands and you succeed, he'll never be convinced that he wouldn't have done as well. And if you fail, you've failed both the salesperson and yourself and you've weakened your relationship with him in the bargain.

Let him do his job. If he succeeds, celebrate. If he fails, sit down with him quietly and get the thorough feedback mentioned earlier in this chapter, letting him tell you what he thinks went wrong. He may ask you how you'd have done it. He may suggest ways in which he will do it differently next time around. In either case, he's learned through his failure which is a growing process available to each of us in no other way.

Types of Motivation

Managers often stand in the way of good management because they tend to motivate others the way they would like to be motivated.

Gil comes to me with a problem. I listen and after pondering for a few minutes, turn to him and say, "Well, Gil, if I were in your shoes I guess this is what I would like to have happen." Unfortunately, I'm not in Gil's shoes and in any case the motivation I give him is completely unsuited to his personality. However, Gil will seemingly accept my answer but never use it and probably never ask my advice again. I tried to motivate him the way I would like to be motivated instead of the way he should have been motivated.

Fear Motivation

There are three basic types of motivation. The first is known as fear motivation and it has been around for many years. It's not unusual for a manager to address a sales meeting and threaten a salesperson by saying, "If you don't have three more listings next month, you're out" or, "If you don't have four sales next month, you're out.

Obviously, if the threat is carried out, pretty soon there won't be anyone left on the sales force to motivate because somewhere along the line they will not meet the demands put upon them and it will be necessary to dismiss them. If the threat isn't carried out it doesn't take long for the salespeople to find out that the manager is just blowing off steam and they won't worry about his demands. When this happens there's no motivating factor at all. If one individual is terminated because he doesn't perform and another one who didn't perform isn't, it doesn't take long before the manager is accused of favoring one person over another.

About the only time fear motivation should be used is when the manager has told the salesperson what is expected of him and he hasn't performed. Then the manager has to give him one last try. For example: when Gil joined the company, he was told that the company required salespeople to earn at least $8,000 in their first year to cover minimum desk costs. Gil has been with the company six months and has generated only $2,500. The manager has a counseling session with Gil and says, "Gil, for the last six months you've sold only $2,500. You know we need approximately $8,000 to cover our minimum expenses. Therefore, Gil, in the next 90 days it is important for you to meet the following goals: we would like to see this amount of listing activity and x-amount of sales activity. If you're not able to make that particular goal then I'm afraid it will be necessary for you to take your license elsewhere." This is a form of fear motivation but it's directed to an individual who was told at the beginning what was expected of him. The manager didn't call Gil into the office and say, "You're out." To Gil's question "Why?" the manager would say, "Well, you didn't do what I expected" and then Gil would say, "But you never told me what you expected." In this case, the salesperson was told what was expected of him, had not performed and was given one more try through a type of fear motivation.

Incentive Motivation

This is used quite commonly in the real estate business. It usually employs sliding scales of commission, bonus plans or sales contests. Incentive motivation is frequently used because it's probably the easiest and requires very little thought. If a salesperson wins the contest he gets a colored television; if he makes $10,000 he's given a bonus and so on. Incentive motivation is a type of motivation in which a manager finds love instead of respect. "I'll give you a trip to Florida if you'll love me." "I'll give you a bonus if you'll love me." Basically, the manager's trying to buy his people rather than setting up respect that will stand the test of time. If a manager depends exclusively on incentive motivation, whenever difficult decisions are made that are not agreeable to the salesperson, he'll simply leave the firm. When another company has a better incentive plan than his present company's he may also leave.

Incentive motivation can have a positive effect when used for morale reasons or to accomplish a specific goal. It is seldom successful when management is trying to increase volume. Real estate does not lend itself to this type of reaction. One can't stay out an extra two hours and work in the evening and be sure to come home with a listing or make a sale.

Sales contest incentive plans are good to raise morale in general or to get specific duties done by stating, "If you make five calls a day for the entire week we will give you a small incentive." Giving a small incentive to one who makes five calls a day for a week or whatever may serve to get specific projects started. Incentive motivation has only limited capabilities. The manager who tries to buy his salespeople will soon find that they will be buying their managers in other companies. It doesn't take long before salespeople feel that incentives are their right and are no longer turned on by the incentive itself. This is seen in comments such as "You owe me the trip to Florida because I won the contest," or "You owe me that $500 bonus because I made $15,000."

Personal Motivation

The only true form of motivation which can be used day in and day out in the real estate business is personal motivation, where the manager gets inside the salesperson's head and finds out what turns him on and what turns him off. When this occurs, the manager can truly stimulate and motivate the salesperson the way the salesperson thinks instead of the way the manager thinks. The reason this technique is not used frequently in real estate is that it takes a tremendous amount of time to get into somebody else's head and find out what his action and reaction to certain situations will be.

Selling sales managers in real estate find their own sales work requires so much time they are not free to devote the time and effort necessary to be personally aware of each one of their salespeople.

When Gil has a problem the selling sales manager is present. When Susan has a problem he is also present. But when Gil's and Susan's problems are solved the sales manager goes into the field to do his listing and sales work; he does not find time to sit down with his salespeople and chat with them on a casual basis to really discover what kind of people they are.

Specialists in the field of personal awareness say there are three types of subliminal motivation managers should be aware of.

Negative Motivation

When a manager employs negative motivation he gets things done through a negative reaction which can be well typified in fear motivation. Constantly saying "If you don't do this," and If you don't do that," is a negative motivator. Generally, the success pattern of a negative motivator covers a short period of time, giving people two weeks or thirty days at the most, to accomplish something. But once it's accomplished that negative motivator cannot continue to be used because its negative style can give only short-term positive results.

Neutral Motivation

Neutral motivation does not necessarily mean that the recipient is satisfied. But if it is not present it will very likely cause stress. An example of this could be a real estate company in a ten-year-old office that has never been decorated or painted inside or outside and has huge chuck-holes in the parking lot. Some of the salespeople may leave the firm because they're embarrassed to bring their clients into a shabby office. They leave and go to other offices that are better kept. However, if that broker filled the chuck-holes and repaved the lot and painted the property inside and out today, it does not guarantee the salespeople will stay with him. He has simply done what is expected. Therefore, it is known as a neutral motivator.

Time after time it has been shown that certain incentives are basically neutral motivators. Though there may be a short burst of enthusiasm when an incentive is won by a salesperson, it won't be long before he takes that incentive for granted and is wondering when he will be given more.

Experiments in industry have shown that raises may stimulate the recipient for one to two weeks. But the recipient soon takes it for granted and wonders when the bosses are going to give him another raise which of course, he well deserves, at least in his own mind. Therefore, incentive motivation many times becomes an unending circle of giving and giving for only short-term responses.

It's been shown in this country that incentive motivation really hasn't been successful in long-term economic results because we continue to increase people's salaries and yet find that they give us less and less production which eventually results in economic crisis.

Positive Motivation

The final type of subliminal motivation that one may be concerned with is called positive motivation. This type of motivation creates and maintains positive results. Positive motivation can best be exemplified by personal motivation mentioned earlier. Getting into somebody's mind, finding out what makes it work, being able to talk and respond, talk and react to that person as they would like to have you react and to motivate that person as they would like to be motivated is certainly positive in nature and can have good long-term results. In addition to building successful friendships, it also provides a level for dynamic leadership because it builds respect.

It is true that at any one time a manager may employ all three forms of motivation, as well as all three forms of subliminal motivation. However, he should be conscious of how he uses them and what he is trying to accomplish each time he's confronted by a people problem.

Moving from "The Bunch" to "The Boss"

An almost universal plea from people moving into management positions which require them to supervise their former peers is "tell us how we become boss after we've been a buddy."

Four works may sound like a pat answer to this important query but they are a guide:

Know yourself

Be yourself.

Neither is easy. Achievement of each comes more easily to some than to others. But it is important to do both to the best of your ability.

Know Yourself

As you move into management to supervise people with whom you once worked side by side, accept the premise that they already know a great deal about you. They may even know some things about you better than you do yourself. They are likely to know which parts of your old job you enjoyed most, which things you did because they had to be done and what you put off until the last moment or maybe never got around to at all. Recognize and admit to yourself what others may know about you that you don't like to face up to yourself.

Were you great on listings and sales but reluctant to keep a daily time sheet? Don't be surprised if this work/procrastination pattern emerges in those you supervise. As you discipline yourself to get more things done on time so will those who report to you.

There is no definitive study of the business of upward perception and performance (how you look to your subordinates and how they react to how you look to them). Informal observations in the general field of management suggest that appraisals of the boss by subordinates are most accurate; appraisals by the boss of subordinates are less accurate, and self-appraisal is least accurate. Such perception applies in real estate management just as it does in any other business.

If you listen sensitively to what others try to tell you about yourself, you can learn a great deal. Observe which of your communications elicit fast action by the group and which have to be pushed. They may reflect your own strengths and weaknesses. The best practice is to seek upward appraisal from sales associates closest to you whose judgment you trust and who will not substitute praise for appraisal.

Be Yourself

You were chosen for or chose a management role because of your skills and what you are. Don't try to be somebody or something else. And if the offer of promotion to management is conditioned on a remake of your personality, shun it like the plague. It is better to continue what you're doing, your own way. Let no one turn your whole world topsy-turvy as they try to fit you into their mold.

If you've always come on strong, keep on coming on strong. Don't try to switch to a Casper Milquetoast approach. It will only throw your sales associates off. They'll be smart enough to know it won't be long before you revert to type. The thing that will frustrate them is trying to time your switchback. They will know it's coming but they'll not know when. Thus, your world and theirs will be slightly off its axis until you get back to being yourself.

This doesn't mean you should not sometimes and in some ways adjust to changing conditions or adapt to new ways of doing things. To do this is a management strength. But adjust and adapt in your own way. Don't try to change yourself. Your sales associates know how to react and work with the real you. To be other than your authentic self will throw them into a state of confusion and will weaken your efforts in your new job.

If your company does not offer a training program, take advantage of courses and publications that are available. They will help you achieve a management frame of mind, add to your skills and strengthen your self-confidence and enthusiasm for the job.

Only as you train for management and gain experience in the daily operation of a business can you hope to rise to a position of leadership in your field. If you become a truly successful leader you will carry along those whose success depends upon you and upon whom your future success depends.

Other Transition Changes

Following are some frequently asked questions from people new to management and one possible answer.

How can I organize my time so routine work and personal things can be handled after spending necessary time with salespeople?
By learning to delegate routine chores, reserving only the most difficult, sensitive problems for your attention.

How can I overcome resentment of men who are managed by a woman?
Forget your sex and focus on your job.

How can I remove myself from competition with other salespeople?
Go into another area of selling such as commercial-industrial or concentrate on referral business only. Don't seek out new clients.

How can I learn to assume responsibility in management when my previous responsibility was only to my customers?
Involve your salespeople more; you'll have to make some decisions but let them make some of their own.

How do I learn to handle disputes or terminate salespeople without tearing myself up emotionally?
Look at these responsibilities in a positive way. You're working for everyone's benefit. Above all, be consistent.

How can I motivate salespeople so they are as goal-oriented as management?
It's your job to constantly remind salespeople of the company goals as well as their own and how they will benefit. Be sure they have the whole picture.

How do I establish guidelines that will constitute success for the company? As a salesperson they were my own goals. Now others are involved.
You've got to know what you are trying to achieve. Too many man-

agers have no goals at all; others have too many goals. Establish overall goals for the company then decide on primary objectives for the next three to six months. Keep the sales staff informed.

How do I assume responsibility for administering policies I had no part in making, particularly in a branch office where all decision are made in the main office?

You can't motivate others to do something you don't believe in yourself. There will always be minor differences. Some of these can be resolved by discussing them with top management. If a firm's policy is wholly negative to you, you ought to consider going elsewhere.

How can I show leadership over friendship?

Friendship involves two factors: leadership or respect and loving or caring about the other person. If you are consistent in your decisions and as fair as you can be, you'll gain the respect of your staff. Then the quality of caring about each other is a natural result.

Leadership 4

The power of your firm to attract and hold good people will be only as strong as the leadership you provide and your effectiveness as a teacher.

Leadership involves not only the operation of a real estate business today but what will happen to it in the future. Five, ten, fifteen years ago the industry faced problems that now fade into insignificance. But the leaders who solved those problems are in the firms that survived. Today they face new dilemmas. What today's leaders do to meet today's problems will be a factor in their survival to meet and beat tomorrow's difficulties. Thus, the technique of leadership and problem solving is a great and continuing concern.

It's a credit to the vision and spirit of today's leaders in real estate that tomorrow's standards are being thought about and formulated now. Problems change greatly. The concepts of leadership are little altered over the years.

Leadership

Leadership is a word often given a variety of meanings and applications. It is used to describe certain attributes. In the context in which it is used in this book, the word relates to administration and management as it applies to the real estate business. Even here there is no all-encompassing, perfect definition.

Ask a group of people to define leadership and you'll get as many different answers as there are people. Then ask those same people to name one or even several people, from any time, past or present, whose names occurred to them as they were defining leadership. It is highly probable that no more than one or two of the same names will appear on any two lists. That's how diverse our interpretation of leadership is.

Consider the names of people who at some period in the history of the world have been spoken of as leaders: Caesar, Napoleon, Patton, MacArthur, Grant, Lee, Lincoln, Washington, Churchill, Eisenhower, Lenin, Mao, Christ, Mohammed, Gandhi, Socrates, Thomas Aquinas, Rothschild.

Which of these people would you accept as true leaders of their time? Why? Which would you reject? Why? Do these people share the same qualities? Can you identify a common denominator among them?

There is a never-ending need for men and women who possess the skills and that special inner drive that propels them into positions of leadership.

Definitions of Leadership

What is this elusive, exclusive quality called leadership? There are many definitions today. Whether wholly new or reflecting some change from past concepts, all are germane to the job to be done in the real estate business today.

Leadership has been called the ability of a person to influence other people to create, perform and actuate results. This is done through reasoning, integrity, compassion, understanding, credibility and confidence of direction and not through fear of change.

Batten, in *Tough Minded Management,* says "Positive leadership, simply defined, means the kind of direction which assumes a job can be done, the problem solved and the negative attitudes overcome until proven otherwise."[1]

The authors of *Leadership and Organization* define it as "interpersonal influence, exercised in situations and directed through the communications process toward the attainment of a specified goal or goals."[2]

All these indicate the art of leading requires creativity, positivism, problem solving, goal setting and achieving, communication, confidence, integrity and empathy.

58

Leadership is what you hope you provide. It is what people expect from you. But the definition of what you provide and what they expect you to provide can be quite different.

Most people in business today are managed, not led. They are treated as staff or personnel and not as persons. Management cannot create leaders. It can create conditions that encourage people with the potential to become leaders. Or, it can stifle them.

Leadership, says Peter Drucker, "is the lifting of a person's vision to higher sights, the raising of a person's performance to a higher standard, the building of his personality beyond its normal limitations."

Leadership is not a chevron on the sleeve or a title. It is a functional process.

Leadership Styles

There are currently at least three styles of leadership: authoritarian, democratic and laissez-faire. And there are styles that combine elements of two or all three. No matter how a real estate manager functions, it is a certainty that he cannot manage or lead from behind an "iron curtain." He must deal with his subordinates.

To illustrate the options of the first two categories, Fig. 1 presents

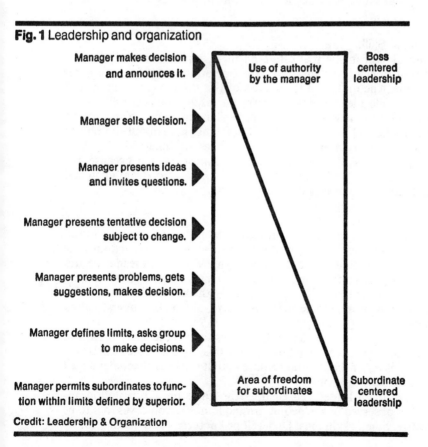

Fig. 1 Leadership and organization

Manager makes decision and announces it.

Manager sells decision.

Manager presents ideas and invites questions.

Manager presents tentative decision subject to change.

Manager presents problems, gets suggestions, makes decision.

Manager defines limits, asks group to make decisions.

Manager permits subordinates to function within limits defined by superior.

Use of authority by the manager

Area of freedom for subordinates

Boss centered leadership

Subordinate centered leadership

Credit: Leadership & Organization

the "Continuum of Leadership" as discussed in *Leadership and Organization*.

The third style, laissez-faire, is presented in *How to Develop Better Leaders.*[3] These authors suggest the leader help establish a climate of cooperation, help the group organize itself, help them determine procedures, keep responsibility for decision making with the group and help members of the group learn from experience. Many brokers believe this style impractical in real estate because control must be trained by management.

Management's role is to prepare the ground for leadership through a spirit that confirms in the day-to-day practices of the organization strict principles of conduct and responsibility, high standards of performance and respect for the individual in his work.

The Concepts of Leadership

Robert L. Katz, consultant in the field of corporate strategy, wrote about the skills of effective administration (leadership) in a *Harvard Business Review* article in 1955. The soundness of the approach he set forth in that article is attested by the enduring popularity of the piece.

Professor Katz examined the three basic skills he believed to be essential to successful administration: technical skills, human skills and conceptual skills. All three are interrelated. Each is important in itself.

Technical Skills

Technical skill in the real estate business implies understanding of and proficiency in all phases of the operation for which one is responsible. The tools and techniques of this discipline are many and varied. While a leader may not carry the responsibility for all phases of the business, he will know a great deal about the phase assigned to him; and he will be concerned with learning more about the phases of the business that are not his assigned responsibility.

Of the three skills, technical skill is the most familiar because it is what we live and work with every day. In the past, job training in real estate has been concerned most with sales skills.

Human Skill

Human skill in a leader requires self-understanding as well as keen perception of the thoughts and actions of others. It also requires the ability to communicate what he wants and why. Such a leader creates an atmosphere of trust and enthusiasm which reflects his sensitivity to the needs and goals of his people. With this understanding and sensitivity he is able to act in ways acceptable to and understood by others.

It may take time to develop the sensitivity necessary to skillful leadership. But no matter how long it takes, each day's efforts will come a bit easier than the day before until it gradually becomes a part of the leader's behavior.

Everything a leader says or does (or leaves unsaid or undone) is heard or observed by the people around him. Katz observes that to be effective, human skill must be developed naturally and unconsciously as well as demonstrated consistently in the leader's every action. What he says and does must be genuine. It must become an integral part of his whole being.

People who are good salespeople may fail completely as administrators. A wise leader will not try to persuade such a person to leave the field in which he excels and is happy. A good leader will let such a person stay in sales and become a leader there. Real estate will always need great leaders in selling.

Conceptual Skill

As used here, conceptual skill involves the ability of the leader to see the real estate business as a whole. He recognizes how the sales staff, office personnel, buyers, sellers and the people in all the outside services necessary to the business are interdependent and how a breakdown in any phase of the business affects the whole. Understanding these relationships and the significant elements in any real estate situation enables a strong leader to act for the good of the whole firm.

The success of any decision depends on the conceptual skills of the people involved in the decision-making process and those who must implement the decision. When, for example, a broker decides to change the firm's sales commission rates, he should be sure to take into consideration all the elements involved: office costs, all other financial considerations, the people involved and his competitive position in the marketplace. The leader who recognizes all the relationships involved in such a decision and the significance of the change he is planning is almost certain to be more effective in administering it.

The leader who is constantly creative, thinking of ways to improve his present business and new directions that may be open to the firm, contributes positively to the general tone of his organization. But he is not autocratic.

In the words of David Berlo, a management consultant, we are living and working in a time when information has displaced authority as our main control system. No longer can a leader tell his people to do something with any assurance his orders will be carried out. Today's business people want to be told how it all came about, how it will affect their lives, both business and personal. And if they like it and if the leader has done his homework well, they'll buy it happily and productively.

Human Relations

Man's basic instinct for self-preservation is very strong; his need for self-esteem is normal. A good leader understands this and finds ways to make maximum use of each person's style in a creative way.

In the organization of any group, three basic concerns need to be interwoven into its relationships for the well being of the whole. These are:

The manager or leader and his own psyche

The individual or subordinate and his needs, wants and desires

The actual situation (be it sales or other) in which the manager and his subordinates function.

Group therapy advocates suggest that people can only understand each other and themselves through concentrated interpersonal group participation sessions. Since most business firms could not afford the luxury and inconvenience of this form of understanding human relationships, it is incumbent upon them to provide opportunities for individual growth.

Self Insight and Analysis of Our Subordinates

If the leader is to understand other people, he must first have a thorough understanding of himself. That is, he must understand his own personality, goals, motivations, wants and needs, prejudices, attitudes, knowledge, concepts of ethical behavior and his reactions when he is in a subordinate position.

Second, the true leader must understand the people he is to manage. He has to be empathetic and able to put himself in the other person's shoes. A leader must know what makes people tick. Why are they motivated? Why do they resist? Why do two people respond differently and sometimes oppositely to the same situation?

When a leader wants to motivate his subordinates, Maslow's "Hierarchy of Needs" provides an excellent key to people's needs. (The chart is presented in Chapter 1.) According to Maslow, the pyramid of individual needs ranges from the base physiological needs (food, shelter and air), then security (no harm, continued earnings), social (sense of belonging) to ego (self worth and confidence, recognitions). At the top of the pyramid is the greatest need of all—that of self-actualization (a sense of accomplishment).

Maslow's hierarchy can guide a leader in his thinking as he asks himself the following questions, found in Paul G. Buchanan's *The Leader and Individual Motivation.*[4]

Why do people behave as they do?

How can I get people to respond the way I want them to?

Why don't people understand things that to me are simple and clear?

Why do they sometimes act against their own interests, resisting changes that may benefit them?

Why do they sometimes react one way in a given situation and very differently in the same situation at another time?

Forming impressions of others is part of our daily experience. What do I think my salespeople think of me as a person, a leader, a helper? A positive leader trusts his motives and actions, has confidence in his ability to understand himself and others and exudes self-discipline in controlling his personal feelings so as not to blind his perceptions. He will check his impressions against facts before reaching a conclusion. He will be open-minded and willing to listen to suggestions of others.

A leader's knowledge of himself and his empathetic understanding of the people he manages work inseparably in dealing with situations and problems faced by management and salespeople.

Need for Personal or Human Direction

Once a managerial leader recognizes the differences (sometimes small, sometimes immense) in the individuals under his direction, he must develop an ability to diagnose and fully understand each one's unique behavior. He must be able to sense when individual egos are threatened, personal relationships between salespeople are on the threshold of a breaking point or feelings appear to overwhelm sensible objectivity.

It is sometimes suggested that a well organized and implemented policy and procedure manual will preclude any major occurrence of management-personnel breakdown. It is true that such a manual sets forth the firm's modus operandi and thus prevents many disputes. But this dispassionately written document of company goals and policies can never replace a strong leader. His leadership talent can transform potential conflict into the more manageable form of a problem to be solved. Here again, a leader guides his people into determining what is right, not who is right.

If the leader of any group is to accomplish his role as a coordinator and not a manipulator of human behavior toward a common goal, he must determine the abilities and attitudes of his people in a given situation. He gets the complete facts of why, where and what through proper communication. He is a good listener. He draws on past and present experiences with the salesperson. He determines the self image of that person. Then he develops that person's abilities, and alters or enhances his behavioral attitudes to rectify the situation. In consequence, the salesperson is led toward fulfilling his needs.

The ancient Chinese philosopher, Lao-tzu, said, "To lead the people, walk behind them." A modern use of the exhortation is found in the example of how one leader helped "coach" his subordinates.

When Benjamin F. Fairless was chairman of U.S. Steel Corporation, he coached his subordinates by responding with searching questions when they came to him for an answer to a pressing problem. Said Fairless, "When one of my vice presidents or the head of one of our operating companies comes to me for instructions, I generally counter by asking him questions. First thing I know, he has told me how to solve the problem himself."

Fairless knew how to lead his people from a possibly self-destructive encounter with the boss to a positive, creative exchange that resulted in the growth of the person's self-esteem.

Need for Positive Direction

We are brought up to find out why an idea won't work rather than how to make it work. What a negative concept on which to base our lives! Yet we've done it traditionally.

Leaders know how to organize situations so that people do not have to defend either themselves or their ideas. Relieved of the burden of self-protection, people can be taught how to expend their energies on positive action.

Those who learn to bypass the traditional, negative approach and attack problems and possibilities in a positive way are our real leaders. They are our time and money savers. They are the people who move America and its businesses off dead center and onto the mainstream of progress.

If you have a person on your staff whose standard response is negative (not infrequently one who considers himself an expert is especially prone to this), call on him in the next staff or sales meting with a restricting lead-in, "Tell us what you like about the suggestion just made." You'll accomplish two things with this approach. First, you'll show the whole group you are alert to this person's negativism and can manage the situation. Second, you teach them one of the ways to keep what might be a weak idea alive until it gains some strength.

People are conditioned to think and act critically and accept criticism for bad ideas, as long as it is done with a minimum of personal reference. They tend to suppress their hostile reactions by covering them with humor or to withdrawing from the conversation unless, of course, they do come out and shout another person down. Either of the two foregoing reactions are not productive of the result you seek: ideas, and how to make them work.

Positive leadership need not be clothed in complex terms or abstract concepts. Simply defined, positive leadership means the kind of management that sees what needs to be done, assumes the job can be done, explores the possibilities and decides how to accomplish it.

The best leadership motivates people to work by telling them why they are working and how essential they are to the success of the business. By relating job processes to company, department and personal goals, a good leader stretches the imagination of his people and sends them out to meet the challenge of today, alert to the potential of tomorrow.

A positive leader asks aloud and often the questions that seek out problems. Then he asks those involved to concentrate on what solutions are possible. He is receptive to every solution suggested no matter how improbable it may at first appear. Having strengthened the self-confidence of his people by sharing the problems with them and asking their help in finding solutions, he has shown courage and his own self-confidence. People have a right to expect this of their leaders.

The Listening Leader
A good leader listens. It is said that a person ceases being a supervisor and become a leader when he stops talking and starts to listen.

A leader listens as problems are conveyed to him. He listens with eyes as well as ears. He sees tension. He sees anger building. He sees indifference. And everything he sees converges into the total knowledge he accumulates as he listens.

One of the most important ways a leader listens is to ask mirror type questions that lead a subordinate to understand why a problem exists. Feeding the question back to the salesperson often results in his supplying his own answer.

Good leaders also listen to themselves. They ask: why am I doing this? What will it accomplish? For whom? Do others understand both the questions and my answers?

As good leaders listen to themselves with both eyes and ears, they learn to their surprise that many of the things being done may be unnecessary, unproductive or even downright harmful to morale.

Is all the data you ask your people to assemble really useful? Is it used? If so, could it be gathered with less time spent by each person? Could the data thus assembled be used more productively than it is now? If it is not used at all, how soon can you eliminate the procedure? Will you remember to tell everyone involved why it's being dropped and how they'll benefit?

Another point most people fail to recognize or admit is the degree of destructiveness in each of us. We each think of ourselves as the exception to the rule, the one who behaves decently. And we are shocked when someone has the temerity to point out how damaging are some of our most common actions.

This enters the leadership picture when the staff meets competition from their leader. A leader is sure to have ideas, too. And he may feel they should be put forth for the simple reason that the firm can't afford to lose any idea that could prove useful. So what does a leader do?

If he contributes his ideas throughout the meeting he will unconsciously favor them. Subordinates are hypersensitive to this and it reduces their commitment and the probability of success. The leader is destroying their creativity.

According to George M. Prince, author of *The Practice of Creativity*, there are specific times when the leader may contribute his ideas.[5] They are welcome during the discussion of early possible solutions and when pressing for ideas later in the meeting; but he should offer them when there is no other action. If a member voices an idea the leader should support it, restating it to make certain he understands what the member had in mind. If he can then add to, build on or strengthen the idea, he should do so. After every member's ideas have been explored thoroughly, the leader may introduce his own. However, the general rule is that the leader always gives the idea of every member precedence over his own.

Assume there is value in any notion a member offers. Search out that value no matter how wild the statement may sound. Humor and laughter are often used as a before-the-fact defense against attack. You can easily retreat to "I wasn't really serious about this idea." A good leader probes laughter not only for the above reason but also because the elegance of an emerging idea may be intuitively pleasing before anyone is consciously aware of what the idea really is. The value of such intuitive urgings must not be underestimated.

How a Leader Looks to Others

If one were to ask, "What is your opinion of your manager?" one could get answers like: "Willing to listen," "Do not always agree with but we respect," "Firm but fair," "Lets us know he cares," "Rules with an iron hand," "Doesn't get along with the group as a whole" or "Never bends, even when wrong."

A good leader knows he cannot please all his people all the time. He understands that his greatest challenge as their leader is to make work so interesting that they will go at it with real motivation to succeed. The techniques of good management, handled with skill, can help a leader guide his people to achieve personal goals as well as the firm's goals.

Listed below and on the pages that follow are some proven techniques that real estate business leaders have found effective in recent years.

Twenty-one Suggestions for People Who Want to Lead[6]

Let each person know where he stands; do not fail to discuss his performance with him periodically.

Give credit where credit is due, commensurate with accomplishments.

Inform people of changes in advance. Informed people are more effective.

Let people participate in plans and decisions affecting them.

Gain your people's confidence; earn their loyalty and trust.

Know all your people personally. Find out their interests, habits and touchy points and capitalize on your knowledge of them.

Listen to your subordinates' proposals. They have good ideas too.

If a person's behavior is unusual for him, find out why. There's always a reason.

Try to make your wishes known by suggestion or request whenever possible. People generally don't like to be pushed.

Explain the why of things that are to be done. People do a better job then.

When you make a mistake, admit it and apologize. Others will resent your blaming someone else.

Show people the importance of every job. It will satisfy their need for security.

Criticize constructively; give reasons for your criticism and suggest ways in which performance can be improved.

Precede criticisms with mention of a person's good points; show you are trying to help.

Do as you would have your people do. The leader sets the style.

Be consistent in your actions; let your people be in no doubt as to what is expected of them.

Take every opportunity to demonstrate pride in the group. This will bring out the best in them.

If one person gripes, find out his grievance. One person's gripe may be the gripe of many.

Settle every grievance if at all possible; otherwise the whole group will be affected.

Set short- and long-range goals by which people can measure their progress.

Back up your people. Responsibility must accompany authority.

Ten Practices of Successful Leaders[7]

Observe with application. Observe and absorb.
Know how to listen. Want to hear.
Take copious notes. Capture ideas as senses respond and react.
Welcome ideas. Be open minded.
Value time highly. Use it skillfully.

Set regular goals. Strive to attain them.

Try to understand first. Then and only then, judge.

Always anticipate achievement. Build on your people's strength.

Know how to ask clear, courteous, incisive questions which are creative and intelligent.

Know how to organize your people's approach to challenges. Focus on what is important.

Meaningful Leadership[8]

Study the art of directing people: Know how to lead, direct, manage. The mark of a good leader is not how well he can drive his people but how well he can lead them.

Study ahead of them: Leadership is drive. Lead by pace setting. Work harder and smarter than your people do. See the problems first and think ahead to solutions.

Study the art of persuasion: Learn how to bring people to your way of thinking. Read books on persuasion and sales psychology. Apply sales psychology in leadership the same as you do in selling.

Seek your salespeople's advice: Ask for their opinions. Encourage them to express themselves. Consult with them and accept their ideas. Don't think you know all the angles.

See their viewpoints: Learn to listen to their problems. Hear them out, even when you don't agree. Try to walk in their shoes. Understand before you decide.

Help them to see your viewpoint: Explain your point of view better. Don't just state it. Justify and support it. Give your reasons. They will help and cooperate more readily if they know the background and reasons for your decisions.

Get the job done well: Don't just be agreeable. Be effective also. Be liked but also be efficient. Follow through on plans. Get things done. Know your business. Speak from knowledge and with authority. Have a positive mental attitude at all times. Demonstrate your ability often. Manage by being a manager.

Be democratic: Be humane in thought and action. Be a part of your sales force rather than head of it. Put yourself on the other side of the fence. Know your people. Lead by serving. Get others to want to do what you want done.

Be kind and considerate: Be sympathetic, not petty. Treat as you would be treated. Be kind to beginners, never rude to anyone.

Be courteous: Be courteous to all salespeople. Courtesy pays off.

Be even-tempered: Hold your temper. Cultivate an even disposition. Be calm. Don't blow up.

Be patient with imperfection: Have the patience and tolerance of a saint. Be patient with human frailties.

Be fair and impartial: Have no favorites. Treat all salespeople equally. Be fair but firm.

Be honest: Be sincere and truthful, straight from the shoulder. Don't hedge or cheat. Never ask a salesperson to be dishonest. Build leadership through character. Keep faith, keep your promises. Be conscientious.

Be helpful: Always be ready, willing and able to help. Help a person to see his need for help. Be tactful in criticism. Help coordinate the salespeople's activities. Remember, guiding is better than pushing.

Be friendly: Be a friend and advisor. Be a manager with a smile. Have friendly conversations with your salespeople.

Be approachable: Make yourself easily available for complaints. Help cement human relationships by letting your people know they can bring their problems to you.

Be dignified and yet a little distant: Be polite and businesslike, friendly but not familiar. Do not be an intimate friend with salespeople. Be their leader, not their buddy or pal. Be sufficiently aloof to command respect.

Be well acquainted with your salespeople: Be interested in and get to know their families and their family situations. Show a sincere interest in them.

Be punctual: Be dependable. Always be on time for appointments.

Build loyalty to the company and yourself: Give salespeople a feeling of belonging in the company. Stimulate personal loyalty. Have them wholeheartedly behind you. Help them to feel close to the company and to you, the manager.

Cultivate their respect for you: Win the respect of your salespeople. Gain their confidence. Maintain a good reputation by a clean life, clean language. Dress well. Be presentable. Be faithful to your duties.

Make harmony an important aim: Unite your sales force in their common purpose. Develop esprit de corps. Develop a happy group. Develop a feeling of interdependency within the group. Work toward unity and harmony in the team. Watch for and avoid or eliminate trouble makers. Discuss the need for harmony. Eliminate any cause for jealousy.

Face unpleasantness frankly: Air troubles. Have bull sessions when necessary. Permit and encourage suggestions when things aren't going smoothly.

Hold meetings often and regularly: Make them inspirational and interesting. Keep them brief but constructive and educational. Use a little humor occasionally. Plan and organize your meetings and conduct them according to the rules. Leave yourself out of the meetings. An "I" attitude can hinder your image. Ask a salesperson what he would have done. Give salespeople a chance to talk about their problems and methods. Encourage them to present their ideas.

Leadership in the Future

It has often been said that to achieve one's goal through others, we smile at some, swear at others, counsel most. But never forget to treat each as an individual.

Frank Nunlist, Chairman of the Board of Worthington Corporation, was quoted in *Tough-Minded Management* in considering the future. As Nunlist looked toward the year 2000 he said, "I believe the characteristics of our society will be far more varied than they are today and that Big Brother and Big Father will not be wanted or accepted.

"What will be wanted will be thoughtful, creative, imaginative, understanding, intelligent leadership—leadership that will be effective because its reasoning toward the common weal is valid, sound and thoughtfully conceived; leadership that shuns the use of power, manipulation and fear. There is no doubt in my mind that leadership by thought will replace leadership gained through the power of money, the power of politics, the power of military might or the power of personality."

Nunlist continued, "He [tomorrow's leader] will realize the great strengths that lie in the point and counterpoint of individualism. He will spend more time in creating satisfactions for people as individuals and will tend to destroy some of our present concepts of mass management."[9]

Today's smart leader will keep uppermost in mind that he needs all the help he can get. This can be one of his most important discoveries in establishing his role in leadership. And he will remember that he is not permanent. No one is. One day someone else is going to succeed or replace him. The best leaders will have prepared that someone else for a very exciting, rewarding role.

[1] Batten, *Tough-Minded Management*, p. 19

[2] Tannenbaum, Weschler and Massarik, *Leadership and Organization*

[3] Knowles and Knowles, *How to Develop Better Leaders*

[4] Buchanan, *The Leader and Individual Motivation*

[5] Prince, *The Practice of Creativity*

[6] Batten, *Tough-Minded Management*, p. 75.

[7] Schultz, *Bits and Pieces,* November 1973.

[8] Chinelly, Sr. REALTORS NATIONAL MARKETING INSTITUTE® COURSE

[9] Batten, *Tough-Minded Management*

Functions of Management: 5
Planning and Organizing

Managers of many real estate firms operate on the theory that if they do everything right and work hard they will make a profit. That is literally true. But effective planning and organizing could make the job a great deal easier and success even surer.

This chapter will examine the planning function and how it can help you avoid the nervous anticipation that comes when one is not prepared to cope with changing market conditions, pressures of competition and the independence of salespeople. Effective planning and organizing will enable you to channel more of your energies in more positive ways as you come to understand and use the resources available to you.

Functions of Management: Planning and Organizing

The planning function for a real estate firm consists largely of determining what business the firm is going to be in (the mission statement) and then developing an operating system for the enterprise. It isn't enough to say simply, "We're going to be in the real estate brokerage business." Management must establish goals or objectives and must determine the areas in which real estate brokerage will be practiced. The manager for example must define whether this is to be a business of residential real estate sales and leasing; or a business of residential and commercial real estate; or a business including insurance; including financing; including the activities of subdividing and construction or a business exclusively devoted to any of these. The principal planning decisions of the manager have to do with determining the limits of action for the firm.

The planning function also includes the determination of the major policies that will guide the firm in the conduct of its business. The policies will govern the general behavior within the principal functions, although policies do not outline procedures to be followed. A firm's policies on listing might define the kinds of listings acceptable and the duration of listing contracts. Other policy areas would include the guidelines to advertising, including media and expenditures; advertising budgets; policies on training and compensation and policies covering interoffice cooperation.

The Organizing Function

A second major function of top management is organizing the business at large. Organizing means determining the department structure, the allocation of efforts and the assignment of duties or responsibilities.

A third function of management is to develop key business resources. The real estate business is not only human resources in the form of sales staff and office personnel, it is also the capital and real estate resources necessary to the business.

Finally, management implements all the planning and organizing into a working organization which operates within the policy framework.

A strategy statement for a real estate brokerage firm might go like this:

This real estate firm is to be a single office dealing in residential and estate brokerage, operating in the northeast quadrant of the city, dealing in properties of the middle- and upper-value class primarily for owner occupancy through a sales force of independent contractors. The sales force will engage in general service. The firm will participate in the multiple listing service and will take exclusive listings only. The managing broker will be active in listing and prospecting,

72

taking outside general office calls and specializing in high value residential properties. He will not participate in unrestricted calls to the office or in floor time. The sales goal of the firm will be X million dollars per year for the next two years with a minimum quota per salesperson of Y dollars.

Central management strategy decisions of what business the firm will be in and what the policies of the firm will be are usually the hardest to make. And they have to be made with the least tangible evidence in hand. Of all types of management decisions, planning and policy decisions usually have the greatest impact on the firm.

The need for central strategy decisions is usually the most obscure of all top management decisions. Symptoms of difficulty in the firm usually appear in operating problems. For example, an advertising campaign goes awry, the listing system isn't working or open houses are not productive. The usual reaction is to attempt to repair the difficulties in those particular business functions or to make repairs in the organization or in policy relations, whereas the difficulty may lie in the total concept of the firm, namely, the identification of the business in which the firm is engaged.

Setting Overall Direction

To set an overall corporate strategy, the manager has to make an evaluation of predictable, probable and possible environmental conditions and changes having to do with factors such as economic, social, political, technological, population and general competitive forces.

In making strategy decisions, the manager tries to determine the firm's strengths and weaknesses, its present potential, its unique competencies and its own special resources and circumstances. He settles on his own objectives and finally outlines possible options and courses of action and chooses from among them.

Some real estate offices operating today have an income and expense factor of approximately $25,000 per month or almost $300,000 per year. This commitment is made with little information as to expenses over and above the rent and other very basic expenses to which they are committed, perhaps an advertising contract with one or more major newspapers and some form of agreement with the salespeople affiliated with the firm.

A broker in such an operation generally does not try to estimate year end profit that will result from his and his salespeople's efforts. He sees too many variables, too many things beyond his control to predict income and profit.

The fact that these variables exist is the reason to plan for a profit figure. If you do not have a total operating plan, both short- and long-term, with all the pieces of the puzzle put together to develop a profit picture, you will not know what moves you must make in order to reach your goal as changes take place in both your organization and your budget.

It makes little difference whether you are opening a new office, expanding into a branch office or offices, setting up a plan for the coming year or the next ten years or if you are new to the business of management in an existing office. No matter what your situation, it is important to understand the need for a good operating plan.

Sales Objectives

A sales manager has two objectives:

To make sure this month's sales are higher than last month's sales

To make sure this month's sales are lower than next month's sales.

But ask yourself what you can do when sales go down. And what you can do when the sales force is temporarily cut back, no matter what the reason. Here is where advance planning includes the element of flexibility. It's usually easier for a small firm to maneuver quickly to respond to changing market and staff situations. But no matter what the firm size, a total plan, thought out carefully and implemented with continuing supervision and regular evaluation, is much more likely to be a flexible plan. The more thoroughly you know what you are doing, the easier it will be to adapt to changing needs.

Let's see how you can start by analyzing and determining your personal goals, then your firm's goals as you begin to develop your plan.

Personal Goals

While it is not the purpose of this chapter to explain the value of personal goals, it is important to understand that the personal goals of the owner are key to planning the future of a real estate firm. The plan and organization of a real estate firm should reflect the goals of the owner. Clearly defined goals of the owner, including profit and personal involvement in management and/or listing and selling by the owner must be set before planning and organizing phases are developed.

One must decide if the office is going to be one of specialization. If it is, the market the specialization will serve and the limits within which the firm will operate must be decided. For example, a residential office may or may not take listings on duplexes, triplexes and quadruplexes. On the other hand a commercial and investment properties office may decide to establish a minimum dollar figure for listing on properties of not less than a certain amount.

Planning to Achieve Goals

Goals set by the company and its principals must be attainable. They must be set up in order of priority. Alternatives to reaching these goals must be explored. Not only must a first choice be made but provision for switching to a second choice must be kept in mind.

For example, let's say you have an operating office that is doing a gross of $120,000 from brokerage. In other words, this is the income you get from your sales and listings after you pay other brokers their co-op shares. That means you have about $10,000 gross income per month, your company dollar. You have five salespeople. This averages $2,000 gross income from the production of each salesperson.

As you begin to think along these lines you will understand that gross income production per salesperson is the key to the total gross for your office. If your problem in planning is how to increase your gross income for the office, you want to study ways to expand the gross income per salesperson.

74

Examine several of the alternatives open to you.

Enlarge the Staff

The first way to increase gross income that occurs to most people is to increase the sales staff. If you have been skillful in developing salespeople who consistently bring in $2,000 a month gross there is little reason to believe you could not go ahead and hire more salespeople and have them do the same thing. However, increasing your sales staff brings you face to face with some new considerations.

Can you maintain the quality of your sales staff? If you increase your sales staff from five to ten, can you reasonably expect that all ten will average $2,000 per month?

You are going to have to recruit five new, qualified salespeople. You are going to have to train them. You are going to have to provide physical facilities for five more salespeople.

Increase your Commissions

Another possible way to increase gross income is to increase your commissions. If you have been negotiating for six percent, you might increase it to seven. Can you do this and keep up the same volume of sales? What will your competitive position be? Could you maintain your income and decrease the amount of work you have to do? How? Do your salespeople believe their service is worth more? Can they negotiate the higher commission if other brokers are negotiating for a lower one? Is your advertising and merchandising program sufficiently better than the competition to warrant a higher fee? Can you persuade potential sellers how they may be able to actually benefit by paying your firm more? What are some of the valid reasons you can give?

At this point you might have another thought. Instead of increasing your fees across the board, you might think in terms of a minimum fee based on your cost per sale. If you find in analyzing the financial structure of your existing business, or one that you plan, that the average sale is costing you $1,400 or more, selling a $20,000 property at a six percent fee results in a net loss. So you may consider setting up a fee structure which basically requires a six percent fee or $1,500, whichever is greater.

Increase Sales Volume

Another way to increase your income would be to increase sales volume and/or sell more expensive properties, or change your internal or external commission splits. How can that be done? You might do it by developing some sales promotions, more contests or incentives or more advertising. You might shift the salespeople's work load. Salespeople have the same time limit as everyone else: 24 hours a day. Work with them to see how you both can get more out of their day. If your salespeople are doing a good job selling but bog down in handling clerical work, you might add to your clerical staff so salespeople can spend their time more productively and thus yield a higher profit to your firm. The overhead for hiring one person and adding a little desk space to handle clerical work for your salespeople may be much lower than finding two or three more salespeople and providing desks and training for them.

You may want to aim at selling more expensive properties. You many want to develop a commercial/investment property department. You may even want to set a minimum on the size transaction your firm will handle.

Adding a commercial/investment property department may take some additional training and development of salespeople. And it may take a special type of salesperson. If you've been specializing in residential properties, you will change your image as you expand into other types of business. This will require more advertising and promotion.

Even when you move from lower priced homes to higher price ranges you may find some of your salespeople are more adept at handling lower priced properties. If so, you will have to find new salespeople to handle properties in the higher price range.

In summary, you can see that to plan for greater gross income you have a choice of increasing your sales staff, the number of sales, your commissions or your dollar volume, adding new services or some combination of these choices. As you plan, consider the pros and cons discussed here and decide which new efforts are most likely to help you reach your goal.

How Salespeople Relate to Company Goals

If you are starting a new company or a new branch office it is relatively easy to find salespeople who concur with your company goals. But if you have inherited an existing office and sales staff, it will be important to understand their goals and see how they relate to the company goals before you develop a plan. This is especially important if you are setting an annual goal for the first time. Each year thereafter you should consult with your sales staff about their goals. In helping them plan, show them how to translate income goals to the actual function of listing and selling. Show them how to break down annual goals of listing and selling to the monthly and daily canvassing and showing needed to achieve their annual gross income goal. Again, the salespeople's goals must be understood and attainable by them. The best way to make this happen is to have the salespeople get involved in the process of setting their own goals. Management must understand that salespeople's goals are far more important to them than company goals. At the same time, salespeople should know the company's goals and take pride in helping reach them. But it is much more important to each individual to fully understand his personal goal and to know that management is anxious to help him attain it.

It simplifies the entire process if you can translate the combined goals of your salespeople into the goals of the company.

Helping Salespeople Set Goals

How do you help salespeople set their goals? Develop forms to get information from your salespeople. Show them how to chart the information and then how to translate it into listing and selling goals and finally how to record their progress toward their goals. Figs. 1-3 show some suggested forms for developing useful data.

Based on your compensation policies, you might want to prepare a chart that enables each salesperson to evaluate the listing and selling effort needed to attain his financial goal. While this chart will never be an exact replica of what happens month after month, it will enable salespeople to assemble the data necessary for Fig. 2, the record of monthly and yearly goals.

The Budget

The budget is a graphic form of detail planning. It is the summation of all plans and takes into consideration seasonal and business cycles. The budget includes all expense items that can be anticipated and reveals the gross income needed to provide funds to cover expenses and assure the desired profit.

In most cases a budget should be prepared at least a year ahead. In larger companies where it is more difficult to react quickly to changing conditions, budgeting is frequently projected two or three years in advance.

It is in the budget that one learns how to relate gross income to the costs of promotion, communication and training. And it is within the budget one makes adjustments if income should drop for any reason. A carefully projected budget makes it much easier for management to do a successful job in carrying out plans.

Levels and Types of Planning

There are two basic types of planning, survival or short-term and long-term.

Under the survival plan, your goal is strictly to be in business at the end of the year. The mechanics of a survival plan can simply be to have more income and personal or company credit than your expenses for the year. Even the best real estate firms find themselves operating at the survival level at times because of severe changes in market conditions, staff situations and the like.

Short-term planning exploits current opportunities. One example could be to find a unique situation such as a land development project, a new subdivision or some recreation land where you decide to set up a small office or branch on a temporary basis. Another kind of short-term plan is really just a portion of a long-term plan. Many good real estate offices operate this way.

The long-term plan provides for growth, horizontal and/or vertical, in line with the goals of the firm's owners. A long-term plan takes into consideration such things as community involvement, participation in nationwide referral services, future branch operations, expansion of departmental activities or the addition of new departments within your existing office.

Many brokers, busy with the demands of the day, fail to plan far enough ahead. In long-term planning you must think further about the future of the total company. In fact, a good long-term plan should include plans for retirement. It also includes plans for your replacement in the event you meet with sudden death or total disability. Ask yourself, "If I were to go away on a trip next week and not re-

Fig. 1 Goal planning questionnaire

TO: Sales Staff

_____begins our new fiscal year.
In order to set our company goals for the year we must know your plans.
The following questions are designed to help you plan your year and thereby
help us to plan and budget for _____ real estate company.

1. What learning process or educational activities do you expect to participate in during the next twelve months?

   _____

   _____

   _____

2. Enumerate (outline) the boundaries of a potential listing area (listing
   farm) you would like to work in and be responsible for:

   _____

   _____

   _____

3. State areas and ideas which you think would help in the improvement of
   your office. If you desire this to be confidential, mark it so:

   _____

   _____

   _____

   _____

   _____

4. What are you doing for client follow-up?

   _____

   _____

   _____

5. What non-real estate oriented group(s) will you actively participate in to
   expand your sphere of influence during the coming year?

   _____

   _____

   _____

6. What do you realistically expect to earn in the next 12 months?

   $_____

7. Taking into consideration your personal strengths, time availability and
   seasonal market conditions, please outline how you plan to accomplish
   your goal in paragraph #6 above by completing the two (2) attached
   forms.

Fig. 1. A simple questionnaire asks salespeople to think about their
goals for the coming year in relation to their personal desire to attain
it. It includes questions of what they are going to do for personal development and community involvement and asks them to make some
recommendations for changes whereby management could improve
the entire company's volume.

Fig. 2 Personal income and activity goals

Salesperson's Personal Income Goals

Salesperson_____ Year_____

Based on:_____ brokerage fee; $_____ average sales price,
$_____ listing commission per listing sold, $_____ sales
commission per sale.
Total yearly income goal $_____
Yearly listing income $_____ (No. of listings sold_____)
Yearly sales income $_____ (No. of sales_____)

Activity Analysis:

Listing:
_____ Contacts = one qualified appointment
(when you ask the questions)
_____ Qualified appointments = one listing taken
_____ Listings taken = one listing sold

Selling:
_____ Showings = one sale (a showing is one buyer—one house)

Activity Breakdown for Average Month:

Monthly:
I will work _____ months during 19_____, this means I must average
$_____ monthly income to meet my yearly goal.
Monthly listing income $_____ (No. of listings sold _____)
Monthly sales income $_____ (No. of sales_____)

Bi-weekly:
I will work two bi-weekly periods per month. This means I must average
$_____ bi-weekly income to meet my monthly goal.
Bi-weekly period listing income $_____ (No. of listings sold_____)
Bi-weekly period sales income $_____ (No. of sales_____)
In order to achieve my bi-weekly income goal, I must make the following con-
tacts per bi-weekly period, based on my activity analysis: (work backwards)
Listings: _____contacts = _____appointments = _____listings taken =
_____listings sold
Sales: _____showings = _____sales

Daily:
I will work _____ days per bi-weekly period during 19_____; realizing I
must achieve my goals one day at a time, I must average the following
contacts and showing per day, based on my activity analysis:
Listing: _____contacts
Sales: _____showings

These are my personal goals for contacts, listings, sales and income for
19_____. They are not merely wishes! They are reachable goals. I will do
my best to attain them.

_____
Signature

Fig. 2. A form used by salespeople to translate financial goals to listing and selling goals and the canvassing and showing volume that will
lead to the necessary dollar volume.

Fig. 3 Personal goals and performance

Listings and Sales

Self Imposed Quota & Actual Evaluation

Name _____

19___	Listings Taken		Listings Sold		Sales		Earnings	
	Quota	Actual	Quota	Actual	Quota	Actual	Actual	Quota
January February March								
¼ Total								
April May June								
½ Total								
July August September								
¾ Total								
October November December								
Total								

Signed _____

Fig. 3. A chart to spread listing and selling goals over 12 months, providing for seasonal patterns and vacations. This form is also used to post actual earnings, listings and sales. It records progress toward the annual goal.

turn, what would happen to the business?" "What would happen to the salespeople and the rest of the staff?" Think about that. A good long-term plan would include the provision for these needs. It should also set up a chain of command. If you don't come back, someone else takes over. If you are the sole proprietor this might be difficult. If you have a partnership or a corporation you should include this provision in the legal framework developed with the aid of your attorney.

One firm has its business organized in such a way that the corporation itself has a chain of command or succession for someone to take over if the broker is temporarily disabled or out of the picture permanently. The owner's will contains a trust wherein all stock is deposited immediately and the administrator or executor of this trust is directed to name a designated broker. In this case, the executor knows who the qualified people are. In many states the designated broker can run the business without any actual ownership in the business. He can take over in a matter of hours and continue the business as usual with no apparent delays or inconveniences for salespeople or clients.

You owe it to the people who work with you as well as to your clients to have a plan to cover all eventualities. No matter how suddenly something happens to you, their personal needs and problems will continue. For example, having money tied up in your trust account can create a hardship on these people. While your competitors may politely regret your firm's hardship for a time, they will soon develop a competitive advantage if your firm cannot rebound quickly from any tragedy that might beset it.

Looking at the brighter side, you must consider who is going to manage the business and be responsible for the daily routine as you have a need or desire to spend more time with your family, in recreation or travel.

Long-term planning is important in providing physical facilities too. You spend money developing space for a residential office. Your whole floor plan and operation is centered on a residential business. Yet in a few years you may want to have additional departments which will need additional space.

The long-term plan must take into consideration the fact that growth usually means you are going to suffer an immediate (if temporary) income loss. Increased overhead and expansion costs are going to reduce immediate income. By going to a growth pattern, thinking in terms of what is going to happen in the next five to ten years, you must be able to accept lower short-term income, a figure you can realistically live with for a limited time.

Community Involvement

Community involvement is a part of image building and cannot be put off to a later date. If you expect to be part of the community, you must put things into it on a continuing basis. Principals and staff people should get into key organizations such as service clubs, the Chamber of Commerce, civic groups, local referral groups, fraternal/social organizations and whatever recreation or country club you find congenial. Be prepared to participate, to "go through the chairs" in organizational parlance, in whatever group you join.

Basic Business Decisions

One of the early decisions that must be made is the choice of a firm name. Should it be a personal name or an impersonal one? Would Charlie Smith, REALTOR®, or Charles Smith and Associates be better than Builders', REALTORS®, or City Realty? Consider name possibilities in terms of what your goals are and the goals of those working with you. An impersonal name is perhaps more suitable if the firm is to be sold at some time in the foreseeable future. In many cases, an impersonal name is easier to work into certain kinds of advertising. On the other hand, the real estate business, particularly the small residential or investment firm, is a personal service business much like law and accounting firms. In these, clients feel quite comfortable with the personal name.

The form of ownership—sole proprietorship, partnership or corporation—has no direct relationship to the success of the firm. But the form of ownership is very important when it comes to deciding how profits are to be paid and shared, how taxes are to be paid and how liability is to be assumed and shared. Choosing a form of ownership compatible to all the owners' goals is important.

Another necessary decision is whether to lease an office or purchase a building. How long should the lease run? How much can you afford to invest if you purchase a building. How much can you afford to spend to renovate an old building if you plan to use it as an office only a year or two. Every one of these considerations requires a thorough analysis of expense factors. Many brokers who say they have no interest in long-term plans will sign five- or ten-year leases for office space. That surely means they expect to be in business for at least the term of the lease.

Organizing People and Time

Having decided the range of services your firm will offer and the strategy for operating your business, the next logical step is to plan the organizational structure of the firm and how both management and staff can allocate their time to be most effective.

Organization Charts

The importance of a chain of command in relation to succession in management was mentioned earlier. An equally important reason for a chain of command and a thorough understanding of it by all who work within it is to assure as smooth a day-to-day operation of your business as is possible.

The illustrations here provide a graphic chain of command for two firms of widely differing sizes, one of medium size and the other a large organization. There is little or no need for having an organization chart for a small real estate firm. All lines obviously lead to the owner or manager. In such an operation, carefully written job descriptions can very well replace a chart. With these available to the staff, there can be no question to whom everyone turns for information and guidance.

It is likely that if conflict exists among management people they do not understand where they are located in the organization chart. Thus a chart should be developed to fit your particular firm. Everyone should know what responsibilities he has and should be given authority to carry them out. This is generally accomplished through job descriptions.

Fig. 4 is an organization chart for a residential real estate brokerage firm with four branches. All department heads and managers report directly to the president. Weekly staff meetings are held with managers and staff department heads to coordinate activities. Beyond that, sales offices operate under the supervision of the respective managers; departments are managed in the same way. There are 11 salaried employees including the president and 55 independent contractors working in sales.

Fig. 5, the organization chart of a large, diversified real estate firm with 25 offices shows how the work of 50 salaried employees and 215 independent contractors is organized. The board of directors is composed of all department heads, the general sales manager and the president. The board meets monthly. Meetings of sales management, division management and other departments are also held monthly. Sales meetings of the entire company are held quarterly. Additional sales meetings are called when special situations indicate a need or when worthwhile outside speakers and programs become available.

Time Management

Good time management practices are essential to success in real estate sales. Yet one of the most common occupational faults in real estate salespeople is the lack of self discipline and more specifically, the poor management of their time. People who sell a service really have only two things to offer: time and knowledge. It is the manager's job to help the sales staff see the value of managing their time better.

Many people selling real estate have come from other fields; most have worked in a structured day where they came to work at a specific hour, had lunch at a certain time and had their day end at a scheduled hour. In short, their day was planned and organized by someone else.

Two major incentives for entering the real estate field are the opportunity to make more money for the time spent at work and the freedom to be one's own boss.

Once into this self-managed field, many people find it difficult to make their time profitable; many find they work for a very generous and accommodating manager. Time management thus becomes a serious problem.

Time management may not have a true meaning unless we know the value of each hour in dollars and cents. The value of time is the first determination that must be made by the salesperson. This determination can be made through several analyses: 1) the value of a salesperson's time; 2) how time is wasted; and 3) how to make maximum use of each hour of the day.

The first step is for the salesperson to know what his time is really worth. A survey was conducted in which five real estate salespeople were asked to keep a log or diary of their day for seven consecutive

Fig. 4 Organization chart for residential firm with four branches

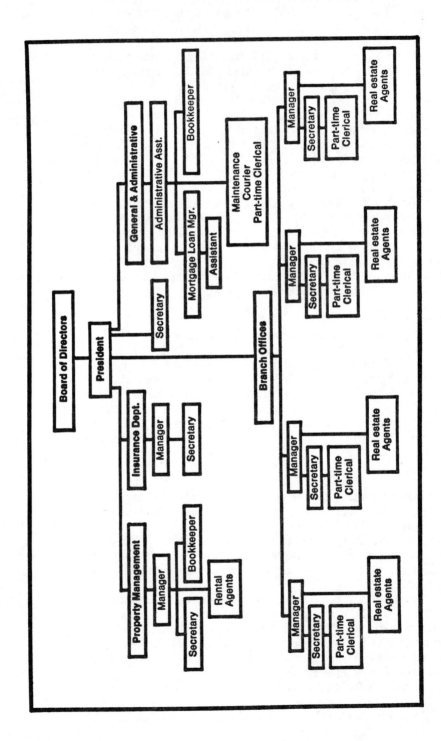

Fig. 5 Organization chart of a large diversified firm

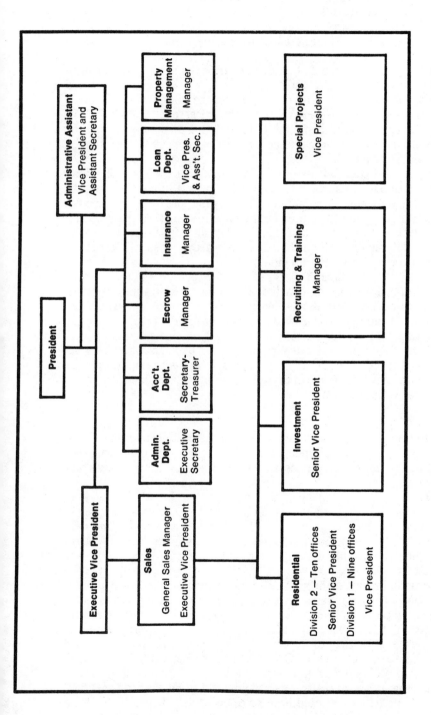

Functions of Management: Planning and Organizing

days. They were given a log that divided the day into 30-minute segments beginning at 8:00 a.m. and continuing until 8:00 p.m. and asked to write down their activities by half-hour time periods. Each was asked to be absolutely accurate and was assured that the record would be kept in confidence.

After the logs were completed, an analysis was made of the salespeople's activities. These activities were categorized into four types of usage.

Class "A" time was that amount of time the salesperson spent in face-to-face contact with a buyer or a seller, someone who could make a decision that could directly affect the salesperson's earnings. This represented time spent to show properties, solicit and obtain listings, get listings extended, qualify prospects and negotiate contracts. The survey showed these salespeople spent 15 percent of their time in Class "A" activity.

Class "B" was that amount of time salespeople spent in direct preparation for or as the direct result of Class "A" time. This was the time spent to make appointments for showing, pre-inspect properties in advance of showings, prepare a competitive market analysis on a prospective listing, take loan applications and close escrow transactions. The survey showed that these salespeople spent 14 percent of their time in Class "B" activities.

Class "C" time was that part of the day spent in all other real estate activity. At work time included sales meetings, training sessions, correspondence, writing ads, placing listings in their books, driving time and waiting time. This was a catch-all activity of real estate work that accounted for 35 percent of their daily business activities.

Class "D" time was categorized as their personal time. This accounted for lunch hours and dinner hours, time with family, time for leisure or any "off" time in that 12-hour day. It consumed 36 percent of total working time.

Evaluating Time

With this analysis of how their time was spent, it next became possible to place a value on their time. (Since this survey is 14 years old, adjust for inflationary factors, if so desired, to reflect today's values.)

These five salespeople had an average income of $15,000 per year. The analysis showed they spent an average of 50 hours a week working in real estate. This was the total of their Class "A", "B" and "C" time. If they worked 50 hours a week, their annual projection was approximately 2,500 hours each year. This meant that each hour was worth $6.00.

Proceeding under the assumption that the most direct way a salesperson can generate earnings is to be face-to-face with a client or customer who can make a decision, we can transfer all value of time to Class "A" time. It follows that since the salespeople averaged only 15 percent of their time in this activity, projected to approximately 375 hours a year, each hour of Class "A" time was worth $40, each hour of Class "B" and "C" time worth nothing. The assumption is also made that if a salesperson spent 100 percent of his time in Class "B" or "C" activities he would have no opportunities for earnings. Ergo that time has no value. Those precious few hours spent with someone who could make a decision to buy or sell have the highest dollar value. However, without the other three classes of time, there would be no Class "A" time.

The following table can show what a salesperson's time is worth for a fairly wide range of income or earning goals:

$10,000 per year—"at work" hour worth $4.00—
Class "A" hour worth $26.66
$15,000 per year—"at work" hour worth $6.00—
Class "A" hour worth $40.00
$20,000 per year—"at work" hour worth $8.00—
Class "A" hour worth $53.33
$25,000 per year—"at work" hour worth $10.00—
Class "A" hour worth $66.66
$30,000 per year—"at work" hour worth $12.00—
Class "A" hour worth $80.00
$40,000 per year—"at work" hour worth $16.00—
Class "A" hour worth $106.66

This leads to the conclusion that Class "B" and "C" time must be managed well to result in the most effective Class "A" time. The entire work day should be planned to get more face-to-face time with clients and customers.

Once the salesperson understands this concept of the real value of time, he should be able to avoid the many time-wasting interruptions he may fall prey to in his self-disciplined world.

It's easy for a $15,000 a year salesperson to take a 15-minute coffee break if he knows it is worth $1.50 in time. But if Class "A" time is robbed by a coffee break, that cup of coffee could cost $10.00. An hour in the barber shop or at the hairdresser's may only be worth $6.00 unless that hour could have been spent with someone who could make a decision. Then it becomes a $40.00 haircut. An afternoon playing golf instead of showing homes could consume $100.00 worth of time.

Here are six steps salespeople can take to more effectively manage their time:

Keep Records on How Time Is Spent

Any salesperson can follow the steps taken in the survey outlined previously in this chapter by keeping a log or diary of his time each day for one or two weeks. This can be done easily in an appointment book or on a tablet. Activities are listed by half-hour increments during the whole work day whether it be from 8:00 a.m. until 8:00 p.m. or from 10:00 a.m. to 5:00 p.m. or whatever hours are included in the typical work day. He can analyze his time as Class "A", "B", "C" or "D" just as in the survey.

The log has to be both accurate and honest to produce the desired information.

Salespeople will learn very quickly how much time is actually wasted each day. They may discover where they have used time inefficiently by making two trips when one would suffice or when a phone call for an appointment could have saved them precious hours waiting for a client.

They may find they don't really work much at all and that much of their time is spent just playing office or going through a lot of wasted motions. They will probably find out why they aren't making as much money as they expected for the time spent.

If they take an objective look at their work habits by keeping accurate records on how they spend their time, they will become much more time conscious and may be amazed at the results.

Use an Appointment Book

Instead of being governed by the clock as they were in previous jobs, real estate salespeople should use appointment books to plan their time. A detailed appointment book, available from any good business stationer, can be an effective tool in organizing a work day to make the most efficient use of time.

The salesperson should learn to schedule his day on paper. This can be done early in the morning or even the previous evening. This visual scheduling can eliminate time-wasting duplication of effort. With a little planning the salesperson can possibly schedule one trip into a specific area (such as downtown) instead of two or three.

A typical work day could begin with scheduling two definite appointments. Let's say one appointment is for 10:00 a.m. for a loan application, another at 5:00 for a listing appointment. Those should be scheduled first. Now let's plan the balance of the day. What should be done before 10:00? Let's say we schedule 8:30 a.m., arrive at the office, check the mail, make some phone calls confirming appointments or gathering information. At 9:00 a.m. write three classified ads. At 9:30 a.m review the file for the loan application appointment and drive to the appointment. After the loan application in the downtown area, about 10:45, we might schedule a prospecting call to a large employer headquartered in the downtown area. At 11:15 a.m. on the way back to the office, pick up a sign at a sold listing and possibly call on the new owner. We might arrive at the office at 11:45, check for phone messages, make some telephone calls and go to lunch.

We're back at the office at 1:00 p.m. to check phone messages and put new listings in our sales book. At 2:00 we could schedule a door-to-door canvass for new listings in a certain area. At 4:00 p.m. return to the office to check for messages and double check the latest sales to add to the competitive market analysis for the listing appointment.

This now leads us to our 5:00 p.m. appointment for the listing. After the listing, it's home for dinner and possibly an evening appointment or time on the telephone contacting prospects and planning future appointments.

Some of these appointments may seem trivial or mundane when they are scheduled in writing. However, a definite time schedule assures their being handled and not put off to be done "later when I get the time."

Once a salesperson learns to use an appointment book and performs his work on schedule, he will be able to accomplish much more in less time. Non-productive interruptions can be avoided along with many of the time-wasting traps salespeople are subjected to every day. It is a matter of planning and discipline.

Put Priorities on Time

In planning the course of a salesperson's day there are certain activities that have higher or lower priorities than other work that must be done. One method to insure effective management of time to perform the most important activities is to place high priorities on those activities.

Generally, all activities can be divided into three priorities:

Must do

Should do

Could do.

These activities can be listed in priority at the start of each day. An appointment book, plan book, or even 3" x 5" cards can be used to write down the general order of work to be done. It is important that these be in writing so they can be checked off.

Obviously, top priority tasks should be listed in the "Must do" list. Here are the things that must be done that day. They could include a loan application, an appointment to take a listing or an appointment to show homes. Sales meetings and training or educational sessions could be listed in this category.

"Should do" priorities occupy second place. Correspondence, ad writing, canvassing or calling on corporate accounts are some of the activities that could be listed here. While these tasks are not tied to a specific time, they must be done if one is to be an effective salesperson.

The "Could do" jobs might better be labeled "some day when I have time" category. These are the things every salesperson intends to do but always seems to put off until another day. Calling back on former buyers, building a listing kit, setting up a prospect file or calling on the lukewarm prospect may be some things that need to be done but are easily put off. Many of these seemingly unimportant jobs are put off continually unless they are scheduled until completed.

Many times the salesperson will not complete the tasks outlined on the daily priority schedule. They are then rescheduled for the next day and until they are finally done.

This system helps keep a salesperson on the job and can eliminate days when there seems to be nothing to do. It brings self-discipline and organization to each day and maximizes the effectiveness of the work day. This system can also be used in conjunction with the appointment book by placing priorities on each appointment. Having this list of priorities in the salesperson's pocket or purse for easy reference is strongly recommended.

Have a Definite Goal

Very possibly the goal is the most important ingredient in time management. Nearly every goal is set within a framework of time. A salesperson is going to earn so much money in a year, is going to get so many listings in a certain month, solicit a definite number of listings in a week and make a set number of phone calls on a given day.

Without a goal, time has no meaning. If a salesperson doesn't know where he is going or what standard he must meet, he won't care much about whether or not he achieves anything.

Once a salesperson knows what his goal is in terms of dollar earnings, number of sales, number of listings or however else he may express it, he can plan to manage his time to reach that goal.

In order to reach the goal, the salesperson must understand his own efficiency and understand how he has performed in the past. This will be defined in detail in the following pages. Once he understands how he has made his money in the past, he can define what must be done on an annual, monthly, weekly and daily basis to achieve his goal.

Time organization becomes easier to understand once the goal is clear. The salesperson becomes disciplined to the goal. Every wasted hour becomes a deterrent to achievement.

Management counseling on the setting of realistic goals and periodic review of salespeople's goals is necessary to help them organize their efforts and manage their time.

Take Advantage of the Law of Averages

Nearly ever salesperson or company that markets any product or service should have a working understanding of the law of averages. Marketing experts know that exposure to buyers or clients is vital to success.

Real estate salespeople are no different. The only way they can sell or list is to be with someone who can make a decision. They can't sell anything sitting in the office or in their home. They must have a plan to get maximum exposure to get into the market place.

The first step in the plan to take advantage of the law of averages is for the salesperson to understand himself, his job efficiency and his effectiveness. Here are some of the statistics he needs to know about his work:

Average price of sold listings

Percentage of his listings that sell

Number of appointments needed to get a listing

Number of calls needed to get a listing appointment

Average sales price

Average number of showings needed to make a sale

Number of prospect contacts needed to get an appointment to show.

Once the salesperson has these facts, he can begin to direct his daily activities toward achieving his goal.

Let's say, for example, a salesperson wants to make $42,000 in commissions in the next 12 months. His average sale and sold listing is $60,000. If the commission rate is 7 percent, it produces $4,200 gross commissions, of which he receives 20 percent or $840 for a sold listing, 30 percent or $1,260 for a sale.*

One of the ways the salesperson can earn his goal of $42,000 is to have 20 sold listings which would produce $16,800 in listing commissions and 20 sales would produce $25,200 in sales commissions.

If approximately two-thirds of his listings sell, he has to obtain 30 listings in a year to have 20 of them sell. If he gets one listing for every two listing appointments, he must get 60 appointments to get the 30 listings. If it takes five calls to get 60 appointments, he must make 300 listing calls to get the necessary appointments. The listing call now becomes the lowest denominator and the most basic task.

He must now make 25 listing calls each month (about six a week) or average at least one each day in order to achieve the listing goal.

Let's now examine his sales effort. The record shows that he averages one sale for every 12 showings. A showing is defined as the physical introduction of a prospect to a property. Only the initial showing of the property is counted. Second look or repeat showings to the same prospect still count as one introduction to a property.

If it takes an average of 12 showings to make a sale, this means the salesperson has to make 240 showings a year to make 20 sales. If it takes five prospect contacts (either by inquiry on ads or signs or by the salesperson's initiative) in order to get a showing, he must make 1,200 prospect contacts in a year to reach his goal. The prospect contact now becomes the basic task.

This computes to an average of 100 prospect contacts per month (about 25 per week) or at least three a day in order to make 20 sales.

In this example, the salesperson wanting to make $42,000 in commissions in a year has to have a daily work plan that calls for at least one listing call and three prospect contacts. His weekly plan must include six listing calls and 25 prospect contacts. He now knows what must be done with his time. He must get that necessary exposure to sellers and buyers in order to let the law of averages work for him.

Create Good Time Habits

Salespeople, like all humans, are creatures of habit. Time-wasting habits are easily formed by people who are disciplined only by themselves. Good time management habits must be formed with a great deal of self-discipline and self-motivation.

One important habit to cultivate is promptness. Being on time for appointments not only shows consideration for other people but compels the salesperson to be a slave to his own plan. Being habitually late or borrowing time from other appointments leads to sloppy time management.

Separating work time from leisure time is another time-saving habit. Allowing mini-vacations to creep into our work day causes

---

*In citing this example and any others throughout the text having to do with commission percentages, the REAL ESTATE BROKERAGE COUNCIL™ publishes them only to enable the manager to plan how to help a salesperson reach a goal. He should adapt figures cited here to whatever percentages he uses. These published figures should in no way be considered as the average, accepted or recommended percentages for any real estate firm anywhere.

costly interruptions in the daily plan. There are many temptations to take a break for some fun. These pitfalls rob the effectiveness of the day and lead to habitual procrastination.

Leisure time should be scheduled along with the work plan. If a salesperson wants to take a day off, he should schedule a day off! If he needs to spend a few hours with the family or working in the yard, he can schedule the end of his work day at mid-afternoon. Salespeople who manage their time efficiently can actually spend more leisure hours than the person who is taking every day as it comes.

Time management is a very individual and personal challenge. Each salesperson must make his own decision about how his time will be spent. It is management's role to provide the leadership, training and counseling to demonstrate to the sales staff that time and therefore time management is very valuable. Besides knowledge, it's the only thing they really have to sell. By providing them with methods and plans, the manager can significantly help his salespeople become more productive and self-reliant and the firm more successful.

Determining Staff Size

Let us assume that you, as manager, have made an extensive market analysis, have established company goals and your personal goals. Now you have to determine how many salespeople are needed and what each one must produce in order to meet the company goals.

One common, effective method to determine how many salespeople you need is to establish a territory, sometimes called a farm, for each salesperson. You arrive at this based on the number of properties in each territory, the percentage of turnover and the percentage of that market the salesperson is going to have to capture in order to make the desired dollar income.

For example, let's imagine the desired goal for the salesperson is $24,000 income, the average sales price in the territory covered is $60,000 and your commission is six percent.

This means that each sale would produce a gross income of $3,600; a 25 percent listing fee would be $900 and a 25 percent sales fee would be the same. By dividing $900 into $24,000 you determine that the salesperson must make 27 units of $900 to produce $24,000 income. Assuming that two-thirds of the salesperson's income will come from listing commissions, you then determine that 18 of the 27 units of income must come from listing commissions. If research and records of the market area indicate there is a 70 percent salability factor (i.e., of all the listings taken, 70 percent will sell) then this means the salesperson must make 26 listings in order to sell 18.

Before you can apply these factors to your business, you will need to determine the average turnover in the market area in which you are to be dealing; or, taking a given number of homes, know how many are placed on the market and sold each year. Your research reveals there is a seven-year turnover. This means approximately 15 percent of the homes in the area are listed and sold each year, and about 20 percent of the homes in the are come on the market each year. Then, determining that the salesperson would capture somewhere in the neighborhood of 13 percent of the market, give or take a point, you can determine that each territory must contain approximately 1,000 homes.

1,000 homes $\times$ 20% turnover = 200 $\times$ 13% = 26 listings

26 listings $\times$ 70% saleable = 8 sold listings $\times$ \$900 a unit = \$16,200 listing commissions

Deduct this \$16,200 from \$24,000 = \$7,800 needed from sales commissions

From this base, you can determine the number of salespeople you need to cover the market area that has been established for the company and this particular location. For example, let us assume there are 20,000 homes based on the above market data. Using the foregoing calculation method, you will be able to determine the number of salespeople to cover the market area.

The Manager's Job Functions

Lead and coordinate the group. In other words, your first and foremost job function is *leadership*. This includes your ability to induce sales associates to work with confidence and zeal and to imaginatively direct, guide and influence their work in choosing and attaining particular ends. It is the ability to get the best out of those you are leading. As a basic principle, you must be believable. No credibility gap can exist between you and your staff lest it make them skeptical of you and your ability and contributions. Leadership by example is best: "Don't just preach me a sermon; live me one."

Make decisions and solve problems. You must have a basic philosophy that you are not only going to be confronted with problems but that you accept them and to a degree relish them. You know it is your job to solve problems. In effect, a problem is a question that requires an answer. You make these decisions by

Recognizing the problem and meeting it head on and not avoiding it

Getting the facts and deciding on the facts and not on emotion

Determining the objective, the desired achievement

Considering the alternatives

Weighing all the above

Making the decision now

Correcting the decision if required as facts and time dictate.

Mobilize both physical and financial resources. You secure help, either immediate or by anticipating the future so you have competent people and organizations to assist you: bankers, mortgage lenders, newspaper personnel, etc.

Risk funds for accomplishment. Seeing an opportunity to capture an increased portion of the market due to a combination of direct mail, institutional and classified advertising, you are willing to set forth a specific program and communicate it to your people. And you take the capital risk after getting the commitment from your people to attain the desired goal.

Use human resources effectively. You are extremely sensitive to their personal needs, desires, ups and downs and individual problems. You are quick to give recognition and praise and less so to criticize. You praise in public and criticize in private. You have a strong pride in the effective and intelligent use of physical resources.

Provide a favorable administrative climate. You provide a strong climate of progressive drive and growth based upon the desires of the individual and the group. Your staff and your salespeople believe you know what you are doing in the firm's area of activities. You are an effective planner, study financial trends and market data, make comparisons and analyses of the competition and base these decisions on facts. You manage by objective, not by crisis.

Measure, analyze, evaluate and plan for the future. You recognize that with each program that is installed or plan that is put in motion there must be a commensurate program or plan to measure the results. You counsel with your salespeople and help them set goals in writing. You have scheduled interviews and consultations with each salesperson in order to evaluate performance, shore up the weak points and further develop the strong points. Together, you plan for the future of the individual salesperson and the result thereof collectively for the company as a whole.

Management functions in the external environment, the forces that will influence your operation, as well as the internal environment or the way in which you organize your operation. The chart, Fig. 6, presents a systems approach to management's sphere of responsibility. The dotted line indicates the boundaries within which a manager can exert the major influence.

All of these functions and the manner in which they are performed determine whether or not you are a professional manager: one who is trained in the skills, competent in the use of the tools, orderly in your approach and working within the climate of a progressive philosophy. You are recognized by your team as their leader, not because you are the owner or entrepreneur (you may not be) but because as a professional you are performing the very essence of management: the development of people.

Once the major tasks of planning and organizing are completed, you're next—and continuing challenge—is to communicate it all to everyone involved in the firm's day-to-day operation.

Planning Questionnaire
Ask these important "What is our business?" questions while you are successful. To delay asking them until trouble comes can be fatal to any business. Involve your staff in this company examination too.

What services do we provide?

Which are most profitable? Why?

Should the least profitable services be continued?

Do they provide a supportive role to other parts of the business?

Do they bring us prospective users of other, more profitable parts of our business? List some examples.

Fig. 6 Management functions and responsibilities in a typical real estate brokerage office

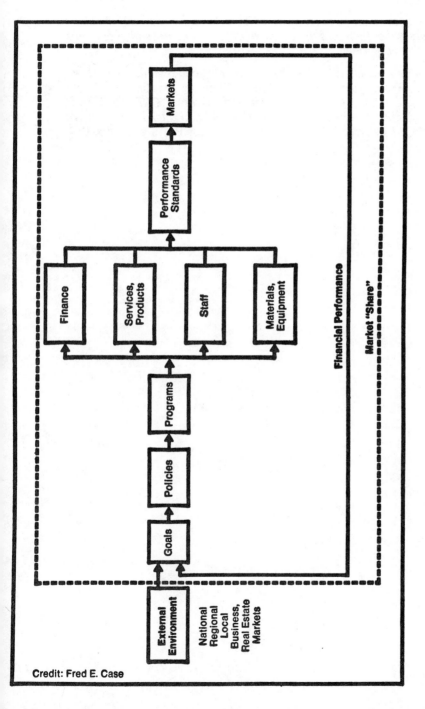

Credit: Fred E. Case

Functions of Management: Planning and Organizing

Can any changes be made to make these services more profitable?

What changes? How could we implement them? How would they then bring an increase in profit to other parts of the business?

How can changes affect our objectives, strategies, organization, behavior?

Will any decision we make be based on a conscious choice of the alternatives rather than on suppression of different and dissenting opinions and points of view?

[*For a more detailed examination of planning and organizing a real estate brokerage firm, consult* Strategic Planning for the Real Estate Manager, A Step-By-Step Guide *by Ken Reyhons, CRB, CRS, published by the Real Estate Brokerage Council™, or attend the Council's CRB® 301 Course,* Planning: How to Plan for Profit and Growth.]

Functions of Management: 6
Communicating

The broker, salesperson, manger, or any individual in the field of real estate who aspires to be successful needs good communication skills. There are few fields or areas where communication plays such a critical role.

Other professionals have other primary tools which help them attain their objectives: a scalpel, a slide rule, dental equipment, computers, etc. But the person engaged in real estate activities is almost completely dependent on his communications with the people in his organization as well as with prospects, financing officers, government representatives and community members outside his company. Because his day is made up of sensitive listening, persuasive writing, thoughtful speaking and analytical reading, he must be an expert communicator.

Functions of Management: Communicating

How do you rate in the areas of speaking, writing, reading and listening?

If you are like most of us, you will rate yourself quite high for surely you speak easily, you write quickly, you hear everything that is said and you read quite rapidly.

But How *Effectively* Do You Do Each?

Obviously the standard by which we can measure effectiveness is not easily available. And furthermore, who is to judge? If that prospect does not buy, it is because "Mrs. Jackson has peculiar ideas about residential housing," and if Barker doesn't purchase that multiple unit from us, it is because "nothing will satisfy that nut," and "Salesperson Betty Brown... well, it's not really me; an angel couldn't work with her...." And so it goes.

The fault is rarely ours, we say. And when we hear that Mrs. Jackson purchased a home from a competitor; Barker secured a multiple unit from another firm; and Salesperson Betty Brown works successfully with someone else, we brush it off with a "Well, you can't win 'em all."

You can't win them all. But by improving your ability to communicate, you can be more successful not only in your real estate office but at home, on the golf course and in almost every other aspect of living.

The Process of Communication

Perhaps the first step in becoming a better communicator is to understand the process. Is it simply that one person talks and another hears? Or is it more complex than that?

In the highly emotional areas of interpersonal work relationships and real estate sales, it is imperative that we keep in mind that a speaker transmits more than words. Of course the words carry his ideas. But through the inflection in his voice, the intonation of his words and the non-verbal aspects of his body, he also transmits his feelings and attitudes. And it is in the non-verbal area that both speaker and listener communicate constantly.

Thus we can define communication as "the transmission and reception of ideas, feelings and attitudes, verbally and non-verbally, which produce a response."[1] It is this feedback (or response), both verbal and non-verbal, which permits both parties to evaluate the effectiveness of their communication. However, feedback must be interpreted with care. Often it is unreliable as in the case where the broker explains for five minutes to the new office secretary that "whenever a sales associate secures a listing, he or she will submit to you a form 42 which you should record in the office log as well as the salesperson's record book and then complete one of these form 65's for the main office. The next step is to complete a sales breakdown to include commission percentages according to our Schedule 4 unless the salesperson is in either category 2 or 3, if that is so, use Schedule 5. However..."

And at the conclusion of this peroration, he says to secretary Dorothy Dunbar, "Of course you see how all this works?"

And poor Dorothy, who was lost after the first reference to "form 42" calmly, clearly and confidently answers, "Yes, of course I see," and doesn't understand the explanation at all.

Why do people "feed back" to the sender, "Yes, I understand" when actually they do not?

Perhaps there are two reasons: they often think they understand and do not or, more frequently, they do not wish to appear stupid. In any event, the expert communicator learns to interpret verbal and nonverbal feedback very carefully.

Objectives
In all of our communications, we attempt to secure some end result: to persuade the receiver to "buy" (an idea, a home or an object), to inform him, to motivate him or to convince him. However, the response which the transmitter seeks can only be attained if he communicated well in the first place.

Thus, in order of achievement, we may say that our objectives are:

To secure understanding on the part of the receiver as we intend him to understand (does he understand "an equal division of advertising costs" the same way we understand that statement?)

To secure a response (hopefully positive but a negative one can be informative)

To maintain or build favorable relationships with the receiver.

Why Communications Break Down
It would seem that the objectives of communication are simple to achieve. If that is so, why do so many people have "communication breakdowns" with clients, wives, children, friends and business associates?

There are many reasons for the breakdowns: emotional, psychological, linguistic, environmental, conscious or unconscious. We can't hope to solve all breakdowns, but knowing which barriers occur most frequently and why they arise will assist the concerned individual to avoid them or deal with them when they do surface.

Barriers may be major or minor. A barrier such as a distracting noise or smell may cause the communication interaction to slow or stumble; a barrier such as unreasonable bias tactlessly communicated may cause interpersonal communication to halt or break down for a significant period of time.

Let's briefly examine some barriers. As we do, you may wish to ask yourself which two or three or four played a role in your last lost sale (communication breakdown) or the problem you had with someone with whom you live or work.

Perception

Differences in perception of a situation may cause imperfect communication. Our previous experiences largely determine how we will react to specific stimuli. Viewing the same thing, individuals of different ages, cultural backgrounds and national origins will each perceive something quite different. Each uses his learning, his culture and his experiences to interpret what he sees. Not only do we see things differently from the way another person sees them but if two of us hear a statement, we may also interpret (hear or perceive) it differently.

Let's look at Company President Anderson, Sales Manager Foreman and First National's Loan Officer Thompson. They have just returned from lunch and as they walk into the main office of the Anderson Realty Company, a group of salespeople burst into laughter.

How did Anderson, Foreman and Thompson perceive that incident?

Anderson, who sees himself as the tough but beloved boss, hears a little steam being let off. Sales Manager Foreman, who has been having more and more trouble controlling his weekly sales meetings, hears derisive laughter. And Mr. Thompson hit the high point of the story he was telling at the moment and didn't hear the salespeople at all!

Let's take another example. Salesperson Kelly feels that his three listings should be heavily advertised in not only the daily but also the weekend editions of the newspapers. However, Senior Partner Humphrey, who is also in charge of marketing, knows the limitations of the company's advertising budget. There are some 28 other current residential listings besides Kelly's. In addition, some of the budget must be conserved for commercial and industrial properties.

If Humphrey can appreciate how Kelly feels and articulate that to him, perhaps Mr. Kelly will be more likely to see Humphrey's point of view. If this takes place, then perhaps communication between the two can be carried through.

Honestly appreciating the perceptions of others, and saying so, goes a long way in keeping the lines of communication open.

Of course we can't hope to perceive every situation as the other person does but if we make an honest effort to appreciate his point of view, we will improve the possibility of achieving effective communication.

An effective way of opening the lines is sometimes called "the mirror approach." If Barton says heatedly, "Every time I come into this office I find a stack of stuff on my desk and 99 percent of it has no business being there. Sometimes I think people just drop their junk on my desk because they know I only come in every other day and I think it's terrible!"

Rather than remaining silent, offering a rebuttal or telling Barton to turn off his stupid "alarm button," better results might be achieved by responding with, "You certainly feel upset by this. I would probably feel the same. Can you tell me more about the situation?"

Note that we have said it is (1) important to appreciate the other person's perception, and (2) articulate that appreciation to him. But nowhere have we said that it is necessary to agree with his perception. You may, if you feel such agreement is warranted but that step (agreement) is not necessary to open the lines of communication. Appreciation of his perception and articulation of that appreciation are.

Knowledge

Lack of fundamental knowledge can be another barrier to the clear communication of ideas. How can you intelligently discuss a problem with those who do not have the background to understand or appreciate the basic concepts of the discussion? Certainly there will be a breakdown in the communication of ideas if a nuclear physicist attempts to explain various high-level principles in his field to individuals who do not have the background to appreciate the material. The same may be true if an engineer attempts to give a technical explanation of a process to a production line worker. Conversely, it is conceivable that the speaker's or writer's knowledge of his subject is superficial. This also becomes a barrier for it is always apparent to us when we listen to someone who is, as the saying goes, only one chapter ahead of the class.

Associated with this might be those cases where the communicator's knowledge in a field is so thorough that he makes unconscious assumptions that the other person can't follow. The danger is to assume that the listener has adequate background or fundamental knowledge and then to try to communicate on the basis of this false premise. To overcome this barrier, determine how much knowledge of the subject the recipient of the message possesses before you speak or write to him.

This determination is not always simple. As was indicated earlier, we usually depend on some type of response, verbal or non-verbal, to indicate understanding or lack of understanding. But the response of the recipient to our message may not always be accurate.

A simple case that we can identify with is Broker Burns who meets with the young, successful surgeon, Dr. Franklin. The doctor has been told by his accountant that he must find a good tax shelter. The doctor is now in the midst of a discussion with Broker Burns who has been explaining, "...and therefore, Dr. Franklin, with a 'down' of $40,000 we can get a first at $60 M. and a second at $20 M. This will give you an equity of...and a yearly depreciation of...and a tax savings in your tax bracket of...percent plus a cash flow...and with the price of a multiple of 7 plus the 2 points...a deal...extremely advantageous to you and of course...you can see how all this adds up!"

Dr. Franklin is an excellent surgeon, respected by his colleagues, but he isn't knowledgeable about the financial details of real estate transactions. However, chances are nine out of ten that when Broker Burns says, "You can see how all this adds up," Dr. Franklin will say, somewhat vaguely, "Oh yes, yes." But chances are good that he won't buy from Burns.

Prospects seldom buy if they don't understand. Therefore, the real estate communicator must be especially adept at interpreting feedback accurately.

The emotions of either the sender or the receiver can prove to be another obstacle in the communication of an idea. We have all been in situations where the atmosphere became so emotionally charged that reasonable discussion broke down. When any of us has deep emotional reactions such as love, hate, fear or anger, we find it almost impossible to communicate coherently anything but that emotion. The lesson learned here is obvious: calm down before you send or receive ideas. Of course this is easier said than done. It is precisely when our emotions are at a high level that we are most strongly motivated to communicate.

Emotions can be an extremely strong factor in assisting or blocking communications. In the case of the broker/salesperson association, emotions frequently play a critical role.

The relationship between a salesperson and the couple buying or selling a home can be demanding on the former. He or she must deal with the different perceptions of husband and wife, changes in their attitudes and a dozen other factors.

When that salesperson returns to the office, it is imperative that the broker communicate with him in a way that will relieve any emotional frustrations which have been established and reinforce the positive feelings which the salesperson has gained. Perhaps the best way is for the broker to listen understandingly and skillfully, to try to appreciate the salesperson's perception (not necessarily agree) and to commend where commendation is deserved.

Prejudice

Bias and prejudice can also seriously impede the transmission of ideas. We usually think of bias as being confined to race, color or creed. But how do you communicate with an individual who says, "I just don't like to participate in 'sales caravans' where 20 salespeople go out to visit the new listings. It's time consuming, boring and bothersome to me." And so you don't invite that person to go out on "caravans" but take him out in your car in the evenings. And what happens? It's the same person who asks you two weeks later, "Why won't you permit me to 'caravan' with the other salespeople; I really like to get together with the people I work with."

How does one overcome bias? Surely not by attacking it or by rejecting it as unreasonable. Understanding it and appreciating the other person's perceptions is usually an effective method.

Distraction

Distractions can certainly cause ineffective communication. The two Martin infants crying while you're trying to show Mr. and Mrs. Martin a series of available homes is almost sure to cause communication breakdowns. Or the lack of time Mr. Carter has available to really look at the multiple unit can prove to be a barrier. Trying to hold an important counseling session with new Salesperson Cory with other salespeople nearby and typewriters clattering is unwise. Obviously a private office is required for this or a lunch for two in a carefully selected restaurant. In either case, office or lunch, the climate for the interview must be correct. If it is not, that in itself can prove to be a distraction.

Almost anything which impinges on our senses negatively or disturbs us emotionally or psychologically will result in a communication breakdown. Therefore make every effort possible to eliminate distractions.

Appearance

The appearance of the communicator or the instrument with which he communicates, the letter or report or descriptive flyer of the home for sale, can prove to be another factor. A person whose coat or dress is awry, whose tie is askew or whose general personal appearance is poor is not likely to arouse a favorable response in listeners.

Conversely, the broker must be careful he does not evaluate the prospect unfairly if that prospect's appearance or attire doesn't conform to his standards. The client dressed in blue jeans, T-shirt, and sandals who asks, "How much bread up-front does that pad take?" may be a rock musician with a seven-figure bank account.

Inattention

Poor listening is perhaps one of the most serious barriers to the communication of ideas. All too often we think of communication as encompassing reading, writing and speaking. When we consider that approximately 60 percent of our time is spent listening, it is difficult to understand how or why training in this skill is so frequently overlooked.

Poor listening is often a natural result of the disparity in the time it takes to communicate ideas and the time required to assimilate them. Most of us speak at the rate of about 140 words a minute but we can assimilate approximately 500 words in the same time span. It is no wonder, therefore, that the listener's mind begins to wander as he moves further and further ahead of the speaker's ideas.

Often a listener is busy thinking of what he is going to say rather than listening to the speaker. Or perhaps his bias permits him to hear only what he wishes. However, we can train ourselves to better assimilate the ideas directed to us. We can learn to listen actively, to concentrate on what is being said, to listen for the ideas beyond the words and to appreciate the desires and needs of the speaker.

It is so important for the person in real estate to listen effectively, to staff, prospects, customers, community members, financing officers, that we will want to look at this area later in more detail.

Competing Communications

The complexities of our busy society present still another barrier. The communicator must recognize that he is competing for the full attention and loyalty of the prospect. That prospect has seen a half-dozen other properties from a half-dozen other brokers, he has read dozens of ads, and he is competing for time himself. All in all, he is so inundated with communications that it is simply a matter of competition to get through.

The partial solution to communicating effectively in a world of communication is to make yours so superior that it beats the competition. No presentation, written or oral, should be made without careful planning, thought and evaluation. And always keep in mind who the receiver is and appreciate his likes, dislikes, biases and emotions. In this way, your presentation can prove superior to those competing for your receiver's mind.

Language is perhaps the most critical factor for the broker or salesperson in communicating effectively. Obviously, this short chapter does not permit us to go into a detailed discussion of semantics; nevertheless, we must keep in mind that words make pictures and symbols in the minds of people. And we must further remember that the symbol for a word which appears in the transmitter's mind is almost never the same as the one the receiver has. What the broker envisions for "home filled with charm," "spacious," "traditional style," "excellent tax benefits" or "significant cash flow," may not conform at all to what the receiver pictures (or symbolizes). But the effective communicator makes allowances for that.

Sales can be won or lost through word choice. Think if you will of the couple who impressed the broker with their need for a "3-bedroom, 2-bath home with a modern kitchen, nice yard, 2-car garage and above all, not to cost more than $95,000." What happens to that prospective sale when the broker visits them and says, "I've found just the place for you: brick ranch, 3 bedrooms, 2 baths, large 2-car garage, modern kitchen, beautiful yard and best of all...it's a real cheap house!"

The sale may well be lost as a result of the use of "cheap" and all its possible implications. But to that salesperson at that moment the word "cheap" carried a connotation that differed from the prospect's. And the sale was lost. Had the broker used the word "inexpensive" or "reasonably priced" or "attractively priced" the sale might have been made.

Or the owner-broker who rather carelessly said to the new salesperson after the latter's first trip out with a prospect, "Well, you've got to sparkle when you present the selling points rather than just sit and listen and nod your head back and forth like a...like a...sort of like a ventriloquist's dummy." And the salesperson flushes.

Although the broker can now add lamely, "Well, I didn't mean dummy; I mean...," the damage has been done.

When one considers that the person engaged in the field of real estate, residential, industrial, commercial or investment, constantly communicates to achieve his ends, then he will choose each word, each gesture like a nugget of gold.

As Mark Twain said, "There is as much difference between the right word and the almost right word as between lightning and the lightning bug."

There are other barriers that cause breakdowns between sender and receiver. Lack of interest on the part of one or the other or the conflicting personality of either transmitter or receiver. A dozen other aspects of the internal and external environments influence the communications of real estate professionals. We must be sure to recognize and understand the role of non-verbal as well as verbal communication.

Non-verbal Communication

The science called body language deals with behavioral patterns of non-verbal communication. Those who understand its basics are aware that what we do with our bodies is frequently in disagreement with what we are saying. A classic example, according to Julius Fast, writing in *Body Language* is the young woman who told her psychiatrist that "she loved her boyfriend very much all the while shaking her head from side to side in subconscious denial."[2]

Body language can enable business people to shed new light on the dynamics of interpersonal relationships. Those who study it carefully learn to observe the mixture of body movements ranging from the deliberate to the completely unconscious, what each conveys and how to put this knowledge to good use in their daily working relationships.

It is probably no exaggeration to say that we communicate as many ideas non-verbally (and sometimes informally) as we do verbally. The way we stand, the way we walk and the manner in which we shrug our shoulders, furrow our brows and shake our heads all convey ideas to others. But we need not always perform an action for non-verbal communication to take place. We also communicate by the clothes we wear, the car we drive or the office we occupy. It is true that what is communicated may not be accurate but ideas are communicated.

The broker must be especially sensitive to non-verbal signals from the other person: the pained or delighted look on the prospect's face as soon as the first step is taken into the home; the nervous tapping of the fingers on the table top; the voice inflection of confidence or insecurity when price is discussed and the physical tension in the individual's posture as he walks around the property or sits in a chair reading an offer, listing or legal papers.

The same is also true when the broker and salesperson hold a critical interview on compensation, promotion or company strategy. The broker must be sensitive to the crossed arms, tapping heel on the floor, voice level and perhaps the perspiration on the salesperson's forehead.

The broker announces the formality or informality of a situation by where he sits during the interview. If someone comes in whom he wants to treat in an informal manner, he could come around from his desk and guide the visitor to the couch while he takes an easy chair. In this way, his positioning indicates what type of interview he will have. If it's to be an extremely formal one he will remain seated behind his desk.

All these non-verbal signals communicate a message and we must attempt to decode them.

Conflict Between Verbal and Non-verbal Communication

One of the interesting aspects of communication is the task of decoding two messages transmitted simultaneously. This happens quite often in the verbal (or formal) and non-verbal (or informal) communication situation. We have all been in a situation when an individual has greeted us with "How are you? Good to see you. Come into my office and chew the fat, you old son of a gun." But the non-verbal communication, consisting of a surreptitious but pained glance at the clock, says something else. Or the guest who says, "Of course we want to see your slides of Europe," as he stifles a yawn and sprawls in the chair.

Then there is the employee who tries to sound relaxed and comfortable when he talks to the boss, but his toe tapping the floor like a machine gun tells a different story.

Interestingly enough, whenever the meaning of the non-verbal message conflicts with that of the verbal, the receiver is most likely to find the former more believable.

Does this mean that we should bend every effort to communicate the same message both verbally and non-verbally? Generally, if we are transmitting an untruth verbally, it will conflict with the non-verbal communication. And the alert receiver will almost always be able to determine that a problem exists. Most of us can quickly see the fearful person who truly exists behind the good-humored, back-slapping, joke-telling facade that is displayed. We somehow know quite well how dismally Betty and Joe's marriage is progressing, even though their protestations of undying love for one another are voiced loudly and clearly. The non-verbal message is usually obvious; and if it does not agree with the verbal one, the receiver quickly and almost invariably recognizes the one that is true.

Media of Non-verbal Communication

Most of the non-verbal messages that we receive come to us visually. We are quick to see the hurt in one's eyes, the triumphant smile on a face, the twisting nervous fingers on a lap or the confidence in one's posture. We also decode the message that is transmitted in a sudden, frightened tug at our arm when we cross in heavy traffic or the barely noticeable touching of fingers of two people in love.

Our nose or olfactory sense also plays an important role in non-verbal communication. What a wonderful message we decode when we walk into the cozy comfort of the warm home where a huge Thanksgiving dinner is about to be served. The tantalizing aroma of a roasting turkey, dressing and pumpkin pie requires no words to transmit a message.

These, then, are some factors in the process of verbal and non-verbal communication. Now let's look at several factors, which when followed, assist us in the entire process of communication.

Factors to Improve Communication

Three major aspects can make a tremendous impact on our ability to communicate successfully with others:

Be alert to feedback and learn to decode it correctly

Listen with understanding

Improve your ability to perceive.

Decoding Feedback

Because feedback is so vital a communication factor in the real estate transaction, the topic deserves added emphasis.

The purchase of a home is highly involved with emotions and may often be more psychological than logical.

Although the garage workshop adds little to the value of the house, it is something the prospect has dreamed about for years. Did you note the look on the man's face when you walked into the garage with him? And the woman has thought a thousand times how wonderful it would be to have a little hide-away sewing room and this home has one. Did you observe her face when she saw it?

In commercial, industrial and investment sales, the non-verbal communication may be a little harder to spot but it is there: the drumming fingers, the hidden smile, the look of satisfaction or frustration and a dozen other manifestations of inner feelings.

Check for feedback from your staff. Do you have a secretary or salesperson who does a job but whose communication with you is routine and only concerns work details, the weather and small talk? Why doesn't that individual feed back to you problems on sales, situations with you that are frustrating or important details concerning assignments? If you're not getting feedback that contains significant information there must be a reason. Find out what it is and open the lines of communication.

All in all, don't take feedback at face value. Make certain that what you receive is the true message. Try to verify feedback. Does the verbal agree with the non-verbal message? Request a demonstration. Ask questions where you can. Very often the answers will prove how well you communicated initially.

But most important, be sensitive to feedback, not only the words but also the inflection in the voice, the emphasis of the comment, the speed of the reply, the gestures.

Listen With Understanding

Although most people have had extensive academic training in how to read better and faster, how to speak persuasively and effectively, how to write compellingly and correctly, few have had instruction in how to listen. And yet most people spend about 60 percent of their communication time doing just that!

The broker must listen in two areas: for facts and for feelings.

Feelings are much more difficult to hear because they are usually not expressed in words. However, the sensitive listener hears them in the words that aren't said, the tone of the voice and the look on the face.

Here, for example, are Mr. and Mrs. Jackson. He had told you that they need 4 bedrooms, 2 baths, ranch style, with a range of about $95,000 to $40,000 but a maximum, absolute maximum of $16,000 down.

The broker found the home but the present owners have 2 dogs and 2 cats, none of which are trained. And here is Mrs. Jackson, satisfied with the house itself but now standing in the middle of the living room saying, "I just couldn't live with such stained, smelly carpeting. And look at those drapes, every one stained yellow at the bottom. And you said there were 84 square yards of carpeting and 14 pairs of drapes...sure the rooms are spacious and the kitchen is lovely—but

84 yards of carpeting...No, the house won't do, but we'll think about it...."

Did you hear the feelings which did not say directly but obviously, "We like the house but can't live with these drapes and carpeting and can't afford to replace them."

The sensitive listener hears those feelings and responds with a partial or complete solution to the stain problem. The insensitive listener might say, "Oh, that's minor. The home's got everything you want. Why not take it? In a couple of years you can replace the carpeting and drapes." But the Jacksons will never buy the home in its present condition.

And here's another case. We requested our new assistant, Bob Drake, to secure data on that Van Buren Street eight-unit listing. Four days later Bob hands us a sheaf of papers and says (or shouts) "Holy smokes, was that a job. I had to go through a million city records, a dozen files and I was down here Thursday and Friday night working on this thing. I don't think you realized what you were asking for. Here it is right on schedule but what a job that was!"

If we respond with a "Good, now what about the tax info on the Ferguson 12 unit?" we haven't heard Bob Drake at all. He was probably saying, in his long tirade, "How about giving me a pat on the back? I need the encouragement." Of course, the effective listener will hear those feelings.

It's often the unspoken words, the feelings, which we must respond to. And it is not necessary to agree with them. But it is necessary to hear and respond.[3]

The effective communicator listens actively, objectively, analytically, to another person's meaning for words and to the non-verbal communication.

Sharpen Your Ability to Perceive

While this recommendation overlaps into listening, understanding, sensitivity to feedback and other aspects, it is important in the field of real estate.

Most brokers perceive working on weekends as vital for most of their salespeople because 80 percent of homes are shown on weekends. But if Mrs. Farnsworth, an excellent salesperson, who has a husband and three children, sees it as an impossible imposition, communication will certainly break down.

You do not have to agree with Mrs. Farnsworth's perception and expectations. However, you must (1) appreciate them and (2) be able to express your perception.

Once you have done that, you can meet on common ground and perhaps find a solution. And that solution may be acceptable and advantageous to both.

"Yes, Mrs. Farnsworth, I can appreciate that with three teenagers and a husband at home, you would want to spend your weekends with them. However, those weekend periods are critical in real estate. What about working every other weekend? In addition, if you have a special situation that only you can handle, you may want to come in on just a Saturday morning on those weekends that you're scheduled to be free."

This is where communication must and can begin, on common ground which both parties perceive similarly. Again, we emphasize that we do not have to agree with the other person's perceptions and expectations. We do have to appreciate them and articulate that perception.

These are just a few ideas in the highly complex area of human communication. For individuals whose vital tool is communication, knowledge and expertise in this discipline are absolutely vital. The real estate broker, necessarily involved with the people in the firm and dozens of individuals outside, must constantly polish his ability to communicate if he is to be successful. There is no better time to start than today.

---

[1] Sigband, *Communication for Management,* p. 10.

[2] Fast, *Body Language,* p. 1 and ff.

[3] Sigband, "Listen to What You Can't Hear," *Nations Business,* June 1969.

Recruiting Salespeople   7

Recruiting sales and office personnel in real estate today reflects the challenges that face every industry in the United States: rapidly developing technology, the requirement to avoid discrimination and the changing average age of the population. Changing lifestyles affect not only the product most real estate firms have to sell—housing—but also bring a whole new work force into their selling market. Surely in no other industry has the emergence of the woman played a more significant role than in real estate.

How well your firm responds and reacts to these changes will depend to a large degree on how well you plan and organize your staffing program. Starting with the first considerations—the jobs to be filled, the lead time desired, the kind of people you want, where you'll recruit them and the compensation you'll offer them—to the final and continuing challenge to keep the best people with your firm, a carefully structured program promises a good return for the time spent on it.

Management's challenge is to plan its personnel and program thoroughly, recruit the needed staff skillfully and present the opportunities the firm offers with such enthusiasm that applicants will not only be drawn to the firm, but newcomers will be drawn to the field as well.

Application of the material in this chapter is dependent on your own office. Specifically it applies to a careful delineation between staff members who are employees and those who are independent contractors.

Recruiting Salespeople

The foremost challenge that faces a broker is that of recruiting and selecting the right salespeople and an effective, efficient ancillary staff. If the broker does this well, a strange phenomenon occurs: he will be forced to run a better company. High caliber salespeople expect and demand high caliber management. The benefits that derive from this phenomenon are many. The broker makes more money, has fewer problems, gets more sleep and in general is happier. His reputation, his company and his industry all benefit. When these benefits are compared to the alternative, it becomes readily apparent that staffing a brokerage office is an area that demands the broker's serious attention.

Wendell French explains the staffing process as "A flow of events which results in the continuous manning of organizational positions at all levels.... In a sense, this process is the flow of human resources into, within and out of the enterprise, although these activities are highly interdependent and all can be occurring within an enterprise at any one time."[1]

Just as real estate has adopted sophisticated, modern methods in selling, it is acquiring equal sophistication and technical know-how in personnel practices.

Industry Considerations

The real estate industry of the 1990s will be more complex and technical than at any other point in its history. Before a broker chooses his first salesperson, replaces normal turnover or expands his sales force, it is important that he employ the strategic planning process, taking into account the state of the industry and the direction in which it is moving.

He will be keenly aware of the changed attitude of the courts from the time-honored "let the buyer beware" policy to one of consumerism. He will recognize the steadily increasing role government is playing in areas such as environment and pollution control, redevelopment, financing, equal rights and in general managing the economy. He will consider the increased level of competition developing through large multi-office firms, franchise operations, national referral networks, equity purchase companies and guaranteed sales plans. Alternative types of housing such as town houses, condominiums, cluster homes and second homes must be recognized. Furthermore, he will develop a keen feeling for his local market area, its trends, special situations and brokerage competition. Only after analyzing these and other factors and evaluating their resultant costs and complexities can a broker begin to assess whether he should remain small, specialize or expand. Also, it is at this point the broker begins to develop a feeling for the type of operation he will run and the kind and caliber of salespeople he will need.

Company Goals and Objectives

It is important that the broker examine and define his overall company goals and objectives before he begins a recruiting program. Recruiting cannot be planned until questions such as the following are answered.

What are our long-and short-range objectives in terms of size, services, markets, profit, image and numbers?

What will the estimated monthly desk cost be?

What will the company policy be?

What will the company provide salespeople in terms of facilities, advertising, commissions, draws, fringe benefits, management, professional services, investment opportunities and personal growth opportunities?

What will the minimum acceptable income for salespeople be?

Personnel Inventory

After you analyze the firm's goals and objectives as they relate to staff needs and have incorporated them into your company plan, you can begin to develop a timetable and budget for whatever money it will require.

A personnel inventory includes the following:

Analysis of the skills in the organization. Who does what and why?

Current and anticipated vacancies in the staff. What staff positions are now open? Are any staff people planning to leave? When? Will you want to replace them?

Current and expected expansion or curtailment of departments. How many people will you need to add if the firm is to achieve its goals and objectives? Can any of these positions be filled by present personnel or will they all have to be recruited? If you plan to curtail any part of your present operation, can people so displaced be moved to another department? If expansion is planned, what are the personnel needs to get the new department or office underway? Are there people now on the staff who could be moved into any of these positions?

Internal shifts or cutbacks in personnel. Even if you plan to keep the firm at its present size, adding no new services, should you be thinking about shifting some of your staff into new positions or cutting back where work production has proved inefficient and ineffective?

One good way to double check the completeness of your inventory and begin to think about additions, shifts or possible deletions is to use your company organizational chart as a worksheet. It will give you a quick picture of who is responsible for what is being done and it can suggest possible changes to make and special strengths or potential weaknesses in the organization.

Personnel Plan

A personnel plan includes developing the following:

Job analysis

Job evaluation

Job description
Job specifications.

Job Analysis
Firms with well developed personnel practices use job analyses to develop job descriptions. A good job analysis includes such data as:

What is the fundamental purpose of the job?

Is the person an employee or independent contractor?

What are the job's specific tasks and responsibilities?

What does the job accomplish toward company goals?

What are the working relationships of this job, including supervision given and review of accomplishment?

Job Evaluation
Job evaluation is the process of determining the relative worth of the various jobs in your firm and where each job will fit in the hierarchy of your firm. Job evaluation assumes that it is logical to pay the most for jobs contributing the most to the firm's goals; that people feel more fairly treated if compensation is based on the relative worth of jobs; and that the company goals are furthered by maintaining a job structure based on relative job worth. Some of the variables examined in a job evaluation are responsibility, skill, working conditions, effort and compensation scale.

Job Description
Writing in *The Practice of Creativity,* George M. Prince expresses the belief that top management that rethinks work assignments from manager to salesperson will reap enormous rewards. It will need the active help of those involved and much creative behavior to design into each job the maximum in personal achievement and satisfaction.

Job descriptions are summaries of the basic tasks performed on a job. They have several important uses. They are useful in personnel planning, counseling and recruiting. Management can plan more intelligently if it knows the basic duties of a job as well as the qualifications required of the worker. Management can recruit more effectively if it is able to describe the job activities and responsibilities to applicants.

Job descriptions should be flexible as well as accurate. Rigidity destroys their value because if a person is to grow and contribute to a firm's growth, his job should be dynamic, not static. Both the supervisor and the staff individual should agree on the content of the description and that it fairly reflects the job. Some of the points to include in a real estate brokerage job description are: what salespeople do in your firm; hours of work each week, including nights and weekends; floor time; cold canvassing and similar duties; office employee working hours and duties (inclusion depends on whether salespeople are employees or independent contractors); who staff person reports to; any staff position reporting to him.

A growing number of firms prepare two descriptions for each job. One is written by the manager, based on personal knowledge and the operations manual; the second is written by the staff person, based on his experience and how he sees his job. As the manager sits down with the staff person to review the two descriptions, lines of communication are often strengthened as each learns how the other views what is being done and why. The two then develop a single job description which details duties, time schedule and how the job coordinates with the work of others in the firm.

Job Specifications
Job specifications translate job descriptions into terms of human qualifications. Specifications are written by management based on job descriptions and the qualifications appropriate and reasonable to expect in the person who will do the work.

The job description outlines the duties involved. The specification details the education, experience, resourcefulness, responsibility, contacts and mental and physical effort involved in performing those duties. The specifications also cover the supervision and the general job conditions in performing the job.

Because job specifications usually result from a combination of management planning and job descriptions, they are subject to most of the same influences. The validity of job specifications is proven by the success of the person hired for the job and the degree to which the characteristics listed are predictive of performance.

Your Working Plan
Now you can begin to get your recruiting plan organized on paper. Start by asking some important questions:

What kind of people do we want?
Expand present staff?
Initiate new services?
Replace normal attrition?

Where will we find them?
Internal recruitment
External sources

How will we compensate them?
Commission
Special bonuses
Straight salary
Fringe benefits—insurance, car, travel expense
Incentive programs

How much should we budget to cover recruiting costs?
Advertising
Printed forms and records
Recruiting brochure

What is the target date for the program?
Beginning recruitment
Job performance evaluation analysis

Selection interviews
Starting date for going on staff.

Short Range Personnel Planning

Under such a program, major emphasis is placed on filling an immediate need, whether for a salesperson, clerk, secretary or accountant. This stop-gap method of planning works for small organizations that intend to remain small. It is an approach that gives little thought to company objectives, expansion, whether horizontal or vertical, competitive influences and the like. It is concerned with filling positions that have been or soon will be vacant, whether though resignation, death or retirement.

Small real estate firms can survive on short range personnel programs. But they are dependent on stability and may be unable to respond quickly to changing market conditions. They focus on getting maximum production from existing staff.

Long Range Personnel Planning

This type of planning in the real estate field finds more emphasis being placed on population trends, market projections and possible expansion (vertical or horizontal) as they affect the growth of the market being served or one that may be included in a general expansion program.

The numbers and qualifications of persons presently with the firm are a matter of concern and study by top management. The success of various departments and special projects, if any, become an important consideration in any long range plan. Long range planning may focus on growth, per se, of the present organization or on designs to change the business character of the firm in the future.

Lead time is an important factor in any personnel program. What are the pressures to get the job filled? If you have a particular person in mind for a job, will he need extra time to sever his present ties? How will factors like your location, commission or salary structure or the general economy affect the time needed to find people you want?

Here is where long range planning pays off. The better it is, the more likely you will have enough lead time to find the best people. Good long range planning often prompts management to add a person they really want before he is actually needed to avoid losing him to a competitor.

If you have a sizeable group to recruit (such as when staffing a new department, division or office) consider the services of an ad agency or an employment agency. The former can help you develop display ads for newspapers or text for radio ads; the latter often prove a good investment of the dollar cost in recruiting and doing some preliminary screening of applicants.

Where to Look

There are two kinds of sources: internal and external. These include the following.

Internal

Sales staff referrals are one of the best sources. Salespeople are often more selective about who they work with than is management. Also, top producers attract other top producers. To be effectively used, this source must be cultivated continually.

Most companies have built a substantial list of satisfied customers over the years. Many well-qualified prospects may be found from this source.

An outstanding basic and/or advanced training program is hard to keep quiet. Develop one and many well qualified applicants will find their way to your firm because of it.

Office walk-ins are a source of applicants from a broad cross-section of people. Some are standouts but many are not qualified.

Individuals with access to a specific personnel market such as universities, medical centers, schools, or local industries.

External

Salespeople from other industries are another excellent source. Proven salespeople from other industries are often well trained in the fundamentals of selling, are fast starters and are often really turned on to real estate.

Sales and motivational courses are an outstanding source of applicants already interested in sales and making an extra effort in that direction.

Career seminars can be effective if they have not been overused in your area.

Pre-licensing schools are an excellent source for applicants already oriented to real estate. As with career seminars, local usage greatly affects results.

College and university placement bureaus are often concerned with placing both current graduates and alumni. Financial assistance plans may be necessary to compete for new graduates.

Employment agencies are often overlooked as a source. Some are good at pre-screening, using your criteria.

Advertisements provide a source of applicants from a broad cross-section of people.

Direct mail and cold calling is a final source for when you really need sales help.

How to Look

Recruiting is more effective if done on a continuing basis. Even when you have a full staff it is wise to encourage a continuous stream of inquiries. The lead time from selecting a new salesperson and getting him into production is long enough, without having to add more time to get your recruiting machinery going again. It is a rare office that can't find space for an especially promising recruit. The manager should keep in constant contact with his sources through personal visits, mail and the telephone. The image and program of the company as well as the benefits of selling real estate should be stressed.

Recruiting Brochures

An attractively designed, well written brochure can be a valuable aid to a recruiting program. Most real estate firms spend thousands of dollars advertising properties to bring prospects to the point of inquiry; yet many fail to develop even an inexpensive brochure to highlight the advantages of selling real estate and affiliating with their firm.

Brochures can be a valuable tool to leave with applicants; they can be used as a mailer or stuffer or handed to the applicant to help him and his spouse make the job decision.

Key elements of a good brochure include discussion of career benefits (high income potential, limited financial investment, high degree of independence, personal growth, investment opportunities, challenge and prestige, it's fun and a people business) and company benefits (training program, experienced management leadership, high caliber sales staff, good company image and reputation, potential income, fringe benefits, personal growth possibilities, facilities, exceptional history and growth record, member of Multiple Listing Service, member of Board of REALTORS®, member of referral and relocation network, closing department, commercial department, insurance department and professional services).

Keep Recruiting Records

Whether you use just one or a combination of recruiting sources available, keep accurate, meaningful records of the results. They will be useful in the future as you continue to add to your sales staff. Good records will reflect the effectiveness of the source. What you're after is not a record of the number of applicants any one source generated but which source brought you the best people.

Such records can also suggest what recruiting techniques worked best and any changes or improvements that occur to you as you go through the process.

The opportunity for high earnings attracts many people to real estate sales. Because of the independent contractor relationship, it is important that a compensation plan be carefully structured and explained to anyone seeking to join your firm.

Commission

The payment of straight commissions is still the most popular and effective method of compensation for salespeople. Several observations may be in order.

First, an important factor to remember when evaluating commission splits is that if you do not retain enough of the commission dollars to provide the services salespeople need to do their job, you will be unable to attract or keep the caliber of salespeople you need.

Compensation should satisfy emotional as well as financial needs. Money may be a symbol to some; to others an absolute necessity; and to still others it offers a way to show that they are the best. In most cases it should be remembered that a salesperson is usually interested in total income and the commission split can be less important than the total number of dollars he can earn in a year's time.

Commission schedules should be agreed upon formally by broker and salesperson. They should be detailed in writing. The best plan is a combination of things that work, motivate, get results and are fair and show a profit for the company. While it is the nature of the real estate business to believe you must meet the competition, it does not follow that when a competitor goes to an unrealistic commission rate his figure must be met or bettered.

Commission rates should be changed only after long and serious consideration. It is usually unwise to change them with the market. The temptation to take from the listing salespeople and give to the selling salespeople in one market, then take from the selling salespeople and give to the listing salespeople in another can have an unsettling effect on the whole sales staff.

Other Forms of Compensation

Salespeople's financial situations and the state of a firm's business sometimes cause management to look to other methods of compensation. There are several, some possible with independent contractors and some limited to salespeople employed by the firm.

The following alternative ways of compensating salespeople have been broken down as they apply to independent contractors and employees. A full discussion of this relationship follows in Chapter 9. Whatever compensation form the broker chooses, he must be aware of the full meaning of it.

This material is not meant to be used as a legal guideline. It suggests the need for legal counsel in planning and instituting any compensation plans. Laws change constantly and legal counsel is needed for the broker's protection. Brokers can obtain direction by contacting the legal services department of the NATIONAL ASSOCIATION OF REALTORS®, and many state associations provide legal services for their members as well.

Draws—Independent Contractor

The compensation arrangements between a broker and an independent contractor salesperson must be carefully described and should be in writing. Under no circumstances should the form of compensation resemble a salary. This is why "draws" against commissions, whether or not earned, are extremely dangerous and should be carefully examined with legal counsel before they are initiated. If a salesperson requires compensation beyond that which he can generate through commission income, he should be "employed" at a salary until he can become self-sustaining at which time he may become affiliated on an independent contractor basis.

While it is not generally advisable, a broker may make a loan to an independent contractor salesperson. If he does so, however, such loan should be evidenced by a note, should be at interest and the broker should insist upon full payment and enforce payment if necessary. One should always be cautious about a note secured by "future commissions" and the broker should only withhold payments on the note from commissions due the salesperson with a written understanding to cover it.

It is critical that compensation arrangements, to the extent they deviate in any respect form a straight commission basis, be reviewed by legal counsel prior to implementation.

Draws—Employees

Draw systems can be used against future commissions, against earned commissions or against the possibility of earned commission. Draws are regular payments made very much in the nature of a salary.

In a draw against future commissions, there may be no commissions currently earned but the draw continues. It is a flat, even rate and is not increased or reduced according to current earnings. In such cases, the sales associate may be ahead of the company or behind it, changing position many times during the year. All he is concerned with is that X number of dollars will be available to him at a certain time each month. This is the simplest form of draw and perhaps one of the most dangerous because such a draw will probably be interpreted as being a salary in disguise.

In a draw against earned commission, payments derive form commissions that have been accumulated. They may be drawn in part or in full but the sales associate has the comfort of knowing that even if a sale does not close for several months, he can draw the money on that sale at any time.

The pitfalls here are that in such a system the sales employee usually draws on future commissions as a matter of practice rather than emergency. A bookkeeping problem arises and trouble surfaces when sales fall through. Another difficulty of this system is that the company's cash position may be jeopardized if the draw is over-used.

Another draw is against the possibility of earned commission. Under this plan, a sales associate can draw against a possible earned listing commission simply by bringing in a listing. The broker evaluates the listing. If it is a good one, the draw would be allowed. This, unfortunately, adds one more dimension to a rather complicated draw system.

In both the above types of draw, the broker should take precautions to protect himself and have a clear understanding of the agreement with the sales associate. Specifically, there should be some evidence in writing as to repayment, payment of interest and the status of each of the parties in the event of termination of the independent contractor. Some brokers who offer draws not only charge interest but require that a note be signed covering each draw. In some cases, brokers require that the sales associate's spouse co-sign the note.

A third type of draw system is against the possibility of earned commissions while the associate is in a training period. In this type of draw a sales associate earns while working, perhaps part time, through a training period. He may earn some commissions during this period. A typical draw of this type pays one half of the earned commission and the other half is deposited by the broker in a custodial account in the salesperson's name. At the end of the training period, a reserve is accumulated upon which the new sales associate can draw until fuller production is achieved.

A fourth variation on financing methods in draws is the minimum guarantee. In this system, the broker either by an oral or written promise or in writing puts a floor on the earnings of a new sales associate. He simply guarantees that the sales associate will earn a minimum number of dollars in a specified time and if he does not earn that amount, the broker will pay the difference.

A fifth alternative for getting new sales associates over a financial hump is for the broker to go with the associate to a bank, credit union or other lending institution and co-sign his note. The sales associate repays the lender and, as he does, establishes credit so future loans can be made without a co-signer. An advantage of this system is that the broker need not tie up his own funds, need not pay interest and can keep a close watch on the progress of the new sales associate. In some instances, a broker will issue two checks to a sales associate on a closed sale. The commission is paid one-half in the name of the sales associate and the other half in the name of the sales associate and the lender. When the check is endorsed to the lender, the debt which was co-signed is partially liquidated. This system demonstrates the faith the broker has in the sales associate, but it does assure repayment and the reduction of the broker's liability.

Salary—Independent Contractor
A salary form of compensation is inconsistent with the independent contractor relationship.

Salary—Employee
The straight salary method is still used rather sparingly as a means of compensating sales associates. A system of salary-with-commission is not so unusual. This plan gives the sales associate the advantage of the economic certainty of a basic salary. A danger in this system is that a sales associate may not be adequately motivated to achieve an optimum production level.

Fringe Benefits
As for providing security for salespeople in a real estate firm, the best security is within the person himself. A well-trained salesperson should be able to do well selling in any market, anywhere. In addition to this personal security, which can be build up and nurtured, some fringe benefits will help provide additional measures of financial security. Some of these benefits can accrue to independent contractors and salespeople alike; some are limited.

Profit Sharing and Pension Plans—Independent Contractor
Independent contractors are not qualified to participate in a broker's profit sharing or pension plan. On the other hand, they can set up self-employed retirement programs. Such plans may be arranged through banks, insurance companies, trust companies and other financial institutions. Under such programs, the amount contributed to the retirement program, within specified limits, is excluded from the independent contractor's taxable income. Earnings on the sums contributed are likewise not currently taxable. Brokers will find it desirable to encourage their independent contractor salespeople to set up such retirement programs in consultation with their legal counsel.

Profit Sharing and Pension Plans—Employee

Employees are entitled to participate in company or firm pension and profit sharing plans. The difference between a pension and profit sharing plan is basically a difference in the nature of the broker's commitment to contribute. A pension plan usually involves a commitment on the part of the broker to contribute to the plan each year whereas a profit sharing plan will normally require contributions only in those years in which a profit is made by the company.

Pension and profit sharing plans must qualify under the Internal Revenue Code in order for the broker's contributions to them to be deductible. The requirements governing eligibility, participation and essentially every other feature of such plans are extremely comprehensive and specific and competent legal counsel should be consulted in their development and implementation.

Pension and profit sharing plans for sales or other employees of a broker can significantly reduce labor turnover and increase employee job satisfaction. They do not involve continuing obligations and costs, however, and therefore should not be established without extensive prior analysis of the commitment and the wide variety of forms such commitment may legally take.

Sliding Scale Bonus Plans—Independent Contractor

Bonuses paid to independent contractors must be a bargained for, predetermined reward for achievement. They should not be discretionary payments lest they be considered salary and jeopardize the independent contractor status of the salesperson. Bonus plans must be carefully designed to achieve their purpose which is motivation of the salesperson to optimum productivity. They are usually set up on a sliding scale basis.

Bonus Plans—Employee

It is not easy for a broker with a staff accustomed to receiving commissions on a fixed schedule to initiate a bonus plan. In most cases it is necessary to adjust the commissions downward and this is invariably a painful procedure. It is especially difficult to initiate such a plan because of its effect on the present schedule of commission. Bonuses are usually most rewarding to high producers and may be resented by less productive employees.

The best bonus plans are those that do not encourage sales employees to either leave or loaf. They do not make a lump payment once a year because this might suggest a target date to leave the company or tempt a salesperson to take it easy until that sum is used up. They should be rewards and not merely a gift to an employee for having survived another year with the firm. The basic requirements of a good bonus plan are that it rewards achievement and motivates.

Insurance Programs—Independent Contractors

Legal counsel should advise the broker which, if any, insurance programs may be open to participation by independent contractors who pay their own premiums. When such arrangements are possible, the independent contractors enjoy the benefit of group rates and the possibility of getting better coverage than they might obtain under individual policies.

Insurance Programs—Employee
Many brokerage firms provide insurance programs for their employees. Group insurance programs for live, medical, dental, hospital, accident and health coverage are available. Employed personnel are eligible for insurance benefits, whether the broker provides them as a wholly subsidized fringe benefit or on a contributory basis by the employees. However, such programs must be reviewed with legal counsel to assure that they satisfy the requirements of the Internal Revenue Code. Otherwise, payments for such benefits may not be deductible to the company and may be taxable to the sales employee.

Other Fringe Benefits—Employees Only
Paid vacations and sick leave are benefits confined to an employee/employer relationship.

Salaried Office Personnel
Much of the broker's success results from the efforts of the office staff. It is the broker himself who determines whether the office staff will be an asset or a liability. If he gives them the feeling that he cannot be bothered with them because he has more important problems—such as his own listings, sales or salespeople's problems—they will reflect his indifference and he may find disorganization and chaos prevail in the office.

When office personnel are efficient, responsible and well organized they give salespeople confidence, knowing that they can rely on the office staff to back them up while they are out in the field. Your office staff can play a leading role in maintaining friendliness, goodwill and keeping office morale high.

Office Personnel Needs
In planning office personnel needs, a broker should carefully spend time determining the type of people he wants and what training and experience they should have to maintain the quality and integrity he has established in his organization.

A carefully thought out job analysis for each office position is just as important as in the selling staff.

Job analysis can be handled in three ways: by observation, by interview and by questionnaire. Many companies use a combination of all three. One common practice is to have each employee describe his job as he sees it, including his duties responsibilities, and the lines of authority. When this course is followed, one should provide guideline questions. Some suggested questions are:

What is the title of your job

Who are your immediate supervisors

What experience or education qualified you for your present job

Who do you work with inside the company

Who do you work with in outside firms on company business

What other persons tell you what to do

What duties do you perform without supervision

What machines are used in your job

A person in your job would normally be promoted from what job

A person in your job would be promoted to what jobs

Do you clearly understand the extent to which you have authority to make decisions

Do you have access to confidential information—why—how do you use it

What duties do you perform that you feel should not be part of your job

Please list as many items as you can which you feel are part of your position and how often you perform them.

Once the employees have written their job analyses the broker has a clearer picture of how the employees view their roles. The results are often surprising. The broker often has a far different perspective of the employee's roles within the organization than that held by his employees.

The completion of this job analysis form provides an excellent source of material for an in-depth interview. During the job analysis interview it's easy to review those areas where the employee and the broker are not on the same wave length. Here is where upward communication can be of great value. Listen well. Repeat back to them what they've said so they know you're listening. This interview can result in a very effective job description, a better understanding and a vastly improved working relationship between office employee and broker.

Developing a Source of Office Personnel

An important internal source for filling positions is by promoting staff. People within your own organization may be capable of meeting the challenges of more responsible positions. Many brokers have adopted a philosophy of first trying to promote from within, rather than seeking outside talent. Thus the only openings that must be filled from outside are the job classifications in the lower strata of the organizational structure, which normally require the least amount of skill. Promotion within the office staff is an important means of building and/or maintaining morale.

Another source for recruiting office personnel is through your employees. Many times your own employees know qualified people who are seeking people. The broker who takes the attitude that people are the most important asset will develop a sense of pride among his employees. Employees will be proud to recommend applicants who want to work with other highly competent people. But it should always be stressed that your firm is not interested in pirating employees from other companies.

In seeking employees from outside sources, they most commonly used medium is newspaper classified advertising. This can be a very effective source because it usually elicits the largest volume of inquiries but demands a lot of time to screen and interview them. Office personnel do not always seek a change in employment for money alone. In writing copy for classified advertising stress that you have an exciting atmosphere in which to work. Stress the opportunities for advancement.

Some experts in the field of office personnel recruiting feel that newspaper classified advertising is not always the best source for recruiting office personnel. Some local junior colleges and business schools have placement offices that will work with a broker to help give guidance on job descriptions and salary ranges in addition to providing qualified applicants. In some areas they pre-screen applicants for the employer. Also do not forget employment agencies for office personnel needs.

Compensation

Most brokers are conditioned to dealing in commissions rather than salaries. This can cause one of two problems. Either he will have a high number of morale problems within his office, resulting in less productive employees or high turnover; or in order to hold his employees, he pays far more than his competitors. To avoid these problems, have a realistic plan to establish salary ranges for your office personnel on a systematic basis.

Research the going rate for comparable positions in your area. Many times large companies in your area will provide data on salary ranges they pay for comparable positions. Some Chambers of Commerce conduct annual wage-salary surveys in their communities. The Small Business Administration is of help, too. The Civil Service publishes guidelines on salary ranges for each job in your office. Adopt a formula for a base salary based on what you consider fair compensation for a new person starting within that position. Be fair and honest with your employees when establishing base salaries, but take care that you're not such a nice guy you put yourself in the red on your profit and loss statement. Some brokers think the answer to all personnel problems is giving a raise. This is usually only a temporary solution to a deeper problem.

The best way to handle staff compensation is to explain at the beginning of employment exactly what the salary will be. Most brokers do an effective job at this point. What causes problems is a lack of regularly scheduled reviews and raises. It is not likely that any raise given to an individual employee will be kept secret within the office for very long. The best way to handle compensation and avoid problems is to establish a policy on salaries. This spells out salary policy for the entire length of time of their employment. This policy should stipulate beginning salaries, when salary reviews will take place and under what circumstances raises will be given.

Once the base starting salary for each position within your organization is established it becomes a simple matter to set the top limit. When the top limit your company is willing to pay for each position is established, it's necessary to determine how an employee reaches the top level.

Employees should understand how they can move beyond the established limits for the job they hold. This might be achieved by adding greater responsibilities within the job held or by qualifying for promotion to a higher job.

There are incentive programs that reward office staff on the basis of performance. Profit sharing programs are probably the most common. In such programs, salaried employees share a percentage of the gross profits, split equally among all the salaried employees.

Many companies provide investment opportunities for salaried office employees. These opportunities provide employees a vehicle for investing in their company on an everyday basis and promise exciting opportunities for future economic growth.

Fringe Benefits

The possible list of fringe benefits that a broker can offer his office personnel is endless. Among the most popular are health, life and disability insurance and special discounts on commissions or fees on the sale of employee's homestead or investment properties.

Paid vacations, retirement plans, stock options, expense accounts, travel allowances, contests and prizes, free memberships in fraternal and business societies, country clubs, health clubs, counseling and psychiatric counseling are among the fringe benefits currently offered.

Many brokers are not aware of what these programs cost. It is easy for a company to "fringe itself to death." Many brokers give employees benefit upon benefit only to have the employee leave to take a position with another firm because of higher take home pay. Many large corporations feel that if fringe benefits total more than 10 to 15 percent of the gross earnings of the employees they exceed normal limitations. Many employees, despite demands for fringe benefits, prefer higher take home pay.

Before implementing a fringe benefit program make certain that the entire employee group is enthusiastic about it. A broker may respond to requests from a few employees only to find out after implementing a costly program that the majority of the employees actually do not want it. This is particularly true when fringe benefits are given in lieu of a salary increase.

Research has indicated that many fringe benefits do not provide the employer with the intended original objective of acting as an employee retention device. The most important concept to remember in compensating employees, is to give them an environment in which to work where they are comfortable, have a strong sense of security and exciting possibilities for future growth with an employer who truly cares about them and their problems.

The important concept to keep in mind in your firm's recruitment program is to make careful plans as far ahead as possible, organize the way you will proceed with the plan and be prepared to do an effective selling job of your firm so you get the best people available. Then both sales and office staff will respond to your comfortable working environment, enjoy a strong sense of security and be motivated to learn all they can to assure their own needs will be filled. As they succeed so will the firm.

Selecting Salespeople and Office Personnel 8

The most critical financial investment a real estate broker makes is in his sales staff because he is almost totally dependent on direct sales for revenue and profit. Effective management recognizes this fact in selecting the best salespeople to be found.

The selection process works best when it is carefully organized. When management understands the logical steps to follow, what is involved at each step and how the applicant either moves to the next step or is disqualified (or disqualifies himself) and is dropped, the entire selection process operates more smoothly. Because the human element is ever present, mistakes will be made; but errors can be minimized by following a step-by-step selection procedure.

Selecting Salespeople and Office Personnel

A number of managers cling to the fallacy that when salespeople operate on a straight commission there is no financial investment involved. These managers are not yet aware of the desk costs of supporting the sales organization. Desk costs are the total expense of operating an office divided by the number of salespeople being supported, both producers and non-producers. If, for example, the desk cost is $1,000 per month per salesperson, in a three-month training and start-up period, a non-producing salesperson would in six months represent an investment of $6,000. This economic reality is called the "lost revenue rule." The lost revenue rule involves an estimate of dollar sales lost over a period of time by a non-producer occupying the space that could have been used by a producer. It is activated each time a potential non-producer is recruited.

Change

Besides the reality of the sales staff investment, another fact must be recognized: we live in a world of accelerating change. Business norms and standards of twenty or even five years ago do not apply today.

Change can occur internally through growth, maturity and enlightened management. For example, X Company began business twenty years ago with two people. It has grown to a force of more than a hundred salespeople operating out of ten branches. There is a general sales manager, branch managers, a director of recruiting and training and an administrative staff. X Company has diversified into commercial properties, investments, insurance, leasing, farm and ranch brokerage, all calling for people with special abilities, experience and training. The selection standards X Company used even less than ten years ago could not possibly serve today.

At the same time, Y Company is struggling to get started. Operating with a limited budget in a highly competitive market (not only competing in sales but also in finding and keeping capable people), Y Company's selection standards will differ significantly from those used by X Company.

But X Company and Y Company have something in common if both have alert, progressive leadership and management, aware of the impact of change in the real estate industry and the necessity of adjusting to it.

The forces of external change, often beyond the control of management, call for adaptations and modifications in the way things are done. This is especially true in the development and utilization of human resources and in the standards and procedures used to acquire on-the-job producers.

External changes affecting the goals and decisions of management can occur in the marketplace as new psychological, social and economic factors influence the attitudes and needs of buyers. Changes brought about by increased government regulation of real estate licensing and laws covering employment practices have a marked effect on screening and selection procedures. The manpower market could undergo a radical change with the trend to offer financial assistance to new salespeople. The increased presence of corporate giants in real estate sales could intensify competition for both revenue and manpower. The real estate franchise organizations with their mass advertising techniques, extensive communications systems, supportive services and pooling of effort and information continue to bring about significant change in management perspectives and methods among their members.

Some of the most important changes, at least with reference to human resources development, are a result of the wealth of information coming from management and behavioral sciences. These include:

New approaches in determining manpower needs

Guidelines for establishing realistic performance standards

Techniques for appraising and predicting on-the-job potential through more effective interviewing and testing

Improved learning and skill development training systems

Increased personal motivation and improved performance by implementing behavior modification methods.

These techniques and procedures are being used by many real estate firms with remarkable results. Measurable changes include higher levels of individual and group performance, reduction in turnover and increased sales and profits.

Why People Fail

The principal reason people fail on the job is because management has failed to do its job.

Some failures are beyond the control of management. Even then, it is likely the reasons for failure are also beyond the control of the person who failed, if management has done its job.

In the real estate industry the turnover rate of salespeople, coming into and then leaving the business, has been estimated to range from a conservative 30 percent to as high as 70 percent. There is a saying among real estate managers that, "There is one-third coming, one-third staying and one-third leaving." If this is true, staff turnover is more in the 60 to 70 percent range since two-thirds of the salespeople are in a state of flux, either coming into or going out of the business, all the time.

Many industry leaders agree that the largest volume of turnover occurs within the first six months. This period is not much more than a minimum start-up time in any career. In the life insurance and financial securities industries, a sales agent is considered a neophyte until he has passed the two-year mark.

During the first six months a great deal of the energy and attention of a new salesperson is directed toward training, gaining working knowledge and experience. This is especially true today with the rapidly increasing technical and legal complexities in real estate. An initial six-month period is not enough time to develop the momentum, motivation, self-confidence and professional skills vital to a successful career in selling real estate.

In other words, if industry estimates of turnover are even reasonably in the ball park, the vast majority of people who enter real estate sales as a career either quit or are phased out before they really get started.

Information Feedback and Decision Making in the Screening Process

All decision making operates by a process called information feedback; and whether a decision turns out as good or bad is totally dependent on both the quantity and quality of the information which is fed back into the decision-making process.

Information feedback is most valuable when compared to some predetermined value or standard, a performance specification, inherent in the decision-making process itself. The source for performance specifications is the job description and job specification. By comparing the information fed back against the performance specification, a prediction is possible. Based on the prediction, a decision can then be made on the most effective course of action. This concept can be diagrammed as follows:

Information$\leftarrow\rightarrow$performance specification$\rightarrow$prediction
$\rightarrow$decision$\rightarrow$action

Job Analysis

During the fall of 1987, the Real Estate Brokerage Council™, in conjunction with the Life Insurance Marketing and Research Association (LIMRA International), conducted a study to investigate the life experiences that real estate recruiters feel facilitate success. Three hundred recruiters and sales associates identified the following life history (biodata) dimensions as critical to sales success: work ethic, sales temperament, maturity and responsibility, sales prospects, vitality, investment in career, organizational ability, and establishment in the community.

Other studies have found that those having a potential for success in sales share certain, basic personal qualities: interest in people, good mental ability, dominance, enthusiasm, aggressiveness, self-confidence, self-discipline and ego.

These life experiences and characteristics vary in degree from person to person. Since they are considered essential to success, they are entered into the performance specification along with other critical standards.

Now, assume there exists an evaluation procedure which can reliably and validly identify and measure an applicant's life experiences and characteristics. The information feedback from the evaluation procedure is compared with the most acceptable standard embodied in the performance specification. From this comparison, actual to ideal, an estimate can be made of possible future performance in this step in the screening process. At this point, based on the prediction obtained from information feedback, a decision can be made either to proceed on to the next step or stop and begin again with another applicant.

Two important requirements must be met in using the information feedback approach in the screening of sales applicants:

The information being fed back into the decision-making process must come from objective, reliable sources

The performance specification should be practical and reasonable with realistic goals and objectives in mind.

The prediction-decision-action sequence involving information feedback is not restricted to the screening and selection procedure in the overall management function. It is equally essential to the subsequent or related procedures that follow selection such as training, sales and expense forecasting, supervision and guidance. All are dependent on feedback for accuracy, efficiency and profit.

Writing the Performance Specification
The performance specification is the basis for decisions made using information feedback. As stated earlier, the performance specification for interview purposes combines information contained in the job description and job specification.

Matching to Management as Well as to the Job
The job analysis is the hard core of the performance specification. It is the specific, defined standard against which feedback from the screening process is compared. On the other hand, the management analysis describes the climate surrounding and strongly influencing ultimate job performance. What if, for example, management selects salespeople on the basis of a job analysis calling for, among other things, "dominance, enthusiasm and self-confidence," then by its very nature fails to encourage or perhaps even restrains these characteristics in the selling job itself? The net result will probably be that a number of qualified people will come into the organization only to leave shortly because of their inability to adjust to the management climate. From this, it is easy to see that the overall purpose of the performance specification is matching people to management as well as to the job.

Selection Ratio
The real objective of the screening and selection process can be summarized in one sentence: to find a very special person to do a very special job under very special conditions.

Only a small percentage of the applicants for real estate sales work will have the personal qualifications to meet the specific demands of the job within the management framework of a real estate sales organization. This relationship between the small number of people who qualify and all others who fail to qualify is called the selection ratio.

It has been estimated that in all types of businesses involving all types of occupations, the average selection ratio runs about four or five applicants for every person selected. When the ratio drops below this level, the qualifying standards for selection are probably less than desirable. In real estate sales work the selection ratio will be much higher than this across the board average. It will be more like one out of ten or greater.

A high but reasonable selection ratio is almost always joined by a low turnover rate. This leads to a fundamental rule applied to the screening and selection process: within practical limits, the higher the selection ratio the higher both the retention rate and the resulting return on the manpower investment.

A high selection ratio is an effect, not a cause. It happens when skilled management chooses only the people who have acceptable qualifications. This has great psychological significance in management's self-image.

To find the selection ratio for past and present recruiting operations, go back through the past two years and pull the application forms of persons who got through at least the initial interview phase of the screening process. Separate the applications of those who were selected from those who were not, even though some of those chosen may have left. The numerical relationship between those who were selected and those turned down is the selection ratio.

If the ratio is one out of twenty or greater, there is a chance that past and current selection standards have been too rigid. If the ratio is less than one out of five, no doubt the standards have been lax, undefined or non-existent.

Validation of the Screening Process
Accuracy in decision making calls for a close relationship between information feedback from the various steps in the screening process (application form, interviewing and testing) and the performance specification. The degree or extent of this relationship is called "validity."

A valid screening process, or any of its sub-parts, will provide only that information having predictive value about future performance. Information which does not bear directly on anticipated performance is surplus and not valid for selection purposes. Surplus information may have value in helping a manager develop a keener insight into an applicant's potential; and it may have significance later on in training, supervising and counseling a person to higher levels of performance.

Information has predictive validity when it can show some relationship with future performance. Education, work history, financial responsibility, physical health and certain observable or measurable traits and characteristics (mental perception, temperament, enthusiasm, self-confidence and self-discipline) are some of the valid indicators of potential performance. Information about hobbies and pastimes, political preferences or favorite colors rarely bears valid relationship to the ability to do a specific job. Indeed, some inquiries of this nature are no longer legally permissible.

Because of the complexity of human behavior and other variables affecting performance, the accuracy of information feedback from the screening process is almost entirely dependent on probability. The more extensive and valid the information obtained, the greater the probability of making the right decision. No screening and selection procedure will predict with absolute certainty that an applicant will succeed or fail. This is especially true for sales work. Whenever someone claims to have a method, whether it be some special interview technique or some type of test that will measure sales potential with absolute accuracy, they are either ignorant of the facts or devious in their intent. Such claims are usually made to influence gullible, indecisive, uninformed management.

Screening Process

All decision making is the result of some form of information feedback. Whether a decision turns out to be right or wrong depends largely on the amount, relevance and accuracy of the information and how well it zeros in on the desired goal or standard.

In the screening process for selecting salespeople, information can be obtained from six basic sources:

Pre-screening

The application form

The screening interview

Testing

The background investigation

The evaluative interview.

Each of these sources of information can be viewed as consecutive steps leading toward a final decision.

How these six steps can be organized into an information feedback system is shown in Fig. 1. In this illustration, the first information from an applicant is screened for its valuable parts during Step I, prescreening. This data is fed back and compared to the performance specification. At that point a decision is made to reject or proceed. If the decision is to proceed, further information from the applicant is processed through Step II and looped back through the comparison procedure. This process continues on with either rejection or continued acceptance by either party being made during each succeeding step until all possible information has been processed and compared with the ideal. In the meantime each step serves to verify, amplify and refine the information coming from the preceding steps.

If this approach in its basic form is used, error in decision making can be greatly reduced, resulting in much higher selection efficiency.

Pre-Screening

In Step I the vast majority of applicants who would ultimately fail are eliminated or eliminate themselves. They can be grouped into four categories:

Those unable to meet basic requirements of the performance specification

Those with only a passive interest or idle curiosity about a career in real estate

Fig. 1 Decision making by information feedback

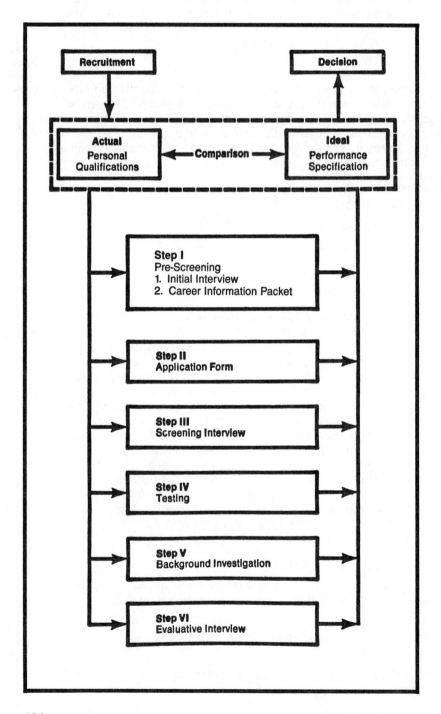

Those with misconceptions about the business

Those who lack the desire, courage and self-confidence essential to succeed in real estate sales.

If Step I is followed consistently, most of the applicants who survive have at least some potential for success. This first step in the screening process requires only a minimum of management time.

Step I involves the use of two sources of information, part of which includes information for applicants to use in making their decisions about real estate sales work. These are the initial interview and the career information packet.

The Initial Interview

Many applicants contact a company in response to recruitment advertising or referral. In fact, when advertising for salespeople, applicants should be encouraged to make their first contact by telephone and schedule an interview appointment.

The initial interview serves four purposes:

It conserves time for both the applicant and the manager

It avoids the risk of making impulsive judgments caused by the "halo effect" and "stereotyping," discussed in Step III

It gives management an opportunity to evaluate the applicant's telephone personality: his forcefulness, tone and skill in communicating with a stranger, which will be important in telephone listing and sales prospecting

It enables management to quickly gather some personal data and history to use in qualifying the applicant for further screening.

A uniform information checklist or outline should be used in the initial interview. It serves as a guide in obtaining pertinent data and keeps the interview from straying into areas not related to performance qualifications. A number of telephone interview checklists are available in standard forms or the manager can create his own.

An adequate checklist will include information such as: name, address, telephone number, present employment status, education, financial ability, and any other information that could have a direct bearing on performance. There should also be space provided for brief note making on how the applicant responds and reacts in the telephone interview.

This part of Step I enables the manager to make the method of compensation clear. Applicants having little or no knowledge of the business may not realize that most salespeople operate on a straight commission basis.

Ordinarily, the interview should not take more than 30 minutes and should always be conducted by the manager or the personnel department.

There will be times when an initial interview will be possible and even practical, such as with walk-in applicants, as a result of career night presentations, or during telephone interviews. Then the manager can implement the second part of Step I, the career information packet.

The Career Information Packet

As the initial interview ends, the applicant, even if disqualified at this early point, is told that he will be provided some information to help him understand more about the job. Whether they choose to take it with them or to have it mailed can be evidence of their motivation and interest.

The career information packet consists of four pieces.

The first is a brief discussion of the real estate industry. It can include a description of the various divisions and related careers, types and levels of certification, and legal and ethical requirements. This information is available in printed form from a number of sources. The NATIONAL ASSOCIATION OF REALTORS®, most state associations and many boards of REALTORS® provide such material for use in recruiting. A resourceful manager can create one tailored to his own firm at a very little cost.

The second is a brief history of your company, its growth, competitive position, types of markets and future plans. This information can be arranged under an attractive heading, typed and reproduced in quantity at moderate cost.

The third is a brief statement of company policy and procedures which must be observed in the event an applicant is selected.

The fourth piece is a personal cover letter for the packet. It can be typed and reproduced on quality company letterhead, leaving room for the applicant's name and date. Each letter is signed individually by the broker. Because it will help less-than-desirable applicants disqualify themselves by putting the onus of making the next step on them, it can represent enormous savings in time.

A cover letter for the career information packet might read like the letter reproduced on the next page (Fig. 2). Notice how this letter pulls no punches in making perfectly clear what is expected of the recruit, and what the recruit can expect from a career in real estate sales.

This approach, as an initial step in screening salespeople, is not unique or new. It has been practiced in top sales organizations for years with great effectiveness.

Management scientists have verified that individuals with high personal standards are attracted to and look for situations with the same standards. People with a clear self-image prefer to work with people who share their attributes. Company management with a clear self-image and high standards has a natural appeal for success-oriented people. In addition, the more difficult the qualifying standards, the greater the esprit de corps, dedication, loyalty and cooperation of the people. All this adds up to high individual and group productivity and greatly reduced turnover.

For the same reasons, people who lack the characteristics for success will shy away. Lacking adequate self-confidence and an intense desire for personal achievement, they will go where less is expected of them. Thus, pre-screening not only acts as an effective recruiting technique but also allows those who cannot survive to eliminate themselves gracefully.

Fig. 2 A cover letter for the career information packet might read as follows:

Date
_____

Dear_____:

Thank you for your interest in our company.

Because I want you to give serious consideration to a career in real estate sales, I am enclosing some information to assist you in understanding our business. I will appreciate the time you take to review this material and feel sure it will help you make a positive decision.

A career in real estate can be both financially rewarding and personally satisfying. It is sales professionalism at its best. At the same time it demands hard work, long hours and the capacity to deal with frustration and disappointment. In short, it calls for the highest degree of personal courage, determination and stamina.

We are fiercely proud of the people who represent our company. In order to qualify they had to meet the toughest standards possible. They had to undergo a thorough background investigation, intensive interview sessions and take penetrating tests to determine their qualifications for selling real estate. They spent countless hours in training in order to meet rigid licensing requirements. They are truly exceptional people. We need more like them!

If after reading the enclosed information you are interested in discussing a real estate sales career with our company, I would consider it a personal favor if you will contact our sales manager, _____. He will be happy to arrange an appointment with you. This may be the rare opportunity both of us have been looking for.

Cordially,

President

The time and costs involved in Step I appear insignificant when compared to what is at stake.

The Application Form

The application form, Step II, should include all legally permissible biographical data that relates to future performance. It is the first official document to go into the personnel files. This form is also the only source of information other than testing that can be validated.

There are two ways to handle an application form. It can be included in the career information packet, giving the applicant time to fill it out at his leisure, or it can be given to him to fill out if and when he arrives for the screening interview (Step III). The second way is perhaps preferable.

Application forms can be purchased or the manager can create one. Be sure the application form you use satisfies the requirements of applicable equal employment statutes and regulations.

A good application form will ask for detailed information in six basic areas: personal data (name, address, social security number, education and training, domestic and family status, employment history, financial information and health).

With the exception of personal data this information can reveal some relationship to potential performance. Since the application form serves as the best guide for conducting interviews, it should also provide open space for notes by the interviewer.

Other information that may be sought in an application form includes character references, hobbies and pastimes, organizational affiliations, etc. This information may have little relevance to job ability but is useful in helping the manager gain a better overall view of the applicant and in preparing for the personal interview by identifying common interests.

Information contained in an application form can be a reliable indicator of an applicant's character and stability. A history of domestic problems, frequent job changes and transience or lack of credit references should be cause for concern and explored carefully in the screening interview. Personnel specialists say that strong signs of instability in a person's background almost always correlate with unpredictable or unstable performance on the job. Many managers do not take negative information at face value and proceed to select a candidate simply because he looks good. When this happens, management has failed and not the employee.

The Screening Interview

When Step II is complete an enormous amount of vital information regarding an applicant has become a matter of record. Before proceeding to Step III, the manager should review both the telephone interview checklist and the application form, paying special attention to chronological gaps, contradictions or inconsistencies in the data and appropriate notations made. If possible the review and note taking should be done without the applicant being present. Before the screening interview begins, the manager should have all previous information well organized and highlighted. This will help keep the interview structured and on track, save valuable time and provide a businesslike climate to the proceedings.

There are two basic interview techniques: structured and casual. The structured interview is designed to elicit specific information about the applicant, generally following a printed outline or list of questions. Structured interview forms can be purchased. Probably the best is the application form itself, provided there is a space for making notes. The casual interview, although guided or patterned, is intended to help the applicant speak freely and volunteer information about himself. Step III, the screening interview, is usually structured; Step VI, the evaluative interview, is casual.

The screening interview serves two purposes. First, using a structured approach, the manager can quickly verify or clarify existing information on the application form.

The second purpose is observation. This may be the first time the manager has met the applicant. All information accumulated up to this point has been objective in content. Now he sits before the manager displaying physical characteristics and personal mannerisms. This is where the element of personality enters the picture. It is historically the weakest point in the screening process because it is at this point all prior information feedback, positive or negative, is likely to be dismissed.

First impressions have a dynamic and often misleading effect on one person's judgment of another. Skilled interviewers recognize this pitfall and go to great pains to avoid being trapped into forming impulsive, subjective opinions on the first meeting. The adage that beauty or truth is in the eye of the beholder has no place in the screening and selection process. Poise, charm, charisma or physical attractiveness have little bearing on self-confidence, self-discipline or how hard a person will work. In this regard there are two psychological effects the manager should keep in mind during the initial interview. They are called "halo effect" and "stereotyping."

Halo effect is present when some single facet in a candidate's outward physical or personality make-up tends to overshadow all other considerations. A prominent nose may turn an interviewer off for no explainable reason. A winning smile may have the opposite effect.

Stereotyping occurs when the interviewer tends to classify people on some notion that physical characteristics determine personality and behavior. Thus, red-headed persons are quick tempered, fat people are easygoing, a sloping forehead means stupidity and a receding chin signifies lack of character.

Some traits or mannerisms can provide clues to general behavior. They should be carefully noted in the screening interview. Positive attributes to look for include personal neatness, good-natured responsiveness, interest and enthusiasm, communicative skill and self-assertiveness. Negatives to watch for are lack of good grooming, evasiveness, undue restlessness, an unusually subdued or timid manner or excessive bravado. Later on in Step IV observations made in the screening interview can be compared with test results for verification.

Step III should be conducted in privacy if possible and should not take more than 20 to 30 minutes. If the manager feels the applicant has been eliminated at this point, he should thank him politely for his time. If the candidate is still in the running or a borderline case, the manager should proceed to Step IV, which is testing.

Testing

This is the most controversial and misunderstood step in the entire screening and selection process. Much of the confusion and resistance involving testing has been caused by those who publish and market tests. Exaggerated claims of test effectiveness in predicting job performance cause some managers to rely too heavily on test information, often with unpleasant or discouraging results. In addition, many test publishers prefer to shroud their particular product with an aura of mystery and omniscience in an attempt to justify unreasonable prices or fees. This attitude has obscured the rationale of the test methods and has led to the alienation of many business executives who are concerned with the risks of adverse or discriminatory selection.

In spite of the criticism testing has generated, a well designed and validated test, used properly, can prove to be a meaningful source of information.

Why Use Selection Tests?

All individuals are not equally suited for all types of jobs. In other words, different individuals have different probabilities of success in different occupations. The great benefit of selection tests is that they can be used to differentiate well-suited applicants from ill-suited applicants *before* they are placed on the job.

In addition, because the results of computer-scored selection tests such as interest inventories and biographical data are tabulated objectively, the bias of the manager is minimized.

Test Validation

Before using a test to select a sales associate, you should make sure the test has been validated. The validation procedure involves determining how closely the test corresponds to actual on-the-job performance. A statistical analysis can be done to evaluate the degree of correlation between an applicant's success on the test and his or her success on the job. The statistic, called a correlation coefficient, can range from -1 to 1 with 1 indicating the highest correlation. A coefficient of .2 is considered to be acceptable and .3 or above is very good.

For example, let's say you administer an intelligence test to applicants for the position of sales associate. Some applicants receive a high score, while other applicants receive a low score. Three months later, on-the-job sales performance is measured. If the intelligence test is a valid test, then there would be a high correlation between a high test score and a high score for actual performance.

Types of Selection Tests

There are many different types of tests for selecting sales associates. Let's turn to a brief discussion of some commonly used selection tests.

Interviews

The interview is the most commonly used selection technique.

However, the record of employment interviews as a valid selection procedure has been rather poor over the years. The validity of the interview is typically low, with an average validity of just .14 (Hunter & Hunter, 1984). But despite the poor performance of interviews as a selection technique, they are still universally used because employers want face-to-face interaction with prospective employees. Interviews are best used in conjunction with other, more valid selection methods to tell you how well an applicant will fit into your company's culture.

Work Samples and Situational Tests

Work samples and situational tests are relatively new approaches to personnel selection. Applicants are asked to perform some of the actual tasks a person on the job would do every day. These approaches generally have been shown to be highly predictive with validity coefficients of about .40.

For example, one commonly used situational test is the "In-basket Exercise." Here, an applicant is presented with an "in-basket" of memos, letters, reports, and so on, which require immediate attention. The applicant's ability to prioritize and perform the tasks is then assessed by raters. Situational tests like this one have shown good validity in the selection of managers, but tests of this nature have not yet been used to evaluate sales associates.

Work samples and situational tests, however, can be time-consuming and expensive to administer. In addition, they only give a measure of the ability the applicant brings to the job—not the potential the individual has if given additional training. For this reason, work samples and situational tests are much better suited for hiring experienced rather than inexperienced associates.

Intelligence Tests

Mental abilities (or intelligence) tests have long been used for personnel selection. It is generally believed that the more intelligent a worker is, the higher the individual's productivity will be.

Mental abilities tests have been demonstrated to be valid predictors for a wide variety of occupations. In fact, the average validity of mental abilities was found to be a quite-high .53 (Hunter & Hunter, 1984). But these tests may not present the whole story, because there are other important qualities that a good salesperson should have such as motivation and honesty. As a result mental abilities tests tend to be less predictive of success in sales than in other occupations.

Personality and Interest Inventories

Unlike mental abilities tests, personality and interest inventories have neither right nor wrong answers. Applicants answer questions about their various likes ("I like to play sports") or how much they agree with different statements ("People who work hard get ahead"). Scales composed of such items are used to assess the degree of interest in a particular activity or the presence of a certain personality characteristic, such as aggression, extroversion, confidence, and so on. The scale scores are then used to predict job success. The basic rationale is that successful workers have certain interests or personality patterns and these patterns become the basis for their selection.

Personality and interest inventories have been demonstrated to have relatively poor validity for predicting success across occupations. The average validity of interest inventories was just .10 (Hunter & Hunter, 1984), while personality measures did slightly better with an average validity of .15 (Schmitt, Gooding, Noe & Kirsch, 1984).

Biographical Data

Using biographical data (also called "biodata") is a popular selection test method that has a long history of successful prediction.

The use of biographical data for the selection of workers is based on the assumption that "the best predictor of future performance is past performance." Biodata are used as a means of identifying which life experiences differentiate successful from unsuccessful employees. Biodata measure stable, enduring traits that predict success in a given occupation. Biodata typically take many different forms, including questions about personal history (e.g., education, past employment); present situation (e.g., income, club membership); and self-reports (e.g., attitude toward employers, self-ratings of social skills).

Biodata also can be scored consistently and fairly using computers. If scoring is done at a centralized facility, the scoring key can remain intact because people won't learn the "correct" answers (meaning, the answers shown to be predictive of success). Centralized scoring also allows for the creation of large data bases which can be used to update, improve, and enhance the scoring procedures over time.

Biodata have an average validity of .37 across occupations (Hunter & Hunter, 1984). In particular, biodata have proven to be *excellent* predictors of success in sales.

One disadvantage of biodata is that very large numbers of sales associates—typically in the thousands—are necessary for the development and validation of biodata measures. For this reason, biodata inventories cannot typically be validated on a firm-by-firm basis.

In sum, there are a number of tests available for the selection of real estate sales associates. Each technique has its advantages and disadvantages. You must weight the benefits and the costs before choosing the selection method best for your company.

Evaluating Selection Tests

With the many brands of selection tests available on the market, you may feel confused about which tests to incorporate in your selection program. Here are some guidelines for evaluating a potential test.

What Does the Test Cover?

All *good* tests provide extensive information outlining what the test is supposed to measure, how the scores should be interpreted and the research undertaken to support it.

Why Should You Use the Test?

There should be a clear statement of the purpose of the test. What is the test intended to measure? For what types of people is the test intended and in what situations can it properly be used? If you are looking for a test to select real estate sales associates in the United States, then a test designed to select car salespeople in Canada is not appropriate.

Is the Test Valid?

There should be a detailed accounting of the test's development and supporting validity evidence. If the authors of the Canadian car salesperson test claim their test can be used to select American real estate sales associates, they must provide validity evidence supporting this claim. The validity evidence should inform the potential users of appropriate and inappropriate uses of the test. Remember, a correlation coefficient of .2 is considered acceptable and .3 and above is very good.

Is the Test Designed for Real Estate?

It is important to use a selection test which has been designed for use in real estate. A test which is useful for selecting other types of employees (such as other sales occupations) my not be valid for selecting real estate salespeople.

How Do You Use the Test?

There should be clear guidelines for the interpretation of the test results and for its use in personnel selection. The appropriate use of the selection test and its placement in the overall selection process varies depending on the design and purpose of the individual test. The author should provide guidelines for the use of his/her specific selection test.

Are Instructions Clear?

There should be precise instructions for the administration and scoring of the test. If the test is administered or scored in a fashion which deviates from the instructions, the validity and utility of the test will be jeopardized.

Another point to remember is to be wary of sales pitches which make extravagant claims such as "we'll help you select the right sales associate every time." The chances are these tests do not provide evidence and information to substantiate the claims.

Also, do not let price influence your decision. An inexpensive test may provide ineffective results. On the other hand, an expensive test may not be the most valid either.

Finally, managers should also note that the relationship between the selection test and on-the-job performance is never perfect, but using a valid selection test can substantially improve the odds of selecting successful salespeople.

[This section on testing was extracted from an article by Michelle Mosher Crosby, Ph.D., an associate scientist in the Marketing Resources Research Department of LIMRA International in Hartford,

Connecticut. The article initially appeared in Vol. 3, No. 3, of Management Issues & Trends *newsletter, published by the Real Estate Brokerage Council™. Crosby used the following references in her article:*

Hunter, J.E., and R.F. Hunter (1984). Validity and Utility of Alternative Predictors of Job Performance. Psychological Bulletin, *96.*

Schmitt, N., R.Z. Gooding, R.A. Noe, and M. Kirsch (1984). Meta-analysis of validity studies published between 1964 and 1982 and the investigation of study characteristics. Personnel Psychology, *37, 407–422.]*

The Background Investigation

Step V, checking a candidate's background, accomplishes three things:

It verifies or contradicts the details on the application form or elicited in the screening interview

It supplies additional data prior steps have not developed

It helps establish the candidate's credibility or memory for particulars.

The background investigation is usually confined to two essential sources of information: financial status and employment history. There may be times when a manager will want to check the character references offered by an applicant; however, information from these sources usually lacks objectivity.

A check of financial references enables the manager to determine a candidate's fiscal responsibility. It also helps in evaluating financial self-sufficiency for the period before commissions are earned.

Probably the single best source of financial information is the local credit bureau. They usually have a detailed analysis of an individual's credit rating for at least seven years. They are also a source of evidence of past lawsuits, bankruptcies or criminal involvements of a serious nature. The manager must receive the candidate's permission to verify financial information through a credit bureau.

Verifying previous employment is often more complicated and less productive than checking a candidate's financial background. Many employers are reluctant to give out information on a former employee especially when a negative appraisal is involved. Furthermore, when an ex-employer reports negatively on an individual, there is always a chance it is due to a personality conflict or some other less-than-objective opinion of past performance. It is the policy of many companies that all such inquiries are handled by the personnel office. This is always an accurate source of the person-to-person relationships or the work habits you want to verify.

The main reason for checking an applicant's employment history is to substantiate the information coming from the application form, including dates of employment, wages or salary, job title and responsibilities and reason for leaving. The secondary purpose is to determine as nearly as possible the quality of performance, job attendance and ability to get along with others.

If convenient, the employment investigation should be conducted by telephone by the manager. At least the last two or three jobs

Fig. 3 Telephone check

Selecting Salespeople and Office Personnel

Applicant_____

Former
Supervisor_____ Title_____

Company Where   Telephone
Applicant Worked_____ Number_____.

1. _____(name)_____ has applied for work with us. I would like
   to verify some of the information given us. When did he work for your
   company?

   From_____ 19_____To _____ 19_____

2. What was his job when he started to work for you?

   _____

   When he left?_____

3. He says his earnings were $_____per_____Is that correct?
   ( ) Yes   ( ) No $

4. What did you think of him? (Quality and quantity of work, attendance,
   how he got along with others, etc.)

   _____

   _____

4a. What accidents has he had?

   _____

5. Why did he leave your company?

   _____

   _____

   _____

6. Would you re-employ him?
   ( ) Yes   ( ) No.   If not, why not?_____

   _____

Additional Comments:_____

   _____

   _____

   _____

   _____

Date of Check_____19_____Made by_____

should be verified. Use of a telephone checklist is the best approach (see Fig. 3). Since it is a structured form, it keeps the investigation on track and more businesslike. Background investigations that tend to meander and pry rather than obtain substantive performance-related information waste valuable time and can cause the former employer to be less responsive.

If a candidate is currently employed, his permission to contact the present employer must be obtained. To omit this might prove embarrassing and damaging and expose the broker to legal liabilities.

The Evaluative Interview

During the first five steps of the screening process most unqualified applicants have been eliminated. For example, an initial group of fifty applicants may now be reduced to ten. Your ultimate goal might be to select the four or five most qualified.

At the end of Step V, data on each remaining applicant has been assembled. All along the line, well organized information feedback has been consistently compared with the most acceptable standards embodied in the performance specification, to be verified and supplemented in succeeding steps. A complete file of critically useful information is now available for reference in Step VI, the evaluative interview.

Step III, the screening interview, was for its own practical purposes, structured. It followed a particular outline, looking for as much specific, detailed information as possible in the shortest period of time, verifying and amplifying the objective data from the application form. The evaluative interview should be far less structured. It should be casual, giving the applicant ample opportunity to speak freely under only subtle guidance of the manager.

There is no special formula for conducting an effective evaluative interview. It should always be carried out in privacy. The applicant should be helped to feel at ease. The principle objective is to develop open, frank but always friendly discussion encouraging him to take the initiative.

The personnel file, containing all the information accrued from the preceding five steps, is the best guide in keeping the evaluative interview alive and providing the necessary cues to keep the applicant talking about himself. Every opportunity should be given him to sell himself to management. Close observation and accurate mental note taking is the key to the successful evaluative interview. The manager should constantly analyze and compare what is being seen and heard with the information gathered in the previous steps. He should be alert to the smallest fragment of information that may be of significance in the selection decision, developing any topic this might suggest.

A multiple interview in Step VI is always best. As a rule, the sales manager has initiated and controlled the screening process and no doubt will make the final decision. But observations and opinions from other levels of management, especially top management, can add a critical dimension at this time. Others participating in the evaluative interview should be provided full information gathered on the applicant in advance of such participation.

A Home Interview

Management has every right to know as much as possible about a candidate's personal life that might have a bearing on ultimate performance. But it is important that the candidate not feel his privacy is being invaded. The home interview should always be by appointment so the applicant has every chance to put his best foot forward on the home front.

In most cases, by the time Step VI in the screening process has been reached, the die has been cast as far as the selection decision is concerned. All the facts are in. The largest part of the final judgment will be based on the objective information feedback developed in the preceding five steps. Step VI allows management to view this information in a more subjective light as it relates to outward appearances, characteristics and life style. This is the point where management skill in selecting potentially good producers gets the acid test.

The Selection Decision

It cannot be stressed enough that the objective of the screening and selection process is to find a very special person to do a very special job under very special conditions. The only way to achieve this objective is by matching organized, factual information about a person with a realistic performance specification. Then effective decision making becomes a matter of reducing the probability of error between what is and what is desired.

Just as there is no single reason why a person is eventually selected, there is no one reason for eliminating someone. Once an individual has been eliminated there is no reason for further personal communication other than the courtesy of a letter thanking him for his time. This letter is a courtesy and permits the applicant to feel free to pursue other opportunities.

Selecting Office Personnel

The primary objective of a real estate sales office is to sell real estate. The primary function of every person employed in that office is to achieve that objective, directly or indirectly. A top-flight real estate sales force cannot operate at peak efficiency without a qualified office staff backing it up. This goes far beyond having people with certain skills sitting behind desks answering telephones or processing paperwork. Every member of the office staff should realize that the only justification for every job is optimum sales and profit.

Management can and should apply the same basic screening and selection process to office personnel it applies to salespeople. In the six steps leading to the selection decision, the only differences would be in the job analysis and performance specification and in testing.

As in the case of salespeople, the job analysis should spell out in detail the required skills and responsibilities which are critical to satisfactory performance. The personal traits and characteristics necessary to job achievement should be defined. Sales support people would in fact possess many of the personality traits looked for in salespeople. A cool, unfriendly receptionist or a tense, high-strung secretary, no matter how skilled in the particular job, can create serious problems. Compatibility among the people in an organization enhances the spirit of mutual concern and cooperation and overall morale.

Testing may evaluate skills such as typing, shorthand, clerical, computer and computational abilities or whatever the job requires. But such tests should be valid and relevant to an applicant's ability to do the work required.

The final proof of effective hiring and selection procedures lies in the performance of the people chosen. Job competence is the final objective. Having chosen well, management's next concern is to train people well and motivate them so they are most likely to succeed and stay with the firm.

Written Instruments Between Broker and Salesperson 9

Two major written documents govern the relationship between brokers and their salespeople. One is the operations manual; the other is a contract or agreement between a broker and the individual members of his sales staff who are independent contractors or employees.

The operations manual is the written instrument that provides guidance to salespeople who are independent contractors and directives to employee salespeople and other employees.

The written contract between independent contractor salespeople and the broker spells out the salesperson's rights and obligations. It also enables the broker to discuss problems in particularized terms, minimizing the risk that independent contractor status will be lost through inadvertence and misunderstanding. Contracts may also be written to cover the relationship between brokers and employee salespeople, but these are not as common as the first-mentioned type.

This chapter examines the need for and content of both types of written instruments, what they can and cannot accomplish and/or control, and the wisdom in having legal counsel in all contractual matters.

Written Instruments Between Broker and Salesperson

It is sometimes felt by people in real estate that their offices are unlike those of other sales organizations because the relationship between management and staff is different in this business. This is true for the most part. However, to use this as a reason for not having modern management controls and techniques is illogical. On the contrary, the unusual relationships in real estate indicate an even greater need for good management. It seems basic that brokers and salespeople should have a clear understanding of what to expect from each other and the conditions under which each will function for their mutual benefit.

That understanding is usually spelled out best by a contract and implemented by an operations manual.

Company Size

Any question about how large a company must be before it should have written policy and procedures can be put to rest because the operations manual is probably more important for the small office than the large one. This is true because in a small office the broker often also lists and sells. The likelihood of policy and procedures problems increases when the broker is wearing two hats. He could conceivably be involved in a disagreement with a salesperson and be expected to judge himself—an almost impossible situation.

Purposes

Just as a broker is charged with winning approval, respect and good will of many groups outside the company, so he must establish and maintain good public relations among his employees and salespeople. A good operations manual is a great aid in this regard.

Many brokers practice management by crisis and not the wiser method of management by objectives. In the latter, establishing a written policy is necessary to set the pace in a company large or small. It should also reflect the company's strategic plan objectives.

What the Manual Should Be

A properly written manual is not easy to compose and is difficult to make complete enough to cover every situation; further, it is often subject to interpretation on even the items included. These are arguments against having written policy. But the benefits far outweigh the negative factors.

The manual should:

Provide a clear understanding of the relationship between broker and salesperson, management and employees and the relationship of administrative functions and sales functions

Permit the anticipation of and resolution of controversies before they arise

Stabilize both management and sales as it builds confidence that management as well as the salespeople know the rules by which the game is to be played

Prohibit favoritism since all must operate within the framework of the manual's predetermined rules and guidelines

Provide stability of organization and permit the staff to function effectively in the absence of management.

(The alternative is to have the policy statement in the broker's head; and when he's not there, it's not there. What's more, he might forget it.)

Uses

The operations manual has many uses. Besides setting forth the rules under which the business operates, it serves to back up management decision. It becomes the uninvolved "third person" that is sought out to give an unbiased opinion on the matter under consideration.

It is a valuable aid in recruiting, interviewing, selecting and/or hiring and retaining good co-workers. In recruiting, the prospective salesperson can be told that the company has a written statement of policy. In interviewing and selecting, the manual can serve to let the prospective salesperson know what he can expect and the framework within which work is done in the company. Fear of the unknown is a great obstacle to success in the sales field. A good, clear statement of policy helps to give the prospective salesperson a feeling of security. It is important these facts are all understood before a contract is signed or a person is employed.

In training new salespeople, the operations manual is an essential tool. A specific period of indoctrination should be spent with each new salesperson covering every aspect of the manual in detail. If no other formal training is given by the broker, the manual at least serves to give the new salesperson the orientation he needs.

Sales meetings present a particular challenge to the average broker and the manual becomes a priceless tool in making such meetings meaningful. A review of one item of the manual each week will pay valuable dividends in communication, feedback and understanding between all members of the team.

Parts of some operations manuals are concerned with the salesperson's liability in certain seasonal changes, conditions under which property is shown or the problems of unoccupied properties. It is important to review these matters regularly and the manual is the reminder to do it.

One thing that should be avoided in the use of the operations manual is getting the public involved. Many of the problems between salespeople involve the public. But while the public is not concerned with a broker's internal policies they might turn salesperson against salesperson by favoring one salesperson in a dispute. Therefore, brokers should bring in the client to determine the facts only as a last resort and then exercise great discretion.

There are some things an operations manual is and some things it is not. It is a statement or declaration of the company business philosophy, procedures, rules and regulations and generally will spell out what is expected of the salesperson in his day to day activities as well as what he can expect from the company. It can include an organizational chart and job descriptions. It should be a viable tool, a constitution and a declaration of interdependence.

It should not be a contract and should not be interpreted as being under the law of contracts. For example, the broker-salesperson agreement which is a contract would spell out the commission split. The operations manual would describe the procedure in the event of a dispute between salespeople about commission splits.

Contents

Just as an architect could not build a structure successfully without a plan, the operations manual must have a plan. And all good planning starts with clear objectives. So the author of policy must begin with company goals. These can be stated in general or specific language in the preamble.

Next comes the outline or index of items to be covered. It should be alphabetical and in sufficient detail to allow for ease in finding specific provisions.

No two real estate offices are alike and it is unwise to copy another's operations manual exactly. However a manual from another company can provide a good starting point.

A list of possible subjects to consider might include:

Advertising and promotion
Associates' sales kit
Bonuses
REALTOR® Code of Ethics
Compensation policies
Cooperative sales with outside brokers
Description of associate's job
Escrow
Floor duty
Growth opportunity
General
History of company
Inquiries
Interoffice exchange of clients
Introduction
Listing procedure
New homes and tracts
Newspapers
Offer procedure
Office cooperation
Open houses
Other departments

Prospects
Qualifications
Residential sales department
Salesperson-client relations
Sales meetings
Screening prospects
Selling policies and procedures
Signs
Termination

Somewhere in its make-up the manual should refer to and incorporate already published statements such as the REALTOR® Code of Ethics, MLS rules and License Authority rules. A simple reference to these is not enough. Copies should be put in the loose-leaf manual and they should be covered in all discussions of policy.

The broker must use good judgment in including in policy such matters concerning the day to day practice of his business which have become part of the law. It is not realistic to assume that all members of the staff are aware of and familiar with local, state and federal laws that concern discrimination, signs, business solicitation, lending of money and such items. In addition to this, most license authorities issue bulletin rules and findings that are matters of policy for the broker. He must keep abreast of them and be sure his staff is informed.

This does not mean the manual must be revised every time a city ordinance is passed; but it is good to republish the provision, discuss it and add a copy to the looseleaf. At a later time some added wording may be necessary if it affects policy.

It should be limited to matters of policy and procedure such as who pays for long distance phone calls. It should not be a training manual in the sense that it spells out such things as telephone technique, how to list, show and present offers. The danger in including sales training material is that the manual becomes unwieldy, policy statements are lost in the mass of words, and simple variations in sales procedures become violations of policy. None of these is desirable. A bare bones policy statement works best.

The manual cannot be made the total answer to each policy matter. When a decision cannot be made easily about a specific problem, it should clearly state how it is to be interpreted and by whom.

Format

The size of the manual is not important. Usually from 15 to 30 single-spaced typewritten pages will cover everything. However it is usually wise to limit each page to only a few items, leaving space for changes or additions. If space is allowed for changes they are made more easily because only one page is affected. For example, a policy statement on the handling of keys to clients' homes might change with the added use of lock boxes of some type. This might involve adding a paragraph. Space should be available on that page without redoing the entire manual. Incidentally, that page should be signed and dated when reissued.

The index is most conveniently set up in alphabetical form, cross-indexing some items that may come under several categories. For example, "Earnest Money" could be mentioned under contracts, trust accounts, responsibilities of salespeople and cooperative sales.

Writing the Manual

Others in the company besides the broker can be helpful in preparing the manual. A partner, manager or salesperson can offer valuable viewpoints in some instances. When asking for help in setting policy or in composing the language, the broker should not give the impression that he is abandoning his responsibility and privilege of policy making. He can get good ideas from staff, give recognition for their help and still not risk a strained relationship that could arise if such cooperative policy making is not handled with tact and skill.

Before asking for help he should carefully determine which items he will open to staff opinions. It would be inviting disaster to have a sales staff decide such items as commission splits.

The best approach is to prepare the "proposed statement of policy" in each matter and submit it for discussion—not necessarily for approval or change. It could be reworded, clarified or expanded to make it more clear but that is all that should be discussed.

The method of building an operations manual in this manner is going to get much better results than trying to make it letter-perfect. Begin with the obvious requirements, the "must" provisions, and then build it one page at a time.

When the time comes to write, the broker need not worry that he will not do a good job of composition. One need not be a Hemingway. It is sufficient to set down in plain terms what he thinks should be said, have it reviewed by someone else and then publish it and put it into effect.

Tips On Writing

In writing policy it is best to use "thou shalt..." as much as possible, rather than the "thou shalt not..." approach. Positive statements are more persuasive than negative ones. For example, the provision on sales meetings should read that salespeople are "encouraged to attend and to remain for the entire meeting" rather than to state that they "should not miss the weekly sales meeting and are discouraged from leaving early."

Write carefully, then read and reread to determine if it is too vague or too limiting. Some provisions concern matters that require a certain amount of good judgment and must necessarily be left open to reasonable interpretation. One such concern is long distance telephone calls. Most companies allow such calls under certain conditions for business reasons. The broker might err by making the controls so tight that salespeople could lose business in trying to comply. However it is equally unwise to be too vague. For example, a provision that "long distance calls may be made if for a business reason" with no further guidelines or procedures for control could result in misunderstandings and abuses leading to serious budget problems.

The broker has a responsibility to create policy for his firm that is workable, understandable and as complete as human nature will allow. To be too strict is only going to set up daily violations of policy and the entire project becomes an exercise in futility.

Manual Revisions

Frequently in a growing company the need arises to add to or to revise policy to keep it meaningful and viable. A good habit for the broker to form is to put items and articles relating to policy in a file to be considered in future revisions or additions to the book. Thoughts he might have or topics that come up at meetings should be noted and put in the file. Such things are often forgotten when entrusted to memory and they could prove valuable in future revisions.

Publications of local, state and national REALTOR® associations often contain statements, findings, warnings and other good general material that could be made a part of policy or form the basis for new provisions. The decisions made by the broker in current disputes within the company should be duly noted, dated, spelled out and filed for future reference in similar situations. This leads to consistency in management and adds to the sense of continuity and fairness on the part of the staff.

When making major or minor changes or adding provisions to the operations manual it is always wise to do it with an eye on the relative importance of the change. Lead time, the time to get used to the new provision before it becomes effective, is usually of some reasonable length. For example, a change in policy concerning compensation might require a lead time of several months to allow salespeople to accept the change. The newer the idea, the more people it affects, the longer the lead time required.

A wise broker tries to make any change less traumatic, any transition smoother. Most brokers find it advisable to first draft a "proposed policy change" and at an informal meeting get the agreement of the managers if it is a large company. In a smaller company or a branch office the broker might meet with the leaders of the sales force and explain it to them so that they know what to expect when it is presented to the entire staff. This provides a chance to get direct feedback on the proposal and gives the leaders a feeling of being part of the management team.

Distributing the Manual

A looseleaf binder is usually the best form. The master copy should be kept by the broker with reference copies available to all the staff. When a new manual is to be introduced or a major revision made, it is usually best to get a copy to each of the staff, have it approved and call in the old copies. The larger the company, the more important it is not to have many copies floating around because they are frequently in various stages of completeness and confusion is the result. A small company with tight controls may find it workable to have a copy in the hand of each salesperson and employee. When changes are made the manuals should all be turned in, amended and reissued. This is usually done at one meeting.

It may seem unnecessary to have every page of the manual initialed by each salesperson but this is an effective way to achieve evidence of understanding. The "independent contractor agreement" between the broker and salesperson (if he is not an employee) should be signed by both parties but the policy need only be signed by the salesperson to indicate his acceptance of it.

Contracts and Agreements

The threshold question which must be answered before any consideration can be given to the form and terms of contracts or agreements between a broker and a salesperson is whether the salesperson shall be an employee of the broker or shall be affiliated with the broker as an independent contractor. The answer to this question will depend on a wide range of considerations:

The degree of control which the broker desires or needs to exercise over the salesperson

The type of work in which the salesperson will be engaged

The personal and professional qualifications of the salesperson

The nature of the broker's business and the techniques he uses to project himself to the public

The type and terms of the compensation arrangements offered by the broker and his competitors

The legal liabilities and rights accruing to the broker and salesperson under each status.

There is no "right" answer as to whether or not salespeople should be employees or independent contractors. On the contrary, any effort to generalize with respect to the proper status of salespeople can be dangerous, if not disastrous, for the broker.

This is because there is no such relationship as an "independent contractor employee." A salesperson may be an employee or an independent contractor but he may not be both simultaneously. For a broker to misconceive the true relationship between himself and his salesperson is for that broker to fail to recognize and fulfill the legal obligations which are attributable to that relationship. Every broker must appreciate that the employee relationship is not legally interchangeable with that of independent contractor. Nor is one superior to the other in all cases. Employees enjoy many rights denied by law to independent contractors and independent contractors have legal rights not available to employees.

Evaluating the Proper Relationship

It is wise to have a contract between the sales associate and the broker specifying whether the associate is an independent contractor or an employee. Typically, the courts weigh practices and activities more heavily than the language of the contract in determining the relationship.

Employee vs. Independent Contractor

How associates are compensated, how they pay and report taxes, and whether the broker has the right to control their activities are the key issues which help establish whether a sales associate is viewed as an independent contractor or as an employee.

Most employees receive wages based on the number of hours they work. In contrast, independent contractors receive compensation based only on their production (i.e., commissions for sales, listings and rentals).

Another factor involves reporting taxes. A broker withholds taxes from an employee's paycheck and forwards those taxes to the government. A broker does not withhold taxes from an independent contractor's income—independent contractors are responsible for paying their own taxes.

The last key issue involves the broker's right to control activities. A broker may exercise control over the activities of an employee or a statutory independent contractor without jeopardizing the salesperson's status. However, a broker may not exercise control over a common law independent contractor's activities, such as attending training seminars or participating in floor duty.

Types of Independent Contractors

There are two types of independent contractors: common law independent contractors and statutory independent contractors.

The statutory independent contractor status was created in 1982, when Congress added to the Internal Revenue Code a three-part test to determine the status of a real estate salesperson. One major difference between common law independent contractors and statutory independent contractors is that brokers can control the business activities of statutory independent contractors, but not those of common law independent contractors.

Under federal tax laws, statutory independent contractors must have a current real estate license, and at least 90 percent of their income as a licensee must be based on production. The statutory independent contractor also must have a written contract with the broker. That contract must contain the following clause: "The salesperson will not be treated as an employee with respect to the services performed by such salesperson as a real estate agent for federal tax purposes."

In examining the differences between whether an employee, statutory independent contractor or common law independent contractor relationship exists, there are various indicia which have come to be recognized as relevant considerations. While a comprehensive and all-inclusive enumeration of such considerations is impossible, it is possible to list those which have been recognized by the courts as among the more significant.

Training

No common law independent contractor may be required by the broker to attend sales training, instruction and indoctrination courses. An untrained or inexperienced salesperson should be employed by his broker if the broker believes training and indoctrination courses are indispensable. This does not mean that the broker may not make available training courses, seminars and other educational opportunities which the independent contractor salesperson is free to attend or not as he sees fit.

Hours of Work

A broker may not control the hours of work of a common law independent contractor salesperson. A requirement that a salesperson accept floor time assignments from the broker is not consistent with his independent contractor status. For this reason, assignment of independent contractor salespeople to fixed hours or days of work at a model home site seriously endangers their status. Similarly, a requirement that an independent contractor salesperson participate in weekly open house caravan tours is impermissible.

Priority of Assignments

If the broker has the right to interrupt the work of a salesperson or otherwise set the order of his services (by, for example, requiring him to work on certain listings or clients in preference to others), the salesperson could well be deemed an employee or statutory independent contractor. The broker cannot reserve first call on the time and efforts of the common law independent contractor salesperson nor should he establish quotas which the salesperson must meet.

Company Identification

A broker may require his employee salesperson to wear distinctive articles of clothing, name tags and to otherwise identify the firm name on their personal vehicles. No such requirement is appropriate for independent contractor salespeople. Moreover, it would be inconsistent with the independent contractor status for a salesperson to be given a title commonly recognized as signifying employee status. For this reason, independent contractors should not be designated by such titles as "vice president," "sales manager" or "sales supervisor."

License Fees and Dues

A broker may not pay the license fees or membership dues of his independent contractor salesperson although he is free to pay those of his employees and statutory independent contractors.

Expenses

The independent contractor salesperson is responsible for the payment of his own automobile and transportation expenses and other expenses incurred by him in obtaining and selling clients. The broker may not reimburse such expenses as he may do in the case of an employee or statutory independent contractor. The requirement that an independent contractor salesperson pay his own expenses does not mean that the broker may not make available to him space, secretarial and telephone service in the broker's office and business cards, forms and stationery on which the broker's name appears. The broker may not, however, pay or reimburse expenses attributable to an office which the salesperson maintains outside of the broker's premises.

Fringe Benefits

Common law independent contractors are not entitled to sick pay or to participate in the broker's pension and profit sharing plans, wage continuation plans, health and accident insurance plans or qualified group insurance programs unless permitted by the broker to pay premiums to participate in group health insurance. Inclusion of a salesperson in such programs or plans is tantamount to an admission by the broker that the salesperson is an employee since such programs or plans, to the extent they are qualified under the Internal Revenue Code, are limited to employees. To include an independent contractor salesperson in such plans and programs is to expose them to disqualification. Similarly, an independent contractor salesperson's vacation schedule may not be subject to the control of the broker. On the other hand, an independent contractor is entitled to establish his own retirement plan as a self-employed person. To the extent he does so, his status as an independent contractor is reinforced. Statutory independent contractors may receive these benefits, but they may not exceed 10 percent of the salesperson's total income from real estate sales.

Taxes and Social Security
All independent contractors pay estimated federal taxes on a quarterly basis, and make self-employment compensation payments using form SE in lieu of social security payments. Brokers must provide a W2 form and withhold social security from any non-production income. Brokers also must withhold federal and state taxes for employees, as well as providing W2 forms and contribute social security payments for them.

Reports and Procedures
While a broker may require his employees and statutory independent contractors to adhere strictly to the office operations manual, such degree of control is impermissible with common law independent contractor salespeople. The operations manual constitutes mere *guidance* to the independent contractor salesperson and this fact should be specifically stated in the manual if it is to be distributed to such salespeople. Reports by independent contractor salespeople, except as to listings obtained, sales made and information necessary to permit the broker to record and close transactions and comply with local, state and federal laws, should not be made mandatory. At the same time, the broker is free to provide such cooperation and advice as the independent contractor salesperson requests concerning the efficient and effective conduct of his work.

Determining the Proper Relationship
Only the broker can determine whether he can effectively function with the limited degree of control required to preserve the common law independent contractor relationship. In making this determination, however, the broker must consider the experience and personality of the sales applicant. If the applicant is experienced, it may be unnecessary to require him to accept mandatory training or persuade him of the value of floor time and adherence to proper office routine. If the applicant is aggressive and self-motivated, it may be unnecessary for the broker to tell him not merely "what" his job is but also "how" to do it.

In addition, the broker must consider the extent to which the applicant will be engaged in activities other than "pure sales." If the applicant will be involved in property management and rental activities, a degree of control will be required which will almost inevitably exceed that allowed in an independent contractor relationship.

In many instances it is desirable if the broker utilizes *both* the independent contractor and employee relationship. Thus, a new salesperson requiring close supervision and control because of his inexperience and intensive training in the firm's policies and procedures as well as other areas of the business should be an employee or statutory independent contractor. When such a salesperson establishes his ability to perform independently, he can change his relationship to that of independent contractor, provided, of course, he is not engaged in aspects of the real estate business involving management functions or detailed supervision.

By having both employees and independent contractors in the same organization, the broker is able to "heighten" the distinction between them and thereby reinforce the validity of the independent contractor status. At the same time he can assure himself of a manpower resource (employees) which he can require to perform duties (floor time, open house attendance) which he could never appropriately require of independent contractors. The availability of such resources reduces his need and hence his temptation to violate the independent contractor relationship.

Any additional cost attributable to the employee status of salespersons can be recovered through an adjustment in the terms of their employment vis-a-vis the terms under which independent contractors are associated. Such adjustment can also provide a significant inducement for the employee salesperson to seek independent contractor status when otherwise trained and qualified to be on "his own."

Establishing the Relationship

Once the broker has determined the type of relationship he desires to establish with the sales applicant, he must determine whether he desires that relationship to be established by oral or written agreement.

If an employer-employee relationship is desired, an oral understanding can suffice if there exists a clear and comprehensive operations manual to which the broker and salesperson may refer for a definition of their respective rights and responsibilities. An oral agreement may also be satisfactory if the rights and responsibilities of the broker and salesperson are well defined by custom and practice in the community in which the salesperson is to function.

On the other hand, a written employment contract, properly drafted, is almost invariably better than an oral agreement. The value of any written agreement rests in the fact that it sets forth the terms of the employer-employee relationship with a higher degree of precision than could be achieved orally and thereby limits the areas of potential controversy and litigation. Moreover, the development of a written agreement permits contingencies to be anticipated and problems to be resolved in advance. It can include, where legally permissible, a "non-compete" provision; it can spell out in detail what happens in the event of termination; and, perhaps most significantly, it can permit the broker to differentiate between employees in a way which cannot be achieved if the relationship is defined by an operations manual or by custom.

A written agreement becomes almost indispensable if the broker also has either common law or statutory independent contractors affiliated with him if only to provide a clear contrast between the terms of his relationship with his employees and that with his independent contractor salespeople. It also is desirable if the salesperson is to perform certain management or supervisory functions since it permits those functions to be defined and delimited.

In the event of a controversy with the IRS, the written independent contract agreement will be the starting point in the examination. If the agreement is properly drafted to reflect the relationship recognized by the courts and the IRS itself as that of broker-independent contractor, the task of the IRS is immeasurably more difficult since the IRS agent must then establish significant deviations from the terms of the agreement in the actual conduct of the broker and the salesperson.

Most important, however, a written contract provides a salesperson with a source of ready reference about his rights and obligations. It enables the broker to discuss problems in particularized terms, citing chapter and verse. As a consequence it minimizes the risk that independent contractor status will be lost by inadvertence or misunderstanding.

Drafting the Agreement with the Salesperson

No agreement with a salesperson, whether employee or independent contractor, should be drafted without advice of counsel. It may *not* reasonably be assumed that an agreement which is acceptable in one state will be appropriate in another. Nor may a broker assume that an agreement which is found satisfactory by another broker will be automatically adaptable to his own operation.

There is grave danger in utilizing model or specimen forms. Such forms are designed basically for use by attorneys to provide them with a format upon which they may build as the laws of the state and the particular needs and desires of the parties require.

This is not to say that an organization may not develop a standard form which may be used in establishing a relationship with a salesperson provided it is understood first that the form will be used only for those salespeople engaged in the same activities and second that any differentiation between salespeople, however slight, will be reflected in changes to the agreement and will be reviewed.

The cost of securing review by counsel of the terms of the employment or independent contractor agreement is a small price to pay to minimize the significant risks created by a defective agreement. Moreover, once counsel is familiar with the broker's business and his relationships with salespeople, the legal costs of maintaining the agreements in current form and updating them as changes in the law require will be reduced.

Monitoring Adherence to the Agreement

Since an employer normally enjoys substantial control over his employees, the monitoring of the adherence of employees to their agreements involves essentially routine personnel administration.

This is not so in the case of the independent contractor salesperson. As indicated elsewhere the status of a salesperson is determined by his relationship with his broker *in fact* and not by the mere terms of his agreement. The most carefully drafted agreement will not preserve the independent contractor relationship if the parties themselves have ignored its terms.

This means that the broker having independent contractor salespeople must establish a routine or program which will identify and correct any actions or attitudes inconsistent with the written agreement. Such a program may be complex or simple depending on the size of the organization, number of salespeople, range of activities, number of offices, personalities of the salespeople, office procedures, management and other factors. Essentially, however, any program must be able to accomplish the following tasks.

Periodic Review of Terms of Agreement

This review should occur at least annually and preferably more often. The purpose is to fix the terms of the relationship firmly in the minds of the broker and salesperson and to provide an opportunity to make such changes in the contract as are deemed necessary.

Review of Plans, Policies, Forms and Procedures

This review is intended to assure that the relationship with the salesperson is consistently recognized by the broker's organization. For example, this review would reveal that the operations manual specifies that adherence to it is mandatory for all salespeople; or that an independent contractor salesperson cannot be assigned to open house duty; etc.

Review of Salesperson's Representation to the Public

This review is intended to assure that the salesperson does not identify himself as an employee of the broker in his dealings with the public. In soliciting listings or customers, or in making appearances in the community, the independent contractor must be careful to identify himself as being associated with and not employed by the broker. Further, he must not, in his dealings, use a title to which he is not entitled or ascribe to his broker a degree of control over his activities inconsistent with his status.

The manner in which the foregoing tasks may be performed is varied. Some will be performed by the broker himself, some by management and some may involve counsel. Some brokers with large organizations have gone so far as to establish an internal security system whereby the actions of both management and salespeople are tested by persons unknown to either.

Regardless of the complexity of the program or the manner of its execution, its effectiveness depends on systematic and continuing implementation.

Summary and Conclusion

In applying these tests to determine whether an employee, statutory independent contractor or common law independent contractor relationship exists, there are many considerations. Check with an attorney for complete details and to determine the current law in your state.

**Written
Instruments
Between
Broker and
Salesperson**

Training

10

Having assembled the best staff available, the broker now faces the challenge of providing a thorough orientation and training program for them. A good training program not only enables salespeople and ancillary staff members to do their jobs more effectively but also saves management time in the long run.

Training

Stated in its simplest terms, the purpose of a broker's training program should be to teach his sales staff how to market real estate effectively, ethically and profitably as well as how to perform other supportive services. Listing and selling real estate is what brokers and salespeople are paid to do and they cannot do it any better than they know how.

Within the broad framework of this goal, the objectives of the training program can be separated as they pertain to the broker and salesperson respectively.

The Broker's Objectives

A real estate salesperson has time and knowledge to offer. With good time management and training he can provide a better service which results in higher sales and profits. Training also provides many other benefits.

Reduce Staff Turnover

A good initial training program will help prevent early discouragement on the part of new salespeople. A continuing educational program will sell the veteran salesperson on the personal benefits of remaining with the organization. These two factors combine to assure the broker a more stable sales force.

Improve Company Image

Because of the one-on-one nature of real estate selling, a salesperson's performance is often the only way the seller or buyer has to judge an entire firm. The more competent the individual, the better the image of the entire organization. This point should be made early and often. When in the field, the salesperson is not only *part* of the organization, in many cases he *is* the organization. Not only is his reputation on the line but those of his fellow salespeople and the firm itself.

Reduce Need for Supervision

Increased competence on the part of salespeople means less need for the broker to spoon feed and hand lead them beyond the early days of indoctrination. This frees the broker for more productive and potentially more profitable activities.

Make Recruiting Easier

There is no stronger magnet for attracting good salespeople to a firm than word-of-mouth advertising of its training program and the success of those who have benefited from it. Thorough training is promised frequently in real estate recruitment but often it is not delivered. When the promise does become a reality, it creates a continuing flow of new trainees. If for no other reason than to meet the competition for good salespeople in today's market, the best possible training program should be a top priority item for every broker.

Improve Company Morale
A well rounded training program motivates the trainee to better efforts, makes for better communication between salesperson and broker and keeps management in touch with what's happening on the firing line, particularly if the broker himself participates actively.

The Salesperson's Objectives
The informed salesperson is confident and confident salespeople make more sales and have greater security.

Self Assurance
Salespeople who are sure of themselves and unafraid of what they'll encounter in the field are happier, more poised and more productive.

Personal Satisfaction
The knowledge that they are growing in professionalism and know-how gives salespeople a tremendous ego boost which is not completely provided by even large amounts of monetary compensation.

Firm Size
Regardless of the size of a firm, a well planned and conscientiously executed training program is an absolute must, both to achieve the benefits mentioned earlier and because a broker has an obligation to give his salespeople adequate training before they represent the firm in the field. This is not a moral obligation to the public and others in the real estate business but a practical obligation to the broker himself to protect his reputation and avoid the possible danger of losing his brokerage license through the actions of an incompetent salesperson.

For the smaller firm, several alternatives are available to begin a training program.

Training can be combined with that of friendly competitors with each taking a share of the instruction in his particular specialty.

Educational programs are offered by local boards, state associations and the REALTORS NATIONAL MARKETING INSTITUTE®. The Institute is comprised of the Real Estate Brokerage Council™, which covers the brokerage management profession; the Residential Sales Council™, which covers the sales profession; and the Commercial-Investment Real Estate Council, which covers the investment and management disciplines in commercial real estate. The books, films and audio-visual programs offered by these Councils and by other organizations can be used in the training program for new salespeople and refresher courses for both the broker and experienced salespeople. If buying or renting all these materials at once for a single firm proves too costly, they can be purchased on a cooperative basis by several friendly competitors, to be loaned back and forth as needed. Many visual programs can be rented at reasonable fees. Publications are also available through the library facilities of the NATIONAL ASSOCIATION OF REALTORS®.

Training skills can be acquired by attending the management courses offered by the Real Estate Brokerage Council™ and the Commercial-Investment Real Estate Council.

How to Set Up a Training Program

One of the best ways to start structuring a training program is to ask the question: what do I want my salespeople to know how to do after they have completed the course? The broker should record the various levels of expertise of his sales staff. Therefore, the development of a training program should incorporate opportunities for three levels of training:

New for inexperienced sales associates

Intermediate for experienced associates

Advanced for experienced associates.

Salespeople should learn to:

Counsel buyers and sellers

Develop and employ basic marketing skills

Prospect for buyers

Prospect for listings

Prepare a competitive market analysis

Understand the operations manual

Read plat books

Fill out a listing contract

Fill out a sales contract

Understand the REALTOR® Code of Ethics

Handle telephone inquiries

Qualify buyers

Show properties

Develop problem-solving skills

Analyze problems

Present and negotiate offers to purchase

Get signatures on contracts

Service listings

Employ mortgage financing programs.

The list goes on and on and it should. In fact, after you have written the original list, carry it around for several days, adding items as they come to mind.

Categorize the Subjects

The next step is to group the subject items into categories such as:

Introduction and orientation

Personal career planning/time management

Forms and accounting procedures

Preparation of contracts

Listing

Marketing/advertising

Telephone techniques

Qualifying buyers

Showing properties

Financing terms as a marketing tool

Negotiating and closing

Commercial real estate and income property

REALTOR® Code of Ethics

Board activities.

The objective here is to organize things so the training process follows a logical sequence. This will enable salespeople to relate to what they have learned previously and prepare for the next subject.

Next, fill out the groups by listing the topics to be taught under each of the general categories. The first list of details is now integrated into the category outline. Every element desired in the training program should appear in one of the general categories with everything arranged in logical sequence.

Now decide what visual aids, reading programs, films, tapes, recordings or guest lectures are available and pencil them into the outline. Make note of any costs involved in lecture fees and rental of teaching aids.

Plan Time

Now estimate the amount of time to be spent on each part of the training program, being careful to budget the hours so the time devoted to a particular topic is consistent with its importance to the firm. For example, don't spend ten hours explaining every line on intra-office forms, the history of the company or procedures for coffee breaks and then crowd a whole lecture on listing into an intensive half hour harangue. Just because a person can talk for two hours on a subject doesn't mean that he should. Remember, the objective is to teach the salesperson how to do his job and not to showcase speaking talents. A captive audience gives one neither the right nor the reason to torture them.

Once the program content and time segments are worked out, break it up into a comfortable, workable schedule so that each training session is long enough to be substantive and short enough to avoid confusing the trainee with more than he can absorb and put to use quickly.

Choose Location

The last chore in planning a training program is to determine where it will be conducted. Certain environmental elements are critical to choosing a location:

First, there must be reasonable privacy as free from distraction as possible. A training program can be conducted in a real estate office, providing the location and/or time provides for an environment free of distractions. It is better to rent a meeting room in a local hotel if facilities are not conducive to a distraction-free environment in the broker's office.

Provide comfortable seating particularly if the sessions will be more than one hour in length. An overworked cliche but a nonetheless valid fact is that "the mind can absorb no more than the fanny can endure." Make sure there is adequate light, good acoustics and proper ventilation. A prime objective of any training program is maximum attention. Uncomfortable people simply cannot concentrate.

At this point in planning your training program, the broker is well advised to estimate the cost. Nothing pays off more handsomely in future profits than the money spent to recruit, train and retain salespeople. If corners must be cut to meet your budget, cut them somewhere else.

Who Does the Training?

This quotation from Sydney J. Harris, former nationally syndicated columnist, contains a word of caution:

"Bernard Shaw's famous quotation, 'He who can does, he who cannot, teaches,' has been used for decades as a smear against teaching... as if only failures in performance took out their frustrations by trying to instruct others." There is no relationship between the ability to do and the ability to teach.

Just because a person is the boss and/or a fine salesperson does not mean he is automatically the best person to put in charge of training the sales staff.

Qualities for Teaching

The trainer must actually want to teach. It is still better if he is a compulsive teacher who cannot resist helping others. This characteristic is more important than knowing the job well and certainly more important than the ability to actually do the things he wants to teach others to do. A star salesperson is not necessarily a good teacher, nor a successful broker.

The teacher must be understanding. Some will say "patient" is the proper word; but a good teacher appears to be patient only because he understands that it takes time and empathy and that an overdose of either is lethal to the teaching process.

The great teacher does not consider teaching a sacrifice or a chore. He gets his reward from the achievements of those whom he has molded and motivated and sent into the field. The person who would rather make a million dollar deal himself than teach ten people to do the same is not likely to be a great teacher.

None of this should be construed as advocating that the star salesperson be kept out of the training program. On the contrary, nothing could be more stimulating to a group of newcomers than hearing a brief presentation by someone who has succeeded in the field. This is especially true if he validates what is being taught, proving that it really works when salespeople get out in the field. The point here is that teachers are a breed apart (whether a teacher comes from the top, middle or bottom of the sales force or even if he never made a sale in his life) and the single criterion is the ability to instruct others so they understand and are motivated to put to use in the field what they learned in the training course.

If people in your organization lack these characteristics, revert to the earlier suggestion to team up with a friendly competitor. Or find a mortgage banker, a lawyer, a school teacher or even a retired real estate broker to cover the parts of the training program with which staff people feel uncomfortable.

Training Formula

Perhaps the best and most succinct outline for training is the advice attributed to an older preacher when teaching a new minister how to structure a sermon.

"Tell them what you're going to tell them. Tell them. Tell them what you told them!"

The following guidelines expand on this over-simplification.

Assume the trainee knows nothing. Start with the basics. Some will need the ABC's. Others can benefit from a review. Never ask, "Do you understand?" You are not interested in a reply from those who do understand and those who do not are likely to say that they do in order to avoid embarrassment. Instead ask, "Are there any questions?" Then be sure complete answers are given. Asking the trainee to restate the answer in his own way will prove he does or does not understand.

Recognize the fact that while people learn, they don't want to change or to surrender their prejudices. Keep this in mind when they quite naturally resist any ideas which are contrary to their preconceived notions or which might require a change of habits. This is particularly important since the instructor will often be dealing with people who have been away from formal education and study for a long time. They may be set in their ways and not as easy to reach as they once were.

Carefully introduce the point to be made before proceeding. You must define the learning objectives. ("Tell them what you're going to tell them.") Specifically, tell them what they will know how to do after the lesson and tell them why it is important they learn how to do it. After telling them what they will learn, fill in the details.

Take a firm position when expressing an opinion. If the instructor says, "I may be wrong, but" he opens a credibility gap. They want to feel he is sure of what he wants them to believe. Unsure of their own beliefs, they do not want to be led by another uncertain person.

Tell how a thing must be done, not just what must be done. Barking orders without supplying the specific "how to" neither strengthens techniques nor improves the instructor's stature. Tell why each thing must be done by explaining how it will benefit them or how it will help them avoid a problem. Give examples of these benefits based either on personal experience or that of other people. Principles acquire meaning when they can be related to people benefits in real life. Use analogies freely. For example, equate the value of an operations manual to making vacation plans, following road maps or planning meals. The point might be that such a manual anticipates problems and either avoids them or solves them in advance.

Remember that communications involve imperfect methods. An idea is presented in a code—the words used. The trainee decodes the words, not the instructor's thoughts. He formulates a response in his mind and encodes his reply in his words. The instructor hears the trainee's words, not his thoughts. He decodes them and so on. Minds never meet; they merely negotiate through the medium of speech which is encoded. This leads to the vital point that the instructor must keep talking and listening until he is sure the thought has been transmitted. He is never sure of this until it is fed back to him in the listener's words. Be sure to encourage feedback! Never assume they have understood. Usually they have not!

Repeat, repeat, repeat, until the trainees feed it back as being understood properly. At this point, and only at this point, has the communication bridge been spanned.

Sense Mood

Try to sense the mood of the class. Shuffling, coughing, wandering gazes and side bar conferences are signs they have "pulled the shade" on the instructor. Regain their attention by changing the pace, changing the subject, changing the approach, changing voice level, asking questions or inviting feedback.

Be the center of attention, use the full voice range, dramatic gestures, movement, facial expressions and pauses to liven up the presentation. Do not hesitate to dramatize. The job requires it. There is a risk of occasionally feeling like a fool but restraint fosters a doubt of the instructor's sincerity. They evaluate the message on the basis of everything they hear, see and even feel during the presentation. Anyone who doubts this should try reading the most profound truths from an encyclopedia in a monotone.

Even though trainees "get a grade when school lets out," it is the instructor and management who will be judged. The staff has the opportunity to learn but management has the obligation to teach.

The proof of the pudding in education is testing. In addition to oral quizzes and rap sessions which should be part of regular training sessions, a written examination (preferably fill-in-the-blanks) is a good measuring tool for comprehension. Tests can be used just as effectively after a training film as after a live lecture or discussion session. Success in the examination provides the trainee greater satisfaction than he would feel if he merely survived the course by sitting through it.

Measuring the Results

Regardless of the teaching inputs in a training course or the amount of preparation and the skill of the instructor, the fact remains that the most important thing is what happens after the course ends. Only if salespeople use what they learn immediately after they learn the theory can they test its validity and report back to the next class any problems encountered.

Training Techniques and Aids

Visual aids should be an integral part of a good training program. In their most rudimentary form they will include use of blackboards, art pads, flash cards, charts, graphs and even enlarged photographs.

The purpose of such aids and other more sophisticated equipment is to add the strong impact of seeing as well as hearing the message. The ancient Chinese proverb, "One picture is worth a thousand words" is confirmed by studies which indicate that the attention of the viewer is greatly intensified by focusing eyes as well as ears on a message; his comprehension of the materials is also dramatically increased and perhaps most important of all, his retention is greater.

Overhead Projector

Once you graduate from the blackboard and flip chart, your first investment might be the purchase or rental of an overhead or opaque projector. This relatively inexpensive device has several advantages over a blackboard: material projected is larger in size; the instructor need not turn his back to the group in order to use it; complex diagrams, formulas and the like can be retained for the balance of the class or may be photographed and converted to permanent transparencies. Modern overhead projectors can be used in full room light and will project black and white as well as multi-colored images.

The advantage to overhead projection is that the projector will faithfully reproduce on the screen anything written, printed or illustrated on a transparent film placed on its face.

Slide Projectors

The slide projector employs full color or black and white photographic slides usually either from 35mm cameras or "Instamatic" types. Despite the difference in size, the frames on which they are mounted are interchangeable and both types can be used in the same program.

There are a variety of types and makes of slide projectors. The carousel carries slides in a circular "bonnet" which is easily removable so the same slides can be stored permanently in each carrier (which can be interchanged for different programs). Other types mount the slides in a straight column ferris wheel. Activated by either manual control or automatic advancing mechanism, the projector shows each slide in order on a standard movie screen. Slide film projection is best in a darkened room. One advantage of the slide film presentation is that an instructor can, using his own camera equipment and a bit of ingenuity, create his own audio-visual programs.

Projectors which can be controlled automatically by cassette tapes are also available. Once the program has started, the sound is automatically synchronized with the picture on the screen and the slides advance automatically by an inaudible electronic pulse on the tape.

Where the automatic advancing ability is not present, a tone, beep or "cricket" can be recorded on the audio tape which gives the monitor of the class a cue to advance the slide.

Filmstrips are fairly popular and widely used, and can either be purchased or produced professionally. Information about film strips can be obtained from any photographic dealer.

Movie Projectors

16mm projectors are not expensive to operate, and a wide selection of real estate films are available from various commercial and industrial studios. If used properly, these films can be very beneficial in the introduction, demonstration and validation of sales/marketing techniques.

Television Recording and Videotape

One of the most exciting tools in the audio-visual field is the in-house closed circuit television and videotape recorder system. Although a camera, recorder and monitor set can be purchased for about fifteen hundred dollars, the investment could run to more substantial sums. The simplest system allows the trainee to not only hear but also see himself in simulated selling situations.

As in the case of the slide projector, videotape recorder programs can be put on tape permanently to be replayed any time a new salesperson is added to the staff or an experienced salesperson wants to brush up on a particular technique.

You don't have to make your own tapes to utilize video, however. Also available is a variety of pre-recorded videocassettes that enhance training programs. The Real Estate Brokerage Council™ offers an extensive series of tapes through Coronet Films.

Role Playing

Whether used theater style in the training center or in conjunction with a tape recorder or videotape recorder, role playing is one of the most effective training methods yet devised.

The object of role playing is to simulate as closely as possible the selling situations in which a salesperson is likely to find himself. This might include problems as diverse as dealing with an irate seller whose door was left unlocked, a skeptical buyer who wants to be shown why a home is priced at $100,000, a nasty telephone caller inquiring about a classified ad or an intrepid soul who is sure he can sell his property himself and avoid paying a broker's commission.

The situation and the characters involved must be clearly defined before the role playing session begins.

Although it is strictly make believe it must be serious to be effective. No laugh breaks or funny remarks will salvage a difficult selling situation in the field, so avoid them in the training session. One of the purposes of role playing is to portray the pressure of a situation so that players can become familiar with handling it before encountering it in the field.

Lessons learned here cost only the training time. The same mistake made in the field can not only destroy a substantial commission but may foul up the plans of buyer and seller as well and do permanent harm to the firm's reputation.

Following the role playing session, there should be an immediate critique. If a tape recorder or videotape system has been used there can be no question of what was said. It should first be played back for both the participants and those who watched them.

The first critique should be made by the participants themselves who will very likely be keenly aware of their mistakes.

Non-participating people in the class might be asked to make comments and criticisms along the same line: "What was done well or how could it have been done more effectively?" The wrap up might be a run through of the same situation with the characters in the drama attempting to take advantage of their own criticisms and the suggestions of their peers and the instructor.

Finally, the instructor should add any suggestions he may have for improving the participants' techniques and correcting their errors. This must be done tactfully. The purpose of role playing is definitely not to embarrass the participants. A good starting point for the instructor's critique is to ask, "What did he (or they) do right?" Follow up questions include, "How could he have arrived at a better solution" or "If you were in his position what would you have done differently?"

Tips on Role Playing

In the opening situation, it is usually a good idea for the instructor or someone experienced in role playing to take one of the parts. This lends stability to the experiment and keeps the subject matter on target. It also avoids situations where the party playing the customer feels sorry for the salesperson and lets him off the hook by dropping out of character, giving hints that no real customer would ever volunteer, or simply agreeing with him just to ease a tense situation.

For role playing to be effective, the tough customer must remain tough, the silent customer must remain silent and the angry customer must keep on shouting until the salesperson has persuaded him to cool off.

Role playing can be employed to polish telephone techniques, listing solicitations, sales presentations, qualifying inquiries and the like as refresher training for salespeople. It is an excellent idea to mix the veteran performers with novices in role playing situations. Both can benefit, although it may be pretty tough to get star salespeople to submit to the tortures of a live audience and the brutally factual attention of the audio tape or television camera. But anytime a top salesperson can be persuaded to join the role playing sessions he has far more to gain from it than a newcomer to whom even the simplest words of wisdom are useful.

Here are three role-playing situations. They are presented to show you how such situations are used in some training programs. You may use them as they are given here or develop others suited to problems in your market area.

SALESPERSON
Scene: Seller is building a new home. Listing is 60 days old. Salesperson has been told to get the price down to the market. Two showings—eight ads—no offers—listed $10,000 over market.

CLIENT
Mr. & Mrs. Seller's new home is nearing completion. Salesperson has not been in touch. Doors left unlocked—lights on.
Nearby home sold by competitor recently.
Salesperson went to high school with Mrs. Owner.
Husband opens with: "Well, stranger—got our place sold yet?"

SALESPERSON
Scene: REALTOR®s office at 9:00 p.m. Second showing is over. All went well.
Property on the market four days—eight showings—priced right—good motive.
Your own listing and right for these buyers.

CUSTOMER
Mr. and Mrs. "Never-pay-retail" have looked for six months.
Now rent month to month.
No money problem—but no decision either.
Wife opens with: "We sure like that house but we think it's much more than we want to pay. We're really in no hurry you know."

SALESPERSON
Scene: Office of owner who had salesperson check a two-family property for him.
He inherited it and now wants to sell it.
It's a nice $75,000, 20-year-old home—needs work.

CLIENT
Mr. Owner opens with: "You come recommended—that's why I called you. Now, I'll list with you for 30 days at $90,000. Do a good job and I'll extend it for another 30 and I don't want any sign or nosy neighbors and the price is firm—I got an appraisal."

Publications and Periodicals

Every real estate office should have its own library and a portion of its operating budget set aside for the purchase of new books. A growing number of books is being published by the three Councils of the REALTORS NATIONAL MARKETING INSTITUTE®, including the one you are now reading. Trade publishers also have a number of excellent titles relating to the industry. Many are available on loan from the library of the NATIONAL ASSOCIATION OF REALTORS® and your local public library.

After you have assembled even a modest collection, use it to plan a program of recommended reading for salespeople. Salespeople should be encouraged to continue their education by reading the new titles in your library, reviewing older ones and keeping up with newspapers and trade publications subscribed to by the firm.

Introductions Are Important

Introduce a new salesperson to everyone in the firm. Let him find out how others' jobs and responsibilities relate to what he will be doing.

The salesperson should become familiar with the functions and operations of every department. Make sure he has a copy of all the firm's listings. Give him a copy of your company's policies and be sure he understands them.

Make Sure He Knows the Community

It is essential that a new salesperson study maps showing church, school, library and park locations and districts. He should be familiar with shopping centers and public transportation in the area. He should review current listings, particularly those that affect the area he will serve. You might assign him a "farm," a specific territory he will work.

See that he knows within a reasonable time the number and type of homes, school and church locations, distance from shopping and all other information pertinent to the area assigned him. This product knowledge is vital.

Sales Techniques and Tools

Basics are still basics. A manager can help a new salesperson avoid pitfalls but he cannot let him skip the basics. Don't ever assume a new salesperson knows the basics. He will need pointers on sales techniques, deliveries and canvassing, when to talk and when to listen and all the other knowledge he will learn to use that will enable him to become successful.

Make him familiar with sales bulletins and case studies of different sales problems and their solutions. Have him assemble a listing and selling kit which should include whatever you feel is important to effective selling or listing of properties.

Explain local methods of cooperating with other brokers and how they work. This is a good time to acquaint a new salesperson with the caliber of his competition. Explain inter-office co-op relations and company policy for such sales. If he has had an opportunity to study the operations manual, the training course is an excellent time to make sure he understands it.

The Telephone

The telephone is a salesperson's most important tool because it is his best means for arranging a personal appointment with a buyer or seller.

After explaining to a new sales associate how the other office equipment works (e.g., copier machines, FAX machines, computers), what records are kept and how long distance calls and charges are handled, one of the most important sales training techniques begins. Have the associate place near his phone the following reminder:

SMILE—BE COURTEOUS

Get the appointment

Get the appointment

Get the appointment

OPEN END QUESTIONS:

How long have you been looking?

When do you need a home?

Where do you live now?

Train him to smile when answering because a smile is felt even through a phone. It is also impossible to be depressed or discourteous when you are smiling.

The phone in a broker's office should never ring more than three times without being answered. To the person calling there is no reasonable excuse for a longer wait. Customers want information quickly. Train salespeople to give it to them.

Property Evaluation

If it is in line with office policy, teach him the fundamentals of property evaluation. Require that every salesperson prepare a competitive market analysis on all listings. Nothing keeps awareness of the market sharper than constant research. If the firm tours all new listings, make sure non-listing salespeople are not told the listing price in advance. Have them appraise each property, then record their appraisals and the date on the listing sheet. When the listing sells, they will gain better reality between the relationship of price and marketability in a given area.

In filling out the forms required in property evaluation or for any other procedure in the company, be sure the salesperson understands each form. Show him how to use it. He should know what information is required and who needs it.

Financing

Consider asking a local mortgage broker to instruct this part of your training program. He works every day with different types of financing and is most familiar with the nuances. If the mortgage company is large enough to have a settlement department, the head of this department might be the instructor. Training in finance should cover:

Types of financing

Where to get it

When and why financing is necessary

Computations involved.

Listing Procedures

Listing procedures will sometimes parallel information covered in sales technique training. How listings are taken, the company's procedures, what methods are successful and what methods have failed are possible areas to cover.

Sales Procedures
By structuring the sales procedures on a step-by-step basis, training can develop tracks for a new salesperson to run on. One such breakdown is:

Rapport building

Qualifying

Presentation

Objections

Close

Continuation.

Since the prime objective is to develop the raw talent of a new salesperson into a sales professional, he should be taught the differences of approach in each step as well as ways to measure his success in each method. Let's evaluate each step and consider teaching approaches.

Rapport Building
Training should develop methods the new salesperson can use with clients and customers to establish this harmony. Empathy is a key word in building rapport. Must rapport be built? Experienced salespeople insist that any sales process ever developed required the existence of rapport.

Qualifying
How to determine needs, abilities and motivations of the client or customer is critically important. All the subsequent steps of real estate sales depend on proper qualifying.

Presentation
Each presentation should be well planned and similar on every occasion. This does not suggest canned spiels. It does emphasize the need for the salesperson to know what to say, when to say it and how to say it every time. A good presentation will depend on the information gained in the rapport building and qualifying stages.

The presentation is often interrupted to further strengthen rapport efforts or qualifying knowledge. The key question is "Am I presenting the right product?" Once your salesperson learns to identify that he is doing this, he can start to close. Attempting a close on the wrong product often ends in loss of rapport.

Objections
What is an objection? Does "I want to think it over," or "that room is too small" mean the same thing each time someone says it? Not at all. Each person says what he says for different reasons. Teach the salesperson to evaluate whether the objection (for example, "I want to think it over") was just a normal reflex comment indicating a need for more information, a defense against making a decision he wants to make or an indicator of some problem that will have to be solved. Objections must be solved before closing takes place.

Closing
There are many books, tapes and other publications available on the hundreds of methods to close successfully. Each firm should teach the methods it uses and how to use them. Closing is a constant process and affects each step of the sale.

Continuation
Many salespeople learn to go through the first five steps and then are not taught the importance of follow-up. Each successful sale is money in the bank to the salesperson. Beyond the commission earned is the possibility of future referrals. A training program should teach the new salesperson how to follow up, how to develop referrals and most important that his future income will depend on this continuing effort.

Marketing/Advertising
Marketing/advertising training should specify who writes the ads and how to write them well. It should cover how much information is put into ads and how often they are run. Salespeople should be taught to tell sellers of the importance of institutional advertising. Other marketing/advertising programs of the company should be explained.

Legal Aspects
Although a new salesperson is already licensed, licensing laws and particularly those statutes that directly affect the firm should be reviewed and understood. In addition, training should review title insurance (including local costs), particular legal problems such as local zoning statutes, and federal, municipal and state influences on real estate.

Escrow
Pay particular attention to the company's policies on escrow accounts as well as any escrow costs buyers or sellers might incur.

Special Programs
Guaranteed sales plans and home warranty programs, as well as any other special programs, should be explained.

Review, Review, Review
A good way to review the above is field training with the manager. The instructor or sales manager actually demonstrates the basics. Cold canvassing, holding an open house, closing a sale and closing a listing should all be included. Management can establish by example good practices that can be followed the rest of a salesperson's career. Most new people are eager to follow instructions if properly shown and taught. Management's greatest pitfall to avoid is to be too busy to give this most valuable of all training. Field training is the copestone of what the firm has invested so much time and money to build.

The death knell has sounded for the non-professional in real estate. State laws are more stringent and the public is becoming more sophisticated. But above all that, the professional real estate salesperson will succeed because he works like a skilled professional. To maintain this professionalism he must be a well informed and able consultant, thoroughly qualified to advise prospective clients on many aspects of business and personal needs.

His basic training gives him the tools. Experience in the field gives him a strong start. Now it is up to management to provide continual training to keep his motivation strong. **Training**

Continual Training   11

Continual, structured training is one of the strengthening agents of an aggressive real estate firm. The frequency of the training sessions, the time devoted to each and the locale may vary with the size of the firm and the facilities and teaching staff available. Whether it consists of a review of the basics, refresher courses on a specific part of the original training program or is strongly oriented to motivation, continual training is needed by both new and experienced salespeople. It is the way many firms keep the sales and office staff up to the minute on current selling and financial conditions, company plans, policy and procedures and maintain open communication between management and staff and among staff people themselves.

Training induces behavioral changes in trainees, stimulates them to greater achievement, reduces staff turnover, improves the broker's image in his business community and attracts new salespeople to the firm. Finally, it frees the broker to spend more of his time on other work. Underachievers or marginal achievers eliminate themselves through continued training and good salespeople are motivated to keep on their toes and do a more effective job.

Continual Training

After new salespeople have completed their orientation training, what next? Now they join other salespeople in regular workshops. These may be special training sessions or regular sales meetings. They may be round table meetings, panel sessions with a moderator or perhaps a panel of speakers discussing important topics, followed by a question and answer period. Whatever type of training program is planned, allocate as much time as possible for a discussion period that involves salespeople.

Some firms schedule occasional five-day seminars but many salespeople are reluctant to take this much time away from their selling efforts. Unless your salespeople are employees, attendance at all training and sales meetings is on a voluntary basis. One company closes its offices one full day each year and everyone in the company is invited to attend a seminar. The program covers every aspect of residential selling, including condominiums. Outside speakers are featured and a substantial share of the day is devoted to question and answer sessions.

The basic operations manual should be reviewed on a regular basis, at least once a year, but its role in continual training has a minimal day-to-day effect.

Idea Manual

One successful firm has developed a work manual to serve its sales department on a day-to-day basis. Each salesperson receives a 3-ring binder which is divided into two main parts.

The first part covers current policies of lenders, selling techniques which are updated weekly, current tax information and a host of formulas to help get the selling job done effectively. As new ideas are heard of or tried they are shared with others with each person getting an addition to his idea manual.

The second part deals with administrative functions as they relate to sales procedures. This part is critical in sustaining a positive, identifiable and supportive relationship between the salesperson and the firm every day. It is updated weekly. Salespeople bring work manuals to weekly sales meetings for purposes of review and the input of new ideas from the sales staff and management. The quality and usefulness of this manual rely heavily on the sales staff but its basic content is the result of management's accumulating information gleaned from years of experience of successful real estate brokers all over the country.

The work manual's importance lies in the way it deals with current situations and supplies the salesperson with solutions to problems likely to be encountered; but it frees him from committing the information to memory. He carries it with him everywhere on the job. The firm that recommends the work manual reports it has helped create new concepts in selling real estate because salespeople use it as a foundation on which to build.

Sales Meetings

Sales meetings accomplish a variety of purposes including motivation, communication of information and training. More than one purpose can be met at any one meeting.

The content of both continual training sessions and sales meetings will be dealt with jointly for purposes of avoiding duplication. Almost every subject suggested for continual training could also be incorporated in a sales meeting agenda sometime during the year. It becomes a management decision whether to schedule training sessions apart from sales meetings or whether time and money pressures dictate combining them.

Continual Training

The sales meeting is one of the most important continual training programs available in real estate. Over the period of a year, ten to thirty minutes in weekly sales meetings devoted to some facet of training can strengthen both management and staff.

Sales meetings, according to the most successful firms, are held at the same time and same hour every week so they become an integral part of the salespeople's schedule. Some firms hold sales meetings in a coffee-and-donut session in the early morning and schedule them to end just as office hours begin. A regular time, a stimulating agenda and a prompt closing will attract a strong attendance. Give your salespeople something to use that week and they'll be there.

Be certain every training or sales meeting has a primary objective and an agenda and that whoever teaches or conducts the meeting has a detailed outline of the training to be included, knows what is to be said and how it will be presented. Give everyone in attendance a chance to participate. What is said by staff to management is as important as what management says to staff.

Motivational Sales Meeting

Theories abound about the art of motivation and the science of what motivates people. The sales technique portion of training emphasizes how to and skills; the rest of training is to assist in the self development of people who happen to sell real estate.

While some motivation problems are best handled in a one-on-one session, a carefully structured meeting designed to fill human needs can strengthen team spirit. Discussion of common problems by the salespeople promotes empathy and a sharing of ideas.

A motivational sales meeting is structured separately and has different results from a general sales meeting. While the latter covers general business considerations and may feature a speaker on a particular topic, it usually includes an attempt by the manager to induce enthusiasm to perform a general sales function.

This type of meeting is critical to an organization that is dynamic and expanding for it ties both new and experienced staff people together in a feeling of common purpose. It is motivational in the sense that it focuses on general market opportunities and strives to inspire the staff to achieve short-term goals.

The motivational sales meeting is more critical in its structuring, participation and the results it should generate. Motivational meetings are based on the assumption that those in attendance are a more close-knit group and those in attendance know one another's strengths and weaknesses. The problem in such a situation is that they have a tendency to become repetitious and challenge management to keep them well structured and inspirational.

Careful planning of the agenda of every motivational sales meeting is of great importance. Selection of materials is also critical to success. Participation by everyone in attendance is high on the list of factors critical to good motivational sales meetings. Participation can take at least two forms in these situations.

One of the most common types is an award presentation. The competition can range from naming a "winner" who put up the first "For Sale" sign following the last sales meeting to announcing a prize for the salesperson closing the first escrow after the present meeting. Size of the prize is not important when management is motivating well trained salespeople. What is important is the recognition of the peer group and the satisfaction of one element in the person's hierarchy of needs.

Another purpose is to motivate everyone to produce at top capacity in all aspects of sales and service. A clear discussion of company goals can form the background of a motivational meeting. When the sales staff knows where the company is going and why, they are motivated to be a part of it and do their share to reach the goal.

Motivational meetings need not always be conducted by the firm. Think about holding meetings outside the company. Qualified speakers are often scheduled to appear before business and community groups. What they say can inspire and inform real estate salespeople as well as others in the community. Management that keeps its eyes open to such opportunities and suggests that salespeople will gain some useful knowledge from hearing these speakers will also benefit. Local real estate boards are another good source of outside speakers and offer individual firms the benefit of banding together to hear someone with a message germane to the industry.

Communications

The communication purpose of a sales meeting ranges from making sure everyone in the organization gets to meet, know and/or renew acquaintanceship with every other member to disseminating information to the entire staff regarding up-to-date market and finance matters, changes either being considered or to be made in company policy and procedures, and any other daily or weekly function that concerns the sales department.

Communications should function upwards from the staff as well as down from management in good sales meetings. The sales meeting can be one of the most productive meetings within an organization. It requires a strong leader to control the group so the meeting is kept on track, no one person dominates the discussion and each individual is given recognition and a chance to express himself.

Meeting Agenda

A strong agenda for sales meetings will repay every minute spent to develop it. Once the purpose of the meeting is decided, an agenda that explores the best ways to achieve that purpose is prepared. Experienced managers know there will always be people around to tell why an idea won't work or a goal can't be achieved. Management's job is to set an affirmative tone for the meeting, provide opportunities for all to participate and then guide the participation toward positive discussion. Problems should be discussed in a constructive manner and meetings should end on a positive note.

Successful firms report that a continuing, regular review of telephone techniques, listing and market analysis ideas and reminders of how the firm services listings can be handled in sales meetings in a variety of ways that are helpful to salespeople. Straight talk from the manager, a moderated discussion panel or role playing sessions vary the presentation and provide ways to motivate the different types of people in a sales organization, giving them something to use the moment the meeting ends.

How to Prepare an Agenda

A small spiral notebook is an excellent place to collect ideas for sales meetings. Choose a size that can slip into a pocket or purse and keep it ready to record every idea for topics to cover in sales/training sessions. Loose bits of paper too often become lost bits of paper, resulting in the loss of good ideas. Back at the desk, transcribe the ideas in the notebook into the sales meeting agenda.

Keep both the source notebook and the agenda for every meeting on file. Both are valuable references of topics that have been covered. The source book, reviewed from time to time, will enable the manager to spot emerging patterns. The agenda file serves as a record of what has been covered in sales meetings and can be used to convince salespeople that a certain problem or topic was discussed and on what date.

Operations Manual

Firms that use their operations manual as a resource for sales meeting agendas find this also helps them keep the manual up to date, enables them to make quick changes when conditions call for speedy action and to plan long-range changes under more ordinary circumstances. Discuss any change under consideration and the problem or reason that instigated it. Ask for additional suggestions from the staff. Often the greatest input for a needed change originates with an alert salesperson.

Listings

A review of current listings is important to every sales meeting. Where is the firm weak in listings? What can be done to maintain listings in a particular area? Let the salespeople present the new listings they have. Speaking about them to their peers enables everyone to do a better selling job.

Review changes in old listings. Use sales meetings to generate ideas for what can be said or done to help a particular hard listing to sell.

Marketing/Advertising
Are you getting lots of calls on certain kinds of advertising? Is your advertising weak in some area? Where should you be pushing advertising?

Goals/Objectives
The beginning of the firm's fiscal year is the time to discuss goals and establish new objectives in selling. Then review them quarterly so everyone knows where the firm stands in relation to its annual goals. Discuss privately with each salesperson his individual goals. But if one of them has done a great job in achieving or surpassing his goal be sure to compliment him in the training or sales meeting. It's a great morale builder for the individual and can motivate others to catch up with the leader.

"Want" Problems
"Want" problems presented by a salesperson have been known to create a sale right in the sales meeting. Someone may say "I have a client who needs such and such" and another might know exactly where to find it.

Brainstorming/Creativity Sessions
Brainstorm in a positive way. Seek salespeople's ideas in areas where the firm has problems. Ask what they think could be done. Use a blackboard to list every solution offered, no matter how impossible some may appear. Then try to narrow the list down to a reasonable number of choices that seem practical. If a solution does not emerge, ask that the problem be thought about until the next meeting. Get it on the agenda to be dealt with then.

Deal With Problems
Never make a sales meeting into a chewing session. Bring things out but never spotlight the salesperson who has a problem. If the problem is a general one and you believe it concerns the entire organization, present it at a sales meeting. Give the exact facts but never use names. Dealing with problems in this fashion can squelch rumors too. If management explains problems to the sales staff openly, sticks to the facts and presents the solution, the problem seems to fade away. If management fails to do this, the rumor grinds on, creating potential harm to both the staff and the firm.

Review Company Plan
If the firm plans to expand, be sure the staff hears it from management first. When the staff is part of long-range planning, both employees and independent contractors are more likely to make all-out efforts to help those plans materialize.

Referral Service
Because referrals are the backbone of the real estate business, some firms pay a small special bonus to salespeople who bring them in. Sales meetings are a good time to pass out these bonuses. When a salesperson has had a particularly good period of referrals, it looks

like a fine incentive to the others when that person is handed $16 in one dollar bills as his bonus for eight referrals in a single week.

Repeat Performances

When sudden changes in the market occur, some large firms schedule a series of sales meetings to be sure every salesperson is aware of how the firm is geared to meet the new situation. Then if a salesperson misses the session in his office, he can catch it at one of the company's other branches. In this fashion, everyone in the organization eventually attends some class and in a matter of a few weeks the whole organization is geared into change.

Continual Training

Attendance Problems

Sales meetings that are held at a regularly scheduled time work best for many successful brokers. When the meeting time is firm, management's major concern is to develop the agenda and coordinate the participation of everyone involved. Companies whose salespeople are all independent contractors report that attendance of 75 to 80 percent is considered good. If the sales staff is employed and if the ancillary staff is included in sales and training meetings their attendance can be mandatory. If the meetings are stimulating and have a record of providing useful information and strong motivation, independent contractor attendance will be high.

One motivator for salespeople's attendance at these meetings is the knowledge that they will be given time to present their new listings. This has promise of immediate monetary value to the individual salesperson.

Strong leadership in sales meetings also helps attendance. The leader's ability to stay close to the agenda, keep the meeting moving along and close on schedule are positive factors in attendance. The ability to let everyone participate but no one dominate a meeting is also important. Encouraging the participation of individual salespeople often leads to their preparing for the meeting too, knowing their performance will be measured against their peers.

All these facets of the meeting have to be handled skillfully by the person responsible. Many situations will need to be dealt with before the meeting occurs to avoid any unpleasant confrontations within the small working group. Specific personal problems and any matters of a negative nature that are handled in advance of the general meetings will allow management to devote more of everyone's time to positive thinking and working. After all, the goal of any sales meeting is to achieve results through group participation and effort to solve individual real estate situations. The success of the meeting depends on management's ability to draw the best from each person who attends.

Developing People

To adapt an old cliche to the real estate business, no brokerage firm is stronger than its weakest member. Management, whether content with the firm's present size or intent on growth, wants its organization to be strong. It can achieve this by developing people. There are at least three ways to accomplish it:

Expanding present jobs

Training for higher level jobs

Retraining older members.

Expanding Present Jobs

Training new salespeople and expanding the jobs of those already affiliated with the firm can only be achieved through continual training. New salespeople need on-the-job training where the manager goes out with a new salesperson and works with him to obtain listings and sell a property or canvass a farm area. They also need continual on-the-job training through meetings and training discussed earlier in this chapter if they are to keep up to date on what is happening in the business.

Each salesperson requires a different amount of time to reach the stage where he knows how best to use his time. The manager who makes sure his people get the best on-the-job training, prompt and full answers to questions and a full understanding of the firm's objectives is the manager who will develop his sales staff most quickly.

There are other sources of development for individual salespeople. Local college and adult education courses offer salespeople educational opportunities they can pursue in their free time, usually at low cost. The real estate industry, both locally and nationally, offers courses of value to salespeople in the industry. The Residential Sales Council™ offers five sales courses to aid in development of personal selling and human relations skills, and which lead to the coveted CRS® designation. Management should do everything possible to encourage attendance at some of these sessions.

Audio-visuals are employed by some firms for unsupervised learning sessions. Good audiotapes and videotapes can be run as one-person training sessions. A salesperson can sit down and watch a good listing and selling videotape, pick up some new ideas and go right out and put them to work. When viewed by more than one person, these tapes can generate lively discussions.

Whatever training is offered to help salespeople expand their present jobs should be followed with careful evaluation. Management needs to know what the person has learned, how he is using it and what the next potential learning or working situation might be.

Training for Other Positions in Real Estate

Every salesperson has to spend a certain amount of time in the ups and downs and frustrations of listing, selling and performing all the other services germane to the real estate business. He certainly has to have learned how to fail and where to find courage to put one's failures behind him, start over again and learn from his failures.

It is possible to accelerate the learning process for an exceptionally good salesperson or a person who shows promise of having management talent. They are not necessarily one and the same person. But in either case, the person is going to have to work longer hours or know how to use his time most productively. He is going to get involved in more transactions and spend more time with the manager or with other better-than-average salespeople to acquire a wealth of experience and knowledge.

Experience, in the opinion of many successful managers, is really the only solid way salespeople develop the ability to make decisions necessary in the real estate business. Someone who is aiming at a management job must know how to follow the money market and changing real estate values and trends, and he must see a great deal of real estate to be able to judge market values accurately. One good way to help such a person develop is to begin to include him in the decision-making process of the firm. Invite him to sit in on discussions of problems. Encourage him to ask any question that comes to mind. Find out what his decision would be and why. Tell him what the firm's decision is and why. The two decisions often prove to be quite similar.

All this leads up to the person's growing awareness of problems, how they develop, what can be done to avoid them or how to correct them if they cannot be avoided. A good manager is not one who is always running around solving problems. He is a person who sees problems before they happen and is able to help salespeople avoid danger areas.

The emphasis again is on experience. If the broker is looking for someone for a management position, look for an individual who has had previous success in management responsibilities or who has owned a good business of his own or comes into real estate from some other responsible job. Such a person will bring a knowledge of the complexities of the decision-making process, will have a fairly accurate idea of how to evaluate right from wrong and will be better prepared to step into a management role once he becomes well acquainted with the real estate industry.

Retraining Experienced Sales Associates

Real estate management sometimes devotes time and effort on their experienced salespeople only to later lose them to a competitor or have them open their own firm in competition. This can be a difficult and discouraging fact to accept. But more frequently than not, such training and attention results in the experienced salespeople deciding to remain where they are.

When outside speakers appear before the entire staff, both new and older members benefit. Occasionally, having a private session with an outside speaker for a small number of the staff, particularly the older members and top salespeople, results in their feeling they are getting special attention. This serves to fulfill an element in their hierarchy of needs. They also learn more by being in an intimate group where their questions are answered personally and they participate in a lively exchange.

Experienced members often like to be asked to help train newer salespeople or to contribute their know-how to a special sales meeting for new salespeople. The experienced person will prepare for such a session, refresh himself with the basics he has so long taken for granted and relish the teaching experience that elicits the enthusiasm of his audience.

Training Goals

Management that instills in every staff member the belief that he has to be his very best in order to achieve self-respect and the respect of his clients and his peers will help its salespeople prosper. It is management's role to involve everyone in the continual training that builds a professional image for both the staff and the firm. Salespeople prosper in an atmosphere of respect, learning and achievement of goals.

Dr. Maxwell Maltz, in his book *Creative Living For Today*, reminds us of the important role goals play in the lives of people who live creatively. He believes that having goals, daily goals as well as those of longer range, enables a person to live each day more fully. He believes no goal too insignificant if it contributes to one's sense of achievement. No goal is small; only a person makes it small. He quotes the poet Robert Browning:

"That low man seeks a little thing to do,
Sees it and does it;
This high man, with a great thing to pursue,
Dies 'ere he knows it.
That low man goes on adding one to one,
His hundred's soon hit;
This high man, aiming at a million
Misses an unit."

No real estate manager ever hit all the training goals he set for himself and his people. It is human to miss some. But don't let failures keep you from tackling new goals optimistically. Set a new goal for each day. Train *somebody* to do a better job.

Retaining Salespeople 12

Real estate managers are continually aware of their need for a vital, aggressive selling staff. They are just as continually concerned with keeping their top producers, bolstering the efforts of their average people and doing everything they can to help any of their salespeople who are not making it.

Before a management person can deal with his need to retain salespeople, he must understand what their needs and desires are and what he should do to help satisfy them.

Here are guidelines to help management succeed in keeping the best through motivation and counseling. Clues for spotting salespeople in trouble and some suggestions for coping with a variety of situations will help management help the others and when termination seems the only answer how it can best be handled.

Retaining Salespeople

Retention of effective salespeople is a prime concern of all real estate brokers and sales managers. Some managers believe it is the chief factor in whether a company will continue to grow and improve. Consequently, a detailed, workable and ongoing retention program should be an integral part of every real estate brokerage operation.

Need for Retention Program

Recapturing company dollars invested in recruiting and training each salesperson is necessary to continue the process of building and strengthening the company. Enormous amounts of training time and money are expended on each salesperson. To have this investment walk out the door is a loss to the company and perhaps to the person.

In the first few years with a company a good salesperson will have built a clientele that produces about 50 percent of his business as personal referrals. To lose this person is to lose a significant amount of company business.

To lose qualified, productive salespeople with any degree of regularity lowers company morale and inhibits growth.

Recruiting

Retaining salespeople who are a credit to themselves and the company begins with a solid recruiting program. If it is vigorous, comprehensive and selective, the company will attract the effective sales staff it needs.

Management should be aware that they are in keen competition for the services of good salespeople not only with other real estate firms but also with all other types of business that have a product or service to sell. One needs only to read the help wanted ads to note the intense recruiting for and the attractive offers being made by business and industry to prospective salespeople. Brokers need to emphasize the unique advantages of a career in real estate sales and orient their recruiting program to specific objectives.

For example, a good self-starter in real estate sales sets no limit to what he can earn. And while he is handling properties and making a good income, he can combine the two to initiate and develop a personal investment program by buying for his own account properties he finds attractive. His good income from sales provides all or part of the capital needed. When more capital is required, his financing know-how leads him to the right sources where he will be dealing with people who already know him, another unique advantage of the wide contacts made in real estate selling. Thus, real estate sales offers two ways to reach income goals and do it faster.

Meeting Salespeople's Needs

A broker's first responsibility is to create and maintain the best possible working environment for his salespeople and then to provide the tools for getting the job done.

The working atmosphere must be positive and invigorating. No matter what else a broker may provide for his salespeople, the best working climate is one which allows them to realize their full potential in achieving personal goals and objectives. Everyone on the company team, both individually and together corporately, needs to be happy in the business and to experience a feeling of accomplishment.

Here effective management provides leadership to meet the needs of each person in all of the following areas:

Direction

Training

Policy

Opportunity

Recognition

Security

Leadership.

Direction

Before a company can expect its salespeople to understand fully what it is trying to achieve, management itself must know what it is doing and where it is going. This direction needs to be specific in terms of both short-term and long-range goals and incorporated into the company's strategic plan.

According to Peter F. Drucker, renowned management consultant and author of many books on the subject, questions should be raised continuously about corporate purpose and mission. Drucker contends that few companies have any clear idea of what their mission is. He believes this lack is one of the three significant causes of major mistakes. The other two, he says, are that managers have no feeling for what the company is really good at and what it is not good at and that they do not know how to make "people" decisions. Most of the time spent on personnel decisions, he adds, goes into selecting people at the bottom and not at the top. Drucker concludes that "the least time is spent on selecting the colonels and this is the step where you are really picking the future generals."[1]

It is neither necessary nor desirable for salespeople to know all the minute details of a company's operation or all of its plans. However, they do need to know and to be a part of some of the management objectives. This sense of participation on the part of salespeople, understanding where the company came from, where it is and where it is going, gives direction to their daily work.

Training

Firms that seem to attract the most desirable salespeople are those that provide an ongoing training program. This means training for all salespeople on a regular basis. It includes in-house training during weekly sales meetings, special training seminars and outside professional courses. Basics of the real estate business cannot be covered too often. With continuous learning, the likelihood of a slump is lessened and a sense of confidence that comes with new or renewed knowledge will be increased.

John Wooden, U.C.L.A. basketball coach for many years, is considered by many to be the best all-time coach of the game. His record of coaching teams to the national championship will be difficult to equal. He is the only man ever to be inducted into the Basketball Hall of Fame both as a player and a coach. Wooden emphasizes the value of attention to the smallest details and the repetition of the fundamentals of the game. He says, "If you keep too busy learning the tricks of the trade, you never learn the trade."

In his book, *They Call Me Coach*, Wooden states:

"One of the little things I watch closely is a player's socks. No basketball player is better than his feet. If they hurt, if his socks don't fit or if he has blisters, he can't play the game. It is amazing how few players know how to put on a pair of socks properly. I don't want blisters. So each year I give in minute detail a step by step demonstration as to precisely how I want my players to put on their socks— every time. Believe it or not, there's an art to doing it right and it makes a big difference in the way a player's feet stand the pounding of practice and the game. Wrinkles which cause blisters can be eliminated by just a little attention."[2]

When was the last time every salesperson in your office recited verbatim his listing dialogue on discount points, his basic monologue on overcoming various buyer/seller objections, or his basic expired listing or for-sale-by-owner presentation?

Policy

The establishment of an official, understandable policy is absolutely essential for every office. A clear, firm, simple operations manual that covers situations that arise in the course of daily business can prevent or solve most misunderstandings and disputes. Some of the topics that should be in writing, assembled in a operations manual include commission schedules, advertising, open houses, phone duty, arbitration; it covers any aspect of the real estate business that is basic to its success.

Opportunity

Another vital aspect of retention in terms of meeting salespeople's needs is to establish procedures whereby each person knows he has the opportunity to grow. Specifically this means the absence of restrictive policies that could inhibit an individual's earning capacity. It can also mean making him aware of the opportunity to move into a new job such as branch manager or sales manager.

While these positions are often viewed as promotions it should also be recognized that an outstanding salesperson frequently can out-earn an individual at the management level and an extremely successful salesperson will not necessarily make a good sales manager. The success ingredients for each are different. However, if a salesperson's skills and desires lead him toward management, he needs to know that opportunities exist for him through expansion and/or diversification.

How does a small firm accomplish this?

When a manager has a well-trained, aggressive selling staff he finds more time to concentrate on developing a stronger or growth image. He looks for good merger and acquisition opportunities with like-minded real estate firms; or he expands into new marketing areas; or plans diversification into such areas as property management or commercial-investment sales.

He communicates to the sales staff that management and other opportunities are available to persons who can demonstrate ability and who are growth and company oriented.

Recognition

A sensitive manager understands that his salespeople have a basic human need to be recognized through expressions of appreciation and praise for a job well done. When a manager does this, he is taking a big step toward attracting and holding good salespeople. Aside from the professional recognition earned, each of us needs to be recognized for just being there, for being a person of intrinsic worth. How can this be accomplished in a real estate sales office?

Ring an "Action" bell every time a listing or sale is made.

Build a "Sales Column." This can be done on a corkboard. Pin a 3"×5" card with a salesperson's name, amount of listing or sale, name of property and watch the column grow. Some months it may reach a couple feet in length. And when it doesn't, its lack of growth serves as a reminder of action needed!

Sponsor a Residential Sales Council™ course for the top lister of your employee salespeople.

Include data on every listing and sale as a regular feature of the office newsletter, even if it's only a one-pager.

Award a company pin to each salesperson who reaches a target listing or dollar figure.

Explore and use every kind of personal publicity acceptable in your local newspaper: Salesperson of the Month; Million Dollar Listing and Sales for the Year; news of promotions; attendance at REALTORS NATIONAL MARKETING INSTITUTE® or NATIONAL ASSOCIATION OF REALTORS® courses and/or conferences. Publicity possibilities are limited only by your imagination and the type of news used by the local editor.

If you decide to conduct contests, set them up so there are lots of winners. Make contests of short duration so enthusiasm remains at a good level and so you can schedule several contests every year.

A broker tells how the combined merit of training and recognition elicited unexpected results. In a "Salesperson of the Month" recognition award, one of the firm's top salespeople won, as expected. But the next month, a new licensee, only six months into a career, followed everything she had learned in the training sessions and topped the whole sales staff!

Formal recognition programs should include everyone. After all, it is from their ranks that future managers and superstars emerge. The firm will benefit from recognizing and encouraging them. Just as the superstars in any field of human activity need recognition for stellar performances, the average salesperson, who represents the majority in most offices, needs to be recognized and encouraged for his accomplishments.

Security

For most people, security means money; and money can be earned by motivated, well-trained, knowledgeable real estate salespeople. Management provides the security by providing an adequate, competitive commission schedule that is fair and consistent for all the parties involved and training opportunities.

Beyond this, a salesperson must feel that his opportunities to earn money are at least as good and probably better with your firm than with any other. These feelings of security result from many factors.

Reputation

The company either has or is building a good reputation in the community. Salespeople need to be constantly aware that the client's interests are being served; that misunderstandings or problems with either buyers or sellers are resolved quickly. These concerns lead to a good image for the company in any community. On the other hand, when a company's relationships with its clients are not good, it is difficult for that firm to hold good salespeople. Because it is easy for salespeople to reaffiliate with a different firm, one cannot afford to have his firm's reputation hurt.

Sales Program

The company must have a listing and selling program that augments and supports the salesperson's individual efforts. Such a program can include a client referral service, a client follow-up service, consistent advertising programs, recruiting and training programs and a genuine concern for filling the client's needs.

Leadership

While this subject is covered in Chapter 4, certain points should be stressed again.

A crucial cause of losing good salespeople is weak management. Without strong leadership, salespeople experience a free-floating anxiety because, consciously or unconsciously, they look to their broker or manager for inspiration and guidance. He must be the person who knows what the company is doing, where it is going and how it is getting there. A manager sets the pace.

From the salesperson's point of view, effective leadership means that work is done properly, decisions are made when they are needed and company morale is high. When these leadership factors are operating daily, the broker will discover he is able to give more time and attention to planning and executing both short- and long-term company objectives; the salesperson will discover he can devote his time to productive listing and selling.

Motivation

Another important element of retention is motivation. It is important to the success of management and every member of the sales staff. Webster defines motive as "an emotion or desire operating on the will and causing it to act." That is why brokers and salespeople continually search for methods, techniques and programs to keep the staff's motivation level high. The many factors involved in successful listing and selling are well known and can be studied, learned and implemented. But the actual sales production of each individual is a matter of personal motivation. It is in fact the individual's motivation that determines how well he learns required skills. And once those skills are learned, the motivation level of the person determines whether or not he will use the skills he has acquired.

If it is sustained and consistent, authentic motivation comes from within. Motivation is a logical, emotional outgrowth of a self-directed person's attitudes and experiences. External stimuli such as pep talks, sales seminars and motivational sessions can be helpful but they do not get the day-to-day job done. There is an important place for motivational sessions but they provide only temporary modifications in personal behavior or work performance rather than preparing a person to work effectively and enthusiastically over the long-term. This is one reason why in the recruiting process careful screening of individuals is so important. It should separate and eliminate the easily discouraged individuals from the persistent ones who keep going despite the countless hurdles or difficulties they encounter.

The skilled manager will know his people so well and be so aware of their changing needs that he can sense what the next steps in motivation should be. Continued study in motivation is needed.

A leader's understanding of the motivational needs of the individuals in his group and the overall needs of the group as a business-oriented team can be achieved by

Putting his own motivation in proper perspective so as not to tune out his team

Letting everyone know the reality of any given situation

Providing the atmosphere of open communication necessary for each to evaluate his point of view in respect to those of the group as a whole and those of management (this technique allows for a change in position in the light of feedback without a feeling of compromise or frustration) and recognizing that people can change their habits.

The basic motivational process, individual in nature, must be planned and sustained. It must be communicated so ably that it becomes something the individual discovers and does for himself rather than something that is done to him. Then, motivation becomes an inner drive that causes a person to move toward a goal.

A leader knows that motivation, like growth, is inherent in people. His task is not so much motivating others as it is releasing the potential that is already there and directing it to produce desired results.

Dr. Maxwell Maltz, in *Psycho-Cybernetics*,[3] discusses self-image psychology and its relationship to successful achievement. In Maltz' opinion, a person's self-image is important because it defines the limits within which he will work most effectively to achieve his objectives. If one's self-image can be improved, the number and type of his successes can be increased.

Webster defines success as "the satisfactory accomplishment of a goal sought for." Therefore, two factors that a person must possess can be clearly defined: realistic goals and a self-image that makes their attainment possible. Nebulous or inconsistent goals and/or a low self-image would most likely lead to failure. The power of positive thinking can work with some people but not with others. It is effective only when it is consistent with an individual's positive self-image.

Therein lies the challenge of self-image modification: changing and strengthening it with information that is experienced and absorbed. The salesperson experiences by responding actively to new information. Rather than accepting information passively, his whole person is involved. He is dynamic. He comes alive.

Management has a responsibility to assist the salesperson by providing possible success experiences. When this is done, the motivational process becomes so much a part of that person that it is expressed through successful activity. How is this achieved?

Goals

Formal goal setting is an important part of the process. First, the individual, working in private, should set down in writing his precise goals as they relate to real estate. Then these goals should be shared with and reviewed with his broker or manager. A person's goals should be the basis for regular counseling sessions.

The individual's goals should include more than real estate production. While the latter will be dominant in his work, they are only part of his whole range of personal goals: family, social, physical, mental, spiritual. All will bear on his life style as well as his business performance. The broker should be aware of them because they will contribute to his understanding of the salesperson and help him deal with the person's goals as they relate to business performance.

As the individual participates in such a goal-setting session with his broker he is competing with no one else; he is being evaluated by himself. He is being measured by goals he has set and which he believes are attainable.

Many salespeople are reluctant to set business goals. This feeling reflects a fear that failure to attain them will result in ridicule from their peers. When goal setting is a strictly private matter between broker and salesperson, no one but the broker need know if a salesperson doesn't attain his goal.

To be effective, a goal should be

Attainable

Measurable

For a definite time period

In writing.

Attainable Goals

Goals should be realistic. It is folly to set a goal to make $200,000 in one year if the best salesperson in the area has never made more than $100,000 in a similar period. It is just as impossible to set a goal of 50 exclusive listings a month if that figure is more than the total number of listings available in your area in a single month.

Goals should be neither too easy nor too difficult. If the best salesperson in your firm has enjoyed an income of $50,000 per year, a realistic increase to $60,000 might be the new goal.

Goals should be flexible. They should realistically anticipate changes in the market which are almost certain to occur in any 12-month period. A new subdivision may open up unexpected markets or a downturn in the economy could result in a tight money market. Be ready to show your salespeople how to include flexibility in setting their goals.

Goals should include every phase of the business. For example a salesperson shouldn't bypass efforts to increase listings in established neighborhoods as he focuses his whole effort on selling lots in a new subdivision. Show him the value of increasing volume in every service your firm provides.

Measurable Goals

Explain why "more" or "increase" are not goal-setting words. To be measurable, a goal must be specific. If a salesperson sets his goal at 60 exclusives in a calendar year, the goal is measurable. If on the other hand, he says he wants to "increase his listings over the 50 he got last year," a total of 52 could mean success to him. But he might have gotten 65 if that had been his established, measurable goal. Thus, the target should be definite, measurable and realistic.

Show the salesperson how to break down his goals into definite time periods. Make sure he takes into consideration seasonal fluctuations in real estate activity in your market, setting higher goals in the most active months, lower when business is slow. The practical exercise of working out monthly breakdowns on various business goals make them easier to measure and also serve to remind a salesperson how much time has passed and how much more intense his efforts need to be. A sub-set of goals must be set which describe the specific tasks to be accomplished to meet the overall goal.

Time Limit on Goals

The frequency of measuring progress toward established goals rests with management. Real estate people who have used this technique for years believe reviews should be scheduled every three months for a one-year objective, every year for three-year goals and every two years for ten-year goals.

One-year goals are the most common and surely most important. They are also the most easily measured and easiest to structure. Many firms establish longer-range goals of three, five or ten years. The unpredictability of the economy, the times and the variables of today's transient society make long-range goals for individual salespeople more difficult to establish. But they are extremely important for top management.

Whatever the outcome, goals should not be put aside. It has been a tradition in too many real estate offices that when goals are missed, the program is dropped. This is an evidence of management's weakness and is not the salesperson's fault. If the sales staff is missing goals there are two likely reasons: they weren't practical in the first place and the review should have been scheduled at more frequent intervals. Find out why goals were set too high and study the results to discover where the weaknesses are. Spend some time on your own determining how to solve the problem, then spend time with the salesperson involved, discussing what went wrong and why. Work together to find the solution. Set new goals immediately.

Written Goals

Putting goals in writing is important for two reasons: they will be more specific than in the case of conversational goals and they avoid misunderstanding and misinterpretation common to oral communication. The speaker means one thing, the listener is hearing with his own and perhaps quite different needs to be fulfilled. Seldom, if ever, is oral communication on this level accurate. Unless written, goals can be forgotten or may be rationalized or postponed to a later date. Written goals are a stronger motivating factor for a salesperson and are a factual basis for management to present when it comes time to review the salesperson's progress with him.

What should be put in writing? A number of progressive real estate businesses today ask their salespeople to set goals in three areas:

Income—dollars, sales, listings

Personal—house, car, service to community

Professional—schooling, books, organizations.

Fig. 1 Production targets

Salesperson_____ Office_____

19___Income target_____19___Income earned (projected)_____

Requirements to achieve income target

	Income	Units	Leads	Appts
Sales	_____	_____	_____	_____
Listings sold	_____	_____	_____	_____
Other	_____	_____		

Vacation Planned for 19

(Planned dates)

Income

The salesperson states how much money he wants to earn. Next, averaging the past performance of the office, he determines accurately the number of listings and sales needed to reach his income goal. Figs. 1 and 2 show how individual salespeople set their income goals.

Personal

One salesperson may have a new, larger home as his goal; another may want a dreamed-of vacation for his family. To a real estate person a new car could be both a personal and a business goal because it is essential equipment for the job. Service to the community might be wholly personal (at least seem to be) like working with Girl Scouts, being a park district or library trustee; or it could be quasi-business related like being active in the Chamber of Commerce or serving on an area planning commission. Realistically, any community activity of a real estate person can lead to improving his business even though business had no bearing on his desire to participate in that organization.

Professional

Professional goals will add substance to income and personal goals. In setting professional goals, a salesperson can examine the opportunities available to increase his knowledge and skills in the real estate business.

At the very least, the firm should help salespeople who want to expand their real estate knowledge and professional skill. Participation in Residential Sales Council™ courses can enable salespeople to win specific professional designations and certification of professional competence that adds to their prestige in the peer group and business community as well as bringing them personal satisfaction.

It is extremely important the broker himself is motivated and that he set a good example. Also, the more the top salespeople are motivated and the better they perform, the more the average salespeople will improve. It has been stated earlier that motivation can be increased and sustained through a reward and recognition system. It is also important, as indicated earlier, that the opportunity for advancement exists within the company. But because the goal process and self-image development program is continuous there must always be opportunities for continuing education both within and outside the company.

Counseling

Counseling the individual salesperson is a logical and integral part of the retention program. A former sports editor once wrote that "the coach who can get most out of his athletes, who can understand their psychological makeup and motivate them to achieve their goals, is the one who will succeed, given the proper talent."

Top Producers

Counseling needs to be provided on a regular basis for the exceptionally talented person as well as for the average one. Productive people appreciate being told what a significant role they play in the growth

Fig. 2 Production targets (cont.)

Salesperson _____ Office _____

19___ Income target _____

Required target income first quarter _____

First Quarter Projections

	Target			**Actual**			
	Units	Leads	Appts.	Units	Leads	Appts.	Earnings
January:							
Sales	—	—	—	—	—	—	—
Exclusives	—	—	—	—	—	—	
February:							
Sales	—	—	—	—	—	—	—
Exclusives	—	—	—	—	—	—	
March:							
Sales	—	—	—	—	—	—	—
Exclusives	—	—	—	—	—	—	

Review of First Quarter

	Projected units	Actual units	Projected leads	Actual leads	Projected appts.	Actual appts.
Sales	—	—	—	—	—	—
Exclusives		—		—		—

of the company. Successes can be highlighted and shared with the whole staff. Management sometimes takes it for granted that these people are motivated, happy and pleased with their work and with the company. This may or may not be true. But if these assumptions are false, the great risk exists that they may leave the company with little or no notice and often for some trifling reason that could have been prevented. Counseling for these people should be scheduled at various earning levels. For example, you could ask your bookkeeper to notify you when a salesperson's commission reaches a certain dollar figure above his past achievement.

Counseling sessions with top producers can and should determine if there are unique reasons for their success or if any problem areas exist in which management might be of help. Constructive evaluation should be sought. If the productive people feel some aspect of the business operation is in need of attention, be it company procedures or individual situations, their feelings are a much better guide for management action than the run of the mill complaints of non-producers.

Average Salespeople

While the earning plateau is a good scheduling method for counseling top producers, a regularly scheduled method of goal review is more appropriate for the average salesperson. A quarterly review is usually considered best. Frequency of a review should be governed by the company's individual situation. While these reviews should be similar to those of top producers, specific attention needs to be paid to performance, work habits and the production goal the salesperson has set for himself. It is less important to cover company policies and objectives, except as they are influenced by the salesperson's performance. Management difficulties can be avoided if counseling takes place before a salesperson gets into trouble.

The manager needs to determine what he can do to help the salesperson with his problems (whether stated or unstated) and, more important, what the salesperson should be doing for himself. The latter's current methods should be reviewed and his listing and sales procedures should be discussed. Together, manager and salesperson should review the reasons why some transactions succeeded and others failed. The salesperson probably has the answers but they may be ill-defined or exaggerated. It is up to the manager to help him clarify his performance profile so he can arrive at the proper conclusions himself.

After a counseling session, the salesperson should know more clearly what he is trying to accomplish and just how the company is trying to help him do it. Equally important, he will have received renewed affirmation of his value as an individual and his importance to the firm.

Salespeople in Trouble

When salespeople run into trouble there are a host of possible causes and some valuable clues. These may include the salesperson's

Being inflexible

Fighting change or clinging to the status quo

Lacking imagination/creativity

Becoming defensive

Having personal problems

Lacking team spirit

Growing lazy or possible poor health

Being unwilling to take a risk

Being unwilling to recognize value of planning and goal setting

Being disorganized

Passing the buck.

In the real estate business, productivity should almost always increase because it builds on an expanding base of referrals from past clients. Thus, a slump is easily spotted by a falling off or leveling off of production. Whatever the cause, obvious or hidden, the effect usually shows up fairly soon in poor performance. It is important to detect the trend and do something about it before it becomes a serious problem to both the salesperson and to management. Every salesperson has a production level at which he is happiest, most comfortable and most productive for the company. Evidence of a change indicates a need for a counseling session.

Counseling calls for the best communications skills management can muster. A counseling session should be arranged for a time and place where the manager and the salesperson can sit down quietly, free of interruption, to converse freely. The manager should come to the session prepared with the facts and figures that led him to know a problem threatens or already exists.

The manager should be prepared to deal with differences in perception of the situation. It is natural that the salesperson may enter such a discussion with an air of suspicion, a degree of resentment or a feeling of considerable discouragement regarding his ability to succeed in real estate selling. If it is suspicion, the manager will need to put him at his ease; if resentment, the manager will be prepared with facts and perhaps employee the "mirror" technique to let the salesperson tell his story his way; if it's a discouraged person who settles down for the conversation he'll help that salesperson focus on some of the things he's done right and help him find methods to add to his total of successful efforts. But above all, the manager will listen with both eyes and ears. Understanding body language can be a great aid to management in counseling work. And when the non-verbal message disagrees with what the person is saying, ask him to explain what he's just told you because it's not really clear to you yet. You may find that the fault lies in the way you phrased a question; that the information you are getting may be what the salesperson thinks you asked for but it isn't really what you wanted to learn from him.

Once the point has been made that a problem exists, the manager must get to the root of it. This can take time. But it usually results in the manager and the salesperson arriving at a mutually satisfying solution. It might mean some added training or a refresher course in some aspect of real estate sales the person is uncomfortable with. Occasionally it means suggesting the salesperson get away for a complete change for a few days and come back refreshed in mind and spirit. Whatever the outcome, bear in mind that the person in trouble needs reaffirmation of his value, his potential in the firm just as much as, and perhaps more than, the top producers. In his case it will take the form of encouragement rather than outright praise.

New Salespeople

New salespeople should receive counseling similar in some ways to those in a slump. Consideration must be given the details of their work habits and daily activity. Wayne C. Dawson, in an article on new salespeople, wrote, "A recruit accustomed to direction will frequently fail, despite training, if firm day-to-day direction is not imposed. Business executives agree the total worth of a company can be established by the effectiveness of good management. Most aspiring salespeople want to be managed—tactfully. How else can they learn successful habits?"[5]

Thus, concern for the individual, attention to detail and a positive sense of direction begins in the formative stages of the company/salesperson relationship. This is when the foundation for all further counseling is established.

Termination

Terminating a salesperson is never easy. There is no rule book to follow in deciding exactly when and why this step must be taken. Nor is it easy to pinpoint the exact time a manager decides it is simply not possible to motivate a certain salesperson sufficiently to continue the relationship.

No matter how personable he is, how much "fun" he might be, a non-producer takes up valuable desk space, spends company dollars, sets a bad example and lowers the morale of the entire office.

Some of the root causes of failure on the part of salespeople are the inability to acquire needed skills, lack of determination or lack of emotional resources necessary to succeed in the real estate business. When management comes to this determination, the only course of action is termination.

Even when termination is accepted as the only answer it involves trauma for both the salesperson and the firm. No one likes to fail and start over in another life phase. No one likes to admit that he chose the wrong person or the wrong firm. But once the decision is made and management has admitted its mistake, it is time to act.

Deep as his trauma may be at the time, experience has proved that termination brings a genuine sense of relief to the salesperson. In most cases he has been aware (even if only in a vague way) that he has been frustrated and has not been carrying his share of the work. Such a person will seldom leave of his own accord because he does not know what else to do or how to go about making a change for the better. When a strong manager clarifies the issue and forces the decision, he enables the salesperson to do something for himself by finding work to which he is better suited and in which he will be happier. This resolute and sometimes face-saving process serves the best interests of the salesperson and the company.

There will also be times when the salesperson decides he wants to terminate the relationship. It may be for what appear to be inadequate reasons. He may have a burning desire to see his name on the door, to see it in lights and on a letterhead. In short, this person thinks it's time to go into business for himself.

When this happens, wise management will wish him well. Not only has this person been an important part in the success and growth of the firm but his proposed new role will place him in a position to become a valuable colleague in the business. If you try to hold him back, he may leave anyway to be an unhappy or difficult competitor. The maintenance of a continuing good relationship is always the wiser course. It can be mutually rewarding. And who knows, the day may come when that former salesperson will decide he'd like to return to your company or suggest a merger of two very successful operations, his and yours.

Understanding
In today's complex society, many salespeople tend to feel business relationships are temporary and that they must really go it alone. Management's challenge in meeting this personality need is to so understand its people that they convey a feeling of security, a positive sense of direction and a favorable working climate in which everyone can grow. Leaders in management must demonstrate their concern for people by helping them work as mature, responsible adults in a self-fulfilling service industry.

Obviously such things as adequate and attractive facilities, an efficient office staff, sales training and educational programs and complete listing and sales services are essential. Important as these ingredients of the real estate business are, full cooperation and a genuine appreciation of each other's goals are also necessary. When all these are provided, each person can work in his own way to achieve his full potential.

[1] Drucker, "A New Compendium for Management," *Business Week*, February 9, 1974, pp. 48-58.

[2] Wooden, *They Call Me Coach*

[3] Maltz, *Psycho-Cybernetics*

[4] Burns, "Psychologist in the Lineup," *Human Behavior*, June 1973, p. 8.

[5] Dawson, "New Salesman: Handle with Care," *real estate today*, October 1973, p. 31.

Financial Systems and Records   13

Even the smallest real estate office needs to have a method of cost control. By establishing a budget and a matching system of cost accounting, brokers can know at a glance whether or not they are running a profitable operation.

This chapter deals with basic accounting methods, guides you through the important business of determining costs accurately, shows you how to analyze your income dollar and how to reflect these last two factors in an operating statement. There are details on analyzing desk costs for any size operation and how to compute the other costs of running a real estate brokerage business.

Charts and other data shown here can be copied for your own use or adapted in whatever way seems to fit your business best.

Financial Systems and Records

The typical neophyte broker generally has a salesperson's approach to problems and is often prone to overlook his need for a good accounting system. He may operate with only a checkbook (it is hoped he at least watches his cash balance) until it comes time to prepare his income tax returns. His tax service will inform him that his increase or decrease in cash is probably not the same as his taxable income. Since he has purchased equipment, perhaps an office building, etc., he has spent a lot of cash that is not deductible as an expense but must be capitalized and expensed out gradually (depreciated or amortized) as the assets lose their value.

The broker soon learns he must have an accounting system for two main reasons: various income tax reports and good managerial control.

While his business is small, the owner-manager needs only a simple bookkeeping system. He is making all the decisions himself and can adjust rapidly to new conditions. Few, if any, reports are required since he can observe most variables in the making. It often suffices for the small broker to use generalized expense and income accounts wherein he will use as few as 10 accounts to trace his income and expense. However, the beginning broker would be wise to get some help in originating his accounting system so it can expand and become more sophisticated as he grows without starting over on a new system. Aside from the extra cost involved, switching systems causes him to lose the direct comparative value of his past data.

As the broker's business grows, he must delegate authority. Now he must be able to control expenses on which he is not making all the decisions. Each link in his chain of command represents a span of control. Having the proper accounting records gives management the tools it needs to evaluate each span of control—such as each branch office, etc.

Balance Sheet
The balance sheet is really a report of financial condition of an enterprise as of a specific date. Oversimplified, your financial position is made up of all your valuable possessions (assets) offset by your debts (liabilities). The difference between your assets (more technically, your net book assets) and your debts is your amount of net worth or equity. Since assets are generally maintained at net book value (cost less depreciation to date) instead of current market value, the statement of position is accurate for tax reporting purposes but not for an absolutely true financial position. The real value of an operating company is not its net worth but the current value of its probable future earning power (liquidation value sometimes must be considered).

Balance Sheet Relationships

When financial people look at balance sheets, they often note three common relationships.

The first common relationship is current ratio. This is the arithmetic ratio of total current assets to total current liabilities. For example, if a firm's net current assets (current assets are assets readily converted to cash, such as marketable securities) are $50,000 and its short-term debts are $25,000, then it has a current ratio of two to one.

The second common relationship would be working capital. In this case, $50,000 less $25,000 equals $25,000, total current assets less total current liabilities.

The third common relationship is equity ratio. If this company had total assets of $100,000 with total liabilities of $45,000, the equity ratio is $100,000 less $45,000, equalling $55,000 equity or 55 percent equity ratio.

Income Statement

The income statement, sometimes called a profit and loss (P&L) statement or operating statement, portrays the ongoing operation of the company in terms of dollars for a specific period. The income statement must reflect total sales commissions and revenue by each principal division of the company.

The expenses should reflect both operating and non-operating expenses. Operating expenses are those costs necessary for the operation of the business. Non-operating expenses are costs that are not due to the actual operation of the company (i.e. interest and debt and/or income taxes).

Net Income

Net income may be defined as the earnings which management has produced during a specified period for all those who have invested capital in the enterprise. It might also be described as being made up of revenues, a positive factor, minus negatives which are expenses, deductible losses and income taxes. Do not be confused because the word cash has not been used. Cash often has little or nothing to do with the calculation of net income, especially on accrual systems or on any enterprise that owns non-liquid assets.

Net income is the income remaining after all expenses have been paid. The income after deducting only operational expenses (does not include interest and taxes) is called Earnings Before Interest and Taxes (EBIT).

Example: Gross Revenue
    − Operational Expenses
    = Earnings Before Interest and Taxes (EBIT)
    − Interest
    = Earnings Before Taxes (EBT)
    − Taxes
    = Net Income

EBIT measures the business decisions and the efficiency of operation with which the company functioned. If EBIT is a negative number, the operation has produced a loss. If EBIT equals "0," the company has broken even. If EBIT is a positive number, the company has made a profit from operations.

Expense vs. Cost

It is typical for business people to misuse the term expense when they talk of the expense of buying equipment or buildings. Buying buildings or equipment is a cost for an asset. The depreciation of those assets is an expense. Costs of making or buying assets are not expenses; they are "costs of" the assets acquired. Expense means that you have given up something of value to obtain revenue.

Gross revenue or gross income is the total dollars that a firm takes in from all available sources. Gross revenue is 100 percent of the income to the company. Expenses will represent a percentage of gross revenue. If gross revenue is $1 million and commissions paid to salespeople is $530,000, then 53 percent of gross revenue is commissions paid to salespeople. If $80,000 is spent on advertising, then advertising expense is eight percent of gross revenue.

A typical example of a properly structured income statement is seen in the following example:

Expenditures from Gross Revenue

Commissions and fees comprise the single largest category of expenditure from gross revenue. These expenses take more than one-half the gross income, regardless of company's size or type of operation.

The owner/broker should distribute to himself listing and sales splits the same way he does to regular salespeople. Personal income from managerial duties should appear in summary value of the service provided.

Following are other major expenditures from gross revenue.

Advertising. Every year brokers spend millions of dollars advertising the properties they have listed for sale. In addition, they spend a considerable number of dollars on institutional advertising to promote the services offered by their companies.

Selling Expenses. In addition to advertising there are other expenses tied directly to selling, such as "for sale" signs.

Sales Management. This area is becoming an ever more important part of the real estate industry. Manager compensation can vary greatly. Some managers are paid a stringent salary; others are paid straight commission; still others are paid a combination of salary and commission.

Salaries. The real estate industry is using more and more personnel to work on a salary basis. Typical employees include secretaries and bookkeepers.

Communication. Sophisticated telephone equipment is having an impact on expenses in today's real estate business. Brokers should research different long distance telephone companies to find the best services and price for their businesses. Included in these expenses are car phones, answering devices and services.

Occupancy. Payment for office space includes rent, utilities, janitorial services and maintenance. Rent should reflect what the occu-

Fig. 1. Gross revenue chart

Definition: All income received by company

*EBIT = Eearnings Before Interest and Taxes. EBIT is referred to as "bottom line" or profit from operations.

pied space would cost on the open market. Where there is an ownership interest in the building occupied, accounting records should be separated to delete ownership applications and loan retirement items and show only what should be paid as a typical tenant. (Otherwise, profit/loss as part owners of the building would be comingled with the profit/loss of the brokerage business.)

Other Operating Expenses. Other operating expenses include insurance, license, dues, legal and accounting fees, taxes (other than income), equipment, supplies, postage, bad debts, auto expenses and miscellaneous office expenses.

Depreciation. Most owners account for depreciation in the income statement. It is the used-up portion of an asset that must be accounted for to guarantee proper entry for replacement.

Accrual vs. Cash Basis Accounting
The cash basis of accounting means that revenue is acknowledged when cash (or something of value) is actually received. Expenses are recognized only in amounts for which cash has been paid. The cash basis is normally used for small businesses because the accounting is simple and less costly. Current income taxes can be saved if all expenses are paid as incurred. When large receivables and payables are accumulated, the profit or loss picture can be greatly distorted through cash basis accounting.

The accrual basis accounting dictates that one accrues revenue

Fig. 2. Income Statement
CRB Realty, Inc.
Year End (December 31)

Revenue	1988
In-house Transactions	$1,042,574
Other Co. Sale/CRB List	533,784
Other Co. List/CRB Sale	533,784
Co-op Transactions	1,067,568
Gross Revenue	$2,110,142
Operating Expenses	
Franchise Fee	105,507
Sales Commissions	1,002,317
Bonus Commissions	17,446
Advertising	168,811
Selling Expenses	42,203
Sales Management	105,489
Salaries	167,767
Communication	63,293
Occupancy	126,587
Other Operating Expense	142,065
Depreciation Expense	15,800
Total Expenses	1,957,285
Net Operating Income (EBIT)	$ 152,857
Interest Expense	3,210
Earnings Before Taxes (EBT)	$ 149,647
Income Taxes	49,088
Net Income	$ 100,559
Common Stock Dividends	100,000
Addition to Retained Earnings	559

Fig. 3. Profit and Loss Analysis of Company Operation

I. Gross Revenue (from sales and listing fees)
   1. In-house transactions $ _____
   2. Other company sales/your company listing $ _____
   3. Other company list/your company sales $ _____
   4. Co-op transactions $ _____
   5. Gross revenue (lines 1-4) $ _____

Expense Analysis
Operating Expenses

II. Commissions and Fees
   6. Internal sales staff commissions (including
      bonuses) $ _____
   7. Owner's listing fees and sales commissions $ _____
   8. Cooperating broker's commissions $ _____
   9. Franchise fee $ _____
  10. Total commissions and fees (lines 6-9) $ _____

III. Advertising
  11. Newspaper classifieds $ _____
  12. Institutional $ _____
  13. Direct mail and brochures $ _____
  14. Radio $ _____
  15. Television $ _____
  16. Yellow Pages $ _____
  17. Other $ _____
  18. Total advertising (lines 11-17) $ _____

IV. Sales promotion:
  19. Courses, training and conferences $ _____
  20. Travel and conventions $ _____
  21. Entertainment $ _____
  22. Contributions, service activities (including service
      clubs) $ _____
  23. Sales awards, contests, testimonials $ _____
  24. Institutional gifts to clients and prospects $ _____
  25. Other $ _____
  26. Total sales promotion (lines 19-25) $ _____

V. Sales management:
  27. Sales managers salaries and/or fees (if you are the
      owner and also operate as the sales manager do
      not fill in) $ _____

VI. Salaries (do not include owners salaries here):
  28. Managers (other than sales) $ _____
  29. Clerical $ _____
  30. Secretarial $ _____
  31. Other staff $ _____
  32. Payroll taxes $ _____
  33. Employee benefits (include hospitalization, profit
      sharing, etc.) $ _____
  34. Total salaries (lines 28-33) $ _____

VII. Communications:
  35. Total telephone (including equipment and calls—
      excluding yellow pages) $ _____
  36. Answering service $ _____
  37. Other $ _____
  38. Total communications (lines 35-37) $ _____

VIII. Occupancy:
  39. Rent (see instructions) $ _____
  40. Utilities $ _____
  41. Janitor services and maintenance
  42. Total occupancy (lines 39-41) $ _____

Profit and Loss Analysis of Company Operation (continued)

IX. Operating:

43. Licenses (real estate, notary, etc.) $ _____
44. Dues (local, state and national real estate associations, chamber of commerce, professional societies) $ _____
45. Insurance (liability, error and omission, workmen's compensation) $ _____
46. Legal and accounting $ _____
47. Taxes (except payroll, state and federal income and company owned building) $ _____
48. Equipment (depreciation, repair and/or rental) $ _____
49. Supplies, printing, maps, plats and photography $ _____
50. Postage $ _____
51. Interest on business loans (not that included as economic rent on building) $ _____
52. Bad debts (including losses on advances to salespeople) $ _____
53. Auto expense $ _____
54. Other $ _____
55. Total operating (lines 43-54) $ _____
56. Total expenses (parts III-IX) $ _____

X. Summary:

57. Total operating expenses (lines 18, 26, 27, 34, 38, 42, 55) $ _____
58. EBIT (Subtract line 56 from line 5) $ _____
59. Interest expense $ _____
60. EBIT (Earnings Before Taxes) (Subtract line 58 from line 57) $ _____
61. Taxes $ _____
62. Net Income (Subtract line 60 from line 59) $ _____

when the service is rendered or the sale is made. The time of collecting the cash proceeds or commission from the sale has no direct bearing on the timing or the amount of the revenue. To keep the accrual system as realistic as possible, a reserve could be established for lost sales if past experience warranted it. Expenses are recognized in the same manner, when they are incurred or become payable, and not when cash is paid for them. The accrual method allows us to match expenses with revenues in the proper period thereby portraying a truer profit or loss position. Be careful of trying to get the best of two worlds wherein you report revenue only on a cash basis (when the sale is closed) but accrue your expenses and charge them out, although not paid, at the end of the accounting period. The Internal Revenue Service will normally demand that you consistently stay on an accrual basis. All external expenses and revenues are funneled through your receivable and payable accounts when you employ pure accrual accounting. However, many firms operate as if on a cash basis until the end of the accounting period, at which time all expenses and revenue are adjusted to the accrual basis. With the proper procedures established, accounting time can be save through the adjusted accrual method without distorting the interim statements.

It is best to seek professional tax assistance before deciding which method to follow.

Avoiding Fraud

Brokerage owners must always presume that embezzlement could happen to them. As previously mentioned, signing all checks can help prevent embezzlement but the following steps are also recommended.

Full audits with interim unannounced reviews should be conducted by outside sources such as an independent CPA firm.

All bank statements and cancelled checks should be returned to the owners, not to the person in control of accounting and not to the person who balances out the checking account each month. Each statement, together with the cancelled checks, must be examined monthly when received by the owner (they should at least appear as if they had been examined carefully). Occasional calls on checks help support the fact that the owners are looking at every check. This simple procedure alone will probably do more than any other to prevent embezzlement.

Different people should handle the deposits and checks with a tie-in between deposits and checks. Checks should not be made to pay out commissions unless there is evidence of a commission deposit having been made for the company on that transaction.

Two people should sign checks and two other people should handle bank deposits.

Ratio of commission payout to company dollar should be watched. If there is a change in ratio, the owners may have a problem.

Be sure check protection systems prevent digits being added without it being obvious. For example, leaving space behind the figures and wording on a check could make it easy to change $100.00 to $100,000.

Budgetary Control

To run a business successfully, management must be able to plan, coordinate and control its business operation. A budget is a financial formula to operate within for a future period. To exercise the proper control, management must make continuous reviews and comparisons to the budget so that undesirable variances can be noted and corrective action taken.

Steps in Preparing a Budget

Top management must review their medium-range plans (two to four years), note how well they progressed toward those plans last year and what must be done in the coming year to keep on the planning track. If last year's performance together with this year's progress cannot meet the middle range goals, the middle range and perhaps the long-range goals should be re-evaluated.

Assuming top management has decided what must be done to reach their objectives, they should now call in the various people responsible for attaining these objectives and have them work up their own budgets (with a minimum of direction from top management). Often top management can subtly influence middle or lower management to project a budget for both sales and expenses just about in line with what they want. It is important that the budget be set by the chain of command responsible for attaining that performance. A person who has set his own budget is much more likely to stick to it than if it were set for him by someone else.

The budget must be prepared with two considerations in mind:

It must be broken down to areas of one person's authority, such as branch offices or departments and

It must be compiled to comply with the established accounting framework to accumulate and measure the data.

In order to control expenses for budgetary purposes, standard expenses must be determined. Therefore, management must not only know how much the actual expenses and revenue are at the present time, it must know through standards what they should be. Expense and revenue standards can provide these measures to gauge present performance. Generally we look to the past for these standards of performance and expense to obtain the desired future performance. Using these past revenue—expense—profit relationships, a realistic budget can be prepared to obtain a planned profit for the future.

Flexible Budget

Although a target budget will be kept in focus, a flexible budget is more meaningful. This budget will reflect expenses for each level of revenue produced. The flexible budget is far more realistic and usable than a fixed budget because it takes into account both fixed and variable expenses of the operation to be controlled.

In a real estate operation, the following expenses are variable depending on volume of sales: commissions and fees, based on a percentage of gross revenue.

By contrast, the following expenses are relatively fixed (depending on the operation): sales management salaries and fees, salaries, advertising, communications, occupancy and other operating expenses (property taxes, auto expense, insurance, dues, etc.).

Breakeven Point

Knowing how much of each of these fixed and variable expenses will be incurred as a standard for the operation of each office or department, we can now measure and gauge each manager's operation. He not only can be watched to see that he meets or exceeds his production quotas but he is also measured to see that he attained these quotas or positions with all costs in proper alignment. All of this data can be set up in the form of a table(s) and/or graph which can also portray very conspicuously the budgeted "break even point" (the point at which revenue equals expenses) for the office or department. A simplified version of a break even-flexible budget chart is shown in Fig. 4.

It must be understood that fixed costs do not always remain fixed but must at times be shown as a vertical rise, such as when your business grows to a point where another salaried person must be added. When a firm goes all out for volume and bigness at any cost it will feel the effects of the limit of its personnel's capacity or expertise and/or the limit of the market potential. When this happens, the

Fig. 4. Breakeven budget chart

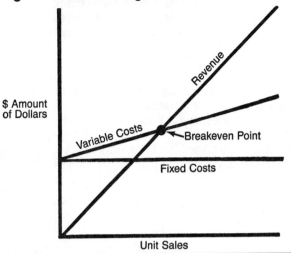

variable costs such as advertising and selling expense become inefficient and skyrocket upwards to the point where profit eventually di-
minishes rather than increases with more volume. This is the opposite
result of the one hoped for.

Rules of Thumb for Break-Even
The broker should know the following by the month, quarter and
year:

Number of exclusive listings

Number of sales and sales volume by own firm on the firm's listings

*Number of co-op sales and sales volume, listings and volume sold by
co-op*

Average revenue per unit

Total expenses

*Number of units produced (sale equals one unit, listing sold equals one
unit).*

The following example illustrates how to find how many units per
month are required to break even. Assume average revenue per unit is
$455.00 and overhead per month is $10,000 (including owner's salary). Therefore $10,000 ÷ 455 = 22 units to break even.

Since there is generally a relationship between the number of exclusive listings and the number of units made the following month,
assume number of exclusive listings last quarter is 157 (a quarter
gives a more reliable sample) and number of units last quarter is 105.
Since 22 units are needed to break even, the ratio, therefore, is

$$\frac{22}{105} : \frac{x}{157}$$

$105x = 3454$

$x = 33$ listings (to break even)

With the proper records on the number of contacts needed on the average to get an exclusive listing or make a sale, calculate how many contacts per day are needed by your office to break even per month and how many contacts it would take per day on the average to make your budgeted profit.

Types of Budgets

As many budgets can be prepared as there are departments or lines of authority to fix responsibility within the framework of a firm's accounting capability. They include budgets for sales, listing, advertising, selling and administrative expense, cash, new office development, overhead and desk cost. Segmented budgets only involve management people who have responsibility and control for a given area.

Marketing and Statistical Controls

Marketing and statistical controls are essential tools of real estate management. Effective records tell a broker where his business is coming from. They are basic to setting sales and service goals and planning the budget that will undergird the operation. Salespeople can be trained, guided and counseled more effectively when management has records of their individual performance. Furthermore, salespeople who understand how good record keeping improves their effectiveness in selling and thus has a positive effect on their income are much more willing to keep necessary records.

Management needs good records as a basis for money planning. Accurate and frequent detail on how performance is meeting goals and budget standards enables management to make short-term decisions on where more money needs to be spent as well as where cutbacks will help adjust to temporary situations.

Finally, marketing and statistical records show growth patterns as they evolve, strengths and weaknesses of people or departments and suggest changes that should be made all along the line. This week's records become next week's guide to management action.

Marketing and Statistical Controls

When management talks to salespeople about controls, the staff often has the impression it means restraints, confinement or rigidity. In this context the word controls implies a certain loss of freedom of movement. Yet everyone is aware that controls are an essential part of the operation of a business. In the present context, controls relate to the data necessary for planning and guiding a successful real estate marketing business. Generally, sales and marketing oriented people will acknowledge that controls are essential over financial aspects of the real estate business but are reluctant to acknowledge the need of controls over its marketing aspects.

The marketing of real estate is concerned with several factors. It obviously requires listings in sufficient quantity to meet sales and income goals. Furthermore, if they are to sell, listings must be priced realistically and be in the price range of prospects to whom the firm has access. In addition, the broker must develop the ability to sell these listings in a reasonable period of time. Just as clothing retailers' inventories must be in sizes, styles and colors appropriate for the market a store serves, so must a broker maintain a listing inventory that fits his market. It is necessary to establish controls over the quantity so the company always has listings. Control of the quality of the listing inventory is also necessary.

Another factor essential to marketing real estate is inquiries or buyers or customer traffic. Does the firm have enough to enable it to achieve its sales and financial goals? A broker cannot leave to chance the fact that he will eventually have enough interested or qualified buyers. A real estate business cannot be conducted from one day to the next.

Controls can be provided over the marketing aspects of the real estate business without confining the salesperson and sales manager. Furthermore, proper controls should help them carry out their responsibilities and achieve their goals.

Listing Sources and Controls

Since all listings start by obtaining a listing lead or information on somebody thinking of selling, the broker should keep accurate records of his listing leads. With this knowledge, listing leads and potential listings can be expanded.

If the information has not been obtained in the initial interview, a staff person can phone the seller a short time after the listing has been taken. During the same interview, the caller can determine if the seller is pleased with the firm's service to date and solicit suggestions as to how the service might be improved.

Listing Work Sheet

Watching some real estate salespeople gather information on a listing makes one wonder if the salesperson thinks he is following in the steps of Abraham Lincoln, jotting all the information on the back of an envelope as Lincoln reportedly did when writing his Gettysburg Address. There is general agreement that a listing must be complete (data on room sizes, taxes, utilities, location, lot size and seller's telephone number) and accurate if it is to serve as a base for a selling package, enabling salespeople to show the property effectively. To most cooperating salespeople, the listing sheet will be their first exposure to a new listing. It therefore behooves the listing salesperson to provide complete and reliable data. This is best accomplished if he uses a form that includes every item he will need to record. The office secretary or whoever processes the listing can be instructed not to process it until all blanks are filled in and every item in the check list is complete. If the listing worksheet is incomplete, the secretary can advise the manager who then carries out whatever follow-up is necessary with the listing salesperson.

Competitive Market Analysis

Any time the subject of listing properties is discussed, the importance of obtaining them at the proper price is emphasized. A responsible broker will recommend a listing price that is likely to assure a sale in a reasonable amount of time and bring the seller the highest price the market will bear.

Using a competitive market analysis or similar system, the salesperson establishes the listing price for discussion with the seller. This gives the office a listing price based on comparables and enhances the firm's professional image.

In many firms, before a presentation is made to the seller, the salesperson submits the competitive market analysis to his manager for approval. In this way management is sure that all listings taken will be priced at such a level that they will sell readily. Thus tomorrow's potential problems of over-priced listings can be avoided by providing controls today.

The very same competitive market analysis form can be used to show the seller not only the price the salesperson recommends but both why and how he arrived at the figure.

Listing Activity Control

When the salesperson makes the presentation he describes the sales activities the firm will provide the seller so his property will be sold for the highest price in the shortest time, with minimum effort, inconvenience and worry to him and his family.

All too often, however, the salesperson tends to act as if his goal has been achieved when he gets the listing. He does not follow through with the same perseverance he mustered to obtain the listing to see that the seller does, in fact, receive the three benefits mentioned.

Activity controls or progress controls should be maintained to enable the salesperson and the firm to be aware of the activity on the listing. Such controls, used effectively, remind the sales department to expand or alter marketing activities as required.

Fig. 2 is a listing progress control which can be kept by either the salesperson or the office secretary.

The form provides a record of facts for future reference. This form first provides for the recording of data that will be essential when offers are obtained and presented. The salesperson will have a record of his recommended listing price as well as his estimated sale price so that these can be shown to the seller if an offer other than full price, terms, etc. is presented. Furthermore, at the time the listing is taken, the salesperson determines the precise dates he will counsel with the seller as to activity data, customer reaction, progress toward a sale and what changes and/or adjustment, if any, need to be made. Unless this is done, the salesperson often procrastinates about contacting the seller until the listing is close to expiration. This causes a bad relationship between seller and salesperson. Here, if the seller insists the property be listed slightly above the recommended price, the salesperson might then inform the seller that if the property remains unsold for, say, 30 days, the salesperson will request a price adjustment. The date for the adjustment being recorded, the salesperson has committed himself and the seller to bring the price in line.

An advertising record is provided as part of this system. The person responsible for placing advertising can reflect on what advertising has been done and determine whether further ads will be run and in what paper.

Estimated showings per week provides the salesperson data to determine whether or not the home has been shown enough to expose it to the market. Estimated number of showings is figured by querying both fellow salespeople and cooperating brokers. If keys are kept in the office, a key book can be checked to see how often the key has been taken out. Or the salesperson may choose to ask the seller how many cards have been left by salespeople or ask the seller to keep a record of how many times the property is shown.

Some brokers provide the seller a record sheet for jotting down the name of each salesperson and firm that shows the property. The listing salesperson collects this data periodically and contacts the showing salespeople to obtain feedback providing the prospective purchasers' opinion of the house.

Real estate salespeople are often reluctant to discuss the number of showings with the seller. It almost seems they think if they don't discuss the subject, the seller will not be aware of a lack of showings. On the contrary, a salesperson has the responsibility of knowing whether the property is being shown frequently enough to result in a sale; and if it is not, he must determine why. The cause can only be corrected if brought to the surface.

Listing Effectiveness
By studying the deviation between listing price and selling price and comparing it to the local market, a broker can measure his efficiency. As an example, a broker might note that his sales prices for the past year were 10 percent below listing price. He can compare this to the record of other brokers. Such records are obtainable through the

Fig. 1 Listing worksheet

Listing office **Date**		**Renewal**	**Code**

By

Owner's name	Town
Owner's address	Phone
Occupied Tenant's name	Phone
Title Taxes Legal	
Special assessments	Incorporated
Living rm.	Fireplaces
Dining rm. Den	Porches
Kitchen	
Breakfast rm. Family rm.	
Bedrooms ( )	
Baths ( ) Powder rm.	
Basement Crawl Slab Recreation rm.	

Utility rm.   Inclusion, remarks, interior finish:

Heat Cost	T
Wtr. htr.	B
Storms - screens	S
Sq. ft. liv. area	GS
Builder	HS
Motive	PAR

Possession Key:	Mtg. info.	Price	
Age Lot Style	Garage		

Rooms   Brs.   Baths   Construction   Owner's name & property address:

Sample ad

Check list

___Taxes	___Listing complete
___Square feet	___Sign put up
___Inclusions	___Referral service
___Special assessment	___Discussed and arranged
___Distance to facilities	___Picture taken
___Comments	___Brochure left
___Triggering features	___Market value appraisal made and presented

Marketing and Statistical Controls

Fig. 2 Exclusive action progress control

Salesperson_____

Seller:_____Address:_____

Date Taken:_____Expiration Date:_____List Price:_____

Salesperson's Recommended List Price:_____

Salesperson's Estimated Sale Price:_____

Target Date for Price Reduction:_____

Advertising Record

Paper A	B	C	D	E			

Estimated Showings Per Week

Week 1	2	3	4	5	6	7	8
9	10	11	12	13	14	15	16

Salesperson's Contact Record

Date	Remarks	Date of Next Contact

Multiple Listing Service or by simple observation. If competition seems to sell homes at five to seven percent below listing price, the broker should review his methods of estimating value. Such a high deviation between listing and sale price means he is probably increasing the length of time required to sell a property.

On the other hand, the broker might find his listings are selling at one to two percent below listing price while typically in the market, homes sell at five to seven percent lower. This might indicate he is being too conservative in estimating value. Possibly he is losing some listings because his estimates of value have been below other brokers' recommendations and less than the seller realistically believed he should receive.

Similarly, the length of time a broker's listings remain on the market should be compared to how long the properties listed with others take to sell. If a broker finds the homes he lists remain unsold for 15 days on an average, while homes in the market are generally unsold for 45 days, this can provide an excellent sales tool when he makes presentations to sellers. Conversely, the broker might find the average length of time his homes are on the market exceeds those of competitors. In this case, steps must be taken to change his marketing and sales techniques.

The percentage of listings that expire is also a measure of the effectiveness or ineffectiveness of the marketing activities. Since percentages of expirations vary with the strength or weakness of the market from one part of the country to another, the broker can compare his percentage of listings that expire with other brokers' as well as with his own expirations from year to year.

Customer Controls: Supply and Demand

As the level of demand (prospects or inquiries) for real estate fluctuates, a broker must change his practices regarding prospecting. Similarly, as the level of supply (sellers) increases or decreases, the broker must alter his activities in securing and servicing listings. Thus far in this chapter we have discussed methods of staying on top of listing sources and marketing practices regarding sellers. Let us now look at the other half of the supply-demand relationship, the buyers, also referred to as inquiries.

The listing controls mentioned have caused no additional work or burden on the salesperson. In fact they were designed to make his life easier. They require no additional record keeping but provide him with easy-to-use forms for data he is already collecting, probably in a haphazard fashion. Now he is able to keep the same data in a time saving fashion. The same can be true of customer or inquiry control.

Fig. 3 is an inquiry form which becomes the salesperson's permanent record for each prospect. Each salesperson is supplied with a pad of no-carbon-required forms in two colors. The pre-punched original becomes his permanent record, kept in a three-ring binder. The colored copy is given to the office secretary and weekly tabulations are made as shown in Fig. 4.

The information on the inquiry form has numerous uses. It enables the salesperson to record names, addresses and telephone numbers of prospects during the first contact. The salesperson is not

Fig. 3 Customer data sheet

Salesperson's Name

Date_____ Name_____

Address_____ Phone_____

City_____ Zip_____

Company_____

Position_____ Transportation_____

Address_____ Phone_____

City_____ Zip_____

Source:
Advertising:_____

Sign   Referral   Walk-In   Rent   Open house   Letter

Property_____ Price_____

Has Worked With_____

Requirements

Style_____ Const_____ When Needed_____

Bsmt_____ Gar_____ FmRm_____ Frpl_____ Bdrms_____

Baths_____ Family Size_____ Boys_____ Girls_____

Lot Size_____ School_____ Church_____

Choice of Towns_____

Present Housing Situation_____

_____ Price Range_____

Income_____ Down Pay_____ Pres. Mtg._____

Other_____

_____

_____

_____

Fig. 4 Customer response work sheet

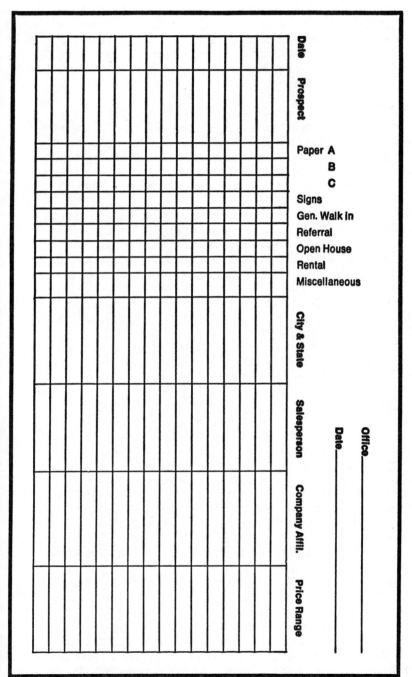

Marketing and Statistical Controls

Office _____

Date _____

encouraged to obtain total information on the inquiry sheet at the time the call comes in. His first objective in receiving a call is to make an appointment, not to qualify on the telephone. He will continue using the inquiry form once he is face to face with a prospect.

If the need for counseling a salesperson arises because of poor production, the sales manager asks him to bring his inquiry book so he can review the progress on each inquiry in an organized way.

The inquiry data as shown in the weekly summary also measures the effectiveness of each advertising medium and the price range of the inquiries the office is obtaining. Are they higher or lower than is typical in the marketplace and has this been by design or by accident?

Sources

A study of home buyers indicates that all buyers fall into three categories from the standpoint of their place of origin: The upgraders are people already living in the community and possibly looking for a larger or smaller place. Maybe it is a new family formation, a young couple just getting married or a couple tired of renting and looking for a home of their own.

The second category is the metropolitan movement. This is a family moving from one section where, unlike the upgrader, the prospect is not familiar with neighborhoods or prices and therefore has different buying habits demanding different servicing.

Generally the upgrader is rather specific on the neighborhood in which he wants to live. But the metropolitan movement prospect can be shown numerous other neighborhoods since he will be less prejudiced. Look for local studies that report on how long these two types are in the market before they buy.

The third buyer is the transferee. This prospect is moving from one geographical area to a totally different one. He is generally in the market for a shorter time. Some studies indicate he will make a decision on the fourth day of his house-hunting trip.

The broker may elect to cater to any one or more segments of the market. By observing the characteristics of customer inquiries, he can determine how effectively his advertising and promotional program is reaching the segments of the market he has chosen.

Another benefit of reviewing characteristics of inquiries is that it enables the broker to establish sales training programs, sales contests and sales management tailored to his market.

As levels of customer inquiries or traffic change, the salesperson must sharpen his ability to execute the steps of the sales and listing process.

As an example, when customer traffic is at a high level, there is no reason for the salesperson to work on inquiries. Canvassing will not be needed when traffic is high enough to supply a constant stream of people with whom to work. On the other hand, during this period, possibly the salesperson should be more concerned with his ability to qualify, making sure he is showing or working with the right people.

By studying levels of customer traffic, the sales manager can plan a better sales program on listings, since increased customer traffic or demand will eventually mean pressure on available merchandise or supply. Management can forecast when tight listing markets will evolve and then give greater emphasis on training in the listing process.

Customer Profile

Equally as important as understanding the characteristics and buying habits of the inquiries is understanding the profile of the people who eventually buy from the firm. Customer profiles can be maintained several ways. The two most popular involve the salesperson completing a brief customer profile report. For firms that prefer the sales staff not to be involved in reports, profiles can be developed by telephone or mail surveys conducted by office staff directly with the buyer.

Fig. 5 shows data typical in a customer profile. By comparing customer profile data with inquiry data, one can see the real effectiveness of advertising media. In one study, while all newspapers accounted for 33 percent of the total traffic, they accounted for 19 percent of the total sales. Referrals accounted for only 14 percent of the total traffic and they resulted in 52 percent of total sales. One out of every two and one-half referrals were sold in this study, while only one out of fourteen advertising prospects were sold.

Such a study gives direction for budgeting expenditures in newspaper advertising. It also influences the money a firm will spend on public relations programs that encourage referrals.

The time lapse between the date of first contact and the eventual date of the sale enables management to plan sales programs. As an example, as Fig. 5 shows, sales follow inquiries in this study by about four weeks. Therefore, when inquiries drop, the sales manager can anticipate that sales will tend to drop if everything remains equal.

The manager, therefore, can institute certain changes to respond to a drop in inquiries, such as greater concentration on converting each inquiry into an appointment, programs of improved advertising and improved referral programs. On the other hand, when inquiries rise, the manager can anticipate sales reacting accordingly. Therefore, adjustments (as indicated earlier) such as a step up in listing performance are called for and advertising can be cut back.

Also if the broker in this study finds himself working primarily with upgraders and metropolitan movement prospects he is obviously doing a mediocre job in his follow up. In other words, since the upgrader and metropolitan movement prospect shops for nine to eleven months, salespeople tend to lose contact with the prospects after 30 days. One way to increase sales would be to improve follow-up rather than promote additional inquiries.

Customer profile data regarding the average age of the buyer can influence selection practices, office decor and themes of advertising.

Sales and Listing Reports

In previous chapters we touched on goal setting. Goals generally focus on incomes. The goal setting method may involve the breaking down of incomes into income from sales and income from listings, the number of appointments required in order to obtain the projected sales and listings as well as the leads or inquiries required in order to

Fig. 5 Customer profile

Salesperson_____

Buyer's name_____

Address of property_____

Town_____

Source: Paper A   Paper D   Walk in

            Paper B   Sign   Open
                                              House

            Paper C   Referral   Brochure Ad

Date of first contact_____

Date of sale_____

Buyer's motive_____

First home purchase?   Yes____   No____

How many homes owned previously?_____

Buyer's previous town, state_____Buyer's age_____

Family size (Include all adults and children) planning to occupy house_____

What did customer ask for?

| Price | Style | No. Bedrms. | Town | Other |

What did customer buy?

| Price | Style | No. Bedrms. | Town | Other |

Fig. 6 Competitive activity report

Marketing and Statistical Controls

Office _____   Month Ending _____

	Office Sales Salesperson-Price	All Company Sales In M.L.S. Area Salesperson-Price	Competition Sales Company & No. Sold	Office X's Salesperson-Price	All New Company X's In M.L.S. Area Salesperson-Price	New Competition X's Company & No. Listed
Total for mo.						
Total yr. to date						
Total for same mo. last year						
% increase this mo. to corresponding last yr.						

233

achieve a needed number of appointments. The use of sales reports are essential to visually illustrate how effective individual salespeople and the sales team are in achieving sales and listing goals.

Sales reports might stack salespeople not only in order of dollar volume produced but also in order of number of units sold. The latter method recognizes that the effort to sell a $90,000 piece of property is often the same, in fact often greater than the effort to sell a $200,000 parcel.

Therefore, in the latter method, the salesperson having sold the greatest number of properties receives greatest recognition. Separate recognition for top selling salespeople and listing salespeople might also be given.

The frequency with which sales reports are published varies greatly. Some progressive companies use a form of daily reporting as a pacing device to illustrate the constant strength of the market. Computers and FAX machines are two means of informing salespeople at all times that there is fast action in the marketplace. Besides informing salespeople of data required to keep their listing books up to date, this gives recognition at a moment's notice to the salesperson who obtained a sale or listed a property.

It is equally important for management and staff to know how the company as a whole is doing in relation to its goals, its performance last year and its competitors. Too often a firm will take great pride in its own sales records or even disappointment in its performance without comparing its record to its competitors. For example, the broker might be pleased with a 15 percent increase in sales when a review of the activity in his market (obtainable through the Multiple Listing Service or local government records) might show that sales in the market had risen 25 percent. This would indicate obviously that potentials had not been achieved. Similarly, in a down market the broker might be concerned at having an increase of only 5 percent in sales; but when compared to the market's decrease of 25 percent due to tight money conditions, his 5 percent increase might be more palatable from the standpoint of protecting his position in the market.

Fig. 6, Competitive Activity Report, shows data that might be accumulated by a staff person and reviewed either monthly or semi-monthly or even several times a week.

Record Keeping

In establishing marketing and statistical controls, management should be sure that a great deal of record keeping is not required on the part of salespeople. If the suggestions made here are carried out, the salesperson only keeps data he needs to service his buyers and sellers.

When a person is asked to provide data for marketing and statistical controls, such as inquiry sources, his cooperation is easier to get if he understands that it will benefit him. When he knows controls can increase his income, he will do his part in making them work.

The accumulation and coordination of the data can be handled by staff people in relatively little time, especially if the company has gone on-line with a computer system.

Advertising

Many companies have prospered and expanded with good marketing and advertising methods; while many more have gone out of business because of overspending on improper advertising than for any other reason. Similarly, thousands of real estate firms fail to grow because they do not realize what good advertising and promotion can do for them and how important it is to get the right message to the right public.

Today's broker can no longer put up a sign, advertise in the local paper and feel content that he is doing a good job of advertising. He needs to expose his listings and services to every possible buyer and seller.

The speed with which all businesses have changed in the last quarter century is mind boggling. Change promises to be even more accelerated in the years ahead. The broker who fails to realize this will be in for an ever-decreasing share of his market. The question today is not can we afford to advertise? It is can we afford not to?

How does a firm begin to develop an advertising program? The best way is to first understand what advertising is and does; have a clear picture of the firm's advertising objectives and the image it wants to convey to the public; and finally, make a thorough analysis of the marketplace and the people it needs to reach.

Once these facets are mastered, management sets the ad budget, studies the media available and decides which it will use. Implementing the program is the next job to be done. It is a continuous task, requiring people with special talents to perform a variety of jobs. Just as important as the implementation of an advertising program is the follow up, measuring the effectiveness of the media chosen and being prepared to make quickly whatever changes media response or market changes dictate.

Understand Advertising

All advertising falls into two categories: merchandise or product and institutional.

Merchandise advertising is aimed at stimulating immediate action for the goods or services the firm wants to market. These ads are written to tell the public about specific properties or developments and are aimed at persuading people to call the broker and get full information. Merchandise advertising is aimed at making the phone ring immediately.

Institutional ads focus on creating a favorable image of or attitude toward a broker's goods or services. Ads of this type focus on long-term results. Unlike merchandise ads, they do not generate immediate action. They aim to keep the firm's name before the public, hoping that when a broker's services are needed at some future date people who have seen the ads will contact the firm.

Understanding the Firm's Image

Know what the people in your marketplace think of your firm. Do they really know you? Have they used your firm? Do they avoid doing business with brokerage firms? Do they rely on real estate services?

The public is seldom interested in the real estate business and the services brokers provide. They have to be told. A broker's marketing program should educate people about the things you can do better for them than they can for themselves.

Search out data, chart it and learn to sense trends as they begin to develop. Surveys made by banks, title companies, industry and schools of business administration are often available for the asking. The first three sources are as interested in a strong local economy as any broker is. Cooperative effort along these lines strengthens the relationship between these groups.

Advertising Budget

Advertising expenditures in the average brokerage run from 15 to 21 percent of company dollar. Fluctuations within these two figures or budgeting a higher or lower percentage of company dollar may be dictated by circumstance. The important thing is to establish a dollar figure. It will be needed before any media choices can be made.

Advertising Media

A practical guidebook, *Marketing Professional Services in Real Estate*, published by Real Estate Brokerage Council™, is a valuable source of information on all advertising and promotion media, how to handle advertising in-house and how to work with agencies.

This book cannot cover the subject in detail but will list the media available and what each can do to serve brokers' needs.

Signs

Dollar for dollar, For Sale and Sold signs give the broker the best return on his advertising expenditure. Signs not only generate calls on properties for sale; they also help get new listings. Many firms fail to recognize the value of Sold signs. Potential sellers have a way of mentally transferring a Sold sign from another house to their own.

Make sure the company sign has good eye appeal, is colorful and easy to read. Keep copy at a minimum. The firm's logo should be on all signs.

Logos

Logo is the graphic arts trade name for a logotype or identification mark. In recent years logo designs have tended to become very simple. Major industries have eliminated complex art work, choosing simple forms that can convey an image in a matter of seconds. The amount of lettering is also reduced drastically for the same reason.

Logos should be consistent throughout a firm's advertising and promotion campaign and on all its business printing.

Newspapers

Newspapers take the biggest share of the broker's advertising dollar. In order to measure newspaper advertising results adequately they should be separated into three parts: display, open house and classified.

Display advertising is more costly than classified but offers certain advantages that may well pay for the added cost. Display advertising captures reader attention by its greater visibility. A well laid out display ad projects a marketing image that can pay off months or even years later when an owner who has seen it decides to list his property.

There are several keys to good display ads. Have the ad laid out professionally. Use a minimum of copy, leaving a good amount of white space around it. Be sure to use the company logo. Write the ad to appeal to clients who can afford the type of property advertised and place the ad in a publication they read regularly.

Open house advertising is similar to classified only to the point that records should be kept on the business it generates, measured against what regular classified brings in. Record should also be made of both the sales and listings such ads bring in. Such records will help a broker decide whether more of his ad dollars and the salespeople's time should be channeled toward open house activities. In some areas of the country open houses are not commonly used.

Classified advertising has been described as the marketplace of the people. Brokers spend the largest percentage of their advertising dollars in this medium. Flexible in cost and size, classified ads offer a unique advantage to all, from the largest multi-office operation to the newest, smallest firm.

How much classified should a firm run? Company size controls this to a large degree. A small office would have a hard time playing a dominant role in classified; a large corporation has little trouble taking command. Small offices can counter this in several ways. They may decide to put all their advertising eggs into this one basket and forget other media. If they do not do this, they will have to put tremendous effort into writing prize-winning, telephone-ringing ad copy. They can determine which day's ads pull best and advertise more on those days. A word of caution is needed here: don't record just the day the respondent calls; be sure to record which day's ad is being checked out. Many brokers find it pays to run double or triple column ads on good response days. Then on days when ads do not pull as heavily, ad dollars are put to work elsewhere.

Television

Big company or small, large city or small, a key question today is should we use television? Much thought must be given to the key objectives of the advertising master plan when a firm considers this medium. Most brokers dismiss television because it is too high-priced. But there might be a place in a company's growth plan for this high exposure medium, especially with the advent of cable television, which is more competitively priced. If the prospect will not get the message from newspapers, the broker can take it to him via television. It is a medium that should be considered mainly by growth-oriented companies. Its main plus is that it is a tremendous image builder. Results are hard to measure but over the long pull listings will be easier for companies who use television than for those who do not.

Television cost is based on the number of families exposed and varies with the size of the city. Buyers usually have the choice of sponsoring a whole program, 60, 30 or 10-second commercials or 5-second station cut-away ads, the latter at a lower cost. This wide price range puts television within the budget of many brokers.

When considering television, ask these questions:

Do we have an adequate sales staff?

Do we cover the major areas where ads will be seen?

Are we growth oriented?

Are we willing to spend more money today in order to have market penetration for future business?

Will a television campaign enable us to show properties or will it just build the company image?

If your television campaign results in showing properties, potential sellers will be more willing to list with the firm.

Give television a lot of thought before you sign a contract to use it. Used judiciously, it can be an excellent growth tool.

Radio

Almost every one of the plus features that apply to television fit radio but at a much lower cost. This makes radio advertising practical for companies of all sizes. The question becomes do we use AM, FM or a combination of the two? The answer to this depends on the type of market the firm is in. A telephone survey of clients, asking what stations they listen to, can be a guide to making a final selection.

Billboards

Outdoor advertising is one of the oldest advertising forms and is certainly an effective one. Most billboards are rented by outdoor advertising companies. The key advantage to billboards is that locations can be contracted at key intersections within a firm's marketing area. Billboards provide advertising 24 hours a day for as long as the space is under contract.

Billboard messages and layout should be prepared by professionals. Most amateurs tend to use too much text. The message should be short and catchy and should carry the company logo. Motorists should be able to read it in five seconds maximum, therefore it must be kept to seven words or less.

Yellow Pages

Advertising in the yellow pages is often overlooked as an effective medium for brokers. The oversight is difficult to explain because real estate advertising is aimed at getting the telephone to ring! Yet many brokers question the need for this form of advertising.

People seldom bother to write down phone numbers when they drive by a For Sale or Sold sign, listen to the radio or watch television. When buyers and sellers want to call a broker they reach for the phone book. Brokers who make it easy for potential clients to find them in the phone book say this relatively modest investment pays off. As one broker puts it, "Let their fingers do the walking, let your salespeople do the showing."

Direct Mail

All advertising to be good must have repeated contact and be on target to the desired audience. Direct mail makes this possible. It is also a medium few brokers use properly. Once a direct mail list is developed, it should be used over and over again, getting the firm name and word of its services and successes into the homes and offices of everyone with whom it does business or wants to.

Much direct mail can be a cross between institutional and merchandise advertising and company public relations. Company brochures illustrate this point. A well-designed, carefully written brochure can tell your company's story and can be used in many ways. It is most effective when a self-addressed return card asking for more information is enclosed.

A sales brochure prepared specifically to promote a new company development or to interest industry in building a factory, warehouse or office building in the broker's market area requires a lot of preliminary work on the part of the broker and the services of professionals in the graphic arts to put it into an attractive package. Brochures prepared for professionals should be prepared by professionals.

Direct mail pieces can also be used to announce a series of institutional or service ads. Backing up direct mail with other kinds of advertising makes sense and provides continuity and variety to a campaign.

Ad Writer

The following guidelines will help determine who should write the advertising and provide tips for writing ads.

Sales Manager

Does he have time? How many salespeople is he managing? Does he have the skills to write phone-ringing ads?

Broker

To the questions above, add this: what other directions of company growth will take him away from consistent attention to this important task?

Advertising Agency

Large companies with big budgets find this the best answer. The agency fee may be offset by better results. Ad agencies may also be the answer for smaller firms that cannot produce successful copy.

Part Time Ad Writer

Brokers and sales managers should ask themselves how much their time is worth. Part time ad writers can be engaged at an hourly rate, freeing the staff for higher paying, more productive work.

Salespeople

Before deciding on this method, ask if the salespeople have the ability, time, inclination and creativity needed to write good ads. Can they write copy that represents the firm in the manner and at the price you will be paying?

Whoever writes the ad copy must keep several points in mind. If a firm's ads are to control the market they must gain the buyer's attention, hold his interest and induce him to call for more information. All this action starts with attention-getting leads. To write good leads requires an understanding of the basic motives of people. The four most important to ad writers are:

Self preservation—the desire to stay alive and well

Money—the desire to make it, the bargain instinct to save it

Prestige—the need to feel important, the matter of pride

Family—love.

People who read classified ads want to know the property's location, number of rooms (or bedrooms), price and terms and design.

Ad copy should have a minimum of abbreviations and it should not tell the whole story. If an ad tells everything, there is little reason to call except to buy the property and the broker misses countless buyers for all the other properties he has to sell.

Measuring the Results

The importance of measuring the results of all advertising was stressed earlier in this chapter. It is important that records be kept regularly so management has an up-to-date picture of the effectiveness of the program. The same data will prove valuable later when decisions must be made to continue certain media or make some changes. Figs. 7 and 8 are two forms that can be used to collect data on ad response. The figures show previously also collect useful data on classified ads as well as other client sources.

Institutional campaigns are more difficult to assess quickly but their effectiveness is proven over the long-term. Good institutional campaigns help a company to grow and they play a strongly supportive role for the sales staff. When a firm has a good reputation, salespeople's jobs are made a lot easier. And when salespeople are content, staff turnover is lower and management's task is also easier, allowing more time to focus on long-term growth and other creative work.

Everyone involved in planning, preparing and responding to advertising should be kept informed of the results of everything the company does to reach its public. Salespeople should know which ads pull strongest, which days of the week are best for classifieds and how the company measures the campaign's effectiveness. When everyone is kept informed, records tend to be kept more accurately and there is a continuing interest in the whole advertising effort.

Public Relations

The image a firm projects through its advertising should be integrated with good public relations, for the two are closely interrelated. Public relations are as diverse as management's involvement in community affairs and organizations, conducting a good publicity campaign with newspaper editors and news directors of radio and

Fig. 7 Weekly report

Marketing and Statistical Controls

Name _____ Date _____

Calls for the Week

Address	Date	Paper A	Paper B	Referral	Other Paper	Other

Results from Open House

Address _____ No. Through _____

No. Names _____ Good Prospects _____

Fig. 8 Advertising and call in sheet

Date	Address	Paper A	Paper B	Referral	Sign	Area Paper	Phone Book	Other	Other Agent-Office	Time & Appointment Date

television stations, sponsoring sports and cultural teams and events and providing giveaways that are of good quality, useful and remind the public of your company.

Every person who gets a good living from a community ought to give back a share of it in personal service and the promotion of good local causes. Every person who joins a service club, country club, PTA or fills an elected or appointive office in local government affairs represents not only himself but the firm with which he is affiliated. Every time a salesperson takes a training course that will upgrade him professionally, wins the company's monthly sales contest or handles an important transaction is a reason for the company to send out a publicity release. New salespeople joining a firm and promotions within the firm should be announced to the public. Talk shows need participants with experience in a wide variety of fields. Management should let program directors know that people on their staff have expertise in real estate and are available for appearances on radio or television. It's all grist for the firm's publicity and public relations mills.

Be willing to speak up about the special concerns of the marketplace. Subjects like home warranty programs or planned unit developments are of interest to the public. Brokers should be willing to discuss them with newspaper editors and radio and television people. Environmentalists and conservationists are always looking for support for their projects. Brokers should look for ways to tell the public they favor the concepts that make the community a better place to live. After all, they are on the front lines every day, selling that community as a fine place to live!

Junior colleges and high school adult education classes are asking for brokers to teach real estate subjects. High school career seminars offer opportunities to tell young people how exciting a career in real estate can be. Their students are, after all, the source of tomorrow's brokers. And while brokers are engaged in some of these public relations activities on their own behalf, they are also being paid for their time which is an interesting twist.

Non-Cash Contributions

What do you do when the budget is spent and there is simply not enough cash to cover further requests? The solicitor is sure to be disappointed. You might offer the front window for a promotional display, if the request is for an antique or hobby show, 4-H or Scouts. Then tell the public about it in your weekly ad, inviting them to come by and enjoy it. That promotes both the project and the firm.

Promotional giveaways can often be used instead of cash outlays. If the PTA is having a book sale, the church a rummage sale, the garden club a plant sale or the school band a bake sale, they all will need tote bags. Offer to supply these (they'll have your logo, of course) and watch you firm name appear all around town, gathering goodwill for both the project and the company.

More traditional forms of promotion and good public relations involve sponsorship of sports teams, balloons for pet parades and other community outings, underwriting award banquets, placing display ads in amateur theater programs and cultural and civic benefit programs. Calendars are among the oldest promotional items in American business. They are still a good way to get the firm name into a great many homes and offices at very low per item costs.

If the firm has a large conference room or training center, make it available for community and non-profit organization functions when it is not needed for business. Garden clubs, voter groups or study clubs will sign up for it. If you have enough extra money in your print budget, provide small memo pads to these groups. They will be carried home, getting the firm name into still more households. Be sure the telephone number is also imprinted.

If space in your office is suitable for the precinct polling place it could be offered for use on election days. Voters create high-volume traffic of citizens concerned about what is going on in the marketplace. Serve them coffee and send them away with a token giveaway with the firm imprint—a pencil, rainhat, memo pad, tote bag or a packet of paper coasters.

Communication Pieces

Annual reports are another form of advertising that crosses over into public relations and promotion. Just as industry prepares annual reports that tell their story to shareholders and the financial community, so real estate brokers can develop annual reports that do a special job for them. Such a report could include details of the firm's growth over the past year, a summary of its listings and sales in both numbers and dollar volume, mention of a few of the most important transactions handled, the services the firm offers, the qualifications of the management and staff and whatever projections it can safely make for the coming year.

Such reports can be mailed to every active client, bankers, attorneys, local government officials, leaders in business and commerce and the civic leaders in the community. It should be a highly professional product.

Newsletters serve in-house as well as external communication and promotion needs. They can be as simple as a one-page sheet written exclusively for staff, telling of goals achieved, new objectives, new staff or salespeople added and promotions within the firm. External newsletters usually avoid the chattiness acceptable for internal publications. They tell in a more formal way what the firm achieved, sales and staff additions and accomplishments, plans for growth or expansion, mention of recent publicity the firm has received and perhaps some promotional copy relating to the marketplace the firm serves. Here again, the broker is the person out front selling the marketplace to newcomers. Why not remind others now and then how a broker does that?

Newsletters can be an expensive public relations tool. When well done they perform a useful service. They should be prepared in a format that makes them easy to keep on file. Banks have discovered that their newsletters are shared by a great many people in the firms that receive them and are kept for further reference. A broker's newsletter could be just as effective a public relations tool, well worth its cost.

Telephone Controls

The use of company telephones for personal and long distance calls should be covered in the policy and procedure manual. How it is answered is covered in orientation training and continual training programs. The importance of answering it promptly and well also relates to the success of the firm's advertising and promotion program.

The dollars spent on advertising are supposed to make the telephone ring. When it is not answered promptly and properly, the result is a loss of advertising money and effort as well as the buyers and sellers it is meant to attract. Everyone in the firm should appreciate the role he plays in using the phone to help reach individual and company goals.

Be sure anyone answering the phone knows enough about the properties advertised to be able to talk about them intelligently. Be sure they answer the phone in a friendly tone. Be sure they keep a checklist of the information they need to get from that first call right by the phone. *Make the telephone a sales instrument.* It can be an instrument of both control and growth.

Effective use of the marketing and statistical controls suggested here have resulted in the strong growth of real estate organizations all over the country.

Appraising and Analyzing the Patterns of Growth

15

When a real estate firm has a well established staff working under good management, it eventually reaches a point where the firm appears to be serving its immediate market as completely as is possible. Then the likelihood is that management begins to think of growth, either in terms of opening another office, expanding its services or enlarging the operation at its present site.

Whatever the reason or the course being considered, it is important that management understand the effect of growth stages and how to appraise them properly. Since World War II the real estate business has come of age. What was once largely a family enterprise is gradually moving into the sphere of sophisticated, scientifically planned and controlled businesses.

Before any real estate broker thinks of expanding his operation he should acquaint himself with the general picture of real estate as it exists in the United States. This chapter outlines briefly what the whole real estate picture is today and suggests how a broker can find his place in it.

Appraising and Analyzing the Patterns of Growth

The reasons for growth and expansion in the real estate industry are the same as in any other business enterprise as they relate to causes and desired results. While the reasons for undertaking growth may be as varied as the people responsible for the undertaking, one basic measurement influencing the decision must be profit: "If we expand and if this growth takes place, what will the increase in profit be, measured against the risk involved?"

Before appraising and analyzing the patterns of growth, it is necessary to establish a base from which growth takes place. What are the physical assets and organizational make-up of typical real estate operations today? They can be broken down into four typical real estate operations:

Five to Ten Person Residential Office

This sized firm represents the majority of the real estate brokerage operations in the United States. The broker is the owner and is a selling broker; his principal source of income is from his own sales.

He also does all the chores: writing ads, training, conducting sales meetings and bookkeeping. He may and often does have limited secretarial help, usually part time or from an outside service. The owner will often also sell commercial and/or industrial property; he may do some work in property management and/or appraisals, all on a limited scale.

25 to 50 Person Office with Multiple Functions

Again the broker is in most cases the owner and he begins to be more involved in management, selling less and becoming a manager-broker. Selling is not his primary source of income. While he still may do some listing and selling, he becomes the sales manager and depends upon the production of his sales team to provide his income.

Three to Five Branch Offices

In this type of operation the owner becomes an administrative broker. He spends his time managing, planning and administering. He has a sales manager in each office. This broker is approaching the third level of management. He manages others who manage still others.

Large Multiple Branch Operations

This is called a full service real estate firm where all phases are departmentalized and there are specialists managing each department: Certified Residential Broker, Society of Industrial REALTORS®, Certified Commercial-Investment Member, Member Appraisal Institute and Certified Property Manager. The head of the organization, while he may be the owner, is more frequently a part owner either through a partnership or a stock ownership in a corporation. His duties are totally and absolutely management and administration. He has at least one level, and frequently two and three levels, between him and the actual sales force.

There is a definite operational philosophy in every type and size of real estate organization. It tends to break down into a small office or a large office approach. The pitfalls and objectives of each are analyzed from the standpoint of physical makeup.

The Small Office
This may vary with the market area. There are generally between five and ten salespeople. They tend to be identified in one area of the market. They tend to become expert in the selected neighborhood area and represent themselves as such. They have full time secretarial and bookkeeping help or perhaps part time secretarial and some outside accounting assistance. The owner is almost always the manager.

Potential Pitfalls
Loose management can result from very close ties with salespeople and a neglect of basic management functions because the owner-manager continues to do what he likes to do best, selling.

Tendency not to have scheduled meetings or staff conferences.

A lack of a line of command and a delay in decision making if the only decision maker is out selling.

A lack of objectives, planning, goals: where are we going and how are we going to get there?

Usually, a lack of budgeting and cost controls; bookkeeping, accounting, and secretarial help is inefficient or ineffective.

A handyman or a jack of all trades approach rather than specialization. Everyone handles some commercial or some industrial or maybe does some management or appraisal in addition to residential.

Objectives
Determine who should be the manager. He should not automatically be the owner. Management is a profession having nothing to do with entrepreneurial position. A wise broker knows whether selling is his forte and desire. If it is, he should be smart and objective enough to find someone else to manage the firm.

Keep a professional image and stay within the framework of the organization's competence. When an opportunity presents itself to do outside work it might be smart to refer it to a specialist and not risk tarnishing the firm's image. This affords much closer control and gives a better opportunity to train people effectively. It also establishes proper delegation of authority and definite job responsibilities.

If the objective of this type of operation is to stay small, it would most likely have only experienced salespeople who require a minimal amount of the manager's time.

Large or Multi-Office Operation
There is a trend toward having more salespeople per office. This has evolved for several reasons: principally, if the sales manager is to

make a satisfactory income he needs a larger sales staff, assuming his income is derived entirely from management and not from his own sales. Also, covering a broader area from one location can keep overhead proportionately lower than it would be with ten people in two offices. Management philosophy stresses a high degree of specialization, the organization is departmentalized and each department stays within its sphere of influence and specialization or has its own management team.

Potential Pitfalls

Expansion can be too fast or departments would start out too small and be wholly dependent on one or two people. If anything happens to one or both of them there is a real problem.

Managers don't manage; they spend too much time selling. Frequently there is not a solid base from which expansion can develop. This is somewhat akin to expanding too fast; there is a jump-in approach rather than a phase-in approach.

A loosely controlled budget results in the profits of successful offices being used to subsidize a new operation for an excessive period of time.

If there is an expansion vertically into related fields, such as real estate management or loans, without experienced personnel there is a tendency to continue to concentrate on brokerage and the others suffer.

There can be a lack of effective communication procedures. The larger an organization becomes and the faster the expansion takes place, the greater the danger of a breakdown or perhaps a total lack of communication. As management levels grow, those who are not in direct contact with the operational people are not as sensitive to communications as they should be and too often make decisions affecting operational people without communicating with them beforehand.

There is also a tendency to make decisions through committees, believing that when the committees are informed everyone else will be informed.

There is a tendency as an operation grows to fill up desks just to fill in space. This creates a morale problem with the people who are producing and is a part of a philosophy that generates problems and resentment.

Being big for bigness' sake is a dangerous philosophy of the big office syndrome, constantly competing with other big offices. The attempt to create that image with the public is frequently the outgrowth of emotional decisions.

While a selling sales manager is an acceptable method of operation, unless it is specifically organized in this manner and clearly understood in the job description of the individual, there tends to be a conflict with the individual as to where his management duties begin and end and to what degree he is permitted to sell.

Objectives

A very strong company philosophy served by organization-oriented management. A clearly defined organization chart.

A detailed policy and procedure manual with job descriptions that support the organization chart.

Close communication at all levels of management, particularly between each office sales manager and his supervisor.

Strong company communications. Company reports that cover goals measured against production communicated to each individual responsible for contributing to sales.

Measured results. Whenever a program is begun a method of measuring results should be set up.

Cost controls. Budgeting of expenses with checks and balances to assure careful observance of budget limitations or necessary adjustments by top management.

Systems and procedures. A basic philosophy of the need for definite systems, procedures and orientation on the part of management for such controls.

Advertising and public relations should be carefully programmed, professionally done, creative and goal-oriented.

Consider Reasons

In any appraisal or analysis of the patterns of growth the reasons for the desired growth should be considered as objectively as possible above and beyond the profit motive at the very outset by those who are responsible for the final decision. These motives and reasons will have a substantial effect upon the successful outcome.

Whatever a firm's reason for considering expansion there comes a time to decide, establish an objective and start the process of fulfilling that objective.

Alex F. Osborn, writing in *Applied Imagination* suggests a series of steps essential to what he terms a process of ideation.

Orientation: pointing out the problem

Preparation: gathering pertinent data

Analysis: breaking down relevant material

Hypothesis: piling up alternatives by way of ideas

Incubation: letting up, to invite illumination

Synthesis: putting the pieces together

Verification: judging the resultant ideas.

Osborn points out that actual work conditions seldom allow management to follow the exact sequence of the steps listed. For example, following the incubation process, one may return to search out more facts (preparation) than were originally gathered. Change of pace is important: first one may push, then coast, then push some more. There will always be unusable ideas and material relating to the problem at hand; but it is very likely to prove usable to solve another problem at some future date.

Stages of Development 16 in Real Estate Firms

Larry E. Greiner, formerly on the faculty at the Harvard Business School, wrote an analysis for the Harvard Business Review in 1972 in which he showed how a company's past provides clues for management that are critical to its future success. The resulting article, "Evolution and Revolution as Organizations Grow" appeared in the Harvard Business Review of July-August 1972. This chapter is a condensation and adaptation of Prof. Greiner's article. It is quoted here with permission of both the author and the Harvard Business Review, with added text written to make it applicable to the real estate business.

Professor Greiner's concept is that growing organizations move through five distinguishable phases of development, each of which contains a relatively calm period of growth that climaxes in a management crisis. Moreover, he argues that since each phase is strongly influenced by the previous one, management with a sense of its own organization's history can anticipate and prepare for the ensuing developmental crisis.

Here are Greiner's concepts appropriate to management action in each of the five developmental phases, translated to show how real estate companies can turn organizational crises into opportunities for further growth.

Stages of Development in Real Estate Firms

Many companies "are rooted more in past decisions than in present events or outside market dynamics," according to Prof. Larry E. Greiner, writing in the Harvard Business Review. "Historical forces do indeed shape the future growth of organizations. Yet management, in its haste to grow, often overlooks such critical development questions as: Where has our organization been? Where is it now? And what do the answers to these questions mean for where we are going? Instead, its gaze is fixed outward toward the environment and the future—as if more precise market projections will provide a new organizational identity.

"Companies fail to see that many clues to their future success lie within their own organizations and their evolving states of development. Moreover, the inability of management to understand its organization development problems can result in a company becoming 'frozen' in its present stage of evolution or, ultimately, in failure, regardless of market opportunities."

As any company moves through developmental phases, each evolutionary period creates its own revolution. "Each phase is both an effect of the previous phase and a cause for the next phase," says Greiner. For example, management practices employed by the firm's owner in the formative stages eventually lead to demands for decentralization as the business grows. "Moreover, the nature of management's solution to each revolutionary period determines whether a company will move forward into its next stage of evolutionary growth." As he shows later, there are at least five phases of organization development, each characterized by both an evolution and a revolution.

Relation to Real Estate Business
One primary goal real estate firms share with other businesses is the desire to achieve personal financial success. No matter what the business, good managers realize that success is not a pinnacle upon which their company will sit for many years. Success is only a temporary level in the continuing growth of an organization. It is this very growth and the change it brings that lead it to become more successful.

When an organization has hit a level of success and stays there for a long time, it could well be that the operation has stagnated; or management may have decided this is where they really want to stay.

If the former, the owners may think they have a successful operation but they have really stopped growing, having failed to keep up with the market trends and with what the competition is doing. Eventually such a firm will find themselves in a very difficult position.

But if they really like the company's present size and pace, they can retain many of the same management practices over a long period of time. Companies that decide they do not want to grow may have top managers who prefer the informal style of a small company. Should they choose to grow, these people could well do themselves out of a job and lose the way of life they enjoy.

The broker who is interested in growth is constantly striving to keep his organization in tune with the market place and the changes going on around him. He realizes that success, being a temporary state, will almost always lead to developmental changes, that change is an inevitable part of growth. Before getting into a discussion of the phases of growth, let us first provide two important definitions from Prof. Greiner's article:

Stages of Development in Real Estate Firms

The term *evolution* is used to describe prolonged periods of growth where no major upheaval occurs in organization practices.

The term *revolution* is used to describe those periods of substantial turmoil in organization life.

Therefore, it is safe to say that when a real estate firm finds success and has built on a strong economic base, the manager will generally start his organization into a new growth cycle. Such a growth cycle might include opening a new office or recruiting several new salespeople for the sales staff; or adding a back-up clerical staff; or initiating a new department such as building or commercial/industrial.

Such growth and expansion usually cause change within an organization. People who have been with the firm for a long time generally resent change. They are secure in the framework of their old job description. They are often jealous of new departments because a great deal of attention is paid to that part of the organization; or they are envious of new salespeople because the broker seems to devote more attention and time to new people and their training than he does to the old. Thus, change often brings with it a sense of uneasiness in the organization. Such uneasiness often leads to a crisis. The crisis can be manifested in a variety of ways.

Several fairly common crises include older salespeople demanding they be given more attention or they will leave the organization; or a money crisis caused by the start-up costs of expansion into a new homes department; or a new commercial-investment division or other type of vertical expansion drains cash reserves, leading to a real financial crisis.

Whether the crisis is in people or finances, a solution must be found by the manager. This solution can take many forms (as discussed in earlier chapters of this book) but he must find a solution if the firm is to survive. A good manager anticipates the crisis and manages by objective; he foresees problems that are likely to arise as the firm enters a period of change and is ready with a solution.

Key Dimensions of Development

A study of four companies made by Alfred D. Chandler, Jr., in his book *Strategy and Structure*,[1] contends that outside market opportunities determine a company's strategy, which in turn determines the company's organization structure. This may well be true, according to Greiner, in a time of explosive markets and technological advances. But he believes more recent evidence suggests that organization structure can play a critical role in influencing corporate strategy. It is this reverse emphasis on how organization structure affects future growth which Greiner stresses.

From an analysis of studies at Harvard and elsewhere, five key dimensions emerge in Greiner's study as essential for building a model of organization development:

Age of the organization

Size of the organization

Stages of evolution

Stages of revolution and

Growth rate of the industry.

We will deal with each element separately but Fig. 1 illustrates their *combined* effect. Each dimension influences the next over a period of time. As all five elements begin to interact, a realistic picture of organizational growth emerges.

It is well to note here that low-growth industries spend longer periods of time in each evolution stage and encounter revolution stages at a much slower rate than is true in medium and high-growth industries. The reverse is true of high-growth industries where companies have to build staff and expand facilities and services rapidly. Such

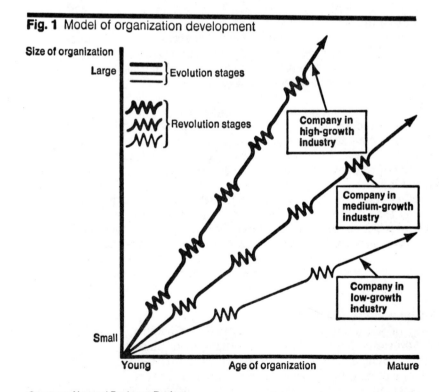

Fig. 1 Model of organization development

Courtesy: Harvard Business Review

firms find both evolution and revolution phases accelerated. Variations in real estate market conditions can also affect the growth pattern of individual firms. Real estate brokerage firms that once were high-growth companies may temporarily encounter slower growth periods. Thus, the reader is cautioned to keep his thinking flexible in using the charts contained in this chapter.

Age of the Organization

The horizontal axis of Fig. 1 shows the base from which an organization grows. A company's age not only determines how much history and data a manager has available to study, it also contributes greatly to the attitudes of management. Thus, management strategy and structure are subject to strong influences because both are strongly rooted in time. The important element to stress here is that good management does not permit its attitudes to become frozen. When attitudes are watched carefully, staff behavior becomes predictable and is easier to change.

Size of the Organization

The vertical axis of Fig. 1 shows the difference in the time span with which both evolution and revolution occur in companies of different size. What a chart cannot illustrate is the fact that as a company increases in size, new challenges and problems are presented, the size of the management team increases and every job becomes more fully interrelated.

Stages of Evolution

Starting with a small, young company (lower left of Fig. 1), we see how growing organizations experience evolutionary periods. This is the time during which they enjoy sustained growth and remain free of major economic setbacks or disruptive internal problems. During these periods only modest adjustments seem necessary to keep the company growing under the original management structure.

Stages of Revolution

As jagged lines on the chart interrupt the smooth linear flow, they mark inevitable periods of revolution. Whether it comes sooner or later (as mentioned above) revolution certainly comes. Study case histories of real estate firms or examine the changes on Fortune's "500" list and you find that periods of turbulence and change come to every company. It is these periods of revolution that call for greatest examination and bring the challenge of adjusting to changing needs.

It is in the stages of revolution that so many companies fail because management is unwilling or unable to effect necessary changes. Those companies that initiate new management practices which respond to changing needs and market conditions are the ones that move into the next, strong period of evolution.

Growth Rate of the Industry

The speed with which a real estate firm experiences phases of evolution and revolution are affected not only by the strength of its structure but by exterior market fluctuations as well. Upturns and downturns in the general economy bring strong pressures on the real estate business. In a rapidly expanding market, real estate management must be ready to add to its sales staff rapidly. When general market reverses occur, real estate management that is prepared to find its way around adverse conditions can still make a profit. Such revolutionary periods will cause companies less well prepared to encounter major difficulties.

In Fig. 2, "The five phases of growth," each evolutionary period is characterized by the dominant management style used to achieve growth; each revolutionary period is characterized by the dominant management problem that must be solved before growth can continue.

It is suggested that you follow the chart and refer back to it frequently while reading the balance of this chapter.

One important thing to keep in mind is that each phase not only results from the previous phase but is also a cause of the next phase. You should also be cautioned that in the real estate business Greiner's five stages of growth do not necessarily occur sequentially. Different departments in your firm may be partially in crisis number two and partially in crisis number three at the same time. It is important that top management recognize the various problems that confront your organization so you can anticipate them and find solutions for them.

Phase One: Growth Through Creativity

This first growth period represents the birth stage of a real estate firm. Characteristic of this period are

An almost total lack of formal management

Frequent but informal communication

Long hours, modest income and

The company responds to the market, hasn't yet learned to control it.

In this stage emphasis on management is almost nil because the leaders are most concerned about creating real estate services and working to market them. The owners are busily occupied getting listings and making sales and working to build up a successful market for future referrals for more listings and sales. Even when they seem anxious to get qualified salespeople, their main effort is really devoted to their own market activities.

The characteristic of this particular kind of organization is that the founders/owners are technically oriented—that is, they spend almost their entire time listing and selling real estate. They usually disdain any type of management activities because they feel they do not have time for such things. Their energies instead are channeled into producing more business for the company and selling their services to the community. Thus it is almost a company without management. Even though the owner's name is frequently on the front door, he is not active in a management capacity.

The few other salespeople who work for such brokers find that communication is infrequent and informal. It may consist of simply the exchange of a few words as two people pass in the hallway or as

Fig. 2 The five phases of growth

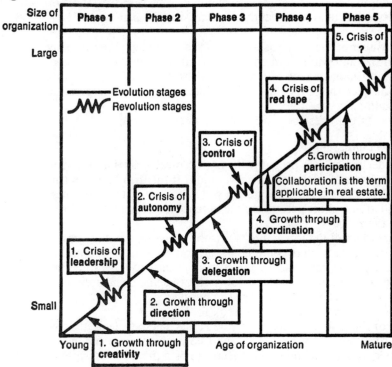

Courtesy: Harvard Business Review

one is going in or out of the office, the one telling the other of a new listing or sale. No formal sales meetings or communications are used because they are considered a waste of time and take away from efforts to list and sell properties. If there are several salespeople working in the organization, they are independent contractors who have little or no direction from the owners.

Such brokers work long hours and their work is rewarded by a very modest income. Their strength lies in the future and in their ability to build an organization.

Their activities are controlled by the immediate market place. As they begin their merchandising program and follow up on listings and sales, they react to the market place. But they never take time to sit down and decide what they are going to do to control it. If the public says it wants one type of service this week, they will run in that direction to provide it; if next week the public asks for a different type of service, the owner will respond to that.

Certainly all good management responds to the public. But good managers also attempt to plan in advance in order to have some control over the market place through their merchandising impact. In the creativity stage beginning brokers do not do this but respond either to what the market offers them or asks of them.

Growth through creativity may continue for many years, depending upon the seriousness of these brokers and their desire to see the organization grow. A great many real estate firms with two, three or five salespeople tend to stay at this level and never rise above it. There are two reasons.

The caliber of their salespeople is not such as to help the company grow in size and win its fair share of the market and the owners are simply not management oriented and therefore refuse to acknowledge the fact that problems may be developing in their growing organization.

This eventually results in a leadership crisis.

Crisis of Leadership

The leadership crisis is probably the most critical crisis that occurs in the five phases of evolution and revolution. If the firm does not survive this first crisis, the organization will never grow. Such a business may fail after a short period of time because the owners did not recognize the crisis.

Essential as all the foregoing "start-up" activities are, they pose a problem. As the owners continue to sell and do a better job and as their salespeople come along, the company starts to have some impact on the community. It is at this point that the owners discover they face a need to really manage the business.

What are some of the signs to look for?

One of the easiest problems to note is that salespeople need assistance. Alert brokers observe that their salespeople tend to run in several directions at one time. There seems to be a tremendous waste of effort.

Some sales are not made because the salesperson was not properly prepared to close the transaction; or some listings are lost because the salesperson wasn't trained to make a proper competitive market analysis and then use it to make a forceful presentation to the prospective seller. Perhaps the owners have had trouble with the Real Estate Board or the Real Estate Commission because a salesperson was ignorant of some state laws—knowledge he should have received through proper training and management control.

The owners become aware of the need for better accounting methods and more complete statistics. At times they feel they are doing well in the number of sales made; but their bank balance continues to decrease and they just don't understand why. They really have little or no idea whether their salespeople are productive, save for a general feeling based on the total number of sales and listings made. They have probably not been confronted with the theory of desk cost, cost per sale or income per sale. All these factors lead to owners feeling a complete lack of control over their organization.

Another major cause of a threatening leadership crisis has its genesis in the size of the sales staff. Many times brokers, hoping to promote the growth of their business, have allowed almost any salesperson to join their organization. Their sales staff may have grown from perhaps three or four qualified people to a collection of 25 or 30 working either full- or part-time. Such fast, uncontrolled growth causes the firm to experience continuing financial losses even as it grows in size and sales. The advertising budget gets completely out of hand and the return for ad dollars spent goes lower and lower because of incapable salespeople who have not been trained adequately.

At this point, the knowledgeable owners realize it is time for them to look around and find a strong business manager. This critical decision will probably have a bearing on the future success of the company.

Greiner comments, "At this point a crisis of leadership occurs. . . . Who is to lead the company out of confusion and solve the managerial problems confronting it? Quite obviously, a strong manager is needed who has the necessary knowledge and skill to introduce new business techniques. But this is easier said than done. The founders often hate to step aside even though they are probably temperamentally unsuited to be managers. So here is the first critical developmental choice—to locate and install a strong business manager who is acceptable to the founders and who can pull the organization together."

Good salespeople don't always make good managers. Thus, the broker may best be suited to continue as one of the top salespeople of the firm, do a strong job in general public relations and strengthen the organization by finding somebody else to handle the business management tasks.

For example, if the broker is a strong listing and selling agent and is bringing in $100,000 to $200,000 a year, his value to the firm is almost certain to be greater in sales work than it will be in management. He will then hire a manager to run the business, using management skills and techniques the broker may never have acquired.

Whether management work is done by the owner himself or someone from the outside hired as the business manager, let us assume that the firm has solved its leadership crisis. The company is now poised to move into a new period: growth through direction.

Phase Two: Growth Through Direction

This new evolutionary period in real estate firms has certain characteristics:

A policy and procedure manual is developed, outlining rules and regulations of the firm

Specific job descriptions are written for each person in the firm which enable sales staff and office personnel to know exactly what is expected of them

Communications become more formal, more frequent

Accounting systems are established and

Budgets are developed.

In this new growth period, management frequently develops incentive programs for the salespeople, outlining minimum quotas necessary to achieve their sales goals. Everyone in the organization is aware of established work standards and accepts personal responsibility to sustain them.

Formalized accounting systems are introduced. They not only provide exact cost figures for the day-to-day operation but also enable the owners to keep track of the cash flow of the business and what obligations it will sustain. Along with this, budgeting is introduced and the practical direction of the company's overall economic policies is begun.

Communications become more formal between management and the sales staff as the hierarchy of titles and positions is initiated. Basically, all decisions must still go through the owner or manager of the firm and rather tight control over the sales staff is established.

One of the dangers of the more formal communication system is the loss of the old policy of just sitting down and talking about problems. The new formality many times results in an overreaction by management as it becomes too directive in its style, telling people what it wants done without bothering to consult them on the best way of doing it.

Another possible danger is that budgets set up under a control system may not be truly goal-oriented. They may be simply figures on a piece of paper. When this happens, growth continues but it has little direction except on an annual basis because that is the time span of the budget itself.

On the positive side, the new management is making firm decisions and this is certainly an improvement over the lack of direction the company suffered in its previous phase. So although there are still problems, the firm does enjoy a period of growth through direction. And management's compensation is basically a salary which generally fluctuates with the increase or decrease of business and the resulting profitability.

With passing time, even these new, stronger directions allow some cracks to develop in the solid foundation alluded to above. It is at this point the company finds itself facing a crisis of autonomy.

Crisis of Autonomy

Greiner comments, "Although the new directive techniques channel sales associate energy more efficiently into growth, they eventually become inappropriate for controlling a larger, more diverse and complex organization."

In the real estate business this can be translated into a situation where the sales staff finds itself torn between following formal procedures and taking initiative. It is during this period perhaps more than any other that salespeople become dissatisfied and terminate their relationship with the firm.

While the new management is more efficient, it eventually becomes somewhat inappropriate for a larger, diversified firm. Those that have grown very quickly find there is too much centralization of authority. The company seems to stagnate because everything must go through the key manager or owner before any action can be taken. And when the company has added lower level managers and salespeople who assist the manager everyone becomes confused by the new hierarchy. Generally it is evident that there is one key manager in the organization. But the rest of the managers or salespeople are confused about what their responsibility is to that particular key person and what his relationship with them is going to be. He becomes almost a "king-tyrant" when nothing can be done without his permission. In this way creativity is often stifled in an organization.

As the key manager becomes more involved in everyday management problems and setting up budgets and controls for the organization he begins to know less and less about the actual business of listing and selling real estate. He becomes increasingly out of touch with the market place and cannot be of much assistance in helping salespeople solve the marketing problems they bring to him. The end result is that salespeople lose their enthusiasm for following this manager's direction.

The crisis of autonomy can be serious when the former managers (or owners) do not want to give up control. In a smaller organization, the former manager may be the broker who has discontinued selling and is going full force into management. He may believe he is doing a good job, not realizing that he has built up a "king-tyrant" image. If in fact delegation does take place, the lower echelon managers (or in smaller organizations, the salespeople) are not accustomed to making decisions and therefore need complete retraining. Many times the key manager moves up to a different type of position, gives up some of his authority and delegates it to others. He expects them to be able to handle it immediately with no additional training. Then he is frustrated to find that others don't do things as well as (or the way) he did. At this point he may step back to resume control because of what he sees as inadequacies of his subordinates. Actually, had he taken time to train those taking over his position he would have found the transition much smoother.

The autonomy crisis is often difficult to identify. When this is so, the company simply flounders. There is either a resultant lack of creativity under the "king-tyrant" management or things go badly when authority has been delegated without sufficient retraining. Because both these situations are difficult to recognize, the manager must be on the watch constantly. If he is getting good feedback from his salespeople, they will bring it to his attention. If he is getting neither feedback nor satisfactory results he must look to himself and the type of training he gave those to whom he has delegated authority.

Phase Three: Growth Through Delegation

"The next era of growth evolves from the successful application of a decentralized organization," says Greiner.

Characteristic of this phase of growth is:

Beginning delegation of authority

Beginning decentralization

Introduction of control systems

Management focus on problems and

Communication becomes less frequent, more formal.

The wise real estate manager recognizes the problems of his new growth and his own management skills and begins to delegate authority and to decentralize his organization. This decentralization or delegation of authority moves the company into the phase of growth through delegation. If during this evolutionary period the firm looks to increasing its share of the market, either through acquisition or expansion of its present facilities, managers will have more authority than during prior phases.

The organizational structure is often decentralized and changed geographically with the opening of branch offices, each given authority to run its own operation. In fact, the company now becomes three, four or five different companies (depending on the number of branches) under one general name, each branch having autonomy.

Wherever possible, duties are delegated to branch office managers or to persons in charge of a specific duty. Rather than directing people as they did in Phase 2 (growth through direction), management now delegates authority to those on the firing line and allows them to proceed to work for the best results they can attain.

Control systems are set up through reports from the branch offices. Top management keeps in touch with what branch offices are doing through their regular reports. It is at this stage of growth a real estate firm is likely to offer bonuses to stimulate the branches to do their best.

Now top management manages by exception. They focus their attention and effort on troubled areas. As long as a branch office is not having a problem, top management pays little attention beyond the regular review of its operation and how the results relate to goals and budgets. Management is paying great attention to those offices that are new, having trouble getting off the ground. They work to solve people problems wherever they occur. This is truly management by exception. It is described by some as management by crisis.

During this growth period communication from top management becomes more infrequent and very formal. About the only time lower level managers hear from top management is when there is a problem. Being called by the boss usually elicits a negative reaction.

What are some of the dangers in phase three that move a company from growth through delegation into the crisis of control?

One of the results of successful growth of an organization is that top management loses touch with lower management. When this happens, top management also loses its empathy for both the outlook and problems of lower management. The nadir of communications is reached when top management loses all real contact with what is going on in the market place and devotes all its attention and energies on being business managers.

Top management runs the risk of losing its empathy with salespeople if it becomes more interested in production quotas than it is in the people who meet them. This can happen when top management tries to push expansion by offering incentives and bonuses as the sole motivation of its people, showing little or no regard for the individual's personal motivation and personal goals.

Finally, the type of compensation or reward emphasis is on individual bonuses. Each manager who is responsible for a particular area is compensated by the firm with individual bonuses or salary increases.

The period of growth through delegation can be a difficult one for the manager because he can never be sure what authority to release, what to retain. Confusion in releasing authority and choosing the proper person to whom it should now be delegated is the root of emerging problems. Though the firm can enjoy great growth through delegation and, it is hoped, an increase in profits, management is creating future problems for itself that eventually are manifest in a crisis of control.

Crisis of Control

Greiner notes that this crisis evolves "as top executives sense that they are losing control over a highly diversified field operation."

In real estate, top management discovers they have given so much authority to local branch offices that they seem to have created little kingdoms within their own larger kingdom. This has two results.

Branch managers leave to start their own company. They've been so well educated in how to run a real estate business that they believe they can do the same themselves.

Top management discovers that branch managers are no longer responsive to the needs of the whole company. They run their own autonomous operation without bothering to coordinate plans, training and other essential facets of the business with either top management or the managers of the firm's other branches.

During this crisis, top management moves to regain control of the situation. Sometimes they try to turn back the clock and return to growth through direction. That usually fails because the firm has grown in size and scope to the point where this form of management no longer works.

What does succeed in solving this crisis is careful planning to coordinate controls. Rather than returning controls to top management, a compromise is worked out. People and practices are coordinated in such a way that top management and branch offices begin to move together as a force. The company gradually works its way out of the crisis of control.

Phase Four: Growth Through Coordination

Phase four, says Greiner, is "the evolutionary period characterized by the use of formal systems for achieving greater coordination and by top executives taking responsibility for the initiation and administration of these new systems."

Characteristics to watch for in this phase include:

A real consolidation of the operation as systems and people are coordinated

Organizational structure changes

Management enters a "watchdog" phase

Control systems and profit centers emerge and

Formal planning procedures are established.

One characteristic of this phase is that the organization actually begins to consolidate and bring leadership back into focus. This is rarely, if ever, an announced action; it can seem to evolve almost by accident but it is actually the result of careful planning. Top management develops new, more formal systems, works with managers on the lower level to coordinate them and makes certain everyone is in agreement before any new system is introduced. Ideas are sought from lower management people but they may not be forthcoming because these people harbor uncertainties caused by the lack of communication during the growth through delegation phase.

The consolidation of this phase may involve closing branch offices; or it may be achieved through consolidation of management itself. Dead wood is weeded out. "Growth for growth's sake" is put aside. The goal of getting a well functioning management team becomes the focus of the organization's efforts.

Now organizational structure changes from a property/service type of organization to one of real estate departments and groups. The groups—such as residential, commercial-investment and property management—are established and for the first time management authority becomes diversified in a vertical fashion. For example, the managers in the residential group will work together as a team; managers in the commercial-investment group will work together as a team where once each worked as separate individuals in their separate offices.

Now the top management assumes a kind of watchdog stance. They watch all departments and their reports very closely and when they see a lack of coordination begin to develop between departments, it is their job to bring them back together.

Control systems become profit centers themselves. But instead of profit centers by branch offices, they now become profit centers by product groups. Where in the past there may have been ten residential branch offices with ten different profit centers, these would now probably be grouped as one. For example, management would now consider residential as one profit center having ten subgroups within it made up of the branch offices. Thus, profit centers now become residential, commercial-industrial, investment, property management and so on down the line. If the business is purely residential, the profit centers may be made up of geographic groupings such as the northern office, main office, southern office and so on.

In this phase reward emphasis may change into profit sharing and stock options. Everyone involved gets a piece of the action because there is true coordination of ideas and resultant sharing in the success of the whole operation.

Probably the most significant trait of the growth through coordination phase is that formal planning procedures are established and reviewed before being implemented. And it is at this stage the management staff is often enlarged to initiate new programs and assure smooth coordination between upper and lower management. Capital expenditures are now budgeted carefully—not only on a yearly basis but on a two- to five-year basis for long-term goals.

Each department or product group now stands and falls on its own—almost as a separate company. If, for example, the commercial division is not doing well, top management spends time finding out what the problem is and how it can be solved. The "cancer" may be cut out of the organization and the commercial division dropped for a time or the department may be revamped completely.

This phase of evolution finds bookkeeping and accounting procedures have become more sophisticated as a greater number of departments must be coordinated. Centralization of accounting systems become almost a necessity.

In short, management coordinates every idea and system throughout the entire organization, making sure there is a check and countercheck to everything before it is acted on. As all these balancing ideas are put together, the company begins to become ultra-sophisticated (with everyone making sure they have a report on what everybody else is doing) and the firm is likely to move into the crisis of red tape.

Red Tape Crisis

Greiner says this crisis is created by "a lack of confidence [that] gradually builds between line and staff, and between headquarters and the field. The proliferation of systems and programs begins to exceed its utility...."

Lower managers begin to criticize the higher managers for not knowing what is going on in the various departments or branches. Upper management is always looking at paper work, making sure the system is working properly. But they seem to have forgotten completely what the business of brokerage is: selling real estate.

Procedure has become more important than the problem. Top management has become more concerned that proper forms are filled out and proper reports are given to the right individuals than they are about production per se. In short, red tape has taken over to the point that when the company goes out of business the managers will be able to tell you exactly why it failed. They are so engrossed in paper work they fail to correct the causes for a threatened business failure.

Although new ideas are well coordinated before being put to use, they almost all originate with top management because lower level managers have never been encouraged to come up with better ideas. And because these same lower level managers are concerned only with production of their individual profit centers and their survival, they spend little time in creative thinking.

Thus, management is now challenged to use the crisis of red tape as the reason for entering a new phase of evolutionary growth through participation.

Phase Five: Growth Through Participation

As Greiner notes, this phase of growth builds around a more flexible and behavioral approach to management. Here are its characteristics:

Greater spontaneity in management

Focus on problem solving and innovation through team effort

Coordination of all those involved in management decisions

Rewarding the whole team for successes and

Management education programs.

Management enters a phase of less formal control and self-discipline. At this point the organization begins to work truly as a team with interaction and creative ideas coming from all areas.

Management's focus is now on problem solving and innovation. All managers are involved with planning for the future and anticipating problems that may result from these particular plans. They truly have learned from experience as they moved through the five phases of growth. They understand that for each solution they have come up with, a new crisis has been created. Now they start to plan anticipating the crisis and how they might overcome it.

The organization structure becomes one of coordination of department teams. The organization begins to use all department heads in management decisions and encourages the respective departments to come up with creative ideas on how better to handle the problems at hand.

The top management style, instead of being delegative or watchdog, becomes participative and therefore they join hands with lower managers in making joint decisions, discussing each one thoroughly before they move ahead.

The control system of the organization is that of mutual goal setting. Goals are set with all management department heads. Each department head understands the goals of every other department and how all are interwoven with the problems of the total company.

The management reward emphasis now becomes that of a team bonus. If the team does well as a whole then the whole team will be rewarded with bonuses. If a particular department within the team does well its members may receive an additional bonus.

In short, the focus is to solve problems with team action, to use more minds to come up with better solutions to problems. In some cases teams may even cross the boundaries of a department. For example, commercial-investment may come into the residential area to help them solve a problem which perhaps the commercial-investment side had encountered at a previous time. Formal systems are simplified. Communication becomes easier from top to bottom, red tape disappears, allowing people to spend more time in creative, productive pursuits rather than simply filling out forms for forms' sake.

Frequent conferences are called to solve problems. These are not formal meetings but they are conferences of two or three key individuals to get their thoughts on any problems that may be threatening to develop. The spontaneity of increased communication is helpful in the organization as everyone realizes they are part of the decision-making process.

For the first time true educational programs for the managers begin so that they are well trained in what their responsibilities are and what is expected of them. Finally, any new ideas that might increase productivity of the whole company are constantly encouraged from each department and each manager. In this way, the company begins to enjoy growth through participation or team effort.

Guidelines

Know where you are in the developmental sequence. Get to know the various stages so you become aware of just where your firm is and are alert to the need to change. Work through the phases in their natural flow. Don't try to skip any phase or to work against it. Each has its strengths and learning experiences that will contribute to the ensuing

Stages of Development in Real Estate Firms

Category	Phase 1	Phase 2	Phase 3	Phase 4	Phase 5
Management Focus	List and Sell	Efficiency of Operations	Expansion of Market	Consolidation of Organization	Problem Solving and Innovation
Organization Structure	Informal	Centralized and Functional	Decentralized and Geographical	Line-Staff and Product Groups	Coordination of Department Teams
Top Management Style	Individualistic and Entrepreneurial	Directive	Delegative	Watchdog	Participative
Control System	Market Results	Standards and Cost Centers	Reports and Profit Centers	Profit Centers	Mutual Goal Setting
Management Reward Emphasis	Ownership	Salary and Merit Increases	Individual Bonuses	Profit Sharing and Stock Options	Team Bonus

This chart has been changed only slightly to relate it more closely to the real estate business.

phase. Don't try to avoid the periods of revolution. They have the positive element of contributing stimulation, pressure, awareness and the challenge to come up with new ideas that will carry you into the next growth period.

Recognize the limited range of solutions. You will learn that each revolutionary stage and your solutions for getting out of it differ from any preceding crisis. If you try to use solutions that worked for prior crises you will find it impossible to move into the next phase of growth.

Look ahead. Be prepared to dismantle troublesome organizational structures before a situation gets out of hand. In order to move ahead you may have to move people (yourself or others) around, either within the company or to a new outside affiliation.

Your ability to sell your ideas will be essential to your success. Your awareness and understanding of the current problem and your foresight in seeing how your solution will fit into the next phase of growth are among your most important management skills.

Realize that solutions breed new problems. It is a natural sequence that solutions for today's problem in a growing organization will eventually cause a new problem. Thus, the ability to solve a current problem through greater understanding of the company's long-term goals (rather than "pinning the blame" on a particular person or factor) will prove a positive determinant of what happens to the firm in the future.

Real estate managers should develop the knowledge and skills that will enable them to predict future problems and so prepare solutions and coping strategies before things get out of hand. Management should be sure they want the company to grow. They may decide their present size suits them well, both in the income it produces and the way of life it offers. If they decide they want to grow, it should be based on a genuine desire and not just because there's more money there to be made.

In conclusion, it is evident there is still a great deal to be learned about the evolution and revolution phases in the real estate field. Changing market and economic conditions demand growing skills. Studying detailed phases in this chapter offer today's real estate leaders one way to meet and overcome whatever new challenges lie ahead.

Market Analysis 17

Customary growth of a real estate organization by expansion either in number of salespeople or by branching out into neighboring locales has historically been a matter of spot judgment. Decisions to expand have been made with a general awareness of what the marketplace offers in terms of availability of listings or buyers. Timetables have been based on availability of working capital or a surplus of cash. The whole process has been based on a "gut feeling" or "seat of the pants" approach. That this approach may be effective cannot be denied because it has resulted in some remarkable successes. It is the purpose of this chapter to examine and then organize the factors which comprise this "seat of the pants" decision so that a logical recognition, interpretation and analysis of the main factors involved can be made.

Market Analysis

We know that regardless of economic conditions as long as there are listings that need to be sold there is a real estate market. The market collapses entirely when either no one wishes to sell, is concerned enough with exterior events to stay put or has no rational need to make a real estate move. Otherwise, whether in a falling or a rising market, as long as people sense a need to move there is an opportunity for real estate sales.

Before making a move into another area or even expanding within your given location, it is essential that a study be made of the market. Records kept of listings obtained can give an indication of an increase or decrease of listing availability within the market area. A look at deed transfers in title companies or county recorders' offices will verify whether the individual business experience correlates with that of the community to a significant degree.

A study of the volume of new building being developed will give an indication of future potential not only in terms of numbers but also in terms of physical direction as well as nature of use.

Changes in Multiple Listing Service statistics on listings procured and sold and a comparison of "by-owner" classified ads can also indicate relative change.

If listing availability seems acceptable, it would be a good indication that there is a market for real estate brokerage services. The feeling for this kind of market should be substantiated with some statistical analysis verifying the belief. In one situation a broker was planning expansion from one location in town to another location on the other side of town. He was dissuaded from doing so after learning that the total potential for listings in the community were running under 100 a month and he was already the exclusive broker for between 30 and 40 of them. The statistical evaluation of an expanding market proved there was turnover, not expansion. Considerable savings were realized by not going to the expense of an additional office which would not have increased his share of the market substantially.

Effect of Population on Expansion

Overall increase or decrease in population as recorded by the Census Bureau, Village Hall or city authorities can provide some interesting data on the growth potential of a real estate company. Any decrease should be cause for concern about what the long-term trend might be.

It is essential that each broker have some concept of the total number of available units for sale during any given period.

The first step in the analysis would be to determine the number of properties that represent the inventory in the trading area. Currently, statistics indicate there are some 3.4 individuals per family unit. Thus, the area population total divided by 3.4 would give the approximate number of living units. Taking out of this number rental apartments, mobile homes or other units which would not serve as a part of the real estate marketplace would result in a net housing inventory available. This inventory should then be converted into the number of possible units that could be sold each year. The result will indicate whether the market is sufficiently strong to support expansion.

Turnover statistics can best be obtained by checking figures in such easily identified areas as water meter turn-ons, phone company hook-ups, club membership turnover, church transfers and country club changes. In one residential area, a swimming club of 350 members indicated a consistent turnover of between 40 and 50 each year. When analyzed, these figures represented 8 to 10 who dropped membership because their children no longer needed the swimming facilities. The balance were transferred out of the area, indicating some 10 to 12 percent of the available housing units were changing hands every year. These turnover figures when applied to the total housing inventory will give some indication of the total market. After applying a factor on the percentage a broker might reasonably expect to obtain, a definite decision can be reached as to whether there is enough potential in that marketplace to support expansion.

Labor Demand

Demand for skilled, semi-skilled and unskilled labor creates a marketplace for real estate which requires either expansion to take care of the inquiries or indicates a need for the creation of a larger housing inventory.

The most obvious source of labor demand is the entry into the community of new manufacturing or service facilities which will create a demand for labor. An experience of this type was the erection of a 2,000 room hotel in Las Vegas, which by its very construction and operation required the need for labor to build, run and maintain it. The rule of thumb in the hotel industry of 1.5 employees per room indicates a need for approximately 3,000 employees in this hotel operation. Such a demand creates a real estate market.

New manufacturing facilities, the establishment of shopping centers or a discussion with personnel directors of already established local businesses about their labor requirement forecasts can verify a strength and demand for people. When brokers are blessed by a growing economy, expansion of their business to meet these requirements can be much greater than a "seat of the pants" feeling might indicate.

As we move into the final decade of the century, the expansion of recreational facilities of all types will develop a sizeable labor market, which will result in increased need for real estate services.

Public relations calls on local industries by the key man in a real estate business can elicit information on their expansion plans and provide an excellent guide to growth potential which would not otherwise be evident. A good example of this is an automotive assembly plant which employs approximately 10,000 people. An increase of 10 percent in orders can be felt directly in terms of new hires which result in a substantial upswing in the demand for residential housing. Under normal conditions, the increase or decrease of 1,000 people in an operation that size could not be measured without direct information from company officials.

Housing Demand

One of the interesting factors that affects a real estate market not only in regard to volume but also influences timing for expansion is the fluctuation in demand. One very interesting statistic that ought to be looked at is the length of time the average home is on the market.

A home buying company from Elizabeth, New Jersey, has measured the length-of-time-of-ownership for the properties purchased on behalf of corporations from their employees. A gauge of the marketplace was obtained by keeping track of the number of days the property was owned by the home buying corporation. Since it materially affected the company's investment in the property, it was a matter of importance. However, for brokers considering expansion, a market that indicates a change either way could be valuable information.

For instance, if the number of days required to sell a property is increasing, it could mean that a substantial increase in exclusive listings obtained from "by owners" would result. Also, a shortening in the time required to sell properties might indicate a demand of such proportion that buyers would be attracted to do business with brokers so they would hear about new listings the moment they come on the market. An analysis of this demand as evidenced by the fluctuation of classified ads in the paper, an increase in signs and a study of Multiple Listing Service records could give statistical valuation to the housing demand.

Geographic Potential

It is interesting to note the geographic factors which influence the expansion of a given real estate market. The historic strength of a community based on accessibility to transportation by waterways of rail has now been amplified by accessibility to raw material resources, power supplies, water for industrial cooling, airports, interstate highways and finally strategic location in surrounding markets. One of the interesting developments in the United States has been the growth of regional centers like Atlanta, whose geographic location has given them a material advantage in the expansion of the community. Add another factor of living desirability in communities like Phoenix where the year round climate has attracted a wealth of manpower. Factors like these make the expansion of all kinds of industry and services a natural sequence of cause and effect.

Conversely, environmental restrictions, especially in areas which are smog prone, can put a damper on expansion. Some areas like the New York metropolitan area are restricted by natural barriers of ocean and water and mountains, a condition which tends to fragment the growth of areas in peculiar ways.

Economic Base for Expansion

The economic base of an area is also an important factor in its expansion potential. A highly diversified economic base or a single unit natural resource base make good economic sense for expansion.

A study of both the geographic and the economic base of a community and a recording of its cyclical nature or its rise or decline could be of definite interest to a broker planning expansion. Expanding in a declining market could bring on economic disaster. Equally important is the filling of an expansionary vacuum in services timed to be made on the upswing rather than at the peak.

Timing of Expansion

One of the crucial factors in expanding an office so that it shows maximum profit in the shortest time is the timing of the expansion.

In one area of the midwest the historic down market is in the late fall and early winter period from November through December. In addition, the strong market is between May and the end of August. Knowing these two factors, timing expansion to coincide with the strong May market would eliminate several months of poor business before meeting the upswing. A prospective facility might be rented or purchased but not actually put into production until the time was as favorable as possible. It might also mean a delay based on timing if the best period of the year had passed.

If in studying the market potential of an area there seems to be a downtrend as a neighborhood changes, the decision to move from that location to another might better be made as soon as practicable. There is little doubt that serious consideration of timing an expansionary move is particularly important.

Another factor of importance in the timing of an expansion program is the national economic climate, which in the past decades has shown us periods of economic crunch which would be an inopportune time to expand. With this cyclical program, the expansion again should be positioned on the upswing to take maximum advantage of the market change.

Restrictive Codes and Ordinances

Many areas of the country today are being adversely affected by stringent building codes, zoning ordinances and "no-growth" policies. Such political interference can seriously obstruct a marketplace.

A typical example of this is a village which has decided against permitting the erection of higher than three-story buildings within its boundaries, delaying much desirable construction which would convert low tax revenue properties into higher tax properties. The resultant increase in tax load on the individual residences is causing a reaction against the price structure and deteriorating market values in this area. These restrictive zoning ordinances can have considerable impact on the desirability of real estate expansion.

On the other hand, if there are some reasonable, sensible master plans or flexible codes that will permit easy construction and maximum use of land, they could be a positive indication that expansion is timely.

Needed Commercial Facilities

One of the potentials for expanding a brokerage business can be found in the imbalance that occurs when large residential tracts are developed without providing commercial/industrial facilities to complement them. Frequently a residential broker can find a large opportunity in supplying commercial facilities to an expanding residential community. This imbalance will be particularly important as we move into the twenty-first century. The number of real estate facilities existing today will need to increase greatly to accommodate the population and its recreation and service demands.

Tax Loads
One factor which has a direct bearing on the potential of an area is its tax load. A light tax burden can easily be translated by a buyer into mortgage payments which permit him to raise his sights on his house economics. Conversely, relatively high tax burdens discourage buyers from purchasing property in such an area. Any broker planning expansion will want to study the tax load potential that might be placed on the community he is considering currently or in the future. Such a study will take into account the projected demand for school services which account for a major portion of the tax load. Ask whether additional facilities will be built, whether there is any demand for improved educational facilities on the part of the taxpayers and even the competitive nature of the school system with those in surrounding communities. In addition to this, the type of village or city government in existence and the kinds and types of people involved in the local administration should be considered.

A low tax rate can be a mixed blessing. A do-nothing city administration can have a stifling effect on the growth of the community. Change in administration can promise progressive, aggressive action which will stimulate the area, even though taxes are sure to increase. The point here is that low taxes are not necessarily desirable if adequate services and good administration are not being provided.

Vacant Land
Just as a lack of geographic restrictions makes expansion possible, so does a lack of expansion within a town cause problems. When a town sees itself as a small individual unit and fails to expand its boundaries as it grows, vacant property soon fills up with construction. Large estates are broken down to provide additional land for a very few buildable parcels. When this happens, a stand off in the increase in deed transfers takes place and the market becomes highly restricted and competitive.

If an area is land locked by mountains or other geographic restrictions, this can become an acute problem. The question then arises: will the town deteriorate or will its desirable features provide for movement in and out, keeping the inventory of real estate in good condition and highly desirable? At this stage, good schools, strong and active churches, up to date shopping centers, viable transportation and strong community, civic and cultural interests will make for a strong marketplace. In the absence of good community services and land for expansion, the end result could well be a deteriorating market which should be judged critically.

Need for Utilities
The inordinate and insatiable demands of the American public today make a good supply of energy and water crucial to an expanding real

estate market. The knowledgeable broker will evaluate the availability of these two resources and the effect the supply may have, either good or bad, on the area he is considering for expansion. Obviously, good water and energy supplies will be a positive contribution to the expansion potential of an area, stimulating interest in that market place by both people and industry.

Along with the availability of utilities is the consideration of waste disposal. Under current Environmental Protection Agency philosophy, the establishment of proper facilities for waste treatment and garbage disposal become important considerations. The expansion potential of whole areas has been reduced drastically by building permit refusals based on the unavailability of adequate sewage handling facilities. A thorough investigation of these services is of prime importance in expansion.

Competition Study

Expansion within an area or to another area can be greatly affected by the type of competition one may encounter.

An in-depth study of who is operating in the area, the kind of service they offer and success they are experiencing can be a strong indication of whether or not this would be a desirable area to move into.

Some areas are completely dominated by one or more very strong brokers and expansion into these areas would be a difficult and costly experience. Where markets are tightly controlled and the competition is firmly entrenched, a great deal of expense in terms of advertising and promotion must be planned if a new broker is to make any kind of impact. By contrast, if the expansion area being considered has very little or no competition or where the competition is primarily in "by owner" sales, expansion can be established relatively quickly, effectively and inexpensively, resulting in great progress in a short period of time.

In some cases the need to expand into an area of intense competition is great but it should be done with the knowledge that it will be more expensive to compete there than it might be elsewhere. In some areas it is recognized that the market is so divided among many poorly trained, unaggressive brokers that while the lure is an apparent lack of tough competition, the costs, time and fortitude required to invade and build up this market must be calculated carefully.

Real estate marketing is undergoing a great many changes and will continue to do so in the foreseeable future. If competition in the considered area is set in its ways and not flexible, it could provide an excellent opportunity to make an expansion move.

Serious consideration should be given to engaging the services of a professional marketing survey firm that can test the quality of the competitors' service, the impact of their name on the community and the strength of their hold on the market. In one interesting case study, it was assumed that a particular broker was exceptionally strong. Then research revealed that the name was unknown to almost 80 percent of the community. This fact largely negated the first impression of a strong organization. The competitor had obviously not penetrated the market as deeply as the outsider assumed.

Prime Need for a Manager

Even if all the aforementioned factors seem positive, expansion into a new area should never be made without adequate managerial support. The word never is a strong one and this is one of the few cases where it becomes a real imperative. Many promising operations start in good locations and attractive offices with all of the background services that could be provided, then fail because of an inadequate managerial staff. Conversely, there have been many examples of success on the part of brokers where both facilities and marketplace were not especially strong; yet a skilled manager was able to pull all the elements together to make the operation successful.

Certainly, promotion from inside the organization is most desirable. As a staff recruitment program moves along, some thought should be given to the management potential of the people being considered. Testing, training and development should be a regular part of any organization that is considering expansion.

While tests indicate basic qualities of a manager, they do not relieve the broker of using his best skill and judgment in the recruitment of management talent. One way management can be developed is through an assistant manager program where a qualified recruit is given a job description of management tasks and allowed to perform them under the guidance of the broker. As these skills are developed and encouraged, the whole expansion program becomes possible.

Market Analysis Checklist

What must you know about the new market area? You cannot know too much, but these points are essential.

What is the population today and what is projected in five years, ten years, fifteen years?

What are the zoning laws, land restrictions, land improvement costs for sewer, water and other municipal services?

What is the type of municipal government? What has been their attitude toward growth? What is their projection for expansion and development of both land and government services?

Is the school system adequate? What is the teacher/pupil ratio?

Can present facilities accommodate expansion?

What is the current and projected tax structure?

What is the total dollar volume of business done in the area each year?

What is the trend over the last five years?

How many new telephones were installed last year? What is the telephone company's projection for the future?

What are the plans of the principal builders in the area? Is land for development readily available?

How many real estate offices exist in the area? How many salespeople work the area? How much of the total market does each firm enjoy?

Who are the leaders? What type offices do they have? Are their techniques modern? Get acquainted with most of the brokers in the area.

What do the opinion makers say about the area and its future? You should talk with: local bankers, municipal officers, hospital administrators, ministers, Chamber of Commerce officials, school officials, builders, attorneys and other key business and professional people.

Spend some time with the local REALTOR® board executive. He can supply you with valuable statistics and vital information about the area.

Determine what the typical home is in the area. What is its selling price? What are the most expensive and the least expensive homes selling for this year? Are homes appreciating in value?

Who is the typical buyer? Determine his age, where he works, his income, occupation, family size, etc.

Market Analysis

Determine what advertising media services the area best. What will it cost to use?

Horizontal Expansion   18

Once a broker achieves a degree of success in a single real estate office operation, it logically follows that he considers expansion. But expansion is complex and risky. With a limited amount of capital and perhaps even more limited experience, a broker should not plunge into horizontal expansion without asking

What are my objectives?

What is the price?

Am I willing to pay the price?

Horizontal expansion, by example, is a residential brokerage opening another residential office, as opposed to a residential firm opening a commercial-investment office, which would be considered vertical expansion. It should be started deliberately. When handled well the first time, it becomes almost a repeat performance each time another office is added. The ideas and information contained in this chapter come from brokers with wide experience in horizontal expansion, whose successes can help others.

Horizontal Expansion

The success or failure of a horizontal expansion program depends largely on the performance of top management. The manager of the original office will no longer be the chief, handling minute details to make sure everything is done right. His ability to motivate, train and delegate becomes critical to the success of the new branch.

Many brokers with experience in expansion report that opening their first branch office was more an emotional decision than a scientific one. It would be fine if one could use slide rule statistics, in-depth analyses and outside professional counseling and expert help. That is just not the way it is. Most of the time an opportunity arises when a selling broker is forced to make the transition to management in order to hold salespeople who resent his competition in selling and his failure to provide them the leadership they want and need. Because this is such a common cause for expansion and because the decision is often made in a fairly haphazard way, the results can be far from successful.

As discussed earlier, the transition to management is filled with frustration and personal turmoil for sales-oriented people. It often results in company production dropping drastically. But given a six-month period for both the selling broker and his old clients to adapt to his new role as manager, company production usually turns around, more than making up for his lost selling production.

There are some hard facts to accept in reaching a decision to expand:

It may take longer than you think to organize and start up

It may cost more than you plan

It may not operate exactly the way you want it to and

It may take longer to make a profit than you expect.

Once these facts are absorbed and accepted, think about the following "don'ts" that will help you avoid costly mistakes:

Don't open the office so far from the main office that there is no company identification

Don't choose a manager who is totally unfamiliar with the marketplace

Don't scrimp on pennies that eventually cost you thousands of dollars

Don't assume that two offices will eventually double your profit.

Brokers who have expanded horizontally recommend that the manager at the new location be involved in the planning all along the way. They state emphatically that if a broker cannot find the right leader for the new office he should abandon the idea immediately.

But before a broker begins to think about staff for a new operation, he must first deal with the practical consideration of the money needed to start up a new office.

Only after the financial considerations are weighed and found adequate can he go on to think about who will manage it. There is still plenty of time to involve the proposed manager in all the other important phases of planning and decision making.

Financial Requirements

Financial requirements for a new branch office will vary greatly with the purpose of the branch office. If it is to be merely a water hole extension of other offices that will contain only two, three or four salespeople, then the start-up cost is probably minimal. The branch office may be located in a construction trailer or a new home in a subdivision or similar type structure that will have minimum initial requirements.

However, if it is to be a full-grown branch office that is fully staffed by salespeople, the rule of thumb for start-up costs around the country is somewhere around $50,000 to $60,000. This figure includes capital and carrying costs needed to start the office and to run it until it generates enough income to carry itself.

Unfortunately, too many brokers consider only the actual physical outlay of cash for the structure, its improvement or remodeling and the furniture that will go into it. Then, as they come down the road three or four months and positive cash flow has not been started, they find that they run out of money and it's necessary for them to close their dream because of poor planning.

This causes a disastrous reaction because the salespeople lose all faith in the leadership of the company.

If the office was properly funded and does not meet the brokers' expectations, he should not hesitate to close it. But to close it because of poor cash planning will cause a negative reaction that will reverberate throughout the entire organization.

In addition to the startup costs the broker should estimate how long it will take for the office to break even or generate a positive cash flow. If the broker's prediction is that it will be six to nine months before positive cash flow will occur and he does not have sufficient monies to cover the office during that time, he would be foolhardy to go ahead. On the other hand, he may have a well established sales force in the area and he's simply moving their physical position from one location to the other. He anticipates cash flow almost immediately after startup and therefore less capital will be needed.

Management should scrutinize the hard cost items such as structure, improvements, remodeling and furniture carefully, relating it to the time estimated for the office to show a positive cash flow. If the two figures add up to more cash than is available, perhaps it would be well not to open a branch office at that time or to obtain additional funding.

Detailed checklists are provided at the end of Chapter 19. Some of the basic requirements one should consider in startup costs are: remodeling, decorating, carpeting, furniture, equipment, phone installation, printing and supplies, office and house signs, impact promotion and specialty items.

Centralized vs. Decentralized

There are operations of both types that work extremely well even in the same area. Management's decision whether to operate the business in a centralized fashion or to decentralize and give each branch considerable autonomy can find arguments favoring both methods.

Advantages of a centralized operation include management's closer control and more direct supervision of accounting, purchasing, training, closing and advertising. Centralized accounting enables management to control expenses more closely. Each profit center is set up with budget and expense records of its own and can be checked regularly by both the branch manager and the main office. Banking that is done centrally often enables the firm to develop leverage factors that prove helpful in expansion. Centralized purchasing and advertising also enable top management to keep closer control of important expense items. When you are centralized, training can be part of an overall recruitment-selection-training-retention program for the entire firm. Or you might consider centralizing only the training segment of your personnel program. If you have someone on the staff who is good in training, have him set up a school for all the new people as they come in. You don't have to have 50 in training. Start a school with as few as three or four. Training is not a numbers game.

Centralized closing is debatable. The positive factors for keeping this part of a brokerage business centralized include financing. Here again, leverage with the local bank can sometimes sustain a transaction that might otherwise fail. If you decide to decentralize that part of your operation only, a closing coordinator from the main office might represent management.

Decentralization has its distinct advantages too. If a manager has the ability to delegate responsibility and authority and get psychological commitments, you can have a branch manager who is not only a sales manager but an office manager and perhaps even a vice-president in charge. Such a person can do everything, including training. He can do his own accounting, posting, pay his own bills and make some impact with his brokerage account at the local bank. He can control his own expenses. He can recruit. He is literally an independent working under the firm's name, perhaps having a share of the operation or some stock in it. Such a branch operation can even be capitalized as a separate corporation.

Decentralized branches not only permit the manager greater freedom to operate according to local market conditions, they also challenge that manager's flexibility, efficiency and ability to develop the branch business according to his own concepts as they fit the firm's general policy and goals. The manager in a decentralized operation also enjoys a stronger image in his local community. Top management in these situations report that such branch operations are easier to measure in matters of efficiency and that this style operation definitely cuts overhead.

Whichever style is chosen, each branch operation should be assigned its fair share of main office administrative costs. Accounting, training, travel and entertainment expenses of top management all relate to basic company operations and should be shared by every office. This is best solved by computing the percentage of time spent by each of these individuals for the benefit of the branch office directly as well as for the benefit of the company as a whole. Then those percentages are allocated back to the branch office in the dollar expenses of the respective individuals.

Administration

Once it has been decided what type of branch office will be added and the type of manager it will require, the next step is to find a manager. It is a well known fact that real estate offices are successful because of good management and not because of good salespeople. In other words, one should not go out and open up a branch office simply because it has progressive, top salespeople. Unless proper management is available, the salespeople will typically be unable to solve their problems without rancor.

The Branch Manager

The characteristics and qualifications of a manager have already been discussed. However, it may be that the branch office manager will not need the entire spectrum of qualifications and characteristics needed to run a full office. Obviously, if he's not involved in cost analysis, budget control, statistics and advertising, these talents will not be needed.

Job Description

In either case, it is important that a complete job description for the manager be prepared so he knows exactly what his job is. Too often the owner-broker-manager assumes the new branch manager will know what his duties are, does not define them and is later discouraged because the branch office manager does not do what he was expected to do. However, when there is close examination of the facts, it's found that the owner-broker-manager failed to give the branch office manager a clear job description. Thus a lack of direction occurred at the inception of the branch office.

It is further suggested that after the initial outline of the job description is drawn, an in-depth meeting with the branch office manager be held to develop a final job description that is mutually agreeable. To assign jobs and duties that are not agreeable to him and then not allow him to give any feedback will probably result in his resenting those duties and not performing them properly. Certainly the branch office manager should understand how the expenses are allocated if he is to be compensated on any type of percentage of the net or gross.

Training

Also, the branch office manager should be encouraged to get proper training by going to the courses offered by the Real Estate Brokerage Council™. Getting him involved in management thinking in the local community by joining the Sales Marketing Executives or the American Management Association and other management-oriented groups will teach him to think more in terms of management than as a salesperson.

Compensation

The compensation of the branch office manager varies greatly with the duties he is expected to perform.

A number of firms pay their branch office manager no salary. In these cases the branch office manager is a selling type manager who has the opportunity to increase his sales volume because he has the title of office manager. Though this arrangement has the advantage of not increasing overhead for salaries and compensation to the manager, it has the inherent danger of encouraging the manager to pick up the cream of the business, short circuiting the other salespeople. It will also be difficult to get that manager to do other work because he may feel that he is not being paid to do it.

Another compensation plan gives the manager no salary but pays a percentage override of the gross sales of his office. This is used for managers who have no say in the cost or expense of that office and therefore should not be penalized for improper expense accounting because he has no control over it.

This approach follows the theory that a manager should be compensated on a percentage of either the gross or company dollar when his main thrust is to increase sales volume. A figure used quite often throughout the nation is approximately five percent of the gross.

No matter what method of compensation is followed, management should first decide the final income range a manager should have and then work backward. For example, if it is common for competing managers to have an income range of $30,000 to $40,000 in your area, determine how much in gross sales or company dollar sales is needed to generate enough volume so that five percent or maybe ten percent of that amount provides the compensation desired. Obviously, the manager's own sales activities would be in addition to those figures.

This approach to compensation is also used for non-selling managers who are paid an override in addition to a base salary. Here again management should calculate the approximate range of income the manager should receive, then figure the base salary plus a percentage override for the manager to be able to earn the total sum.

The third most commonly used method is for managers who are involved directly in the control of costs and overhead. In this case many managers are paid a percentage of the net. It will encourage them to keep expenses down and sales up. This theory can follow the others. He may be compensated on a percentage of net profits plus the sales commissions he earns; or if he is a non-selling manager, a percentage of the net profits plus a base salary.

In all cases, it is possible to increase the percentage and not pay a salary, putting the manager totally on incentive. The problem here is that in very bad years the manager's compensation can be almost completely wiped out by factors beyond his control.

The above suggestions for compensation are just that— suggestions. Compensation should be adapted to the specifics of a situation and adjusted to the individual motivations of the manager as well as what the owner is trying to accomplish through that manager. In short, the compensation method should be designed to reward results and to create the best condition between the branch manager and the owner in order to generate the best results. Compensation must be fair and just to encourage new managers and keep other managers. The owner who tries to skimp on management's compensation is shortsighted for it can have a negative effect on the whole operation.

Cost Computations

There are a few rules of thumb for breaking even in an anticipated office opening.

Compute the average income per sale anticipated times the unknown number of sales needed which will equal the known overhead. For example, if $1,200 (the average anticipated income per sale) times Y (the unknown number of sales) equals $30,000 in anticipated overhead, it means that 25 sales are necessary just to break even. This can be related to the number of salespeople necessary, a topic covered later in this chapter.

The second formula is used to estimate the unknown projected income as follows.

The anticipated average listing price × commission rate × the number of listings projected to be obtained × percentage of the listings that should be sold ÷ by the office commission splits = projected income. For example, a $70,000 average listing price × 7% commission = $4,900 × 20 listings (an average of ten salespeople averaging two listings per month) equals $98,000 × 70% of the listings sold = $68,600 ÷ by 2 (to represent a 50/50 company split) = $34,300 projected income. Please note that the above formula does not include any compensation to cooperative brokers which must be figured in the final relationship.

When one can estimate the projected income or the projected number of sales needed, one is then able to convert it to the number of salespeople needed.

Determining Number of Salespeople Required

There are two basic theories to use in determining the number of salespeople needed in a real estate firm. One is the quantity theory and the other is the quality theory.

Obviously the quantity theory suggests that real estate companies should hire as many salespeople as possible, hoping that each will bring in enough sales for their large numbers to show a generous cash flow.

The opposite is the quality theory in which one has fewer salespeople and trains them thoroughly so that each is able to generate a handsome income for himself as well as a profitable company dollar.

For those striving to go into the area of professional sales representation, the latter has to be the choice. However, this is not to say that the former has not been successful. In some cities it's the tradition of successful real estate operation.

One determining factor is the economics of the proposed office. If the proposed office economics indicate that one needs $30,000 per month to cover overhead and the average sales commission generates approximately $1,200 to your salespeople, on a 50/50 split, it is obvious that 25 sales per month are needed to cover basic expenses. If the rule of thumb in your area is approximately two sales per month per sales agent, you will need 12 salespeople just to break even.

Relationship to Developed Inquiries
Another rule of thumb used is the relationship to developed inquiries. If proper statistics have been kept, the company should have some idea as to how many inquiries come in in relationship to appointments made, which relates finally to sales themselves. Obviously enough salespeople must be available for opportunity time and/or floor time to be able to handle the inquiries and make appointments in order to have final sales; and the final sales should directly relate back to the inquiries so the salesperson is assured of making a reasonable income.

Relationship to Population Turnover
At one time many companies thought in terms of mileage circles— that a branch office should service X amount of square miles per salesperson. However, it is generally recognized now that this is not a safe rule of thumb. It is more important that the number of salespeople in the branch office be in relationship to the population turnover in the area. Obviously this does not include population turnover of people moving into or out of apartments since they do not require sales assistance. However, the population turnover of people in the sales market itself and the anticipated percentage of their share of the market can give a good indication of the number of salespeople needed to serve them.

To the other point of view, if it's an area of very low population turnover, fewer salespeople are needed. One should keep this in mind in arranging the initial square footage at the branch office so as not to end with more space than needed.

Need for Experienced or Pre-Trained Staff
Finally, one should pay attention to pre-trained or experienced people who will form the core of the operation. The success of the office often depends on starting with some experienced people who produce sales immediately. This plan is preferred over an office starting with a completely new staff who need three to six months to become familiar with the market and start generating income. One should also consider the number of experienced salespeople who may want to join the firm in their area.

In summary, the manager opening branch offices should be conscious of financial requirements and how they relate to future projected incomes. The manager should also be conscious of the fact that he must have a successful manager to operate the new branch office and be concerned about the way he will compensate him.

Finally, the manager should pay attention to the salespeople who will work out of the new office and make sure their number is in relationship to the potential of the market in which he is opening.

Opening a Real Estate Office 19

Here are guidelines to follow in preparing to open a real estate office—everything from how to make the very important choice of a general location, how to find the best site available and points to consider in deciding whether to rent, buy or build. Several workable floor plans are outlined and the advantages and disadvantages of each explored. Practical styles of decoration and furnishings and a shopping list of furnishings, equipment and services you'll need to get started in real estate brokerage are included.

Ways to establish your firm's identity in the new market and ideas for introducing your staff and services to the neighborhood are included. Concepts for effective management supervision of branch offices are examined. The control systems—financial, business and physical—necessary to operating a well-run real estate office are also covered.

Opening a Real Estate Office

The site of a real estate office is of prime importance to its success. Finding the best place available at a price you can afford will take a great deal of your time but will be well worth every minute you devote to it. Unfortunately, many brokers don't give enough thought to finding the best location and then getting the best site there, whether for a main office or a new branch operation. Instead, they take what's available in a general area and try to begin a profitable operation from there.

Site Possibilities
Let's first look at the general areas you may consider as you begin your search:

Downtown

Access highway

Highway to an expressway

Shopping center

"Waterhole"

Mobile.

Downtown
A downtown location is generally best for the small residential town or suburb in which the downtown area is the business core of the community. Generally in such a town there is adequate parking, the location is easy to get in and out of, there is little or no traffic congestion and it promises your firm strong identity in the community.

Downtown locations in large cities are usually favored by commercial-investment firms as well as property management companies. However, many residential, multi-family oriented property management companies and investment offices have gone into the suburban areas to be closer to the properties they either sell or manage (or both).

Commercial-investment real estate firms like to be downtown, close to the financial hub of the city and near attorneys and tax accountants who are involved in many of their transactions. Whenever possible, a downtown location should be near the courthouse, where statistical records essential to commercial-investment transactions are available.

On the other hand, large residential companies who have found their fame in the suburbs may decide to have a central office or a flagship office downtown. They look to the downtown area for identification and to prove to the community that their firm has arrived.

Downtown offices for residential firms are usually used for administrative purposes and fewer salespeople work out of those locations.

Downtown space is usually the most expensive available and it may lock the firm into a very high overhead at a time when sales are not too prosperous. In a major city prime downtown space in a first floor location runs from a minimum of $6 up to $20 and sometimes as high as $25 a square foot. Such rental costs can seldom be justified in return for the location itself.

An alternative to this is prime downtown space on the second or third floor with good identification on the first floor or outside on a busy street. This still gives good identification and yet keeps cost down somewhat.

The firm fortunate enough to find adequate space at a reasonable rate on a first floor is bound to have good walk-in traffic as well as good community identification. Obviously there is much less walk-in traffic on upper floors unless good identity is established at ground floor level.

The decision whether to choose a downtown site or one in a suburban area depends greatly on the forces and direction of the community itself. If the downtown area is decaying and most of the businesses have moved to the suburbs, management obviously would not plan to move to the city. But if the downtown area has been renewed or is maintained in a way that makes it an action center for the entire metropolitan community there are obvious advantages to being there.

Access Highway or Highway to an Expressway
The access highway location affords good traffic flow patterns for real estate offices. Such a location also usually provides easy access for salespeople who will use it most frequently. The location may also attract buyers and sellers because of its convenience.

The access highway office should have an easy-in easy-out location. Traffic speed will be brisk and one must allow adequate room for drivers to turn into and get out of the location. Avoid an access highway where a barrier in the middle of the road prevents drivers from turning from the opposite side of the road into the office.

Check with state police or local police departments to get their traffic count for the area and the average traffic speed. Fast food franchises (who choose their sites with great care and research) have found that if the speed is about 35 mph people will slow down and turn into their restaurant. The same would apply to real estate offices. Thus it is well to know the *average actual speed* on the road. Simply looking at the speed limit is not enough. An access road may have a posted speed limit of 45 mph but an actual average speed of only 25 or 30 mph because of congestion. This in some ways could help the broker's location because cars are moving at a slower than posted speed.

Access highways give excellent sign locations which can be utilized to the fullest. Most fast food franchises feel their sign should be seen for a minimum of one-quarter of a mile and preferably one-third of a mile before arriving at the site. This gives the driver adequate time to think about turning into their property. A similar rule of thumb could apply to a real estate office.

Another advantage of the access highway is that it is a well known address. When the address is given to people coming to your office they'll know immediately where it is and perhaps even be able to visualize the building itself.

If the average speed is not too high, the access highway may produce stop-in traffic similar to walk-in traffic in other locations. In today's mobile society, people are walking very little and driving a lot. Therefore the broker must consider the possibility of drive-in traffic as opposed to walk-in traffic.

One further advantage of an access highway site is that because it is on a main thoroughfare in the city, salespeople can cover more territory in less time.

Shopping Center

A shopping center has a definite advantage of high walk-in traffic. The real estate firm in a shopping center with attractive window displays will draw people into their office for inquiries.

However, on the minus side, some brokers have found that they had so much walk-in traffic it forced them to put extra salespeople on duty. This restricts salespeople's time in the field where they could either be doing other work that might lead to sales or be more productive in other ways. Many times the walk-in traffic in shopping centers is similar to window shopping in retail stores. That is, people simply look at the pictures and want a little more information. But they are not serious buyers. Brokers are cautioned to choose a location that will not tie up too much effective manpower for a minimum return.

Generally, the people who walk into a shopping center office are less qualified and less likely to buy property than those who walk into a free standing building at a less convenient location.

Major shopping center space can be rather expensive in relation to the business it generates. Strip store shopping malls tend to cost less per square foot and also give a little better sign identification.

Most shopping centers have adequate parking. Be sure to check whether parking spaces can be reserved near the office. Some brokers have moved into shopping centers believing they had ample parking only to discover the parking lot jammed with cars every day. Their customers had to walk a quarter- to a half-mile to get to their office because closer spaces were all taken early in the day. This also proved an inconvenience for salespeople and discouraged them from using that office as an operating base.

Another thing to check carefully is the identity allowed in the shopping center itself. Many newer shopping centers do not allow exterior or interior sign identification except in a stipulated size which is governed by the shopping center management. If sign identification is to be so restricted that people have trouble finding you, the firm has lost the whole intent of strong identification and the only people who will know you are there are those who come into the shopping center itself.

Small Branch or Field Office

The small branch or field office (often known as a "waterhole") is the type office sometimes installed in a new shopping center or a new area of town in which the broker feels a full-size branch office is not yet justified. Such an office would not have a full-time secretary or any assistants but perhaps employ a part-time secretary several afternoons a week. Generally the salespeople on duty will answer the telephones and type whatever limited correspondence originates there; or all correspondence might be sent to the central office to be typed and mailed.

The small branch or field office is not only suited to new areas and subdivisions but is also a possibility for small satellite towns. For example, a broker may have his main office in a major metropolitan area ten or fifteen miles away but believes there is sufficient promise to justify a limited operation in the satellite town on a trial basis.

Brokers are cautioned to check state regulations and requirements for management of these offices. Many states view them as full branch offices and require that the manager be a licensed broker.

Mobile Office

Another alternative to the small branch field office is the mobile office such as a trailer bus or travel bus like those made for commercial camp vehicles.

These buses retail in a price range of $30,000 to $60,000 and can go even higher if the broker has them customized for his particular operation. They are a fairly expensive solution to the need for a temporary office.

The mobile office can serve temporarily as a "waterhole" office at a new location, a new subdivision or a new town. It is also ideal for a broker who has several subdivisions and wants to move his office from place to place.

Generally, a trailer bus interior is customized so there is adequate room for a typewriter and desk and space for consultation with clients. The outside of the bus can be attractively painted with the company colors. This gives institutional advertising while it is being moved from one location to another.

Another use for the mobile office is by brokers who sell resort properties outside a metropolitan area. In this case, they can transport several prospects at one time right in the mobile office to the location of the resort properties. Once there, the driver converts the bus into an office type setting while agents show the properties. Thus it is ready for whatever negotiations may ensue.

Finally, novelty vehicles such as old double deck British buses or luxuriously outfitted mobile offices may be used for philanthropic activities from time to time. These not only provide strong community identification but are also good public relations for the firm when donated or rented at cost to philanthropic organizations for special events, parades and the like.

Branch Location in Relation to Present Office

There are several rules of thumb on how to locate a branch office in relation to a present or main office. "Rules of thumb" vary almost as much as thumbs!

One long-accepted rule of thumb is that a single residential office can satisfactorily service 25,000 population. This does not take into consideration what the turnover rate of the population is nor does it suggest the number of salespeople who will work from such an office.

So how does one go about establishing one's own rule of thumb?

Brokers can develop their own check list for gathering necessary information. Such a check list should answer the following questions:

What are the physical boundaries of the community this office will serve and does it overlap areas served by our present offices?

What is the population of the area?

What is the turnover rate of housing there?

What percentage of the sales or the total business in the designated community can the broker realistically expect to command in three to four years?

What barriers exist within the area to be served?

Once a broker has computed the percentage of business he hopes to be able to control in three to four years, he can apply that percentage to the population turnover to get an indication of how many sales per year this new office should make. This figure is a guide to the number of salespeople needed to service those sales.

Certainly when a broker considers branch office locations he must look at the city's expressway system. Cities that have good expressway systems both north and south, east and west need fewer branch offices than those with a limited expressway system or none at all. Merely to open another office so he can say he has more offices is an ego trip a broker can ill afford. Unfortunately in the past too many brokers have concluded that the more offices they have the more successful they will be. In difficult markets they have found to their dismay that this is not a workable formula.

Barriers in the Community

There are three kinds of barriers to be aware of: man made, natural and psychological.

Expressway systems are a plus in one sense. But they may be a man-made barrier when it comes to determining the area an office will service. Other man-made barriers are major highway systems, railroads, sports complexes, airports, industrial parks, campuses and the like.

Natural barriers are things that break up an area and make it difficult for real estate firms to transact business across or around them. They include such obstacles as rivers, mountains, hills or land depressions in a city.

One of the best examples of a psychological barrier found in some metropolitan and suburban areas is the refusal of individuals in one area to list their property with a firm in an adjoining area. They may think that because the office is located in an area of $85,000 homes the office has no one qualified to sell $150,000 homes in the adjoining community. This one barrier has forced hundreds of real estate firms to string out their offices, placing them tandem style in a series of residential communities.

Mileage Circles

To make a mileage circle study get a detailed map of your area. Mark your office location (or proposed location) with a map tack. Determine the mileage scale of the map. Using a piece of string tied to the map tack at one end and a pencil at the other, circle the area limits you think your office might service. It might be as little as a half-mile in a densely populated area, as much as five, ten or more miles in sparsely settled places.

Now determine what the population is within each of the circles drawn and the turnover rate for housing in each. Likely sources for this information include city hall, mortgage companies, utility companies, planning commissions and the like. Be sure to note whatever barriers exist within each circle.

Once you've established the circle area around the office your salespeople can service, draw mileage circles around your proposed office. Ideally, the boundary of one circle will touch the circumference of another but will not overlap. Thus you avoid the waste of duplicated sales power or office facilities in overlapping territories.

Finally, the office would ideally be located where outbound traffic moves from the metropolitan area to the suburbs. An ideal site is at a four-way intersection on the far right corner. This is considered best because a stop light or stop sign at the intersection gives drivers adequate time to look across the street, see your sign and pull in.

If the office were on the near right corner, the driver would be sitting parallel at the stop light or sign and might not be able to maneuver his car into the traffic lane nearest your driveway. The near left corner has similar drawbacks and the added difficulty that the driver has to cross oncoming traffic. Finally, the far left corner, though giving better visibility, still presents the driver a problem of having to cross traffic.

Unfortunately, real estate firms are not the only ones smart enough to know that the far right corner of an intersection is an ideal one, so square footage costs are prohibitive in many cases. But when available and affordable they are ideal.

Building versus Remodeling

Obviously, a broker would prefer to build a facility to his own specifications. Building certainly gives the broker what he wants. It allows him to establish his company identity, to project to the community who he is and what he is trying to accomplish.

The relative cost of building versus remodeling is a primary concern. If one costs substantially less than the other, the broker may be forced to opt for it even if this second choice doesn't offer the amenities he wants.

Next, the broker has to consider capital availability. Does he have enough capital available to tie up cash in a down payment on land and also to finance the building contract for an office? The obvious alternative is to lease space, have the owner remodel it and then amortize the remodeling costs over the period of the lease. This gives the broker modernized offices at a lower cost because the expense is spread over a period of years. Basically, the cost of remodeling is only justified when the location is exactly right or if there is no land available for building or if construction costs are prohibitive.

Vacated gas stations offer interesting remodeling possibilities—albeit more costly than some other type structures. They usually have a prime corner location and good on-site parking.

Older homes are a natural for residential firms if they are located in a zoned business area and can be remodeled for real estate use. Another excellent type building is the outdated supermarket. Most of them have clear span ceilings which permit a variety of interior floor layouts. The exteriors can also be made attractive, with facing materials that complement the "flavor" of the neighborhood.

Finally, historic homes and buildings offer the broker both usable office space and the community's gratitude for having saved an historic landmark—fine public relations! This is especially true when the character and important architectural elements are not changed by the broker who converts it into a sales office.

Office Layout

Most real estate office floor plans have several elements in common. They usually have a conference room which provides privacy for consultations with prospective purchasers and listers of property and closings. Most also have a manager's office which may be completely glassed in so he has visibility of his salespeople but can work free of office noise. Draw draperies may be installed to provide privacy when needed.

But real estate offices vary greatly in the arrangement of working space for salespeople and ancillary staff. Some of the most common concepts are:

Separate offices or cubicles and dividers

Standing counter

Minimum number of desks and

Open area or bullpen.

Separate Offices or Cubicles and Dividers

Separate offices can be completely closed spaces that give total privacy to the individual salesperson. Or they can be cubicles, created by using dividers that may be floor-to-ceiling or perhaps only high enough to provide a salesperson some degree of privacy. Thus each salesperson enjoys the security of his own desk and a private area to which he may retreat if he wishes. This concept seems to be used more in commercial-investment departments than in residential real estate sales offices.

The drawback to this plan is that communication within such an office can be reduced greatly. The salesperson goes into his office, shuts the door and immediately closes out his interrelationships with other salespeople. This loss of communication can cause him to lose touch with what is going on. And when a customer walks into an office of this type he has no sense of the excitement or activity that may really exist there. It is much more apparent in an open sales office.

Standing Counter

One floor plan concept is the use of a long counter, at desk height, extending along one wall or around the perimeter of a room. Salespeople are assigned "desk" space (about three feet), a chair, a telephone and perhaps a cork bulletin board above each assigned space. It is restricted to salespeople's use; customers are not admitted to this area but are seen in a conference room or a private office.

What are the advantages of the standing counter plan? It's one of the least expensive ways to set up a working area. The counter top can be plywood or a formica type surface; the chairs may be the folding type. In such a plan, communications are open, information is exchanged quickly and the sales staff is up and on its way. These simple working conditions and the closeness of staff can foster a sense of camaraderie among congenial people.

There are disadvantages, too. Such a floor plan provides no privacy and no storage space unless under-the-counter two-drawer file cabinets are placed between working spaces. It's an arrangement that gives little sense of belonging. When all you have is a counter space, a chair and a telephone, they don't lend much prestige to what you're doing.

But the plan works well with some firms that have centralized computers. The computers occupy space in the middle of the room and are used for research in compiling information for later client interviews.

Minimum Number of Desks

The concept of having a minimum number of desks is a rather outdated one. This floor plan is still seen in some real estate offices; four or five desks are used by as many as ten salespeople with no one assigned to any specific desk. This plan was originally conceived to discourage salespeople from staying in the office so they would be out in active pursuit of business. Such a concept gives no sense of belonging. It provides salespeople no place to keep materials and records. Consequently they either work out of their homes or have no base at all for their work. Management has very little contact with salespeople in such an arrangement.

Communications are lost when only a few salespeople can be in the office at any one time to interrelate their efforts and ideas. Although this plan does keep salespeople on the move, the manager doesn't know where they are moving to. Unfortunately they are soon moving to another firm in some cases.

Open Area or Bullpen

The plan probably in most prevalent use today is the open area or bullpen area for salespeople.

The open area or the bullpen offers a sense of belonging. Each salesperson has an individual desk in this open area and can use the conference room or perhaps a private office off the bullpen to work with clients when necessary.

There is, however, a lack of privacy and a definite increase in the noise factor which can be distracting when a number of salespeople are in the office at the same time. On the other hand, this plan increases communication. Salespeople tend to keep up with what is going on. When a client walks into such an office he may respond favorably to the air of great activity and the excitement it generates among salespeople.

Finally, such an arrangement provides open space for sales meetings, eliminating the need for the firm to rent a meeting place.

Identity

The image your new office projects to the public is very important as you introduce your firm in a new location.

Some older firms choose a colonial building to maintain their image as an old, well-established firm. From the opposite point of view, other older firms choose a contemporary identity to convey the feeling that though they are an older firm, they have modern ideas.

Whatever type architecture or surroundings a firm chooses, it should conform to or complement the immediately surrounding properties so the real estate office is not an eyesore in the community.

Consideration should be given night lighting of the office sign so it can be seen for advertising purposes after office hours. The exception to this rule may be the existence of an energy crisis when commercial night lighting is frowned upon.

Naturally the office setting is part of the image a real estate firm presents to the community. Landscaping should be tasteful, lawns well-tended and parking lots kept clean at all times. Winter snow removal is important in regions where this is a problem.

Graphics

Sign design and colors should be uniform throughout the company. Whatever company design and colors the firm has chosen should be used in highway signs, office signs, car signs and yard signs. The identity should be carried through all print materials—letterheads, business cards, advertising brochures and other print materials.

Furnishings

Furnishings should convey a pleasant atmosphere. Color coordination is critical in the design of a real estate office. Skilled color coordinators can discuss with you color cybernetics—the theory of surrounding oneself with colors that attempt to influence one to do "what the colors say." For example, in sales office spaces one might use bright orange and bright yellows in the open and bullpen areas.

They're "active" colors and will contribute to keeping salespeople active. Just as soft greens, soft blues and soft yellows in conference rooms will help clients feel relaxed at closing sessions.

Low maintenance costs are important in choosing paint and wall coverings. The use of washable wall coverings and washable paints are practical in an office. High gloss paints and wallpapers and fabrics can be distracting to the eye.

Draperies and carpets are important for noise control. They lend a warm feeling to an office and have the advantage of lower maintenance costs.

If possible and practical, identical furniture, carpets and drapery fabrics should be used throughout a firm's offices. Thus when staffs expand or an office is phased out furnishings may be exchanged between locations.

Office machines should be coordinated. When a letter is typed in one office on a master machine, it can be sent to another for individualization on a matching machine. The interchangeability of machines between offices is again an important factor in cost control and continuity of the total decorating scheme.

Whatever the plan adopted, a broker must ask himself if the improvement cost per man can be covered in a reasonable length of time by the expected sales volume. Per unit desk costs are an important aspect of the total planning for a proposed office.

Introduction to the Neighborhood

Introducing your firm in a new neighborhood requires a lot of planning. It's a major undertaking that calls for using the market research you've already done as the basis for deciding how to promote your company in imaginative and acceptable ways and doing the job within the budget.

Use your market research as the beginning point. It will give the information you need about the kinds of businesses and people in the new neighborhood and what their interests, tastes and needs are. With this information, you can explore all the promotional possibilities open to you: person-to-person contacts, direct mail, newspaper advertising and publicity, radio and television advertising and publicity and open house functions.

Person to Person Contacts

First consideration and effort is given to getting acquainted with the leaders in the area. Get around and meet the people who run the local government, both paid employees and citizens who serve on governing boards. Business and industry leaders are also high on the list of people who should be told of your new location and the services you offer. Churches and service and civic organizations offer opportunities to meet people in groups, the kind who are likely to be "movers and shakers" in the area. Tell them how enthusiastic you are about being part of their town. Local leaders like to meet people who are moving into their community because they believe it offers the opportunity they've been looking for.

Always have a supply of business cards with you. A lot of them will be put in wallets or desk drawers and pulled out later when the person is in need of your real estate services.

Encourage your salespeople to make door-to-door visits in the new neighborhood, taking along their business cards or whatever other print promotion material you have prepared. Salespeople can simply introduce themselves and invite the residents to stop in your new office and get acquainted. If you've planned some kind of open house, an invitation to it can be extended orally.

Direct Mail

Direct mail covers everything from the simplest post card announcement, personal letters from your salespeople to their friends and acquaintances to formal announcement folders and invitations to an open house.

The post cards can be a simple announcement of the time and date of the official opening, inviting the addressee to come get acquainted. This is perhaps the least expensive form of direct mail promotion you can use. Done in good taste with important details included, post cards can be very effective.

It is perfectly acceptable for personal letters to be form letters. They are more effective if they are personalized either by a handwritten salutation or signed individually by the new manager or one of his salespeople. If you cannot give them any sort of personal touch perhaps you should bypass this form of promotion letter and consider a more formal announcement card or folder or a printed invitation to an open house.

Formal announcement cards or folders can give the pertinent information regarding your new operation. For example, you can include the firm name, new address, name of the manager, office phone number and hours on one side of a printed card announcement. If you go to a folder, there's more space for your message. In addition to the information suggested for a card announcement, you could add a list of the real estate services your firm proposes to supply. Many people do not realize the broad range of services available from most real estate firms. Keep in mind that what you take for granted as general knowledge is often understood only by those involved in the real estate business.

If you plan to conduct one open house or a continuing open house for a week or so, printed invitations will help draw a crowd. Build a mailing list of the influential people in the area and ask salespeople to assemble their own list of buyers and sellers and other friends in the community. Use this collection of names for your open house invitations.

Whatever form your direct mail promotion takes, be sure your mailing list has the correct spelling and address for everyone on it. People like to see their names spelled correctly. Incorrect addresses mean money is wasted twice, first on printing, then on postage.

Set up your mailing lists so they can be kept up to date. Delete names promptly when people leave the area. Add names as new people move in.

Newspaper Advertising and Publicity

A series of eye-catching display ads in your local paper can be used to make your announcement to the general public. Unless you have someone on your staff who is experienced in writing and laying out display ads, ask the newspaper's space salesperson if the publisher provides such a service, or go to an established advertising agency to have the job done. However it is handled, the information in the ad is your responsibility.

Such a series can tell the location of the new office, date of opening and who will manage it. One of the series might give a brief history of your firm; another might list all the real estate services you will provide. If you need salespeople to work at the new location, one of the ads might focus on this.

Another in the series might picture the best looking properties you have listed in the area. In addition to describing the property, always include information about the new operation. If you're wholly new to the area, consider running a picture of your new office, identifying its location in relation to some local landmark if that is possible—"one block east of the library on State Street," or "on the west side of the new shopping center."

Invite the local editor for a preview visit of your new operation. Be prepared to give him the facts about your firm, the reasons why you chose to locate in the area and how you believe your firm can contribute to the growth of the community. This is a job for the manager and a valuable form of publicity.

Radio and Television

Spot announcements on radio and television can be one of your best advertising buys. Listen to radio and watch television shows that offer the audience you want at the time of day those buyers and sellers are most likely to listen. Off-peak hours are available at bargain rates. Are these the hours of the day when the people you want to reach are listening? Make note of the program and the time and check to find out what a 30- or 60-second spot announcement costs.

A well written 30-second commercial can include all the important facts about your new location. Expanded to 60 seconds, you can include some sales talk about your services, tell about attractively priced listings and inform the public about how you can help them solve their housing problems.

Think of publicity possibilities in radio and television. Talk shows are very popular. Many of them accept telephone questions from the listening audience. If you can interest the host in a show devoted to real estate, you may handle some very interesting questions related to your business and the appearance could very well result in future business. Don't walk in cold and expect to be put on the air. Talk shows are often planned months in advance. Make an appointment to see the show's producer. Go equipped with a couple of ideas for a program that could delve into the real estate business in a way that will interest the show's audience, explain how the host can approach the topic and how you can contribute to it. Then be prepared to accept the producer's way of handling it, should he decide to schedule you.

Open House

An open house can be kept small and simple or expanded to be as large and elaborate as your budget will allow. Its size and simplicity need not limit its effectiveness.

A series of daily coffees the first week or two in your new location can give a feeling of warm hospitality to your official opening. But even the most informal event needs careful planning and continuing attention to details. Who will be in charge of floor duty so there's always someone on hand to welcome people as they come in? Will there be a guest registry; who will be responsible for it? Will you want to have some candid pictures made? Who will take them?

A more elaborate open house can be staged for afternoon or evening hours. Invitations to an open house of this kind should be more formal than you'd need for a coffee. Your local job printer (often an added service of your newspaper) can show you paper and type samples and quote prices for such invitations.

Souvenirs

The premium business today offers a large selection of items and in an equally wide price range. Choose whatever premium you think will help tell the new community about your company and be useful to the recipient. Investigate ideas and prices from several firms.

Investigate costs before you commit yourself to any form of promotion. Determine whether your staff can handle the kind of promotion you'd like to stage. Do as much as you can but don't attempt to do more than you can do reasonably well. Better to underplay your hand as you get started in a new location than to have the event end in confusion. Remember, you are presenting a new image in the neighborhood. A good beginning will convey to the public the standard they can expect from your firm in the future.

Follow Up

What happens after that first burst of hospitality and enthusiasm? How do you use it as a springboard to a successful every day operation?

Your guest list makes a fine nucleus of permanent promotion/mailing list. These are the people who either thought enough of you or were curious enough about you to come get acquainted. They could be future buyers, sellers or people who perform banking, building or government services essential to your success. Keep these people aware of what you're accomplishing.

If your office operates on a listing "farm" system, whereby salespeople are assigned specific areas to canvass in order to create spheres of influence, be sure they get names of guests from their assigned areas. It's important for them to know exactly who came to the official opening functions. These names can come in handy in casual conversation, provide a clue to a potential friend in their territory or be a source of valuable guidance in the area.

Operation

If you are opening a branch operation you will want to make sure that your schedule is planned to include lots of time at the new location. New branches require the kind of management that almost becomes over-management. Why? For one thing, you are identified closely as the leader of the organization. It is important to both staff and customers that you be seen there frequently. Otherwise, the staff can quickly develop the feeling that "the main office is somewhere else and we really don't matter much."

If possible, the new office should be staffed with salespeople who have been successful in other offices. They may stay in the new location only during the start-up period, a number of weeks or months, or they may move there permanently.

Some firms use a temporary incentive program to get a new operation under way. A contest to promote listings or an offer of a small break in the commission split on the first ten or twenty listings taken at a new location are a couple ways to motivate the staff.

One successful firm with a number of branch offices schedules a luncheon session with each branch every 60 days. The broker and his general sales manager attend these luncheons together. The two of them communicate the fact that they agree on goals and progress and recognize problems. Conversation is directed to encourage staff people to discuss their problems, objectives and goals. These staff members look forward to this time spent with top management so much that when a regular date is missed the question immediately is where have you been?

The workable policy and procedure manual is essential in a branch operation. Problems that come up in a branch may be different from those that occur in the main office. You should have regular reviews of this manual with branch office staff. You should provide them with a standard method of making suggestions for revising the manual and this work should be done on a regular basis.

The effectiveness of the branch office management is especially important to the firm's top management whose supervision is likely to be intermittent at best. Experience has proved to many firms that a branch manager who has been with the firm for some time may find the job easier than an outsider who is brought in. The person who has been associated with the firm understands its goals and objectives. He certainly should concur with them if he is to implement them in a new branch operation.

Goals and projections of future company development should fit those of the main office or other branch offices. They should be checked with the same regularity scheduled in the company's other offices. Both the standards of checking and the reporting forms should be identical throughout the whole company.

Staff training should be consistent throughout the company. Where possible, training sessions should be combined to serve as many offices as possible. This not only assures identical teaching of concepts, objectives and goals; it also reduces the total cost of staff training. Other facets of staff education can be individualized by offices or combined to serve everyone. Local education opportunities like adult evening classes, lectures by local people at staff sales meetings (bankers, municipal officials) may serve only a limited area. Sales specialists, psychologists, attorneys and others may speak on topics germane to the total company area. The firm's library may be located in the main office and its materials available to everyone; public libraries may serve a restricted area. Whatever your educational pursuits, be sure everyone in the firm knows what is scheduled and feels free to avail themselves of every opportunity.

When you determine how much training and education you can afford in both time and dollars, be sure everyone knows you are in favor of it. If staff people think they don't have to be trained because you really are not in favor of it, they won't attend training sessions. Here is another place management should maintain a high profile.

Impact

Of course it's always hard to get a new operation started. The best answer to this challenge is to get in there and make it go. If you are thinking of opening a new branch, don't sneak in. Let people know what your plans are. Develop some programs for getting listings and some programs for securing buyers. Have your office as fully staffed as you can afford. Employ the publicity and promotion techniques suited to your budget and compatible to the style of the local market. It's better to spend additional money to get started well than to ease into a market and decide you'll spend money after you are established.

If you have done your research and market analysis work well and chosen a strong manager and a competent sales staff, the new operation will get off to a better, stronger start and realize a profit much sooner than is possible in trying to put it together one step at a time. Get the whole package ready, then sell it with enthusiasm.

Control Systems

Control systems in a new office are usually dependent on the firm's size. For a large firm, most control systems originate in the main office. Daily deliveries to all branches provide each with new listing and sales data and all other information relevant to the branch operations. Some very large firms use computers or FAX machines. Many small firms have someone on the main office staff keep branch offices informed by daily telephone calls. And some brokers have a daily delivery service contracted with an outside delivery firm or carried by one of the employees enroute to or from work. It's important that everyone be kept informed on a daily basis.

Financial Controls

While the techniques for control are similar, methods of implementation vary when the concept of the branch operation is one of dependence on the main offices as opposed to independence from the main office. While only these two extremes of operating a branch office are considered here, the innovative manager can modify these guidelines to develop procedures for operating anywhere within these limits. Emphasis, however, is on methods of control that are financial in nature because an amazingly wide range of activity can be brought into managerial focus by translating diverse plans and objectives into the common language of money. In a real estate sales operation prime attention is given to cash, expenses, income as reflected in sales, escrow requirements and the major non-cash assets of the firm.

The tools available to the manager in exerting control are likewise diverse. Budgets, financial statements, petty cash funds, check authorizations and purchase orders are the hardware. Clearly assigned responsibilities are the glue which binds the control system together.

An operation where the main office retains primary control over the operations of a branch office presents few unusual problems. Office space is leased, necessary office equipment installed and salespeople operate from what amounts to a satellite of the main office. All administration continues at the main office as if the branch were located in an adjoining room. Questions of improved management therefore relate to operation of the business as a whole and are independent of the geographical location of the branch office.

In contrast, however, when the branch office takes on the character of a small subsidiary company, a major concern of management is that "the left hand knoweth what the right hand doeth." When the owner-manager decided upon an independently operated branch, a major psychological hindrance to success had to be overcome. There had to be conscious recognition of a willingness to rely on someone else to operate a major segment of the business. Having made that decision, the next logical concern is "How can I be sure that I know what is going on in the branch office?" To answer this question and ease the pangs of anxiety, reliable tools necessary to measure performance and safeguard assets must be put to use. Almost every management book written has included detailed discussions on authority and responsibility. To reiterate however, the key to a successful operation is to actually give the branch manager the authority necessary to do his job. A major pitfall lies in what is implied versus what is actual. The broker who implies that a branch manager has the requisite authority and responsibility but continues to impose his own authority in routine operations is doomed. Only be setting objectives, measuring progress and working with the manager to both highlight and establish plans for correcting problems can success be achieved.

The day the ship's captain leaves the bridge to run the engine room one of two things can happen: The ship will founder or there will be a new captain on the bridge. Exercising control and meddling are two entirely different techniques.

Once the decision to establish an independent branch office has been made, the techniques for main office control of the operation must not only be established but explained and implemented. The following guidelines are the basic tools for the job. Their interdependence must be kept in mind if a reliable system of control is to exist.

Branch Manager's Authority

Give the manager the authority to operate the branch and hold him responsible for the results. A key to this situation is whether or not the manager will also sell. If he is allowed to sell as well as manage, his responsibility is compromised to a degree. The basic reason for allowing him to sell would appear to be motivated by the desire of management to pay a minimal salary for management services. A human trait on the part of the manager to maximize his compensation leads to a tendency to manage only when there are no sales prospects in sight. Conversely, not allowing the manager to sell isolates his efforts to management alone where his progress can be measured. With this latter arrangement would go a salary and incentive arrangement. Any bonus agreement should be based upon the net income of his operation since such an arrangement has significant built-in controls. First, his total compensation is now related to his effectiveness as a manager and includes his effective control of operating expenses. Second, he is not now competing with his sales personnel but rather controlling and guiding their efforts in meeting the sales goal of the branch.

Dollar Limits on Major Expenditures

A valuable control is to establish a dollar ceiling on selected or significant items of operating expense. For example, it might be feasible to establish a maximum dollar value for classified advertising during a fixed period of time. The means by which this is done, of course, is a budget. The annual plan of operation is clarified by translating it into dollar terms. To establish the budget, list the items of fixed expense such as rent, taxes and depreciation over which the branch manager has no control. Control or not, the branch is stuck with these costs and must cover them from gross income before any thought can be given to the quest for profit. The branch manager now lists his sales objective for the year in terms of dollars which translates to budgeted gross income. Subtracting his budgeted fixed expense from the budgeted gross income highlights the budgeted dollars available to cover the branch's variable expense and to produce net income. The categories of variable expense over which the manager does have control are those on which he must focus his attention. Monthly comparisons with actual operating results and their differences from equivalent budgetary amounts produce the variances which are another prime control tool. Using the "management by exception" technique, the main office can require the manager to explain significant variances from the budgetary benchmarks. A word of caution is appropriate at this point. Far too often only those variances over the budget are ever examined. Quite as crucial to successful control are explanations of significant variances under the budget. If nothing else, such an examination can often prove the validity of the budgetary benchmark. It is also essential that the manager be given monthly financial data in a format that is both meaningful and useful to him in evaluating his operation. Far too often a company will fall into the trap of giving their manager data that is convenient to produce rather than what is necessary for effective operation.

Separation of Responsibility

While the title of this section may appear to contradict the first section, the fact is that it supplements it. The manager must have the authority to do his job, no more and no less. Yet in using the various tools of control, the proper assignment of each is vital to success. The records on which the statement data is based must be valid if the statements themselves are to be reliable. The source data for these records is the same as in most accounting operations. Significant items were previously cited but because of their importance bear repeating. In turn, brief commentary will be made concerning a petty cash fund, check authorizations and purchase orders. These items, as they represent a separation of responsibility constitute a method of control. While the examples are necessarily limited, the underlying principles apply to a large spectrum in the area of financial operations.

Each branch office should be authorized a petty cash fund of sufficient size to meet ordinary operational needs. A large dollar fund is not advisable as this is self-defeating. More frequent fund replenishment can meet most of the needs for petty cash.

Check authorizations and purchase orders are valuable tools of control. The forms themselves should be designed to meet the specific needs of a particular company. But equally important, they must be designed to assure that the necessary information is entered on the form. In this manner, both the check authorization and purchase order can be prepared in the branch office thus aiding the branch manager in controlling his expenses. The branch manager alone is now responsible for expenditures for he must approve each check authorization and purchase order. His file copy serves as his record of the details of these transactions. In addition, authority to incur charges against the branch office accounts is restricted to the man directly responsible for the success or failure of the branch operation. Actual issuance of checks is handled by the main office accounting department.

Escrow funds and sales files can be controlled in a similar manner. Deposits on sales are physically made by branch office personnel with duplicate deposit slips forwarded to the main office accounting department. Withdrawals from the escrow account are authorized using a check authorization by the branch manager and physically made by the main office accounting department. Sales cases are controlled by the branch manager when he authorizes the indicated disbursements. Actual payment of sales associates and other parties is handled by the main office accounting department.

Responsibility for control of major non-cash assets such as office furniture is again split. The branch manager purchases the equipment after such purchases have been approved by the main office. Payment is made by the main office accounting department after the branch manager acknowledges receipt of the equipment and authorizes payment. Annual depreciation is the responsibility of the main office and is a fixed charge of the branch. The branch manager, in turn, submits an annual inventory list to the main office for comparison with the fixed asset listing used as the basis for depreciation.

In summary, the specifics of operations vary by company and the basic principles of control must be implemented within this existing framework if they are to be effective. This operating framework serves as a harness which gives the manager the necessary authority to perform and at the same time holds him accountable for his performance. Definitive measurements of performance are indicated by variations from budgeted activity. Having measured the manager's performance by means of a budget, the incentive arrangement now produces a direct correlation between manager performance and manager compensation.

The main office must tailor their tools of control to properly fit their method of operation. As is true for any system, periodic review and adjustment are mandatory to keep their control tools both sensitive and responsive if they are to serve as reliable sensors of business activity.

Housekeeping Check List

Whether you have a single office or supervise a multi-office operation, it's wise to establish a routine of checking the housekeeping. Tell each person responsible that this is routine and important to a uniformly good impression of the firm everywhere it does business. But don't tell them when the housekeeping checks will be made.

It is only fair to share the check list items with responsible people in each office. They can use it for their own housekeeping checks and as a reminder to the whole staff which things are important in the general impression given people who enter your place of business.

One firm's rating sheet is illustrated in Fig. 1. After these sheets are filled in, the person responsible is given a photocopy of the actual checklist. Commendation for the best points on the check and suggestions for improvements needed are made in a separate memo, Fig. 2. The memo then becomes a part of management's next check to make sure recommendations for correction and improvement were carried out.

Goal Setting

Management techniques in helping salespeople establish goals that fit their own and company needs were suggested in Chapter 5. Let it suffice here to remind the reader that once the company goals are established and salespeople found who understand and concur with those goals, the individual salesperson's goals must originate with him. They are then reviewed with the manager, totaled and projected for an agreed upon time period.

Data Flow

All reporting should be organized so that it becomes second nature to both management and staff to provide the main office with data essential to good record keeping. Reports are valuable only to the extent they provide an accurate measure of how a business is doing. Management should review all reports at least once each year to make a judgment on their value. Any statistics not being used to increase sales or control costs or evaluate growth should be discontinued; and the people who have been gathering this data should be told why such reports are no longer useful to the firm.

Whether branch operations are centralized or decentralized, staff review of listing and sales goals should be handled with regularity. This starts on a one-to-one basis between the salesperson and his local manager and moves upward until top management reviews company goals with the heads of its sales staff.

When organized well, such reporting provides top management with data to handle the entire sales department realistically, to determine whether a branch is contributing its assigned share toward com-

Fig. 1 ABC Realty housekeeping check

	Rating	Remarks
Office: Canada Park **Date:** _____, 19_____		**E — Excellent** **S — Satisfactory U — Unsatisfactory**
Employment question	S	Questioned all independent contractors
Checking accounts		
General	E	Currently posted
Escrow	E	Currently posted
Petty cash	U	$50.00 fund; $18.75 in bills, $16.75 cash, $14.50 short
Files, general		
Arrangement	E	
Condition	U	Many needed new jackets
Files, exclusive	U	Advertising not used
Form letters	E	Being used regularly
Jackets	E	
Progress report	E	Advertising record used and up to date
No. inspected	U	Not kept up
X-taker worksheet	U	5 out of 14 w/out worksheet
Visual aid	E	Checked 3. Well kept and used.
Comp books	E	
Street files	E	
Files, unclosed	S to U	Some loose paper & notes. Judgment note. See comments.
Jackets	E	
Information	S to E	Good information on most files
Use of sales tools by staff	S	Most are being used
Closed files	S	Many w/loose notes & unnecessary paper 8 x 10 photos in many

Fig. 1A ABC Realty housekeeping check

	Rating	Remarks
Office: Canada Park Date: _____, 19____		E — Excellent S — Satisfactory U — Unsatisfactory
Office exterior	S	
Lawn	E	Had just been mowed. Parkway needs trim
Parking lot	U	High weeds, trash and papers. Tools & signs piled behind incomplete shed. Messy!
Windows	S	Clean and shiny
Sign	U	Front sign has old REALTOR® logo
Office interior		
General housekeeping	S	Needs good cleaning. Has just fired janitorial service
Desks	E	Clean and clear
Carpeting	S	Will need replacing soon
Bulletin board	E	Well placed and current
Sign-out sheet	U	Not being used regularly
Arrangement	E	For size
Staff size and potential size	10 12	
Staff	S	1 in 8:30; 1 & Manager 8:45; 6 by 10 A.M.
Appearance	E	
Automobiles	E	
Secretary	E	Summer part-time, very knowledgeable
Supplies		
Adequate supply	E	Small but adequate
Area	E	Small but adequate
Arrangement	S	Needs straightening
Signs	S	Stored in shed. Clean
Key arrangement	E	Kept at secretary's desk, well controlled
Sign out	E	Appears to be used regularly
Equal opportunity poster	S	Posted but book covering

Fig. 2 Office inspection report

To: President, ABC Realty

From: Sales Manager

Subject: Inspection of Canada Park Office

The attached report is the composite finding of the team inspection made

Points of deficiency were discussed with the manager and suggestions made for
correction and improvement.

The janitoral service agreement had just been terminated. The office needs a good
general cleaning. Carpeting is showing wear and should be replaced in the near future.

Closed and unclosed files were examined. Smith-Jones note three days overdue.
Dates of Earnest Money deposits not shown on many files.

pany goals, to change direction when necessary and occasionally
decide that a branch is not making it at present and is not likely to in
the future.

Getting It All Together
There is so much to plan, to supervise and to follow through on in
opening a real estate office most top management people find it practical to prepare a procedural check-off list so all details are covered.
The adapted list here shows how one successful firm makes sure every item from procedures in choosing a location to purchasing pen-
cils and paper clips becomes part of the total plan. Whether you
follow this detailed list or plan one of your own, the time spent on it
will be well invested.

FINANCIAL PLAUSIBILITY
    Determine that corporate funds are available
    Determine that proper business and market conditions prevail
        Check company growth statistics
        Check all Multi-List statistics
        Check national and local financial conditions
        Check national and local mortgage money availability

AREA DETERMINATION
    Check coverage by existing company offices
    Pick two or three most likely areas
    Check all Multi-List sales statistics in key areas

Check company sales statistics in key areas
Check business and industrial expansion in key areas
Check highway and sewer and water expansion in key areas
Check school, police and fire facilities in key areas

MANAGER SELECTION
Determine qualities to look for
Check company personnel
Check other REALTOR® personnel

MANAGER LETTER OF INTENT AND CONTACT
Upon selection of manager, give him letter of intent
State salary and terms
State approximate starting time within 60 days
Sign the contract 30 days before opening of office

SELECTION OF OFFICE SITE
Separate store building
Shopping center
Other
Miscellaneous
Check outdoor sign problems re: municipality and landlord
Check quality of surrounding commercial area
Check trash pickup
Check street and parking lot lighting
Check sewer and water
Check municipal licensing fees
Check proximity to good subdivisions

OFFICE LAYOUT PLANNING
Prepare two-dimension layout of entire building space (four-month lead)
Allow five-year growth pattern re: various work and storage areas
Waiting area
Sales desk area
Manager area
Clerical area
Conference room
Storage area
Coffee and coat area
Allow proper traffic patterns
Allow for proper natural and artificial lighting

STANDARD LEASEHOLD IMPROVEMENTS AND CONTRACTING FOR SAME
Two or more bids unless dealing with known contractor
Carpentry (two-month lead)
Electrical (three-week lead)
Painting (one-month lead)
Heating

Air conditioning
Ceiling tile
Floor tile
Outdoor sign (three-month lead)
Outer doors and windows
Parking lot

FURNISHINGS (four-month lead)
Determination of whether to purchase or lease
Determination of suppliers
Order floor furnishings
Arrival of floor furnishings
Order decor furnishings
Arrival of decor furnishings

INSURANCE
Order package policy
Fire
Liability
Property damage
Products liability
Check of lease by insurance company for "hold harmless" clauses

ORDERING AND INSTALLATION OF UTILITIES

MUNICIPAL PERMITS

JANITORIAL SERVICE AND ORIGINAL CLEANUP

ADVERTISING AND PROMOTION PLANNING AND EXECU-
TION
Tie-in with company recruiting seminars
Kick-off ads—classified
Agency advertising
Agency promotion
Yellow Pages ad
Residential phone book listing
Announcement sign in display window 60-90 days prior to opening

FINANCIAL ARRANGEMENTS
Choose proper bank
Open escrow account, if necessary
Arrival of check ledgers
Arrival of deposit books
Arrival of deposit slips
Arrival of rubber stamps
Enter account resolutions
Set up accounting ledgers

MANAGER INSTRUCTIONS RE: FINANCIAL AND CLOSING PROCEDURES
Bank deposits
Bringing deals to closing department
Closing deals

MANAGER INSTRUCTIONS RE: OFFICE EQUIPMENT

OFFICE SUPPLIES, EQUIPMENT AND STATIONERY
Order supplies

BUSINESS FORMS
Listing forms
Purchase agreement forms
Lease forms—residential and commercial
Addendum to purchase agreement forms
Listing kits
Receipt books
Title folders

MANAGER INSTRUCTION RE: SALES RECORDS AND PROCEDURE
Conference with manager and statistical department
Manager starts collection of his records one month in advance
Complete review of entire procedure one month prior to opening—statistical department and new manager

SELECTION OF SALES STAFF
Check all current company staff
Have salespeople pass word
Recruiting seminar
Newspaper, TV and radio advertising
New manager totally responsible

TRAINING OF SALES STAFF
Thoroughly indoctrinate manager with training department
Attendance at current company program by manager
Attendance at any current recruiting seminars by manager
Register all salespeople in proper REALTOR® Board
Complete policy manual review
Visit other company offices
Spend day in each service department

NOTIFICATION OF REALTOR® BOARDS AND DEPARTMENT OF LICENSING AND REGULATIONS
Notify Department of Licensing and Regulations within 30 days of opening
Notify all REALTOR® Boards concerned within 30 days of opening
Notify all Multi-List associations

MISCELLANEOUS
Order decorative trash can (six-week lead)
Decals-front door
Lettering—front door and windows—logo, notary public, street number (two-week lead)
Mail slot—front door (two-week lead)
Order proper newspapers and periodicals
Manager application for notary certificate—with seal
Clean-up supplies
Coffee equipment

**Opening a
Real Estate
Office**

Mergers and Acquisitions

20

Mergers and acquisitions are ways a company with limited capital can grow. Combining the complementary strengths of companies can increase their total market impact. A merger may be the salvation of small companies struggling to survive.

The material in this chapter applies whether management is looking for another company to acquire or is being acquired.

Before pursuing either a merger or an acquisition, management has to decide whether it really wants to expand. There is nothing wrong with remaining small. Many small companies are very successful and want to remain small. Bigness alone does not guarantee success or prevent failure.

Mergers and Acquisitions

In evaluating the operation of some small companies, management frequently cites the following difficulties:

Lack of adequate advertising and promotional budget

Lack of free time for the broker

Lack of security for the broker

Small impact made on the market

Lack of continuity

Harder to make more money

Difficult to broaden base of operation

Difficult to provide full service to the consumer

Difficult to attract experienced people

Inability to penetrate new markets.

This list can act as a check-off for any small brokerage firm. What can the broker do to improve one or more of these categories in order to have a larger operation? If there is limited capital available, the answer lies in one of two directions: either attempt to merge into a larger firm that offers all or more of the services as outlined above or find other small companies of similar size, merge them into a single operation and effect needed economies yet provide more complete brokerage service to the consumer.

A case history shows how eight small brokers merged into one major operation with minimum cash and capitalization. This merger was brought about in a large metropolitan area where the brokers had offices separated geographically by basic markets. They closed non-productive offices and concentrated on the best ones. Each broker was assigned specific duties, from the president of the merged operation to the training manager. They were able to attract a number of new salespeople by virtue of the merger. They were also able to broaden their services to the public and develop programs such as trade-in and guaranteed sales plans, that they had been unable to provide as individual offices. Since the merger, there have been a number of changes. Only five of the original eight brokers remain. However, their overall success has justified the merger. They were able to do it by a very simple formula dividing the cash and capitalization requirement based on the number of salespeople each broker brought into the merged operation. The most important feature of this merger was that each broker willingly accepted an assignment in the merged operation in the area in which he excelled.

It is admittedly a frightening experience to consider merging with another company or the acquisition of your firm by another firm. But with an honest, fair appraisal and long-range planning a merger can enable the following to occur:

A stronger company image

Sufficient size to assure adequate advertising and promotional budgets

An effective training program

Improved ability to compete for listings

The physical size to offer adequate consumer services

More free time or the opportunity for a vacation for the managers

Shared responsibilities.

The owner of any small- or medium-sized real estate firm should honestly evaluate where he expects to be in his operation one year and five years hence, list all the firm's attributes and deficiencies and then decide on objectives and goals.

Disadvantages

Licensed brokers and real estate salespeople are probably the freest, most independent thinking businesspeople in the United States today. They are independent contractors. There are no time clocks. Their ability to achieve is unlimited. It has always been interesting to observe their broad spectrum of productivity and the fact that there is really no typical salesperson. Some real estate salespeople are satisfied with $15,000 or $20,000 a year in earnings. Yet many top producers consistently earn $45,000 to $100,000 per year. What does this have to do with mergers or acquisitions? It has a great deal to do with it because the typical small to medium broker may see justification in a merger or acquisition but when it comes to deciding to do it, the psychological impact of that decision is overwhelming. No real estate broker, small or large, wants to lose his identity. Cases can be cited of thousands of real estate salespeople who were making an excellent income associated with a good active broker but left to open their own company not just because they thought they could make more money but because they wanted that personal identity, additional independence and freedom of action. How can one rationalize with this type of individual that his ultimate goals could be achieved by merging with another office or offices?

The major disadvantage of any merger or acquisition is the loss of identity and the need to adhere to someone else's direction and policy. Currently a number of franchise operations are trying to overcome the disadvantages by preserving local management identity and responsibility, yet providing the advantages offered through the successful operation of a larger firm without complete takeover.

Another disadvantage could be the basis of compensation in the acquisition or merger. If it is not a straight cash transaction and stock is given in lieu of cash, the broker must consider the market risk involved in holding stock and its fluctuating value based on economic conditions. Once the broker gets past the psychological impact and decides the logical direction is in acquisition or merger, he must approach the decision-making process on as scientific a basis as possible.

What to Look For

The decision has been made to expand by acquisition and merger of other real estate operations. This may be done ideally within the firm's current operation, expanded into new markets and even broadened further into different cities or states. One New Jersey firm, over a period of five or six years, made ten acquisitions which developed into 98 real estate offices in five states and four mortgage banking operations.

Once the broker has determined the direction he wants to take, what is the procedure? Before he can determine the method of acquisition and the price, he has to get a clear picture of the assets (both physical and productive) that will be acquired and how they will affect the continuing operation. In the attractiveness of any acquisition or merger, the firm being acquired must have at least one of several advantages:

A location in a highly productive market area

Recognized productivity by the existing sales organization

Good internal management

The first things to look for are: current production, built-in expenses, management continuity, MLS membership, identity and status and difference in operation.

Current Production

Determine the number of licensed salespeople presently with the firm, what each has earned for at least a period of two years and what goals each has set for his current production. In a number of cases, where adequate records are not available, sit down with the management and list all licensed staff, examine their earnings for the previous year if possible and then analyze their production month by month. Discuss with management the productive ability of each salesperson, whether he has the ability to produce more business if greater advantages are offered through the merged firm. The ultimate price of the purchase of a real estate firm is going to be directly proportionate to the productivity of its sales staff.

Built-In Expenses

Acquisition of a firm includes assuming many of its obligations that cannot be eliminated by virtue of the merger or acquisition. Therefore, it is critical to analyze the operating expenses of the firm in detail, listing all the obligations that are built in and cannot be eliminated. As an example, in most cases a real estate company will have a lease for a period of years. The merged operation may not plan to operate out of that location once the deal is complete. But the lease will be the obligation of the new firm.

In addition, there can be other obligations: group and health benefits for employees or bonus arrangements. A policy on division of commissions that differs from that of the other company can present an immediate problem. Other obligations may include the leasing of various types of equipment. These are some of the obligations that can remain for which the succeeding firm will be responsible. This is why it is absolutely essential that the operating statements be carefully analyzed.

Management Continuity

As outlined here, management may be one of the essential things being bought. This determination must be made in the acquisition of any firm. Will the licensed salespeople remain with the merged firm in the event present management is eliminated? Most merger or acquisition agreements generally insist on some sort of contract with existing management for a period of at least one year, preferably longer. It is very difficult to merge or acquire a firm and put new management in charge immediately. To so do disrupts the operation and has a tendency to hurt morale and affect production. Therefore, it is essential to approach existing management with the idea that they remain for a reasonable period of time until the transition is complete.

MLS Membership

Membership requirements in Multiple Listing Services vary greatly and their operations also vary from area to area. In a tight market it is important that the broker be a member of the Multiple Listing Service. It should be determined early in the negotiations whether membership rules provide that a newly merged firm becomes a member automatically or whether the membership must remain in the existing firm.

Identity and Status

Is the firm to be acquired a recognized, viable operation that shares a major portion of a market? If identity of the firm is changed how will it affect the overall status of the operation and its productivity? What is the market penetration of the firm being acquired? These questions must be answered by in-depth study. In many cases the firm being acquired may have a stronger reputation than the one doing the acquiring, but due to ownership status or retirement the older and more reputable firm would be absorbed. In one case, the company to be acquired had an outstanding reputation, was in existence for almost a hundred years and had represented thousands of clients over that period of time. Because of the advancing age of the broker and the lack of continuing management, the company was acquired by a relatively new broker. Rather than lose valued identity, the new broker incorporated the major portion of the name of the former company in the new firm name in order to take advantage of its identity and status. No acquiring firm should take an arbitrary position that their name must dominate in the merged operation. There are many things the other company may have to its advantage after the merger is complete.

Difference in Operation

Companies vary as much as individuals in their operation. These may range from the way holidays are scheduled, different benefits, divisions of commissions, floor time, use of long distance telephone calls to advertising requirements or listing procedures. Before making a final judgment in the acquisition of a firm, a broker must decide whether the differences in the operation are so severe that it would be impossible to indoctrinate the surviving salespeople and employees into his operation.

Operations may be so loose that by the time the staff of the acquired firm adheres to the acquiring company's policy and procedure most of them are gone and the acquisition then proves to have been unprofitable. If the firm being acquired has an operations manual, compare it carefully with the acquiring firm's. If it has no written documentation, the only way a broker determines the differences is by interview. If this is the method by which the differences have to be determined, interview the management to find out the functions of their operation, the salaried employees to find out if they understand what their duties are and the salespeople to find out if they understand what management expects of them. In some cases after all of the other areas have checked out and the deal looks reasonable, mergers have failed because of vast differences in the types of operation.

A major portion of the firm's value is in the general operation of the business. Unless those areas can be accurately evaluated, there is no reason to go on into the detailed operation to pursue the acquisition.

Evaluating Assets

The nuts and bolts of an acquisition are the fixed assets of the firm. The base by which the purchase price is decided starts with an analysis of assets and liabilities. From this data the evaluation is made about productivity and goodwill. In evaluating the assets of a real estate firm, consider the following items: physical assets, listings, staff, name and reputation, management staff, lease, current commissions receivable and personnel.

Physical Assets

In the majority of cases, a real estate firm leases its space. In addition to space, they must have desks, files, mechanical and other equipment. In many cases the equipment has been depreciated and its current market value is greater than its depreciated value. The value of physical assets is determined by taking inventory with assigned values. All physical assets should be inspected visually. If there is any question about the assets, an office supplier can generally assist in setting current market values. In some cases the real estate company owns the building from which it operates. It could possibly be an office building where there are other tenants. In this event, a current market appraisal is necessary in order to determine the valuation for acquisition.

Listings

When one purchases a business, one pays for inventory. When a broker buys another real estate company, part of the value of the company is its inventory of listings. What those listings will produce in the way of income over a period of time can be determined mathematically with a reasonable degree of accuracy. Take the listings the firm has had over a period of a year or two. Check the number sold against those actually listed and the percentage sold by cooperative brokers to determine what the firm could expect to earn in gross income from the sale of existing listings. It is the listings presently available that will produce the income to carry the office after acquisition. It is not just the fact that one day the business name changes and all kind of great things happen. Remember that there must be continuity in business and that in order for a business to have value, there must be a source of future income under new management. So, listings and their marketability are essential in determining the value of a real estate operation.

Staff

As outlined in the text dealing with what to look for, the sales staff can be one of the most valuable acquisitions. Generally, when a new firm has been able to offer broader benefits, more advertising dollars and a general clean sweep of an operation, the sales staff can become dramatically more productive. It is important to determine the nucleus of the staff, their ability to produce, their desire to stay with the merged operation or which members of the sales staff will leave due to the merger. Be sure the best producers are planning to stay.

Name and Reputation

Measuring goodwill of a real estate company is extremely difficult. Experience of many brokers is that in the vast majority of acquisitions, goodwill has added little to the value of the total package. However, it is essential that this be considered as part of the assets.

Management Staff

Does the firm being acquired have a young aggressive management but just lack capital or training? Can that management staff be productive in the merged operation? Is it willing to stick with the merged operation to give it the opportunity to survive and succeed? Generally, relatively little value is assigned to the management staff because the acquiring firm normally has the management expertise to be applied to the firm being acquired.

Lease

There is a good possibility that the area leased by the real estate company was negotiated over a period of years and that there could be an existing lease value that should be considered in acquisition. It is essential that the lease be examined to determine the remaining term, the rent and any obligations for any increased rent, renewal options, division of cost, who furnishes gas and electricity, janitorial service, snow removal and parking lot maintenance.

Current Commissions Receivable

Determine whether the company is on a cash or accrual basis. An accrual basis provides a more accurate accounting of both the income and expenses of the operation. Most small real estate companies are on a cash basis. Therefore, most of the deferred income is not reflected in current statements. On that basis two things have to be determined. Get current status of all pending contracts of sale including whether they have been financed and commitments issued, when settlements are expected and what commission the sales will produce. In addition, you need a listing of obligations which have been incurred but have not accrued. Current commissions receivable are an asset of a firm that will help defer continuing expenses. These current commissions would of course be off-set by expense obligations.

Staff

In many cases in a merged operation one of the effective savings is the consolidation of personnel. For example there may be an administrative broker who is the owner, a sales manager and possibly bookkeeping and secretarial personnel. In a merged operation the bookkeeping may be taken over by the parent company, eliminating the need for a bookkeeper; instead of having two individuals in management positions, one would be sufficient. The payment of personnel and their benefits are all expenses which must be considered in acquiring a firm. After the fixed assets have been evaluated, determine anticipated productivity. Then decide personnel needed to achieve these goals. Be certain there are no long-term commitments or employment contracts with existing personnel that may not be changed after the merger.

Methods of Acquisition

There is no precise formula for the acquisition of a real estate company and the price can vary substantially based on the method of acquisition. For example, if a broker plans to acquire a real estate firm and pay cash out of pocket for it with no deferred payments, he will look at the cost of acquisition with a very conservative and calculated eye, because once the cash is paid there is no recovery. If all of the facts and figures do not shape up as anticipated he is out of luck once settlement is made, because he paid a price based on his analysis and there are no incentives to continue management of that firm for the repayment of that cash. Most real estate firms do not want to pay cash. They prefer to arrange payment on a deferred basis so part of the value is paid out of the continuing assets of the firm being acquired—the ability of the new firm to produce continuing income out of which the purchase price is repaid.

Determining Value

There are several major steps to ascertaining the value of a real estate brokerage company. These follow.

Step 1: Determine Conditions and Assumptions

Estimating the value of a firm is no different than appraising real property. The purpose for the valuation determines the appraisal process and focus. Your first step, then, is to consider the purpose of the appraisal as well as your strategic plan or "conditions and assumptions" regarding the future of the firm. For example, the value of a firm continuing in its current operating mode can be quite different than the value to a purchaser planning to merge it into a multi-office operation.

Step 2: Reconstruct Income Statements

Reconstruct an income statement (based on the criteria established in step one) for the future operation of the business, considering the following:

• Exclude direct income and expenses from non-brokerage activity (such as investment income and non-business expenses).

• Allocate or exclude indirect expenses for non-brokerage activity, including bookkeeping, telephone and rent.

• Impute a fair market value for all owner's services and support (e.g., wages, rent, auto and loans).

• Eliminate excess owner fringe benefits (club dues, travel and entertainment for example).

• Project income and expenses based on the predetermined strategic plan for operations.

Continually ask yourself: "If I were to hire someone to do the job the owners are now doing, what would I pay that person?" After you review and revise the above points as appropriate, calculate an estimate of earnings or loss before interest and taxes (EBIT).

Step 3: Reconstruct Balance Sheet

Next, reconstruct the balance sheet (again considering the criteria defined in step one), making the following adjustments.

• Include only the assets that support the brokerage activity as defined in the reconstructed operating statement and strategic plan.

• Exclude office building(s), other property held for investment, cash beyond what is necessary for the prudent operation of the firm and vehicles and equipment not critical to the success of the firm.

• Adjust the value of the remaining assets (e.g., phone systems, computers and receivables) to current resale value.

• If the firm is on a cash basis accounting system, consider the current inventory of transactions signed on both sides and progressing toward closing. That portion due to the firm (after co-op splits and sales associate commissions less a percentage for fallout and administration cost) is an asset.

• Consider the listing inventory as another asset based on the gross potential fees adjusted for an expiration factor, co-op splits, sales associate commissions and administration cost.

Step 4: Evaluate Goodwill

Next, a current owner's net worth (or stockholder's equity) should be calculated.

Associate Value. Most commonly, the value of the sales associates is included in the goodwill of the firm. If the firm does not have measurable goodwill, there is no value to the sales force as a group.

Return on owner equity. Next, compute the return (yield) on the reconstructed owner's equity of the firm.

More than 15-25%. If the EBIT on the reconstructed income statement is in excess of 15-25% of the owner's equity, the firm has goodwill. Fifteen to 25 percent is an appropriate range considering 1987 before-tax returns on the alternate investment opportunities with similar risk and liquidity. Choosing a specific number within that range is a subjective decision.

Less than 15%. If the income is less than 15% of the owner's equity there is no goodwill. With no goodwill, the upper value of the firm is the same as owner's equity on the reconstructed balance sheet. This is also known as the "current net worth of tangible assets."

If the EBIT exceeds the calculated minimum return on owner's equity, then there is a value to the goodwill of the firm.

Example. If the reconstructed income statement shows the EBIT is $100,000 and in the reconstructed balance sheet the owner's equity (tangible net worth) is $300,000, that is a 33% (before tax) return on equity. If investors require a minimum 20% return on equity, then 10% (20%-30%) is the intangible asset called goodwill.

Step 5: Value the Firm

There are two recognized processes for determining the value of a firm with goodwill: 1) Value is based on current income using a multiplier or capitalization rate, or 2) Value is based on the present value of the projected income stream over the next 3-5 years. The method used will depend on the purpose, conditions and assumptions of the valuation.

Capitalization Method

Capitalization, or the earnings multiplier method, works as follows:

• Multiply profits from a reconstructed annual operating statement by a factor (multiplier) or divide by a capitalization rate.

• The multiplier or the capitalization rates are arbitrary numbers to calculate. They are established after careful study of many factors (including the business and financial risks involved, the investor alternate investment opportunities and the cost of borrowing long-term operating capital).

• Compare capitalization rates and profit multipliers:

Multiplier	Capitalization Rate
1	100%
2	50%
3	33.3%
4	25%
5	20%

Example: If EBIT for the year is $150,000 and the multiplier chosen is two, then the value would be $300,000. If EBIT for the year is $150,000 and the capitalization rate is 50 percent, then the value would also be $300,000 (150,000/.50).

As shown in this example, it would take two years of profits to recover the purchase price of the business. This is a common method for determining sales price for small business opportunities.

The capitalization rate approach assumes the owners will earn a 50 percent return on their investment and no recovery of their capital until time of sale. Or, in other words, the 50 percent represents 30 percent return *on* investment and a 20 percent return *of* investment.

Present Value Method

The "present value" method states the value in terms of what an investor would pay today for a predictable future cash flow. These calculations can easily be made on most hand-held calculators (check your calculator instruction booklet for details).

To establish the value of a real estate firm using this method, project the annual EBIT on reconstructed operating statements monthly or annually for 3-5 years. A yield or "risk adjusted discount rate" is selected considering the owner's other investment alternatives, the risk involved and the cost and availability of borrowed capital. The present value of the projected income is then calculated in the same way the present value is calculated on other real estate investments. Here is an example of imputing the diminishing residual value of the tangible and intangible assets provided by the former owners when a change of ownership is anticipated. Note the reduced annual EBIT from the second through the fifth year.

Example: Risk adjusted discount rate of 33.3 percent

Year:	Projected EBIT: (at year end)
1	$200,000
2	160,000
3	120,000
4	80,000
5	40,000

The present value is $325,587.

Step 6: Make Adjustments

After you complete the calculations, you may need to make adjustments depending on the nature of the reasons for valuation.

Example. In calculating the value of a firm by the cash flow methods *only*, the assets critical to the operation of the business would be included in the calculated value. If cash reserves and/or investment property is to be included in an ownership change, appropriate additions would be expected.

The valuation of a multifacet firm can be simplified by "spinning off" assets or separate profit centers. For example, if the firm owns its offices, it may put them under separate ownership and lease them to the brokerage company. This should be done with the counsel of your tax accountant or attorney.

Step 7: Consider the Limitations
As you determine the value of the firm, note the difficulties:
- Collection of applicable data on internal and external factors
- Imputing value of owner's services, market rent and office space
- Agreement about capitalization rates and risk-adjusted discount rates
- Uncertainty of future revenue and expense projections
- Limited comparable data
- Subjectivity of buyer (a person may pay more for a business than its estimated value because they are buying a market share or location critical to their expansion plan, or they are simply "buying a job").

Conclusion
Appraisals of business opportunities are very subjective. Considerable judgment is required. It is also important that you begin the process with a stated purpose and strategic operating plan. All determinations and conclusions must be relevant to that purpose and plan.

[*This section on Determining Value was extracted from an article by Ron Schmaedick, CRB, CPM, owner of Rams Realty, Inc., in Eugene, OR. The article initially appeared in Vol. 2, No. 4, of* Management Issues & Trends *newsletter, published by the Real Estate Brokerage Council*™.]

The reader might ask at this point, why would a person be willing to receive repayment of their fixed assets? To answer that question, go back to the reason why a person will sell, whether the motivation is the desire to retire, the fact that a broker has progressed as far as he can go individually or perhaps wants capitalization to continue. All these are motivating reasons why a person will sell and not just because he thinks he can make a profit. In fact, it is unusual for a substantial profit to be made as a result of a sales or merger of a real estate company. In the methods of acquisition, the first is cash and as emphasized here, it must be done conservatively and it is the simplest method. You merely enter into the contract to purchase a real estate company for a fixed sum after a complete analysis. When it goes to closing, the buyer pays cash to the seller and the seller enters a bill of sale for all of the fixed assets, assigns the leases, or in the case of real property, deeds the real property over to the buyer.

Deferred Payments
There are many other sophisticated forms of acquisition. The system most commonly used in the acquisition of small real estate companies is that of deferred payments. Under this system a buyer establishes a purchase price as outlined earlier; a predetermined amount of cash is paid at the time of transfer and a note or legal document is executed by the buyer which specifies deferred payments over a period of years. This has several advantages to both buyer and seller. If a profit is being earned, the seller can spread it over a period of years, limiting the tax impact on that profit. This method will also give the

seller a continuity of earnings over a period of time. The advantage to the buyer is the fact that he doesn't have to lay out all the cash at one time and actually pays a major portion of the purchase price out of the future earnings generated by the acquiring firm. Most real estate firms defer payments over a period of five years and generally do not exceed 50 percent of the net anticipated earnings after taxes.

Exchange of Stock

The third method of acquisition, the stock exchange, has become very popular. For example, a real estate company which has a major impact on a large market area, strong capitalization, and is publicly owned, has created an established value for its stock. When such a firm wants to acquire other real estate companies, instead of paying them either cash or deferred payments for the value of the company, it exchanges stock of their company for the ownership of the company to be acquired. The advantages for the seller are that it is generally a tax free exchange and no tax consequences occur until the sale of the acquired stock. The other advantage is that if stock appreciates the increased value comes without the management headaches. The risk factor is that if the bottom drops out of the real estate market, the stock is also devaluated dramatically. The advantage for the acquiring company is that they don't have to use any cash for their acquisitions. By buying a publicly owned company, they have sources of financing not generally available to a small, privately held company.

The stock exchange can be attractive where there are two major corporations that understand each operation and feel there is a strict advantage through marriage, recognize the management of each company and are willing to exchange stock even though their respective stocks are not publicly held and there is a limited market. For example, X Company is in negotiation with Y Company that has a good market penetration where X Company is weak. Where X has excellent market penetration Y is weak. X and Y have similar operations in mortgage banking and property management. A merger would provide substantial savings and efficiencies in operation. Neither stock is publicly held. Therefore, there is little or no market for the stock but both recognize the market potential and advantages in merger. The logical direction would be a tax free merger so that both could reserve their cash and assets for a more efficient operation. Therefore, it is to their advantage to negotiate under these terms for a tax free exchange of stock rather than a buy-out by one or the other.

New Corporation

The last method of acquisition could actually result in the creation of a new corporation. This could be done very nicely if the separate brokers got together and found it to their advantage to merge their operations. There are other examples that have occurred in recent years where brokers have found it to their advantage to have a merged operation, created a new corporation, divided their responsibilities and developed a successful operation. In a number of cases where firms have been acquired due to management, the purchase price has been established by a guaranteed fixed price in cash with additional funds available based on the ability of management to increase the business. In other words, there would be an established kicker or percentage available out of earnings as an additional purchase price. Also in some cases, options were given to acquire additional stock based on increased earnings. This stock option could be quite valuable in the event the market value of the stock increases.

Forms of Ownership

Every broker considering either merger or acquisition should have legal counsel. Without getting into legal details, the various forms of ownership and some of their advantages and disadvantages will be examined here.

Sole Proprietorship

Sole proprietorship, where the individual owns his business by himself, is a common form of ownership. He may be the only salesperson or he could have a hundred salespeople but it is individual ownership. The obvious advantage here is the fact that the owner is the boss, makes all the decisions and, if those decisions are profitable, makes all the profits. If the business grows it is all to his advantage.

The disadvantage is that the burden is all on the owner's shoulders. He has the responsibility of continuing management, lacks freedom, is tied down to the operation of the business and has no one else to share the responsibility. From a tax standpoint, there is no shelter. Whatever earnings are produced are taxed at ordinary income. He cannot build any surplus other than in the form of fixed assets.

Partnership

In a partnership one or more individuals operate a business as individual partners. Their partnership agreement spells out the percentage of ownership and division of responsibility. All profits and losses are passed on to the individual partners. It does have the advantage of a sharing of both responsibility and liabilities. The natural tax advantage is the fact that profits and losses are passed on to the individual partners without a corporate shell.

The partnership arrangement has the same general disadvantage in that there is no way to build a surplus other than fixed assets. Like the sole proprietorship there is only continuity in ownership by virtue of the partnership agreement.

Corporation

The third form of ownership is the corporation, giving a corporate body structure to the business and stock ownership. The advantage of the corporation is the continuity of ownership. A corporation survives the stock ownership, provides shelter for liability and if there is liability the corporate body is responsible for repayment and not the individual.

The disadvantage is the two-tier level of taxation that must be paid in a corporate structure: individual taxes on any salary plus bonuses collected from the corporation and corporate tax.

However, a corporate structure can build up a surplus. The corporation builds a name and reputation that is a continuing operation and it is generally believed that it is advantageous for any person forming or expanding a real estate company and expecting to be in business on a long-term basis to do so under a corporate structure.

Sub-Chapter S Corporation

Sub-chapter S corporation is permitted under existing tax laws that allow a pass through of income and expenses to the individual stockholders. There are many limitations in the formation of this type of corporation. The advantages or disadvantages of a sub-chapter S corporation should be explored with legal counsel.

There are many times in the real estate business that legal counsel is needed. One of the most important instances of this need is in the determination of the form of business ownership and its legal structure and existence.

Realigning Staff

After management goes through the entire process of determining the advantages and disadvantages of mergers and acquisitions, evaluating the property, arriving at the purchase price and the method of acquisition and determining the form of ultimate ownership, the day arrives to start the new operation. The doors open for business under the new ownership with plans carefully made for a more profitable operation. Several potential assets were identified early in the acquisition analysis, such as continuity of management staff, sales staff and personnel.

Suppose the advantages a firm had to offer were quality of management, capitalization and liquidity, expertise, market impact, physical size, effective training programs, broadened advertising base and management knowhow. The most essential part of the plan before closing and after closing the deal is the realignment of staff operation of the new firm. Perhaps the advantage of purchasing another firm was to acquire its outstanding management. The individual running the other business would make an ideal sales manager for your business or there might be other staff people who would fit into property management, mortgage financing or other staff assignments. The importance of analyzing the personnel of the firm to be acquired cannot be overemphasized. Find out how many people will stay and what their potential is. It is very important to look at the whole picture of the continuing operation.

Will a new sales manager be assigned? Will salespeople be reassigned? If the firm was acquired because of its location in the market, will salespeople from other offices be assigned there or will salespeople from the acquired firm be moved to other locations? How many salespeople will be needed in that operation for market penetration? What staff will be needed to service those salespeople—secretaries, bookkeeper, settlement officer, sales manager?

The following general realignments are common: first, a sales manager is assigned who is familiar with the policy and procedure of the firm, knows and agrees with the sales philosophy of the firm and is prepared to implement those policies immediately. Next, personnel not needed are generally either reassigned or dismissed (such as a bookkeeper and/or secretaries, depending on central service functions; also settlement officers, depending on what type of closing department is organized). Third, salespeople are reassigned. In many cases a salesperson is reluctant to move into a new sales office because he fears losing the security he has developed operating under certain management personnel. The advantages of moving must be established before he will agree to it. The variance in operation and benefits for salespeople can result in animosity between existing staff and new salespeople. Many of these situations can be avoided through the assignment of a well qualified training officer who can explain the advantages of the merged operation. It must be remembered that one of the original criteria in the acquisition or merger of a real estate firm was to develop a more efficient operation for greater productivity and higher profits. This cannot be achieved unless there is a properly motivated, trained staff to implement the policies promulgated by the parent firm.

Franchises
Mention was made earlier of franchise operations that offset the reluctance of smaller brokers to give up their individual identification by use of franchise agreements.

Advantages
One is using a standardized sign that emphasizes the franchise company but also features the identity of the local broker. Because the size, color and logo of the sign is standardized, people driving around the market area see the impact of a tremendous number of listings.

Second, advertising can be merged into a major program, maintaining individual identity in the ads through phone numbers. Again, the impression conveyed to the public is that one organization has a massive volume of listings. In like manner, a heavy institutional advertising campaign promotes the service provided by the affiliated brokerage houses functioning under this one title. This can have a great impact on the market and result in increased production. Small firms can put themselves in a stronger competitive position. When a broker tries to analyze the advantages of franchising, the first thing to study is its market impact.

Third, some franchises provide standard office procedures, standardized forms, operations manuals, training and other educational tools.

Disadvantages
The disadvantages of a franchise, first, are financial. A franchise fee is generally broken down to so many dollars up front in order to set up the system, buy the initial franchise and then some percentages of gross commissions on a continuing basis. This comes directly out of the company dollar and affects the profits of the operation.

Another disadvantage is that certain procedures, guidelines and criteria have been set up by the franchise and unless the firm adheres to them it can lose the franchise. This removes some of the independence and freedom real estate brokers traditionally cherish.

One other disadvantage is the territorial limitation under a franchise. Some franchises will not give any territorial protection. As a consequence, a broker can end up with the same franchise company overlapping in his market area.

Franchise operations have enjoyed rapid growth in the last 15 years. Franchises for the small broker can be their answer to meeting competition from the large brokerage firm and unless there are other motivations such as retirement and capitalization it will cut down the need for merger and acquisition.

Summary

When a broker considers buying a firm, he must determine whether he can absorb that operation without undue strain on present management and accounting personnel. He must be sure he can comfortably finance or obtain financing and working capital for the merged operation.

The many areas to be considered, such as purchase price, method of payment, employment contracts, stock options and fringe benefits cannot be taken lightly. They will have long-term direct commitments on the continuing operation. With the expansion of franchising, the industry will also see an aggressive market in the acquisition and merging of real estate firms in order to remain competitive.

Vertical Expansion   21

A broker spends a great deal of money, time and effort getting people to call, to come in and talk to him. He works hard at developing his firm's reputation for respectability, honesty and effectiveness. As he does this he develops a wide acquaintanceship among a great many people. There are ways to use all these contacts to develop more business through related services. This is called vertical expansion and it involves many real estate disciplines or fields of special knowledge.

Each real estate service is a separate discipline. Most of them interrelate with at least several others. Every discipline a firm adds spreads the promotion of the company name over more units, reduces the cost load on individual profit centers and increases the profitability of the whole business.

It is not the function of this book to provide detailed information on how to perform the related services a broker may add as he adds new disciplines. Each discipline, its advantages and disadvantages, is described briefly and sources for further study are listed for brokers interested in vertical expansion.

In addition, the various institutes of the NATIONAL ASSOCIATION OF REALTORS® offer courses in the disciplines mentioned here.

Vertical Expansion

As the practice of real estate has grown and matured, a trend toward specialization has developed. In the past a broker serviced almost all the real estate needs of a community. Now firms have begun to specialize in a particular phase of the business and large companies have set up separate departments to serve particular areas. These developments have resulted in what is known as a series of disciplines in real estate.

Fig. 1 could be the organization chart for a large, diversified marketing firm. It also highlights the various disciplines or branches of knowledge involved in the real estate business today.

Present and potential users of specialized services may already be customers of the broker's more traditional services. Others are within easy reach, needing to be told about the range of services a firm provides. They may be turning to others for services the firm already performs but has not promoted.

Residential Brokerage
Residential brokerage is the base on which most real estate firms are built. The broker who achieves success in residential work and is interested in expansion may move into another subdiscipline of brokerage or perhaps into one of the other major disciplines or both.

A good residential broker is knowledgeable in appraisals, finance and research. He has need of these disciplines as he evaluates properties for listing purposes, arranges loans and advises clients on probable future values.

Farm and Land Brokerage
A farm and land brokerage office specializes in the sale of producing and non-producing farms and ranches as well as raw land. This subdiscipline of brokerage has become increasingly profitable as investors buy land for future use and appreciation. The broker who understands the tax laws involved in buying and holding raw land, the value of producing farms and ranches and can also envision future uses of the land will find this a lucrative department. Here again the brokerage discipline interacts with appraisal, research and finance disciplines. The REALTORS® Land Institute of the NATIONAL ASSOCIATION OF REALTORS® offers education in this area.

Industrial
Although a residential broker may sell some commercial-investment property, brokerage of this type has usually been found in separate firms that specialize in it. Larger companies often have separate commercial-investment offices.

Commercial-investment brokers must be knowledgeable in major disciplines: appraisal for valuation, finance for arranging loans, re-

Fig. 1 Organizational chart

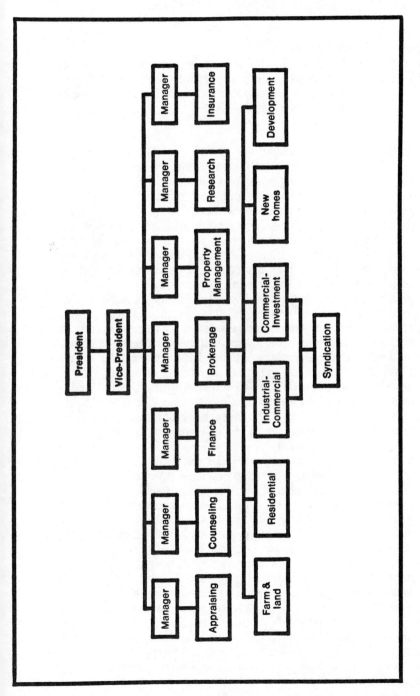

Vertical Expansion

search for understanding present value and calculating future value of proposed income streams or special purpose properties; and in some instances, a knowledge of property management to counsel the client on the operation of a proposed purchase. The Society of Industrial and Office REALTORS® of the NATIONAL ASSOCIATION OF REALTORS® provides information in this area.

Commercial-Investment

Like industrial transactions, this area is very complex, requiring knowledge in the major disciplines. Complicated and ever-changing tax laws as well as the increasing sophistication of investors have created a need for specialization in this field.

Cautions in Making a Decision

Commercial and investment sales generally require more time and effort per sale than residential sales. This can affect the time required to succeed. Also, more education and more market information is required to become recognized as an authority in the commercial, industrial or investment field. A large amount of paper work packaging (the work-up data on properties for prospective clients), more planning and cooperation with state and local authorities is required. Extensive contacts with and association with specialists will be needed in many instances to complete transactions.

A broker must carefully establish the division's exclusiveness of multiple, commercial and industrial listings and the selling rights of residential salespeople. Are residential salespeople to be permitted to handle these types of properties? What will the effect be on sales volume and morale if residential is excluded from these sales areas? What will the effect be on the firm's reputation if untrained, unskilled residential salespeople try to compete with industrial or investment salespeople for the same client? What effect would any proposed restrictions have on the independent contractor status of salespeople? These questions must be dealt with very carefully as expansion plans are considered.

This area provides high company dollar return. While desk cost is higher than in residential, profitability on these transactions is excellent. There is the added plus of the firm's image and prestige being enhanced when major buildings are sold. To be known as a firm that can produce sales of all kinds is a great advantage.

Considerations that favor adding this discipline to an existing brokerage operation start with the fact that a potential clientele is already at hand. A company executive who has bought a home may also need office or plant facilities. If he is coming into the area to handle company expansion or to open a new division he may need a new warehouse, office space or land on which to construct a new plant. A full-service firm can handle all its clients' needs.

A broker's present clientele may have investment property they want to sell. This could be anything from a corporation's outgrown factory or office building to properties acquired through inheritance. A series of institutional ads that focus on basic real estate investment principles have been known to elicit response from wholly unexpected sources. Some of them could come from people you have been doing residential business with for years.

This is not a costly area to get into as far as office space is concerned. A broker will need a desk, some good reference books and files.

Effective communication in selling investment properties is important. Salespeople have to be numbers oriented. The sophisticated terms of the discipline are often foreign to people who have money to invest. The broker should be sure his salespeople have or get special training in how to communicate the terminology so the buyer understands what is being said. To fail to do this has spoiled many a big investment opportunity when buyers turn away rather than admit ignorance of the technicalities of a transaction.

Other advantages include spreading the cost of institutional advertising and other overhead over more profit centers, interdepartmental referrals, opportunities for equity investment by the brokers and less bookkeeping and sales records required.

Recruitment advertising must attract the investment-oriented person and should offer him a challenge in the ad itself. It should probably be placed in the investment section, not the want ads section, of the newspaper. One of the most effective recruiting tools is a one-to-one talk with people already employed in a white collar position with a local non-real estate firm. Real estate offers them a great deal of independence, a higher than normal return on their time and a fulfilling career that will never be tedious or boring.

Some Complexities

Training is long term and harder than residential. As tax laws change and become more complicated every year, tax expertise becomes a discipline in itself.

Salespeople going into commercial-investment need lots of lead time, sometimes as much as two years. And they require management dedicated to giving them sound advice and continuing encouragement.

Commercial-investment sales are complex. Many require intense creativity and determination to get all the pieces together and lots of perseverance and patience to see transactions through. And some transactions never reach the contract stage. Money is poured into research, investigation and travel and the broker never recoups that money. There are long, dry spells. It may be two years between really big sales.

The broker may be called on to put up a lot of front money to support good people through dry spells. There is also the problem of commission splits. Some sales split as many as ten ways and those who claim a share may not have contributed anything to the transaction. To refuse to cut someone in on a sale may throw it all over and result in the selling broker being in trouble.

Desk cost is high and commercial-investment requires more secretarial work than residential work. More research materials are needed.

There is a lack of market control. It is difficult to get exclusives in this area. Owners of this type of property are not interested in being tied up; when they are amenable to it they want to work with a broker who has a long track record of successes. It is a difficult field to break into.

Commercial-industrial work has some public relations hazards that could affect the entire firm adversely. For example, if a broker's commercial department is putting together a transaction opposed by a segment of the public and gets involved in zoning meetings where emotions run high, the end result could be bad public relations that affect every division of the company negatively.

The Commercial-Investment Real Estate Council provides excellent educational courses in the commercial-investment field, leading to the Certified Commercial-Investment Member designation.

Syndication

In many states, security departments are ruling that many syndications, historically considered real estate sales, are now classified as security transactions. More and more people are becoming involved in the ownership of real estate by multiple group ownership, syndication or limited partnerships. This is a coming method of real estate investment involving hundreds of millions of dollars in recent years.

Most firms doing a substantial amount of partnership and syndication type transactions find it desirable, if not in fact necessary, to obtain a securities license permitting them to go in whichever direction is dictated by the final disposition of clients' holdings. Syndications are becoming more attractive than single client transactions. As long as syndications show a good profit, they continually generate the capital needed for more investing and these clients come back over and over again. Syndications appeal to people in the professions who historically invested in mutual funds, stocks and bonds.

The Real Estate Securities and Syndication Institute of the NATIONAL ASSOCIATION OF REALTORS® provides training and publications in this area.

Appraisal

Appraisal services are often sought when present and future property values must be measured with great accuracy. The appraiser must be able to evaluate residential, commercial, industrial and multi-family properties. He needs a strong background in finance, property management and research.

An appraisal, according to the American Institute of Real Estate Appraisers, is a supported estimate of value usually based on one of the accepted methods: cost approach, market data approach and income approach.

A competent appraiser usually has a background in all the disciplines in real estate, gained through training and experience in evaluating various types of property. For example, an appraiser who specializes in residential valuation needs a background in residential brokerage and a knowledge of current and past markets. He must also have knowledge of new homes to utilize the cost approach to value. Such a person also needs to know investment properties in order to calculate income from income-producing properties.

Some four thousand appraisers have a Member of the American Institute or Residential Member designation from the American Institute of Real Estate Appraisers of the NATIONAL ASSOCIATION OF REALTORS®. Senior Real Estate Analyst, Senior Real Property Appraisers or Senior Residential Appraiser are designations of the Society of Real Estate Appraisers.

Record keeping is of prime importance in appraisal work. An efficient filing system for records, maps, data, statistics and correspondence is essential. It is here the broker will keep data on assessments, taxes, zoning regulations, deed and property descriptions. Information on comparable properties, current construction costs and any other data used in arriving at a conclusion should be retained.

Vertical
Expansion

All the foregoing information may be used when the appraiser reconciles data to come to a value conclusion. Then the conclusion is drafted into a formal report and sent to the client along with supporting displays of photographs, maps or plats.

Appraisal fees vary both in content and cost according to their simplicity or sophistication. Some fees are hourly, others per diem and still others on a job-plus-costs basis. It is at this stage of expanding into appraisal work that a broker must know all the costs involved including the value of the appraiser's time, secretarial costs, a share of general office cost, automobile and/or travel expense and whatever miscellaneous costs should be assigned this department. The latter would include the costs of professional photographers, surveyors and other professionals whose work is essential to doing the job.

Advantages of Appraisal Work

What are some of the advantages of adding an appraisal department? It is a low overhead operation, requiring little secretarial help to type reports, many of which are standardized. There is a great deal of appraisal business today and there promises to be more. Every time a highway is built or a school or library built or enlarged, appraisals are needed. In some cases whole towns are being assessed, reestablishing values for tax purposes. Corporations are fine prospects, whether an entire company is moving, building, buying or plans to transfer a number of employees.

Some Problems

On the negative side, starting up an appraisal business is slow. It requires a lot of time to build it to the point where it produces a good income. Anyone considering going into appraisal work should plan a long lead time.

Conflict of interest is a potential problem and should be watched carefully. When a conflict occurs, the broker may find himself appraising a property only to lose the listing to another broker.

It is growing more difficult to get credentials. A number of states are considering legislation to require the licensing of appraisers. The AIREA offers training necessary to obtaining the designations mentioned earlier. Here again, plan a long lead time for training and obtaining the designation.

Property Management

Many brokers move into property management more by accident than by plan. Friends or clients ask them to manage single-family or small multi-family units and from this a limited property management department evolves. Unless it is a full-time operation, property management seldom shows a reasonable return for its cost to a broker.

This discipline is a natural outgrowth of residential and commercial listings. It is almost a necessity for firms that have an investment department. Many investment properties are absentee-owned. It is to the broker's advantage to be able to offer management services along with the investment itself.

Property management interacts with appraisal in evaluating a client's property; finance, to assure the best type of mortgaging; brokerage, to advise whether to sell or hold the property; and research, to indicate when rentals should be raised and to inform the owner on general market trends.

Advantages

One of the advantages of starting a property management department is that it has an even cash flow. A broker with a substantial property management operation need not care as much about market fluctuations because this profit helps offset some of the losses incurred in slow residential work. A long-term management contract is another form of security. If the company does a good enough job in management it is in a prime position to lock in an exclusive when the time comes to sell the property.

People from the residential staff can help rent management's properties, adding to their income too. This increases the total service aspect of real estate brokerage.

The prestige of having the firm name on large buildings is a plus. It is another way of keeping in the public eye and informing people that the firm helps in a variety of ways.

Complexities

What are some of the problems in property management? Prime properties can be hard to get, for one thing. If they are being well managed, only a major mistake or the death of a principal seems to free up the best ones. In a growing area, getting accounts as they are built may be a bit easier.

Fixed salaries are involved for all the people essential to the operation. These include rent collections, repairs, record keeping for the owner (and these can be as detailed as routine bank deposits, check writing and monthly reports). There is a smaller percentage of profit than in brokerage. A company has to handle a great many properties before it realizes a sizeable return.

Inadequate repairs and unsatisfactory maintenance can lead to tenant problems and resultant poor relations with the owner. Certainly anything connected with a negative consumer relationship that results in bad press publicity will have an immediate adverse effect on the whole company. This problem can reach all the way back to the quality of a maintenance crew.

There is higher liability in management and it is absolutely essential to carry good insurance, which can bring some problems of contract cancellation. A great deal of bookkeeping is required in property management and the department or its representatives must be on 24-hour call.

The Institute of Real Estate Management of the NATIONAL AS-SOCIATION OF REALTORS® offers courses and publications in this area as well as the designations Certified Property Manager, Accredited Management Organization and Accredited Resident Manager.

Vertical Expansion

Insurance

Some say that in its truest sense, insurance is not a real estate discipline. But in every discipline measured here some knowledge of insurance is helpful. Like finance, insurance is one element of a full line of services many firms want to offer. In many smaller firms, insurance is the department that pays the bills when listing and selling is not doing well. On the other hand, some large firms have discontinued insurance departments in recent years, citing problems in servicing accounts and a decrease in commissions paid by insurance companies.

Every person who contacts a broker, whether he buys or not, is a potential client for some kind of an insurance policy. And everyone who does buy owns real estate he is going to insure. The kinds of insurance property owners need range from liability, mortgage protection, fire and theft to all manner of special policies that require the broker to find special underwriting. Every insurance service a broker provides adds to his potential value to his clients, another thing for which they depend on him.

Advantages

An insurance department keeps a broker's name before the public. It can increase his public relations image in the simple, routine steps essential to year-round service. Reminders of approaching renewal dates and suggestions for updating coverage are among the best public relations tools an insurance department has. The friendly birthday or anniversary card are the kind of small gestures insurance people are great at and which the recipients appreciate. They also give the broker an opportunity to get his name into all those homes on happy occasions.

Selling insurance adds to the total profitability of a firm because it lays off overhead and contributes to the cash flow. No matter what size the department, the insurance premiums keep coming in.

Negatives

The negatives to consider in relation to insurance in real estate brokerage focus on the cost of doing business. Claims can run ruinously high. There is a low profit ratio per policy. It is often necessary for a broker to concentrate the writing of policies within the office, keeping salespeople's attention and effort on the much more productive activities of listing and selling properties.

Insurance must be a high dollar operation to be profitable. Some brokers estimate that a firm should have a quarter million dollars in premiums if an insurance department is to pay out. Others, arguing that it is a service traditionally expected of real estate brokers, believe it should be continued on a narrow profit margin because of its public relations value to the firm.

New Homes

The new homes subdiscipline in brokerage is a fairly recent development. Brokers have traditionally tried to list new homes but were discouraged or prevented from doing so by many builders. The state of the selling market is a strong factor in a builder's attitude. Brokers have learned that the sale of new homes is very different from selling pre-owned homes and requires a different kind of salesperson. Compensation is also handled differently, often being paid on a unit basis instead of a percentage.

There are several ways a broker can add a new homes department. Some go into development and construction on their own, some sell them for builders and still others joint venture with builders in acquiring and developing land and constructing the houses. All three methods have advantages and disadvantages, depending on local market conditions, land availability and construction costs.

Benefits

The need for a special selling effort in new homes exists in many markets. In one major metropolitan area 13 percent of the buying public who go into a broker's office buy new homes. But a great many who come in to look at new homes actually buy pre-owned properties because a builder cannot provide financing and cost flow. Without a new homes department that broker would lose all or a portion of 13 percent of his market.

Another benefit for a broker in new homes is that as he sells them he gets to know the people and is on the ground floor for resale listings. Also, the buyer acquiring a new house probably has one he must sell, which creates another chance for a listing and sales commission.

New homes are excellent field offices. A desk, phone, heat and light are all it costs a broker. Local home furnishings merchants usually like to furnish models in exchange for promotion of their names and services. Salespeople who work in model homes free up desk space in the main office.

Some Problems

The negatives to be considered include the high advertising costs of new homes. This can sometimes be offset partially by inducing electric and gas utilities to join in a cooperative advertising campaign. Fall and spring home festivals sponsored by metropolitan newspapers are seasonal events in many areas, offering special lower ad rates and substantial promotion during these heavy buying months.

Financing can be a problem. There are often delays in closing. A signed contract may be six months in final settlement and the broker may have to supply interim financing to his sales staff.

Compensation rates can also be difficult to handle. Builders have variable commission schedules and they seldom cover a broker's usual rates. But a broker should keep in mind that the builder is providing him with merchandise his firm may sell many times in the future. One house sold at a first commission rate below standard may bring multiple standard commissions in resales over a fairly limited time.

Staffing model home offices can be a problem. It is often difficult to persuade salespeople to stay on in a model home on a dark, rainy or snowy night. But the agreement between builder and broker may call for the house being kept open and staffed.

Development

Closely aligned with new homes is a development department, used by a broker to find suitable land parcels, then to develop them for sale to a builder or an investor. In some cases the broker may hold the property for his own use, bringing in a builder or constructing new homes himself.

Any broker interested in development needs to be familiar with the finance discipline, to determine the best way to fund the land purchase; with research, to find available parcels best suited to development; with appraisal, to evaluate the property; and in some cases with new homes and industrial-commercial subdisciplines.

Counseling

Real estate counselors have experience and/or knowledge in all the disciplines. They have generally been in the business a long time and have built up a steady clientele. They operate on a fee basis and counsel their clients in all their real estate transactions and portfolio holdings. The American Society of Real Estate Counselors of the NATIONAL ASSOCIATION OF REALTORS® provides information in this area.

Finance

Finance is an allied discipline of real estate. However, large brokerage firms are increasingly integrating finance into their general operation and considering it part of their total real estate service. It can be a profitable part of the operation when managed expertly.

In those areas of the country that close in escrow, the availability of one's own mortgage closing office is a great asset, permitting total control of the sale from inception to closing. A growing number of firms are adding mortgage brokerage service to their general operation.

All the foregoing disciplines in real estate can be operated as separate businesses rather than being under a single roof.

When brokers regard real estate disciplines in the same way they are thought of in the field of education—where special fields of knowledge are grouped under that one word, education—it may be easier for them to focus on the thrust of their particular discipline, aware that the other fields of specialization will contribute to their needs as they arise.

The Challenge of Management   22

One of the first chapters in this book outlined the broker's need for knowledge in three areas: real estate, management and people. The book has dealt with the functions and systems managers can use to expand their knowledge, develop skills and train staff people to be most productive in today's marketplace.

Management's challenge for the future is to stay in the lead in these areas—to read and study as widely as possible in a variety of fields, learning to relate all emerging trends to the field of real estate, then know where to turn for information and training so they are prepared to give full service in a changing economy. Only as management people succeed in these endeavors will the real estate industry be able to sustain its important role in the American business economy.

This final chapter suggests some of the emerging trends already recognized, a number of future possibilities and some of the ways management can meet and deal with these challenges.

The Challenge of Management

What will the real estate market of the next quarter century be? What will brokerage ownership encompass? What technological tools and human methods, introduced recently or still on drawing boards or being discussed in broker seminars and association board rooms will become part of a broker's daily routine and staff action of the future? What new concepts of management will be introduced? What new services will real estate brokers conceive and offer as they work to keep their business viable?

We have become a society of organizations and knowledge in the twentieth century. More people than ever before work as members of managed institutions within a managerial structure and organization. And more and more people make their living by putting knowledge to work. Management is both the carrier and the result of these two developments. In fact, management itself is a knowledge.

All management consists of two major elements: marketing and innovation. The concept may be as old as management but the concept of what marketing really is is new.

For years marketing was accepted as the selling of a product or a service to people. Today's most successful marketing programs begin by asking what it is the consumer wants and then focus planning and sales efforts on the people who really need and want the product or service they market. In this sense, marketing almost makes old-fashioned selling superfluous. The aim of modern, progressive business is to know and understand the customer so well that its product or service fits him and sells itself.

Real estate is in a position to perform marketing services in their most ideal form. The industry is called upon to serve people who are ready to buy and whose demands, needs and lifestyles are outlined in a buyer profile. The broker has a collection of listings from which to suggest properties that fit the buyer's needs, demands and lifestyle. Ergo, he is in a position to perform the service demanded by consumer advocates today: to give the buyer what he wants. Refinements of the logistics of real estate marketing are still possible but the basics are already there. The public has every right to expect the industry to further refine its marketing services.

What the buyer wants is undergoing dramatic change, too, as lifestyles and values shift to accommodate new environments.

Questions to Ask Yourself
Before one considers the future challenges of management it would be well to address himself to the following four questions.

What is my future? One should truly analyze what his future is and whether or not real estate fits in the picture. It could be that you are managing the wrong type of people and the wrong type of business and should therefore consider an entirely different profession.

What's the future of real estate in my area? Once you have committed yourself to real estate take a look at your market area. Does it show promise of future profits or is it an area which has grown stagnant and would be difficult to get started up again?

Where does my organization fit into the future projection? Once you have committed yourself to an area, take a look at your organization and see how it fits within that projection. Is it the right type of organization for the area and does it fit all the needs you think will be challenging you in the future?

How can my firm make more money? Certainly one of the prime motivations of management is to show profit. One must consider if his firm is set up properly to return the risk dollars which must be put forth in order to succeed.

Seven Trends

Once these questions have been answered, one should examine the changes that are taking place in the real estate business in order to try and define the trends of the future. Trends in the following seven areas particularly affect real estate·

Growth of the suburbs

The expanding metropolis

The second-home market

Sophisticated highway systems

Planned unit developments

Non-real estate corporations' entry into the real estate business

Government involvement.

Number one, the rapid growth and expansion of the suburbs will challenge many REALTORS® and managers in the years to come. There has been a significant change in the type of ownership people are demanding. Many Americans today don't want to be tied to the land and the chores it entails. The condominium concept is the answer to some of these problems. To the other point of view, condominiums allow inner city home ownership of a type not available in the past.

Town houses and higher density units involving the concepts of zero lot lines and cluster housing present a different selling concept. Therefore the manager must carefully watch these trends and anticipate them in order to retrain his staff as necessary. The manager whose staff continues to sell as they did in the '70s may well find himself out of business in the '90s.

Number two, the exploding metropolis of the future will challenge those in commercial and industrial real estate and their office management techniques. As the suburbs explode and continue to grow and as the inner city core is rebuilt there will be need for service-type operations which require commercial space. Managers in these areas must be concerned about condominium concepts in commercial and industrial developments and the effect they will have on salespeople and their market.

Concern for better ecological planning and environmental control is also bringing changes in basic commercial and industrial uses. A few areas of the country have gone to underground industrial construction which calls for a completely new look at land value and usage. Other areas of the country now require underground industrial plants to landscape the top of their plants to make them blend better with the environment and be more acceptable to the people in the area.

Number three, the second home and recreational market continues to have a vital impact on the American public. Many areas of the country which in the past had been almost unsalable have suddenly come to life because their environment makes them attractive for second homes. Modular housing or mobile homes have been the answer for part of this market. The alert marketing manager of the future will search his trade area to see if there is an opportunity to start some type of recreational housing or second home building.

Number four is the newer concept of vertical shopping centers, built up and down rather than spread out over a tremendous acreage. Here one can park within the center and be protected from the elements throughout his entire shopping tour. The vertical center is serviced by high-speed elevators that whisk the consumer to the various floors to do his buying. Some developers envision a day when purchases will be sent by pneumatic tube back to the consumer's automobile.

In like manner, sophisticated highway systems result in suburban areas being developed further and further from the inner city. This has encouraged the construction of industrial parks to provide employment within short driving distances.

Number five, planned unit developments are here to stay. The examples of Reston and Columbia on the east coast show how they succeed when planning is done prior to building the city. The integration in those two cities of residential units—single-family, condominium and apartments—along with commercial and industrial structures has proven successful. The PUD office that utilizes cluster housing and tremendous amounts of open space brings new challenges to the marketing manager who must train his people to sell and market them.

Number six, in recent years there has been a tremendous influx of non-real estate corporations into this business. It began with the need for corporations to assist their transferred employees in moving from one area to another. Because the real estate broker was not prepared to fill the void—buying the employees' old homes—many corporations went into the real estate business themselves. In studying the reasons that they came in, some of the following were prominent:

For an inflation hedge

To diversify their investment

To use surplus cash

For public relations.

The manager who knows why major industries are coming into the business can try to capitalize on it for the benefit of his firm.

Most of the major corporations entering real estate have had difficulty understanding the marketing concepts and realizing a good return on their investment. Many are turning to professional REALTORS® to assist them in feasibility and probability analyses for their projects. It is the manager's job to accept the challenge of their interest in real estate and match the investor with the appropriate investment. This will not put the real estate broker out of business but will give him a significant cash influx which, if managed properly, can lead to the betterment of the industry as a whole.

Finally, no discussion is complete without concern about the government and its programs. The manager of today and the future must be constantly aware of government programs and subsidies. Through changes in tax laws, government can affect the marketing and sale of commercial-investment real estate tremendously. Government's change in incentive plans can often alter the course of new home construction. The manager who is constantly aware of changes in government regulations can keep a step ahead of the competition as these changes occur.

Essential Know-How

The residential and commercial broker of the future must have knowledge in four areas.

With the influx of monies from outside the industry, concern for well-planned profit centers as well as environmental considerations, the real estate broker must be attuned to growth trends in metropolitan areas. He must be knowledgeable about commercial activity in the area and what competition he would be confronted with were he to add a new commercial endeavor. This will affect the trends in future investment return. The sophisticated investor of the future will require that the consultant or real estate broker be able to provide reliable information.

The real estate broker must be attuned to financial analyses and understand how to calculate returns on risk capital. The manager of the future must understand net cash flow projections, and how tax laws will affect the persons for whom he is doing consulting work. Also, real estate brokers will be concerned about the return available from competing investments. The manager of the future will need to be knowledgeable in all forms of debt capital, agencies and regulations that govern any sources of income he may tap to build future projects.

The real estate broker will be concerned about probability analyses. He will have a department to project investments into the future, watch trends and predict where they are going.

Finally, he will have expertise in computer technology. The real estate manager of the future will be able to combine economic and financial analyses into a probable result, making sophisticated projections.

There are challenges for every type and size of brokerage firm in the future. The questions the manager today must ask himself is, do I want to stay the way I am now, do I want to expand or do I want to diversify or specialize? There are no pat answers. The answers lie within the manager himself and in what he wants his company to do.

Human Resources Development

However, once the manager has decided which avenue he will pursue, he must consider the human input necessary to accomplish his goal.

As the quality of staff performance becomes increasingly a matter of concern to management, new concepts will be sought. One that is currently being used is called Human Resources Development. Stated in its briefest form, it is a management philosophy that business should no longer go out and simply hire workers but that they must accept the fact that the individual's contribution to the success of a business should be better understood and developed, that productive work also involves the quality of the work-life experience and that a manager must learn from the work force as well as the work force learning from management.

What are some of the factors behind Human Resources Development? Ted Mills, writing in the *Harvard Business Review* of March/April 1975, said, "The U.S. work force, both as people and as workers, has changed and is changing still. The arts and science of workplace communication as well as the impact of technology on what people do and how they feel about work and themselves contribute to its concern. Also important to this field are job security, reward systems and compensation systems."

How can real estate managers begin to use human resources development in their personal planning and administration? Perhaps the first and most basic way is to give thought to new planning and recruitment programs for different kinds of people, keeping an open mind about who can contribute to the firm's success.

It is well understood today that there are three types of sales personalities. The order-taker is proficient at allowing people to come to him and selling a stated product and taking the order. This type of person is probably best at new home or condominium sales, where he has a defined product, where through advertising and perhaps some canvassing people come to his project, and where he has a limited number of products to sell.

The second type is an order-getter who basically has a territory for which he is responsible and goes out to get orders. This individual is not particularly effective in bringing in new orders but is good at maintaining the clientele that is already loyal to the company. A person who specializes in the sale of properties for corporations that transfer individuals could be a good order-getter.

The third type of individual is an order-counselor. This covers most of the activities of the general real estate brokerage firms in America today. This salesperson is good at in working with the client to a conclusion which is in the client's and/or prospect's best interest.

New Sales Types

In the earlier part of this chapter some of the future changes in real estate were discussed. It's obvious that if the suburban areas continue to expand with condominium concepts and planned unit developments, marketing them will take a different type salesperson or the acquisition of new skills by those who traditionally handled pre-owned properties. Therefore, the manager of the future will have to acclimate himself to the different personalities necessary to handle the product he will be selling. In recruiting these individuals the manager will have to subordinate his personal beliefs of what makes a good salesperson.

One of the greatest problems management has is narcissistic hiring. Many managers tend to hire their own image and if the prospective salesperson's personality is not similar to the manager's he often is not invited to associate with the company.

In many cases the manager will be able to learn a great deal from new salespeople about the approach of selling in their specific former field.

Therefore, a healthy mix of personalities in the future sales force might include the go-getters who aggressively seek new business, the super-selling types that come fully motivated, the rather slow starters who show promise for the future but need more training and motivation and the name people who have public relations value for the firm but are perhaps not as income-motivated as the other types. Many types of individuals as well as a variety of selling personalities will have a place in the future real estate organization. Therefore, though this chapter has stressed the changes in the future of the real estate product, which could probably best be described as things and/or systems, it is obvious that as the product the real estate firm sells changes, the people needed to sell the product will also change. Some needs are already evident; the ability to fill those needs will become easier as the firm grows. Constant awareness of individuals and their ability to perform specific jobs will be paramount to the manager's success.

A question can never be answered until it is asked. The challenge of this chapter is for the manager to recognize that there are many changes occurring now and certainly there will be many more complex changes in the future. He must constantly ask himself whether he is prepared to meet the challenge.

Pasteur's sage comment that "Chance favors the prepared mind" is particularly applicable to the role of management in real estate marketing in the future.

As stated in the beginning of this book, you are probably a manager today because you were unusually good at doing something else earlier in your career. Your challenge now is to use the skills, sensitivity and judgment that brought you where you are today to prepare for the challenges that lie ahead.

Bibliography

Chapter 1

Case, Frederick E. *Real Estate Brokerage.* Englewood Cliffs, N.J.: Prentice-Hall, Inc., 1965.

Donnelly, Jr., James H., James L. Gibson and John M. Ivancevich. *Fundamentals of Management.* Austin, TX: Business Publications, Inc. 1971.

Drucker, Peter F. *The Practice of Management.* New York, N.Y.: Harper & Row, 1954.

Drucker, Peter F. *Management: Tasks, Responsibilities, Practices.* New York, N.Y.: Harper & Row, 1973.

Filley, Alan C. and Robert J. House. *Managerial Process and Organizational Behavior.* Glenview, IL: Scott, Foresman & Co., 1969.

Flippo, Edwin B. *Management: A Behavioral Approach.* 2nd ed. Boston, MA: Allyn & Bacon, 1970.

Gibson, James, L. "Organization Theory and the Nature of Man." *Academy of Management Journal.* Sept. 1966.

Haimann, Theo. and William G. Scott. *Management in Modern Organization.* 2nd ed. Boston, MA: Houghton Mifflin Co., 1974.

Haynes, W. Warren and Joseph L. Massie. *Management.* 2nd ed. Englewood Cliffs, N.J.: Prentice-Hall, Inc., 1969.

Hersey, Paul and Kenneth H. Blanchard. *Management of Organizational Behavior.* 2nd ed. Englewood Cliffs, N.J.: Prentice-Hall, Inc., 1972.

Herzberg, Fred. *Work and the Nature of Man.* New York, N.Y.: World Publishing Co., 1966.

Koontz, Harold and Cyril O'Donnell. *Principles of Management: An Analysis of Managerial Functions.* 5th ed. New York, N.Y.: McGraw-Hill, 1972.

Leavitt, Harold J. *Managerial Psychology.* Rev. ed. Chicago, IL: University of Chicago Press, 1965.

Likert, Rensis. *New Patterns of Management.* New York, N.Y.: McGraw-Hill, 1961.

Litter, Joseph A. *The Analysis of Organizations.* 2nd ed. New York, N.Y.: John Wiley & Sons, Inc., 1973.

Lundgren, Earl F. *Organizational Management.* New York, N.Y.: Harper & Row, 1974.

McGregor, Douglas. *The Human Side of Enterprise.* New York, N.Y.: McGraw-Hill, 1960.

Maslow, Abraham H. *Motivation and Personality.* New York, N.Y.: Harper & Row, 2nd edition, 1970.

Michael, Stephen R. and Halsey R. Jones. *Organizational Management.* New York, N.Y.: Intext Educational Publishers, 1973.

Newman, William H., Charles E. Summer and E. Kirby Warren. *The Process of Management.* 3rd ed. Englewood Cliffs, N.J.: Prentice-Hall, Inc., 1972.

Raia, Anthony P. *Managing by Objectives.* Glenview, IL: Scott, Foresman & Co., 1974.

Schmidt, Warren H. *Organizational Frontiers and Human Values.* Belmont, CA: Wadsworth, 1970.

Starr, Martin K. *Management: A Modern Approach.* New York, N.Y.: Harcourt Brace Jovanovich, Inc., 1971.

Terry, George R. *Principles of Management.* 6th ed. Homewood, IL: Richard D. Irwin, Inc., 1972.

Young, Stanley. *Management: A Systems Approach.* Glenview, IL: Scott, Foresman & Co., 1966.

Chapter 2

Batten, J. D. *Tough-Minded Management.* New York, N.Y.: American Management Association, 1963.

Townsend, Robert. *Up the Organization.* New York, N.Y.: Alfred A Knopf, 1970 and Fawcett Crest, 1970.

Chapter 3

Tannehill, Robert E. *Job Enrichment: The Modern, Proven Method to Motivate Your Employees,* Chicago, IL: The Dartnell Corp., 1974.

Chapter 4

Batten, J. D. *Tough-Minded Management.* New York, N.Y.: American Management Association, 1969.

Buchanan, Paul C. *The Leader and Individual Motivation.* New York, N.Y.: Association Press, 1962.

Chinelly, Sr., John V. *The Meaning of Management.* Miramar, FL: Chinelly Real Estate, Inc.

Katz, Robert L. "Skills of an Effective Administrator." *Harvard Business Review,* Sept.-Oct. 1974.

Knowles, Malcolm and Hilda. *How to Develop Better Leaders.* New York, N.Y.: Association Press, 1956.

Schultz, Dr. Whitt N. "Bits and Pieces." Fairfield, N.J.: Economics Press, 1973.

Tannenbaum, Robert, Irving Weschler and Fred Massarik. *Leadership and Organization.* New York, N.Y.: McGraw-Hill, 1961.

Chapter 6

Boorman, Howells, Nichols, Shapiro. "Interpersonal Communications in Modern Organizations." *Behavioral Sciences Newsletter.* Glen Rock, N.J.

Chase, Stuart. *The Tyranny of Words.* New York, N.Y.: Harcourt, Brace and World, Inc., 1938.

Fast, Julius, *Body Language.* New York, N.Y.: Pocket Books, Simon & Schuster, Inc., 1971.

Flesch, Rudolph, *How to Write, Speak and Think More Effectively.* New York, N.Y.: New American Library, Signet, 1963.

Giffon and Patton. *Fundamentals of Interpersonal Communication.* New York, N.Y.: Harper and Row, 1971.

Goldhaber, F. M. *Organizational Communications.* Dubuque, IA: Wm. C. Brown, 1974.

Harriman, Bruce. "Up and Down the Communications Ladder." *Harvard Business Review.* Sept.-Oct. 1974.

Hayakawa, S. I. *Language in Thought and Action.* New York, N.Y.: Harcourt Brace & Co., 1972.

Keltner, J. W. *Elements of Interpersonal Communication.* Belmont, CA: Wadsworth Publishing Co., 1973.

Lee, Irving J. *Language Habits in Human Affairs.* New York, N.Y.: Harper and Co., 1941.

Nichols and Stevens. *Are You Listening.* New York, N.Y.: McGraw-Hill Co., 1957.

Sigband, Norman B. *Communication for Management.* Glenview, IL: Scott, Foresman, 1969.

Sigband, Norman B. *Management Communications for Decision Making.* Los Angeles, CA: School-Industrial Press, 1973.

Chapter 7

French, Wendell L. *The Personnel Management Process.* Boston, MA: Houghton-Mifflin Co., 1970.

Sweet, Donald H. *The Modern Employment Function.* Reading, MA: Addison-Wesley Publishing Co., Inc. 1973.

Yorks, Lyle. "Let's Change the Job—Not the Man." *real estate today.* Jan. 1974.

Chapter 8

Batten, J. D. *Tough Minded Management.* New York, N.Y.: American Management Association, 1963.

Career Proficiency Evaluation Program, The. El Paso, TX: Vocational Research Data Complex, Inc., 1975.

Fear, Richard A. *The Evaluation Interview.* New York, N.Y.: McGraw-Hill, 1973.

Fear, Richard A. and Byron Jordan. *Employee Evaluation Manual for Interviewers.* New York, N.Y.: The Psychological Corporation, 1943.

"Guidelines on Employee Selection Procedures." Equal Employee Opportunity Commission, Federal Register. Aug. 1, 1970.

Lyman, Howard B. *Test Scores and What They Mean.* Englewood Cliffs, N.J.: Prentice-Hall, Inc., 1971.

McGregor, Douglas. *The Human Side of Enterprise.* New York, N.Y.: McGraw-Hill, 1960.

Maltz, Maxwell. *Psycho-Cybernetics.* Englewood Cliffs, N.J.: Prentice-Hall, Inc., 1960.

Mayer, David G. and Herbert M. Greenberg. "How to Choose a Good Salesman." *real estate today.* Jan. 1970.

Multiple Personal Inventory. Princeton, N.J.: Marketing Survey and Research Corp., 1956.

Porter, Arthur. *Cybernetics Simplified.* New York, N.Y.: Barnes & Noble, Inc., 1970.

Porter, Henry. "Manage your Sales Force as a System." *Harvard Business Review.* Mar./Apr. 1975.

Roberts, Don C. "Testing for Real Estate Sales Ability." *The Texas REALTOR®.* May 1973.

Screening and Selecting Successful Real Estate Salespeople. El Paso, TX: Vocational Research Data Complex, Inc., 1974.

Tatsuoka, Maurice M. *What is Job Relevance?* Champaign, IL: Institute for Personality and Ability Testing, 1973.

Chapter 9

North, William D. "How to Choose What's Right for You." *real estate today.* Aug. 1974.

Chapter 10

Behavioral Sciences Newsletter. Sept. 23, 1974.

Stone, David. *Training Manual for Real Estate Salesmen.* Englewood Cliffs, N.J.: Prentice-Hall, Inc., 1965.

REALTORS® NATIONAL MARKETING INSTITUTE. Training films. 1968-1975.

Chapter 11

Maltz, Maxwell. *Creative Living for Today.* New York, N.Y.: Simon & Schuster, Inc., 1967.

Chapter 12

Brown, Stanley M., ed. *Business Executive Handbook.* Englewood Cliffs, N.J.: Prentice-Hall, 1953.

Burns, Bill. "Psychologist in the Lineup." *Human Behavior.* Los Angeles, CA: Manson Western Corporation, June 1973.

Cyr, John E. *Training and Supervising Real Estate Salesmen.* Englewood Cliffs, N.J.: Prentice-Hall, 1973.

Dawson, Wayne C. "New Salesmen—Handle with Care." *real estate today.* October 1973.

Drucker, Peter F. *Managing for Results.* New York, N.Y.: Harper and Row, 1964.

Maltz, Maxwell. *Psycho-Cybernetics.* Englewood Cliffs, N.J.: Prentice-Hall, 1960.

May, Rollo. *Existential Psychology.* New York, N.Y.: Random House, 1961.

Meyer, Paul. "Dynamics of Motivational Development." Waco, TX: Sales Motivation Institute.

"Probing Opinion." *Harvard Business Review.* Mar./Apr. 1974.

Saint Laurent, Henri. "What It Takes to Star in Selling." *Salesman's Opportunity Magazine.* Mar. 1974.

Smith, Charles M. "Goal Setting, the Attainable Dream." *real estate today.* March 1974.

Wooden, John. *They Call Me Coach.* New York, N.Y.: Bantam Books, 1973.

Chapter 13

Accounting System for Real Estate Brokers, An. Chicago, IL: NATIONAL ASSOCIATION OF REALTORS®, 1972.

Backer, Morton. *Modern Accounting Theory.* Englewood Cliffs, N.J.: Prentice-Hall, 1966.

Bierman and Dyckman. *Managerial Accounting.* New York, N.Y.: Macmillan, 1971.

Cost of a Salesman's Desk. Chicago, IL: NATIONAL ASSOCIATION OF REALTORS®, 1972.

Dixon, R. *Essentials of Accounting.* New York, N.Y.: Macmillan, 1966.

Dixon, Robert L. *The Executive's Accounting Primer.* New York, N.Y.: McGraw-Hill, 1971.

Heckert, Josiah B. *Accounting Systems*. New York, N.Y.: Ronald Press, 1967.

Steffey, John W. "Creating a Budget That Works." *real estate today*. Aug. 1974.

Wixon, Rufus. *Principles of Accounting*. New York, N.Y.: Ronald Press, 1969.

Chapter 14

Case, Fred E. "Real Estate Economics: Market Analysis," *California Real Estate Magazine*. Nov. 1974.

Drucker, Peter. *Management: Tasks—Responsibilities—Practices*. New York, N.Y.: Harper & Row.

Peckham III, Jack M. "Real Estate Investment Newsletter," *real estate today*. Sept. 1974.

Real Estate Advertising Ideas. Chicago, IL: REALTORS® NATIONAL MARKETING INSTITUTE, 1973.

Chapter 15

Osborn, Alex F. *Applied Imagination*. New York, N.Y.: Charles Scribner's Sons, 1953.

Chapter 21

Boyce, Byrl N. and Stephen D. Messner. *Management of an Appraisal Firm*. Chicago, IL: Society of Real Estate Appraisers, 1972.

Harrison, Henry S. *HOUSES—The Illustrated Guide to Construction, Design and Systems*. Chicago, IL: REALTORS® NATIONAL MARKETING INSTITUTE, 1973.

Managing an Appraisal Office. Chicago, IL: American Institute of Real Estate Appraisers, 1971.

Real Estate Management Department—How to Establish and Operate It, The. Chicago, IL: Institute of Real Estate Management, 1967.

Chapter 22

Packard, Vance. *A Nation of Strangers*. New York, N.Y.: David McKay, 1972.

Reich, Charles. *The Greening of America.* New York, N.Y.: Random House, 1970.

Toffler, Alvin. *Future Shock.* New York, N.Y.: Random House, 1970.

Index